Soil and Soul

People versus Corporate Power

A LASTAIR M C INTOSH

Aurum

Quarto is the authority on a wide range of topics.

Quarto educates, entertains and enriches the lives of our readers—enthusiasts and lovers of hands-on living.

www.quartoknows.com

First published in Great Britain
2001 by Aurum Press Ltd
74-77 White Lion Street, London N1 9PF
www.aurumpress.co.uk

This revised paperback edition first published 2004 by Aurum Press

There is a website for *Soil and Soul* at www.AlastairMcIntosh.com.

This book is also being published in French translation
by Éditions Yves Michel, 2005.

A catalogue record for this book is available from the British Library.

ISBN 978 1 85410 942 2

Design by Roger Lightfoot
Printed and bound in Great Britain by CPI Group (UK) Ltd, Croydon, CR0 4YY

MIX
Paper from
responsible sources
FSC® C013604

Contents

Acknowledgements

A vast number of people over many years have contributed to the material that has made this book possible. Here I must confine myself to the limited process of thanking some of those who have played major roles while the book was taking shape.

Some of you provided nourishment and care during difficult times or when I was wrestling with explosive material. I think particularly of Lise Bech, Mags Beechey, Mike and Cathy Collard, Christine Davis, Tess and Ian Darwin-Edwards, John Fleming, Tom Forsyth, Samantha Graham, Shirley Anne Hardy, Fred Harrison, David Horrobin, Patrick Laviolette, Babs MacGregor, Maxwell MacLeod, Alesia Maltz, Tara O'Leary, Ian Ramsay, Jane Rosegrant, John Seed, Tina Sieber, Jane Stavoe, Helen Steven, Ninian Crichton Stuart, Bron Taylor, Djini van Slyke, Colin Whittemore and Nick Wilding.

Others provided resources that enabled me either to write the book, or to support aspects of the work that it documents. I think particularly of the Christendom Trust, the Joseph Rowntree Charitable Trust, Cecilia Croal of the Russell Trust, Ulrich and Francesca Loening of the Konrad Zweig Trust, and the late Di Bates and others associated with what is now the Craigencalt Farm Ecology Centre in Fife.

Some of you have given considerable support in brainstorming ideas, or have worked painstakingly through parts of the manuscript. (I should stress that you are not responsible for places where I might not have followed your advice, and for sections of the text that you may not have seen.) These people include Marcella Althaus-Reid, Audley Archdale, Tim Birley, the Beavitts and the Dawsons on Scoraig, Ian and the late Jane Callaghan, Jim Crawford, Camille Dressler and others on Eigg, Ian Fraser, Stina Harris, Brendan Hill, Alastair Hulbert, Alison and Andrew Johnson, Satish Kumar, Bashir Maan, John MacAulay and others on Harris, Joan MacDonald, Murdo MacDonald, Norman MacDonald, John MacInnes, Colin and Gehan MacLeod, Donald Macleod, Norman MacLeod, Steven Mackie, Angus MacKinnon, Mike Merritt, Alex George Morrison and the boys from Leurbost, Michael Newton, Michael Northcott, Indra Sinha, Thierry Verhelst, Andy Wightman and, especially, Richard Roberts, professor of religious studies at Lancaster University.

I first met my literary agent, Sheila Watson of Watson, Little Ltd twenty-five years ago. She held the maieutic faith throughout that long gestation. Above all, she found me, at Aurum Press, a very special editor in the person of Karen Ings. Together with their wonderfully helpful colleagues they have nursed this work to fulfilment.

I am grateful to sources cited for their generous permission where it has been needed; these are credited in the relevant endnotes. Where there may have been difficulty in contacting sources or in obtaining responses, I hope they will not mind my having quoted their material, and having done so with warm appreciation.

Finally, living with a writer can be like having three people in a marriage: the book stays awake and wriggles all night. Thank you, Vérène, for drawing me constantly back to the beauty and peace of presence.

Picture Credits

Page 1   (*above*) Courtesy of Joan MacDonald, Aberdeen; (*below*) Alastair McIntosh
Page 2   (*above*) Donald Campbell; (below) Murdo MacLeod
Page 3   (*above*) Alastair McIntosh; (*below*) Murdo MacLeod
Page 4   (*above*) Alastair McIntosh
Page 5   (*above & below*) Murdo MacLeod
Page 6   (*above*) Computer modelling and photomontage copyright Envision Ltd, Edinburgh; aerial photograph copyright P. & A. Macdonald; (*below*) Murdo MacLeod
Page 7   (*above & below*) Alastair McIntosh
Page 8   (*above*) Murdo MacLeod; (*below*) Maxwell MacLeod

The cover photograph by Murdo MacLeod is of Calanais standing stones on the Isle of Lewis.

*To the past, present and future people of North Lochs
on the Isle of Lewis, to my parents who grafted me there,
and my children, Adam and Catriona,
whose roots are nourished from that place.*

Child go break off from the herd
go beyond the lowlands
leave the valley of shed antlers
the elders are sick
it is your time now

'Listen to the Wind', written in Adam's treehouse
by Barnie McCormack, Bard of Craigencalt

Foreword

In his recent book *The Song of the Earth*, the Shakespearean scholar Jonathan Bate made the extraordinary claim that poetry could save the world. I think Alastair McIntosh has just proved him right.

This is a world-changing book, one of the most important I have ever read, which will transform our perception of ourselves, our history and our surroundings, much as the work of Alice Miller and Sven Lindqvist has done. It is a first step towards the decolonisation of the soul: the essential imaginative process we have to undergo if we are to save the world from the political and environmental catastrophes that threaten it.

Soil and Soul is an extraordinary adventure in theology, economics, ecology, history and politics. It takes us from the Hebrides to the Solomon Islands, gently guiding us towards a new and remarkable philosophy by means of compelling, beautifully written stories. It overflows with ecstasy, quiet wisdom and love – love for humanity, for the world, for our failings and our possibilities.

McIntosh tells the story of his exceptional childhood, the historical destabilisation of the community in which he was brought up and, as he travels and reads, his growing understanding of why and how this happened. He explores the colonisation of resources, of human labour and, most importantly, of our own perceptions. Then he uses this emerging wisdom and experience to develop daring and innovative means of tackling the powers that have deprived us of ourselves.

With the people of the Isle of Eigg, he helped devise a strategy for overthrowing the once-intractable power of the landlord. Their remarkable victory – the first known case in which Scottish tenants cleared a laird from his own estate – galvanised public demands for widespread land reform in Scotland. When a multinational quarrying company announced its intention to turn a Hebridean mountain into a giant superquarry, McIntosh persuaded the Native American Warrior Chief Sulian Stone Eagle Herney to come to Scotland and help assemble the first-ever theological submission to a public inquiry. The publicity converted a local issue into an international one, developing one of the most striking challenges to corporate power in British history.

xiv Foreword

McIntosh draws on these experiences to develop a radical politics of place. He transforms our engagement with soil and soul – once the preserve of the right – into a new and compelling vision of freedom and social justice. His radical liberation theology, rediscovering both the presence of God in nature and the neglected femininity of divine wisdom, is persuasive enough to encourage even such an indurated old sceptic as myself to take another look at God.

By these means, Alastair McIntosh shows us, we can break the spell of consent, unchain our imaginations and challenge both power itself and the anomie and disaggregation on which power's abuse thrives. The work of a great thinker and a great poet, *Soil and Soul* shows us how we can, in McIntosh's words, make 'beauty blossom anew out of desecration'.

Make no claim to know the world if you have not read this book.

George Monbiot
Oxford, 2001

Introduction

Whether beyond the stormy Hebrides,
Where thou perhaps under the whelming tide
Visit'st the bottom of the monstrous world.

Milton, *Lycidas*[1]

In one of his poetic works Hugh MacDiarmid reflects on the waste of a poor woman's life in some Continental slum. Imagine her if you will: 'thin and gaunt, in pink tights despite the cold'; and him, watching, yet realising that it is not good enough only to pity her suffering. There must be more to life, he muses, than for human beings to owe dignity, 'their claim to our sympathy, merely to their misfortune'.

That 'more' is the capacity to see a person's potential for blossoming: to see what they could be and maybe still can be; not just the limitations of what they presently are. 'And I *am*,' MacDiarmid says, emphasising the words with which he concludes his musings: 'And I *am concerned with the blossom*.'[2]

This book is about that concern. It is about the Earth – soil, in a metaphorical sense – and people, which is to say, soul. It is about the interrelationships between natural ecology, social community and the human spirit. It moves away from the mainstream trunk of western culture and goes out on a limb, where the blossom is.

The mainstream manufactures people as a monoculture. It turns us out like cloned rows of apple trees on pesticide-manicured fields. The mainstream 'trains' people by pruning. It forces growth in standardised ways. The song that we sing from within the mainstream is thereby not our own song. It does not issue from the opened gates of the soul. And so our personal branches and cultural roots atrophy away. We yearn for connection with one another and with the soul. But we forget that, like the earthworm, we too are an organism of the soil. We too need grounding.

2 Soil and Soul

Yes, progress and prosperity might have made us richer in material terms. But meanwhile, between thirty and a hundred plant and animal species become extinct each day, and the poor bleed. Such atrocities impact upon the psyche in ways both known and unknown, shaping who we are and what we become. This is a book about those impacts, and about how they can be healed.

The great disease of our times is meaninglessness. If fresh wellsprings of hope are to be found, we must first cut through the collective hallucination that 'there is no alternative' to nihilism. We must dig where we stand. We must get beneath the grassroots of popular culture and down to the eternal taproot. Here new life can grow from ancient stock.

But to make blossoming possible, we must embrace our losses. We must face the reality of a brokenness of heart that is both personal and of the world. Surprisingly, that is when we discover that *the pain is the mantra*: the very suffering of the world can be what repeatedly calls us back to the imperative of its healing. If we can persist and sit with the reality, not running from it, a music may eventually be heard. The fetters of destructive control loosen. Life's dance resurges. And there is joy in spite of everything.

In her poem 'Natural Resources', Adrienne Rich writes:

> My heart is moved by all I cannot save:
> so much has been destroyed
>
> I have to cast my lot with those
> who age after age, perversely,
>
> with no extraordinary power,
> reconstitute the world.[3]

Today, some of us from the older corners of the world look around and ponder. Mine is a generation from the Outer Hebrides off the far north-west of Scotland, standing with one foot in the old world and the other in a new millennium. Historically, we are first and foremost navigators, Atlantic navigators. We know something about how to pilot a boat through storms. If that boat is cultural, perhaps we can make a modest contribution in seeking a more true course. And who knows, maybe there are survivors to pick up along the way. Maybe there are those adrift who had no anchor point. Well, there is room on board, and laughter grows in the sharing. Maybe a new song will emerge when ancient ways inform our times.

In the place where I come from, we see that old people have been robbed of eldership by rapid change. In any case, they are passing on. The time has arrived for the mantle of culture to be placed, with blessing, on our shoulders – premature though it may often be. And something says that what we have to share is not just for little Scottish islands out on an Atlantic limb: it is a matter of world heritage. After all, much of what our forebears learned came from navigating the whole world. Let there be no presumption of cultural superiority here: it is merely the ebb and flow of historical circumstance in the sea of all humanity.

Allow me to say a little about my writing style. Some of the time it will be very personal. The book may read like an autobiography, which in fact it is not. What I have done is to engage the particular to illustrate the general. All the parochial material will tie in, sooner or later, with themes of much wider significance. My approach uses what has been called 'heart politics'.[4] It aims to restore the feeling 'heart' alongside the thinking 'head' and the doing 'hand'. It means living out, perhaps surprisingly for a man, the feminist principle that 'the personal is the political'. Often this requires an impressionistic, multifaceted style of writing. Readers may find themselves left hanging for a while, but not, I hope, for longer than suspense permits. Seeds will be dropped in to grow, resonate and create an emerging pattern, one that illustrates the book's main theme: life, and what causes it either to wither on the vine, or to flourish.

I have incorporated many endnotes, most of which can be ignored in the reading. They are there mainly to suggest further reading, to make due acknowledgements, or to corroborate assertions. I do hope that the reader will forgive any minor irritation they might cause, but there is little point in writing a deeply researched book if I then keep all the sources to myself.

In Part One, I explore the Isles of Lewis and Harris as I experienced them during my youth. Some of my ancestors were rooted in the ancient traditions of crofting and spiritual song; other influences were modern, cosmopolitan and not Scottish at all. I therefore chart the process of growing up with one foot in an apparently dying indigenous world, and the other hard down on the accelerator of progress. I do not argue for going back to the past, but I will be suggesting that the past should be carried forward to inform the future. In this way, fresh light can be shed on the story of modern times and wisdom harnessed to knowledge.

Interwoven with the story of a Hebridean childhood is a dawning awareness of power, and how this shaped the world in which we all live – how it shaped it first through the colonial era of empire, and then through the globalisation of modern times. We will therefore move gradually from the parochial world of a small island and into realms of experience that all of us must today navigate, irrespective of our geography and ethnic origins. Most of us are unaware of our own deep history and its psychological effects – our psychohistory. Many experience a paradox of privilege: we are materially richer than ever before and yet suffer a spiritual poverty that is difficult to pin down. We do not realise how historical forces have shaped the human heart because these things were rarely taught to us; after all, 'where there is no victim there was no crime'.[5]

In consequence we live, but suffer spiritual death. Our very accomplishments cut us off further from the soul. The ailments that we can observe 'out there', in the environment actually have their origins 'in here', in the human psyche. This calls for healing at an individual and a cultural level – a cultural psychotherapy. This, I believe, is what the bardic tradition of the Celtic world has always been about.

Cultural healing entails coming alive to community with one another, with the place where we live, and with soul. This interconnection is, at its deepest level, poetic. Such poetics can be deeply political, which is why, in many parts of the world, the bard has been the king's closest advisor.[6] It is also why the poetic function has been seen as dangerous from Plato onwards. If we are to restore meaning and heal our broken cultures, if we are to be concerned with the blossoming of human potential, then we must learn again to use such techniques that in some cultures would be called 'shamanistic'. These, I will try to show, can be highly effective tools for community empowerment.

Part Two of the book attempts to demonstrate some principles of community empowerment by interweaving accounts of two successful campaigns. I tell how land reform was brought to top priority in Scotland's new Parliament through achieving community land ownership on the Isle of Eigg. And I tell how a Native North American warrior chief and Sacred Pipe Carrier helped the people of the Isle of Harris (adjacent to Taransay of the BBC's *Castaway* fame) to resist their mountain being turned into 'the gravel-pit of Europe' by a multinational road-stone company.

Both these stories generated international media coverage. Here, I show something of what went on behind the headlines and use it to suggest how even Milton's 'monstrous world' can be transformed. While rooted in the Scottish Hebrides, the significance of these struggles reaches out far across the world. They point to a Celtic truth about identity, which is actually a deep *human* truth: a person belongs inasmuch as they are willing to cherish and be cherished by a place and its peoples.

In such a spirit we can all assume responsibility for our lives and for this planet. The unity of soil and soul can be restored. Concern can truly be with the blossom. And even amid all its despair and destruction, I do believe that the world can be reconstituted.

PART ONE

Indigenous Childhood; Colonial World

1. Digging Where We Stand

I must start where I stand. As children, we used to be told that if you dug a really deep hole, you'd come out in Australia. I think in some ways this is very true. If any of us dig deep enough where we stand, we will find ourselves connected to all other parts of the world.

I grew up just 10 miles from the famous Calanais (or Callanish) standing stones. We lived by the village of Leurbost, on the east side of the Isle of Lewis in the Outer Hebrides. The island lies some 50 miles north-west of the Scottish mainland, out in the Atlantic Ocean.

Our first house, before we moved closer to the village, was a little croft cottage called *Druim Dubh*. There was no mains water supply. It had a well, from which our tap spluttered a dark, peaty flow, like real ale, for washing with, and a huge wooden water butt in which we collected drinking water from the roof. Whenever it rained, which was often, we'd hear a trickle running down the drainpipe and into this tar-caulked barrel. Every morning Dad would scoop out the day's fresh supply with what we called the 'water bucket' and bring it into the kitchen.

Sometimes, when outside, I would climb up on the wheelbarrow, edge the lid sideways and peer down into the inky depths of the butt. As my eyes adjusted to the darkness, I'd look for water beetles. These had silky wings beneath an armoured outer shell. Because the butt's lid did not fit tightly, they would fly in and out at night. What made them visible, black against black though they were, was that each carried its own tiny aqualung. Each had a minute bubble of bright air held tight by surface tension in special hairs at the end of its tapered body. This shone with a most brilliant translucence. It shone with that vibrant life that only oxygen can give, trapped and fighting for freedom. For me, then aged four, our water butt meant more than just a drink. It was a magical place. To shift that lid and gaze upon the awesome depths was to see a chest of zooming dancing jewels.

In Gaelic, *Druim Dubh* means 'the black ridge'. In recent years a fallen stone circle has been uncovered by peat digging just a stone's throw from our old front door. It is out by the rubbish dump on the circular rocky hillock where my younger sister, Isobel, and I used to play. We never knew about the pre-historic stones then. If we had, we'd have thought of them nonchalantly as 'just something from the old days'.

To us children in the early 1960s there was nothing exceptional about even the big standing stones over at Calanais. Yes, they were five thousand years old. That meant they had been erected at around the date attributed to events in the earliest parts of the Old Testament. And yes, they were laid out in the shape of a Celtic cross on a site more spectacular by far than Stonehenge. But otherwise they were unexciting. The Stones were just a place to get cold or eaten by midges when we showed visitors from the mainland around the island. We certainly had no sense of veneration towards them. Indeed, the nineteenth-century people of Calanais had taken what seemed a sensibly prosaic attitude. They had used the Stones, or so it has been said, as public conveniences. Accordingly, they were not greatly pleased when the owner of all Lewis, Lady Jane Matheson, decreed that the site was to be cleaned up and treated with respect of a rather different kind.

In fact, our attitude to the Stones differed little from our attitude to the environment in general. We were often cavalier in our treatment of the countryside. I remember how, for a bit of fun, we boys would take matches and set the heather alight. Nobody minded us doing this. It was thought to help the grass grow. My own record was three entire hillsides burnt from one match. In dry weather, underground fires would smoulder in the peat for weeks afterwards. I never thought much of the little creatures incinerated in the process, or of the now-recognised need for any such moor burning to be carefully regulated. That is how it was then.

When I was about six, my neighbour and schoolfriend, Alex George Morrison, taught me how to fish in the river that flowed by our house. Rarely a day would pass that we wouldn't be out there with bamboo-cane rods and a poor earthworm wriggling on the hook. There used to be salmon in the river when we were very small. Now they'd gone. However, one day I did catch a small sea trout, and often we would bring home brown trout the length of our grubby hands – lean, but incomparably tasty when fried in butter with bacon.

The bigger rivers on the island did still take a good summer run of wild salmon, but most people weren't allowed to fish in them. They all belonged to the estates and therefore were the private property of the 'lairds', as landowners are called in Scotland.

My father was the community's doctor. We also had a croft – a piece of land, usually between 4 and 40 acres, that is rented from the laird for small-scale peasant farming. I can remember, when I was about five, telling my dad that when I grew up I wanted to be a farmer. He said that this would not be possible. He did not have enough money to buy a farm for me. Even then, it seemed strange to me that land had a money value. But I accepted Dad's prescription. I accepted that in my life I would have to rely on brain rather than brawn.

All the communities around us were crofting townships, and most were strung out along fjord-like sea lochs. Our eyes were sharp, and from the school bus at half a mile's distance we could see porpoises breaking the surface of Loch Leurbost. They pursued shoals of herring that dappled the limpid shining surface. At various times we kept hens and a cow. In winter we looked after Tommy, the large white horse who in spring ploughed village fields in preparation for planting oats and potatoes. My sister and I cleaned out his byre, and so the manure heap, intended for our vegetable garden, was my pride and joy. This midden, as we called it, got so hot as it composted down that the winter's snow could never last for long, and blackbirds made holes to snuggle down inside for warmth. I can remember taking a lesson from nature one frosty morning when my hands were frozen numb after going out sledging. I plunged them in, almost to the elbows, and warmed them in the steaming heat. There was nothing 'dirty' about this that could not easily be washed off. After all, manure was the stuff of life. It was a precious commodity.

Nearly everyone spoke Gaelic and most folks, except the very old and very young, had 'the English' too. I grew up with one foot planted firmly in the indigenous culture. But that was not the whole picture. My parents were very conservative politically, so much so that when, much later, I left home to go to university in Aberdeen, I thought it perfectly natural to campaign for the Conservative Party at general elections. You see, we were an establishment medical family in the mid-twentieth century. This meant that we had much to do with those who held social power at the dawn of the atomic age – schoolmasters, ministers of religion, and, of course, the lairds who owned the land and often happened also to be corporate magnates or military chiefs. If I had one foot in crofting culture, the other was in the world of the laird's lodge – 'the big house'. Never did I feel there was any contradiction in this. My parents taught me to treat power, especially old-money landed power, with the utmost respect. Indeed, I was groomed to be able to fit in with that milieu in life and was taught how to dress, to behave and even, through elocution lessons (intended primarily, it is only fair to say, to correct a lisp), to speak accordingly. To this day my Lewis accent is pronounced but not strong.

The land on which we lived was in the parish of North Lochs. Looking down on the area from an aeroplane, you might wonder how anybody could live there. It comprises a beautiful patchwork of lochs; indeed, there appears to be almost as much water as land. Most of North Lochs came under the Soval Estate, owned by two English sisters, Mrs Barker and Mrs Kershaw. It embraced 39,000 acres – about 16,000 hectares – from the huge Loch

Langabhat in the centre of Lewis right across to our east-coast villages. To the west was the 12,500-acre Garynahine Estate. That was owned by the Anglo-French Perrins family, of Lea and Perrins' Worcester sauce fame.

Betty Perrins claimed to be an aristocrat; she was certainly a character. She was followed everywhere by a troupe of growling, snuffling, dribbling pugs. Dogs are the only species with which aristocrats are happy to share power. Both, in their respective ways, excel at marking out territory. So it was that Betty decided she wanted a pretty ribbon of white built around the margins of Garynahine Lodge; in other words, she wanted a fence. And this was to be no ordinary fence: it was to be one of those double-banded joiner-crafted wooden jobs that they put around race tracks in England. Her husband, Captain Neil Perrins, refused. It would have cost £1000. So Betty waited until he went away, withdrew £1000 of her own money, had the fence built, and when Neil came back presented it as 'a surprise' for his Christmas present!

It has to be said that Betty's efforts to hitch the Harris Tweed industry to the fashion houses of Paris did make her sufficiently popular to be elected as a county councillor. She and Captain Neil were two of my father's best friends. I remember my sister and I crying the night the Captain died of a heart attack on board his yacht. He was so young – of the same generation as our father – and we loved him.

Up north, towards the town of Stornoway, with its population of 5000, was the relatively tiny MacAulay Farm Estate. This comprised little more than a very good salmon river and some rough shooting. Edmund and Margaret Watts of the Watts Watts shipping line ran it. And south, towards the mountains of the Isle of Harris, was the 27,500-acre Eisken Estate. Rich in deer stalking, salmon lochs and game birds, it was a sportsman's paradise.[1]

Eisken was one of my very favourite places. Driving along 10 miles of a road marked 'Private' into the spectacular mountains of south-east Lewis was like moving a hundred years back in time. There was no electricity. You would be greeted by the howl of hunting dogs from the kennels. Living all alone in the gaunt Victorian lodge was a quaint but kindly, craggy, tweed-skirted old lady, named Miss Jessie Thorneycroft. She was descended from a family branch of the seventeenth-century Edward Thornycroft of Thornycroft in Cheshire. Their fortune was cast from the ironworks of the Industrial Revolution. To this day, the family history and name survives in the yacht, mercantile and warship building company, Vosper Thornycroft.

From time to time our family would be invited down to Eisken for lunch, usually along with the Stornoway Sheriff and his family. Of course, it was his job to punish anybody caught netting Jessie's salmon or popping off a stag. With the Sheriff's twin boys and my sister, there'd be four of us kids huddled around a single paraffin heater in the immense drawing room. This boasted a billiard table, rows upon rows of stuffed stags' heads, a tigerskin rug (or was it a lion?) and works of art including a beautiful little Thorburn sketch of a hind. The hind's eyes gazed out dolefully, straight at the viewer. I can remember my mother, herself an artist of considerable talent, using this sketch to teach me a curious fact. In a picture where the subject's eyes look straight ahead, they appear to follow you whatever angle you view it from. Little Isobel and I felt as though the hind was alive as her eyes softly followed us round the room wherever we went. No wonder my father said that he could see no pleasure in stalking deer.

However, as was his privilege on all the estates within his area of medical practice, my father did love to fish. This was a particular honour at Eisken. Jessie Thorneycroft came from a family line that would not allow someone onto the loch unless they could land a fly from considerable distance into a soup plate. The reciprocal side of Dad's privilege was, of course, that our house was often visited by guests who needed a fish hook extracted from an ear or a thumb – not everybody was up to the soup-plate test!

Such expertise resulted in dinner invitations and friendships that went on year after year. In this way I became familiar from a tender age with the lives of generals, admirals, industrialists, lords and ladies, their chaplains and many of the great and the good who had built up or laid down the British Empire and often lamented what little was then left of it. I have to say that they usually seemed to be fine people. True, I was expected to say, 'Yes Sir, no Sir,' and call the titled ladies 'Ma'am'. But that was not so very different from the hoops we were put through at school, where teachers also expected certain airs and graces. And there was, after all, a bit of pride to be had in meeting such important people.

I still have a school diary from 1966. It offers a little insight into these social encounters. Tangled among accounts of fishing expeditions, rabbit hunts, bonfire nights, candy-making, my mother's exquisite understanding of a small boy's love of food, and watching *Tomorrow's World* or *The Man from U.N.C.L.E.* on the newly arrived television, I recorded the following entry on 31 August 1966:

I went out to play with Derek and Donald. I did not have much time because my mother was having guests. When the guests arrived I opened the doors for them. My mother had told me that the man who had come was in place of the Queen in New Zealand.

In other words, this was Lord or Viscount Cobham of Hagley Hall, the Governor-General. To me, there was nothing exceptional about his visit to our home except that I had to provide the service of doorman! It seems incredible now, but to my child's mind there was no incongruity between hand-scything a meadow and making haystacks on a neighbour's croft during the day, watching the latest pictures of the moon from the *Apollo* rockets on television in the evening, and dining with the royal ambassador at night.

Some of the houses in our village were very modern for their times. Others were traditional – thatched dry-stone blackhouses that reeked of peat smoke. One family near us had no bathroom. It seemed perfectly natural that they should wash their clothes outdoors in the same pools as we fished in.

I can remember waiting for the school bus one day – I think it must have been in 1966, because the village was full of men. They were all at home because of the seamen's strike. This was a community of mariners. Crofting has never been able to provide a living from the land alone. The plots are too small; the ground too poor. The produce of the soil has to be supplemented by Harris Tweed weaving, commercial fishing, local part-time jobs or working away, for example in the merchant navy. Anyway, across the road from us was a family, the daughters of which were my sister's best friends. One of their main sources of income was from their big brother, Neilie. He was a seaman, and, with the lengthy strike on, they had very little money. Yet here they were building a magnificent modern bungalow! How come?

On this particular day the school bus had been delayed. We'd had a late cold snap. Ice covered the road, and so we had to wait for grit to be spread by hand before the bus could make it up the hills. Isobel and I wandered into the new house to keep warm. Nobody ever knocked on doors in those days, and many houses had no locks fitted. You went in and out of other people's houses as if they were extensions of your own. If you were hungry, you would be fed; if you were cold, you would be warmed by the peat fire; if you were naughty, you would be ticked off, because the village was like an extended family.

As Isobel and I stepped inside the half-completed bungalow that frosty morning, we encountered a hive of activity. It was buzzing with men. All manner of building skill was being applied. Every mod con was being installed. And over the open fire a string of salted ling and cod from Loch Leurbost was being cured for consumption later. Much of our diet then was local, and everything was what would now be called 'organic'. Dad would rarely come home from his morning rounds without a leg of lamb, a bottle of milk, home-made butter, new potatoes or even a lobster. He never accepted salmon or venison because, by definition, these would have been poached from our friends, the lairds!

Anyway, there I was in Neilie's new bungalow, standing there in my black lace-up shoes, flannel shorts and long grey socks, with a striped yellow scarf bulging under a navy-blue duffel coat. On my back I carried a brown leather satchel containing books and all manner of essential accessories: a torch made myself from batteries which in those days tended to leak a white powder, magnets, string, nails, penknife, rubber slingshots, fishhooks and line, a tin with holes in the lid full of worms for bait, and often, rattling around among it all, an apple. Dad used to get boxes of apples regularly posted up from England. We'd get one a day – 'to keep the doctor away'.

'How is it,' I asked one of the workmen in the bungalow, 'that Neilie's not rich but he can afford to have all of you working on his house?'

'Ah, well,' came the response. 'You see, Neilie's helped all of us to build our new houses each time he's been back on leave. Now it's our turn to help him.'

I think that may have been the last communally built home in our village. Now, to comply with government regulations for housing grants and planning requirements, contractors put up most houses by competitive tender. But you can't just blame outside forces for the weakening of convivial old ways. Even bringing in the peats – the moorland turf dried to provide winter fuel – is now as often as not a solitary activity. Everybody has easy access to cars and tractors these days. Many people have jobs with hours that constrain the shared use of time. Accordingly, the old custom of making a communal effort in order that many hands might make light work has greatly declined. Yes, people have become richer. But often money has replaced relationships. These days, there are fewer demanding common tasks around which to build community.

2. Earmarks of Belonging

It may have been observed in the foregoing pages that I sometimes make use of the collective pronoun 'we' when 'I' might have seemed more accurate. My urban friends, and acquaintances who have been on workshops about 'owning your own stuff', have often remarked on this. By way of a pre-emptive strike, I would therefore like to offer my excuses. I accept that to speak in the first person is very appropriate in a culture of individuality, but to do so overlooks the big picture when speaking as a person grounded in a commonality – a community.

Writing in 1811, Anne Grant put the point rather more forcefully than might be appropriate some two centuries later, but her words do show where, in Gaelic Celtic culture, this attitude is coming from. Incidentally, I would call what I'm about to share *communalism* rather than communism, though I wouldn't expect that subtle distinction to cut much ice with those who think that any word beginning with the letter C, like collective, co-operative or community, spells gulag. Anyway, we're on safe enough ground here, because this was Mrs Anne Grant of Laggan, a well-bred woman and something of an authority on the mores of her era. She wrote:

> No highlander ever once thought of himself as an individual. Amongst these people, even the meanest mind was in a manner enlarged by association, by anticipation and by retrospect. In the most minute, as well as the most serious concerns, he felt himself one of the many connected together by ties the most lasting and endearing. He considered himself merely with reference to those who had gone before, and those who were to come after him; to these immortals who lived in deathless song and heroic narrative; and to these distinguished beings who were born to be heirs of their fame, and to whom their honours, and, perhaps, their virtues, were to be transmitted.[1]

Such a reflection brings us to questions of identity and belonging. Now, on Lewis, sheep outnumber people, and they are identified by their clipped earmarks. There's a commonly used expression, 'What are his earmarkings?', meaning, 'Where's he coming from; what's she about?' In the cultural context

Anne Grant describes, even in its attenuated modern form, it will be clear why this is an important question and therefore why, as our family did not move to Lewis until 1960, when I was four years old, I should declare my own markings.

My mother was from Warwickshire, an English nursing sister who grew up at RAF Finningley during the Second World War. I always remember her describing the terror she felt when she got off the school bus one day just as a damaged German fighter, which had made an emergency landing, discharged its machine guns in one last blaze of terrible glory. Her mother's maiden name was Jones, but all that was known of her Welsh ancestry was that 'they sung in choirs'. Her father was a businessman of English squirearchial stock, and his father had been a vet, an expert on horses during the First World War.

The unlikely combination of my avant garde mother and Scots Plymouth Brethren-turned-Presbyterian father came together when both were running the children's ward of a hospital serving Doncaster, the West Yorkshire coalmining town. That is where circumstance caused me to be born, and this helps me to bridge more than one culture.

Dad had Gaelic-speaking grandparents on both sides of his family. His father's people were variously in banking and gamekeeping. The line of his mother, Isabella Ewart Purves, provides resonances with a number of the themes that will open out as this story unfolds. She was descended from the MacLennans of Strathconon, north-west of Inverness. These crofting forebears provide me with distant relatives on the Isle of Lewis as well as a rather intriguing cultural background.

At the age of twelve, Isabella's mother, Ellen MacLennan, had migrated south to enter domestic service in Edinburgh. Like so many of that era, she quickly disowned her 'backward' Highland ways. It is said that she never again spoke a word of Gaelic until she was on her deathbed. Ellen's parents were Murdo MacLennan and Mary Gollan. Mary is described in an 1896 newspaper report of their golden wedding anniversary, when she was seventy-four, as being 'hale and hearty, and able to attend daily to her domestic cares'.[2] As for Murdo, he lived his life from 1808 until 1899 at Jamestown by Strathpeffer. He crofted a small patch of land and was a famous 'precentor' of the hauntingly beautiful old way of singing Gaelic psalms. In this oral tradition, dating back to when most people were illiterate, the precentor sings out each line in advance of the rest of the congregation. There is a little book by a Dr Beith recounting another doctor's tour of the Highlands in 1845; in it, Murdo is described as 'the best Gaelic precentor in the North'. The German collector, Joseph Mainzer, wrote down his tunes in 1844, and thus it is Murdo's version of Psalm 65 that is sung to this day in the closing ceremony of the Mod, Scotland's annual festival of Gaelic song.[3]

Scotland had become a Protestant country with the Reformation of 1560 – 'the fundamental fact of Scottish history'.[4] The big issue was the right to challenge spiritual authority, and the nature of salvation. To be a Protestant is to be a 'protestor'. 'Justification' or acceptability before God, protested the reformers, is a matter of faith alone. There was no way it could be bought by doing good works, saying a certain number of Hail Marys or paying 'indulgences' to what, in their eyes, was an institutionally corrupt Roman Catholic Church. This, however, placed a heavy burden of redemptive responsibility on the individual. You were out there on your own in the jungle of the universe, alone before God. No priest or bishop could fix things for you; you could only be saved, as the song puts it, by 'amazing grace'.

At its best, justification by faith was about embracing responsibility and not passing the spiritual buck.[5] The downside was a self-righteous, fear-driven, neurotically pious spiritual individualism, which, in ways the reformers doubtless never intended, chimed in rather too comfortably with the growing emphasis on number one in this world, as well as in the next, that was to become the hallmark of the modern soul.

Calvinist or 'Reformed' principles of church administration were supposed to be democratic: determined by a presbytery – a local body of church members – rather than by episcopacy, or bishops. This is Presbyterianism, and, at its best, it is about bottom–up rather than top–down church government. Inevitably, however, such principles were inconvenient for some of the powers that be. In 1712 a Patronage Act was therefore passed by the landlord-dominated Parliament. It gave landowners the power to appoint clergy. Many of the common people found this objectionable. They believed that it was spiritual corruption. For example, it effectively blocked the community from putting the fear of God into the laird by petitioning him in prayer. In consequence, the established Church of Scotland split in two in what became known as 'the Disruption' of 1843.

According to his obituary, on the Sunday of the Disruption it was Murdo's solemn duty to carry the Bible and psalm book out of the established church at Contin, and to continue the service, disestablished, in the churchyard – doubtless leaving the laird's shocked sycophants behind closed doors inside.[6] Similar defiant acts of witness were conducted all over Scotland, especially in the Highlands. In this way the breakaway Free Church of Scotland came into being. It was a church born out of the defiance of landed power.

Murdo's parents, Kenneth MacLennan and Kathrineea McKenzie, had married in 1787. Records show that Kenneth, a senior elder, never missed a meeting of the parish Poor Fund Committee, and Murdo's obituary mentions that his father was also one of a movement called 'the Men' – *na Daoine* in Gaelic. Throughout the Highlands and Islands in the early nineteenth century these lay prophetic figures followed in the tradition of wandering bards of the past.[7] Their preaching, says one authority, combined 'a harsh and pristine Puritanism with a transcendental mysticism that had less to do with nineteenth-century

Protestantism than with an older faith ... clearly derived from the neo-pagan cultural heritage of the Highlands'.[8] It was the Men's skill with words and spiritual song that had stimulated an evangelical revival in the early nineteenth century, preparing the way for the Disruption.

Kenneth MacLennan's probable parents, my four-times-great-grandparents, were Alexander MacLennan and Mary McNeil. The McNeils were the Scottish offshoot of that great Irish clan, the O'Neils. Alexander and Mary lived at Urray in Strathconon. But in 1792 the Balfours created a huge sheep ranch there which, in due course, would doubtless cash in on wool prices boosted by the Napoleonic Wars. Unfortunately, this made necessary the eviction of tenants like the MacLennans. Their primitive patterns of subsistence would have been inefficient and uneconomic. This was all part of the Highland Clearances, of which more later.

My father's people therefore had strong Highland roots. Following Ellen MacLennan's marriage to a carpenter, William Purves, my great-uncle James was born and rose to be appointed by the Hospital Board of Stornoway Town Council as the first resident consultant surgeon to the Lewis Hospital. Another of that line is said to have been a builder who constructed Stornoway Town Hall. As for Dad himself, he wanted to live where he could practise medicine as both a science and an art. He wanted to help people heal in both body and soul. He told the *Scottish Field* magazine in the early 1960s that he had gone to Lewis 'to start living'.

He rests now, facing east towards our Highland forebears. A growing part of the soil of Lewis, my father rests by Loch Leurbost in Crossbost cemetery, among the old people of the Hebrides, beneath a small rough stone inscribed: 'Beloved Physician'.

I must say a little more at this stage about Lewis and Harris to give an idea of the earmarkings of the place itself. Confusingly, the distinction between the two 'islands' is ancient and administrative, since they are actually only the northern and southern parts of one landmass – the Long Island. However, this distinction remains useful because tourism has become, on top of fishing, weaving and crofting, one of the mainstays of the economy. It offers visitors two islands for the price of one! The 1991 census gives the islands' population as 22,381. They contain some of the most densely populated rural areas of Europe. And as ancient sites like the Calanais stones suggest, the Hebrides have a spiritual pedigree now almost lost to popular consciousness.

Of course, we do not know what Calanais was used for. Evidence points variously in different eras to a lunar temple, an astronomical observatory, a burial ground and even a possible site of child sacrifice.[9] Probably all that we can safely assume is that, like any focus for spiritual power, it will have been used and abused. And who knows, perhaps the many nearby satellite stone circles, like the one over which Isobel and I played at *Druim Dubh*, represent earlier Disruptions and Free Church prototypes. Perhaps there were schisms even in those days! Maybe all that we can say with certainty is that such stones are poetry. We can but let their enigmatic presences affect us as they will.

One of their possible meanings is that Calanais affords fine views of Cailleach na Mointeach, a range of Lewis hills thought to resemble a woman lying on her back. The Gaelic translates as 'The Old Woman of the Moors', but some people call her in English the 'Silver Maiden' or 'Sleeping Beauty' mountain. While these may represent a relatively recent play on the ancient Gaelic name, there are, nonetheless, hints that the Celtic mother goddess was once sacred to these islands. Variously called Bhrighde, Brigh, Bride, Bridey, Bridgit and Brid, she became Christianised as St Bride of Kildare in Ireland, and in the parallel Scottish tradition as St Bride of the Isles. Legend has it that on the night of the Nativity, angels transported her from Iona to Jerusalem, where she became the foster mother of Christ.[10]

John MacAulay, a native Gaelic-speaking historian, shipwright and folklorist on Harris, has this to say about the islands' spiritual significance.

> The Hebrides, or Ey-Brides (derived from the 'Isles of St Bridgit') are now collectively and politically known as the Western Isles. The Gaelic, *Innis Bhrighde*, has long since disappeared from use, having given way to *Innse Gall* (The Isles of Strangers), a derogatory term from the time of the Norse settlement. According to folklore, at one time all of the Outer Isles were committed to the special care of Bridgit, the Celtic goddess of fire, whose temples were attended by virgins of noble birth, called the 'daughters of fire'. When Christianity first came to the isles it proved easier to institute a Christian Order of the Nuns of St Bridgit than to remove the vestal virgins from their post. The Nuns of St Bridgit were the first Christian community of religious women. Various religious sites, parishes, and individual churches throughout the islands have retained this name, in the form Kilbride, or in Gaelic – *Cill Bhrighde* [*Cill* meaning 'cell' or 'church of'].[11]

In recent years there has been heated debate as to whether such a thing as 'Celtic Christianity' or 'Celtic spirituality' really existed. Many such voices are from scholars who are either secular humanists or who have a sincere commitment to institutional church structures, but fear losing ground to movements that they see, often with considerable justification, as vacuous and delusory. The 'Celtosceptics', as some of them call themselves, condemn 'Celticity' and 'spirituality' alike as being 'mere feelings', incompatible with the imperatives of a rigorous rationality. Too much romantic poetry, they suggest, results in the 'cardiac Celt': a Celtic identity existing only in the heart, with no foundation in what it means to be a 'genuine Celt' – this being defined by Professor Donald Meek as 'someone who has been brought up in a country in which a Celtic language is spoken, and/or who has learned that (or another) Celtic language to the point of fluency'.[12]

As for mysticism, the true faith of Celtic lands, concludes Professor Meek, who is an eminent Gaelic-speaking Celtic academic and the son of a Baptist minister, is 'a heavy emphasis on judgement, retribution, penance, self-denial and mortification (of the flesh)'.[13]

Well, I have a respect for many of the scholars making these arguments. Some of them are personal friends of mine. They remind us of the importance of using the head as well as the heart. Without the head we might risk getting sucked into shapeless platitudes and the latest 'druidic', 'shamanic' or 'Wiccan' personality cults. Still, in downplaying the heart's capacity to know by *feeling* – by intuition, vision, poetry, dreams and beauty – I do sometimes wonder whether the Celtosceptics have become trapped in their heads, missing the music, even the magic. I do wonder if they have overplayed their attacks on 'romanticism', forgetting that romance has both a purpose and a reality. Some would even say that this is what having a soul means. And I do wonder whether W. B. Yeats's much maligned 'Celtic Twilight' may not, in fact, be a rather charming poetic depiction of the threshold between mundane and spiritual consciousness; and that those who protest that 'the Celtic Twilight never existed' have yet to allow their eyes time to accustom to a more subtle illumination. As one native Lewis bard told me, 'Well, it has always existed as far as I can see!' And as Ronald Black of Edinburgh University's Celtic Department puts it in a respectfully expressed reservation about Professor Meek's scepticism, 'if theological writings are strong on punishment [as Meek emphasises], there must have been a climate of liberalism to provoke them'.[14] That climate is, of course, the imaginal realm of dream, vision, legend and faerie. The 'imaginal' is something more than imagination alone. It is the source of imagination, of creativity and therefore, as we shall see, the upwelling of poetic reality itself.

The issue, I think, is not *whether* Celtic spirituality ever existed, but the fact that a living spirituality connecting soil, soul and society manifestly can and does exist. This is *community* in that word's most holistic sense. As Professor Meek himself wrote in an outstanding anthology of the nineteenth-century Gaelic bardic tradition, 'The poets' aims can be focused in on one word – "community"'.[15] It is precisely to this 'Celtic' sense of community that the casualties of globalisation, which is to say many people in the modern world, turn for a bit of vision, hope and nourishment. Far from feeling threatened by this attention, the modern Celtic world could perhaps look on it as a continuation of an ancient tradition: one in which these North Atlantic islands have long been looked to by Europe, and perhaps even Ancient Greece, as places of the most profound learning.

The Celtic traditions of Ireland, Britain, France, Spain, Germany, Italy, Switzerland and so on also offer a loose underpinning by which many Western

European peoples can, if they wish, start to connect with indigenous histories and geographies otherwise swept away by mainstream metropolitan influences, from Roman times onwards.[16] 'Celticity' therefore takes on a meaning that can be bigger than ethnographic and linguistic definitions alone: it becomes a code for reconnection with human community, with the natural world and with God. It expresses what I call 'metaculture': a connection at a level of the soul that goes deeper than superficial cultural differences; a connection simply by virtue of our underlying humanity. Such a bedrock of commonality is desperately needed in today's fragmented world. It arises not from 'globalisation' as a business concept, but from the fact of being 'one world'. As a young German musician visiting Iona told me, 'I cannot relate to our more recent folklore because of what the Nazis did to it. But I can connect with Celtic music. It comes from a deeper level.'

There is nothing 'New Age' or new-fangled about this. In Roman times Tacitus recorded his admiration of Celtic and Germanic tribes, some of them remarkably feminist. As long ago as the late eighth century, St Columba's biographer, Adomnán, portrayed the saint's expectant mother as having had an angelic dream. An angel brought her a cloth mantle 'of marvellous beauty, in which lovely colours of all flowers were depicted'. But after a short while he asks for it back, and withdraws it from her. At first Ethne, the young woman, is distressed. 'Why does thou thus quickly take away from me this lovely mantle?' she asks. And the angel replies, 'For the reason that this mantle belongs to one of such grandeur and honourable station that thou canst keep it no longer by thee ... [one] predestined by God to be the leader of innumerable souls to the Heavenly Country.' On hearing these words, 'the woman saw the afore-mentioned mantle gradually receding from her in its flight, and increasing in size so as to exceed the width of the plains, and to overtop the mountains and forests'. Then she awoke.[17]

Perhaps the mantle represents the internationalism with which we are called to make our 'Celtic connections'. I would suggest only three caveats. Firstly, that the process is about listening to, and not imposing upon, the culture of peoples in Celtic lands. It is one thing for a tradition to be shared in an atmosphere of mutual respect, and also for that tradition to evolve as it comes into contact with new ideas. But it is quite another for its direction of growth to be forced, as so often happens, under colonising or commercial pressures. Secondly, it must be recognised that what we may like about the 'Celtic' world is rarely uniquely Celtic. There is no monopoly on beauty, community, or, for that matter, God. The invitation of Ethne's vision is to seek that mantle's beauty not just on her lap, but across the entire world. And thirdly, we must face with honesty the less palatable aspects of Celtic tradition. In other words, we must not romanticise it, in that sense of the word that means denying the hard edges.

After all, as any good traditional storytelling session will show, the Celtic world was not all love and light disappearing into the sunset's twilight. Early Celtic societies had a marked propensity towards warrior cults. Warrior societies necessarily go in for hardening the hearts of their people from a tender age. Tacitus wrote that Saxons ensured their babies were accustomed to the sights and sounds of war by having the camps of women and children deliberately pitched close to the battlefield. Galen adds that the newborn were plunged into icy water to toughen them up.[18] And Plato based his ideas for child-rearing in an ideal military state on ancient Sparta. He said, 'As men try whether colts are easily frightened by taking them near noises and alarming sounds, so we must bring our men, while still young, into the midst of terrors, and then again plunge them into pleasures, testing them more hardly than gold is tested in the fire.'[19]

Celtic warrior practices may have been little different. In pre- and early-Christian Britain and Ireland, children were reported to accompany their mothers into war, flogged and prodded on from behind by their menfolk. On one occasion Ronnat, the mother of Adomnán, Abbot of Iona, found on a battle-field 'the head of a woman lying in one place and her body in another, and her infant on the breast of her corpse. There was a stream of milk on one of its cheeks and a stream of blood on the other cheek.' Such was her outrage that Ronnat would not let her son rest until he had persuaded the powerful patri-archs of his time to enact *Cáin Adomnán*, Adomnán's 'Law of the Innocents', protecting non-combatants, specifically women and children, from being caught up in battle. This is recorded in the *Annals of Ulster* for the year 697, and in a remarkable feminist testimony Article 27 of it states: 'If you do not do good to my community on behalf of the women of this world, the children you beget will fail, or they will perish in their sins.'[20]

Going psychologically deeper than history into mythology, we find the vio-lence of Celtic warrior society culturally anchored in the legends of Cuchulainn, the 'greatest' of the Gaelic heroes, who owes his name to the Cuillin hills on Skye. It was there that the young Ulster prince went to study military excel-lence under a warrior queen, Scáthach, 'the Shadowy One'. We must ponder, of course, whether her alleged love of war was an actual representation of womanhood at the time, or whether male monastic chroniclers invented the witch-like Scáthach to caricature pagan women. Perhaps she is like those highly sexualised high-tech warrior women created today on the computer screens of (mainly male) computer-game designers. But the story goes that Scáthach told Cuchulainn that in order to prove he was worthy of studying at her school, he had to fight a rival queen, Aife. Cuchulainn waited for the virgin Aife in a big yew tree. The struggle took place, he overpowered her, and then offered a choice of humiliations. Either she could die, or she could agree to father his child. Doubtless to Cuchulainn's greater pleasure, she elected for the latter. Scáthach was duly impressed and, being also a prophet and poet, eulo-gised him on graduating from her university of war with these words:

... battle eager, ice-hearted! ...
proud striding raider pitiless
for Ulster's land and virgin women
rise now in all your force
with warlike cruel wounding skill . . .[21]

According to Irish history, it took Bhrighde, St Bride, to 'turn back the streams of war' that such founding figures as these had set in motion.[22] It may have been the Christian theology of forgiveness that caused the early Celtic world to embrace the new religion so dearly.[23] And for my money, if 'Celtic spirituality' means anything, it means showing how a culture ripped apart by violence can again be made whole. That is what makes it a suitable metaphor for what the world needs deeply today. For no place is more sacred, no peoples more worthy of honour, than those that have made beauty blossom anew out of desecration.

When I started school at Leurbost in 1960, there were still inkwells in the desks and a pile of wooden-framed slates, as well as the recently acquired hand-held blackboards, for us to learn to write on. Only three of us in a class of nineteen spoke English. I can remember teachers saying that Gaelic is important, but to 'get on in the world' everybody should learn English, from me and the other two. That meant that, like my great-grand-mother, I grew up thinking Gaelic to be a backward language. I am now deeply saddened that, like so many of my generation, I lost such a golden opportunity to have learned it. There were many other things, however, that I did learn.

The village at that time was one where cows were hand milked, where looms driven by foot filled the air with their clackety-clack, and the atmosphere itself was perfumed with the dusky reek of peat fires. Not until 1974 was the last inhabited Lewis blackhouse vacated. This was in Gearrannan, near Calanais. The housing officials had long wanted to move the old woman who lived there into a modern council house. She refused. She waited until her elderly cow died because, as she said, 'They won't let you keep a cow in a council house.'

My close friend, the late John MacGregor of Gearrannan (Garenin), delighted in showing people the blackhouse in which he was born not far away, in Tolstachaolas village. 'In the really posh houses,' he would explain, pointing to the stone ruins of a bygone age that stand beside every modern villa, 'there were two doors: the cow had one to herself.' In less posh houses cow and people shared the same entrance. I've even heard it said in County Mayo, Ireland, where the Gaelic culture was very similar to ours, that to put the cow out in a separate byre or barn was considered cruel, because such a convivial creature would feel lonely.[24] Similarly, in Scotland I've heard it said that the cow was often greeted with a song. In delight she would lick the milk-maid, much as a friendly dog would do; conversely, she would withhold her milk if anything made her unhappy. Thomas Hardy's *Tess of the D'Urbervilles* portrays similar understandings of cow culture holding sway close to London not so very long ago; Helena Norberg-Hodge's magnificent writings speak like-wise about yaks in Ladakh; and Darrell Posey has collected a vast compendium on the cultural and spiritual values of relationships with other creatures from around the world for the United Nations.[25]

Interestingly, this warmth of relationship was not an impediment to killing animals for meat when their time came. We had never heard of vegetarianism when I was growing up, and there was no awareness at that time of the wider ecological costs that counsel some restraint in the eating of meat. I think that we just took it for granted that life and death were interwoven, and we engaged in local production for local consumption. We all need food, and when the time comes, our bodies too will become food for something. The only imperative is to minimise the period of suffering. It hardly crossed our minds that there could be a conflict between caring for animals and swiftly cutting the throat of a sheep, pulling a chicken's neck or taking a bullet or sledgehammer to the head of a cow as she contentedly ate her last meal from out of a bucket. It might have been a small concern, certainly, but not a huge ethical problem; it was just the way of things. Either it didn't demand a logic or we knew that its logic was ecology, though not that of the Bambification of nature. There was, though, a sense that the business of killing needed to happen in a manner that was timely and appropriate. You knew you ought not take the lobster berried with her eggs (though sometimes we did), or hunt rab-bits in those breeding months that were without an 'r' in their name – the summer season; it was not really the done thing. And I remember, once, the school bus hit and killed a lamb. Its mother wandered around bleating for the next three days. Some of us wept. Such an untimely ending felt out of keep-ing. It was not in the order of things.

Seen close-up, the interconnectedness between people, animals and place can be quite remarkable. A retired vet, David Skinner, told me that shortly after he came to Lewis from the southern Hebrides in the early 1970s, he started to see cases of cows suffering trace-element deficiency, especially cobalt. Why had this not been more common before? He eventually traced it to the fact that, up until that time, nearly every family would keep a barrel of salt herring for the winter. The rock-salt liquid from this, and an occasional herring for good measure, would be mixed in with the cow's feed. These pro-vided trace elements. But when the human culture changed and people no longer 'put down' their barrel of herrings for the winter, the animal relation-ships were also unwittingly affected, and this was revealed in illness. No wonder traditional societies are conservative about change! Now trace elements have to be added to the feed; they come not from any rustic way of life, but from the pharmaceutical industry.

There was no need for people living in a blackhouse to have a toilet as such because they simply made a little hole among the animal dung in the byre, thereby composting human and livestock waste alike to be spread back on to the fields. In the very old houses with no chimney, the open fire was in the middle of the floor and peat smoke filtered up and out through the thatch. One of these can still be seen conserved at Arnol on Lewis.[26] Each spring, the inner thatch was removed and the outer made into the new inner lining. The soot-ridden discarded thatch was then spread on the fields, so the roof recycled fertility that had been captured even from the smoke. While exact practices varied from place to place, this pattern was typical of the olden days. Everything went round in relatively closed-loop cycles. Indeed, an Irish farmer once put it very humorously in telling me that: 'The free-range eggs never tasted the same since we got the flush toilets!'[27] The serious point within this was, of course, that when the bog, quite literally, served as a public convenience, the hens could pick out maggots and thereby enrich their feeding and so the flavour of the eggs. Such are the cycles by which generally poor land had been able to support continuous human populations since agriculture first started in the Neolithic period.

Up until the mid-1960s, Lewis had no municipal rubbish collections, because so little waste was generated. Biodegradable waste was readily composted on the midden. When a tin or bottle was used, it either had a return deposit on it or some valuable reuse in the garage, boat or kitchen. Our house was an exception only because it had the surgery with a medical dispensary attached. We therefore had an incinerator and dug holes out in the moor to bury non-combustible waste.

Television – all of one channel, the BBC – reached us in the mid-1960s. Nowadays, when I go into an old person's house, I'll often ask what most changed the old way of life. They'll invariably point to the TV, which is probably on and turned down so you can't quite hear it except as a distraction. 'That thing,' they'll reply. More than the effects of harsh Calvinist religion; more than the effects of two world wars from which the islands suffered particularly heavy casualties because of the merchant marine tradition; more than the effects of cash economy. 'That thing,' they'll reply, with a guilty air of love–hate resentment. 'That is what has most changed us.'

It was in an encounter with John MacGregor of the posh two-door blackhouse that I understood why modern technology could sometimes have this effect. There he was, seated leprechaun-like, with his ruddy complexion and sparkling eyes, lording it over a ramshackle shed, a sign for tourists outside proclaiming 'MacGregor's Boutique'. Each day, to the clackety-clack 2/4 time of the old Hattersley loom, he would beat out as much as 10 metres of Harris

Tweed, surrounded by one of the world's finest collections of miniature whisky bottles.

'Do you ever get tunes running through your head as you pedal to that rhythm?' I asked him.

'Oh yes, all the time,' he answered.

'And do you not sing to them?'

'Ah, well . . . there was a time when I was younger and you'd hear somebody walking through the village singing to the rhythm of your loom as they went past. And then when they'd get a bit further on and pick up a different loom's rhythm, they'd change the song to suit that one.'

He starts singing 'Am Muileann Dubh' – 'The Black Mill'. I pull from my pocket a two-part penny whistle, press it together, and commence accompaniment. John pedals steadily at the Hattersley and we get a kind of thing going until a thread breaks, and we crack up in laughter.

'So why not now, John? Why do you never hear people singing when they're weaving?'

'Oh, well . . . we'd be embarrassed! People expect it to sound like it does on the radio or television now, and if I started singing they'd laugh. They'd say,' and he puffed himself up as if to make a VIP statement: 'Who does *he* think he's trying to be?'

In her book about southern Hebridean folk traditions gathered in the 1930s when John would have been a boy, Margaret Fay Shaw records how traditional work was often accompanied by song and even dance. 'Those were the days when a wearer could regard his homespun from the Hebrides with the thought of the songs and gaiety that went into the making of it.'[28]

All that said, there are few people who would admit to wanting to turn back the clock. The old way of life was often hard. The new way brought conflict between cultured community and modern economy, but it was easy. With the emergence of the mass-produced carton of refrigerated milk, milking songs to please both child and beast became entertainment on a CD rather than a way of life. The cow is now a unit of factory-farm production – a necessary focus for animal welfare rather than a family member under one roof. Similarly, with the advent of the outboard motor, rowing songs are losing touch with their original inspiration in the body's natural swing. And, as John implied, a shyness crept in; a loss of cultural self-confidence.

As I recount these things, I remember the voice of an old woman from Seaforth Head, beneath the Sleeping Beauty Mountain that reclines near Eisken. She would have been one of Dad's patients, and she's talking – it's very alive in my mind now – about the tractor, which has taken the sweat out of agricultural labour. Oh yes, she remembers well those backbreaking days with just a horse to work the field. And yet, she asks: 'What kind of a music will come from out of a diesel engine?'

3. Globalisation and the Village

During the 1960s many delicious species of fish such as haddock, whiting, and cod could be caught on handlines baited with shellfish in our sheltered sea lochs. The old people were full of amazing stories of even more abundant times. They told of lines with upward of a hundred hooks, good-sized fish on every one. In the 1960s fish were less plentiful. And smaller. Yet throughout my boyhood you could nearly always be assured of an adequate catch.

I suppose I was about eleven when I started putting out to sea in Loch Grimashadar, just north of Loch Leurbost. My mentor was an old crofter, Finlay Montgomery, who lived alone with his sister, Norah. He was small and very dark – one of a type of Lewisman who could have passed as native in the southern Mediterranean or even north Africa.

Various stories try to account for such physical characteristics. Some say that sailors shipwrecked in the retreat of the Spanish Armada were given comfort where they swam ashore. After all, they had been pitched against the 'auld enemy' and perhaps this merited fostership by marriage. Others believe it gives credence to the Irish *Book of Invasions*,[1] which maintains that the first queen of the Gaelic Celts was Scota, the daughter of Pharaoh. The tribe had come to Egypt from the Black Sea region of Scythia. They formulated Gaelic from the seventy-two languages of Babel, a feat that recreated Gaelic as nothing less than the original 'language of Eden'! From Egypt, they migrated through Spain and Ireland, thence eventually to Scotland. With them came Jacob's pillow of Genesis 28 – the Stone of Destiny – upon which British monarchs have been crowned since medieval times. We can tell that Scota was a feminist from the Bible story of how baby Moses was rescued from the bulrushes. She thwarted her father's patriarchal tyranny that would have killed every child. Scota also gave her name to Scotland, which reveals the importance that medieval historians placed upon her legend when they wove reference to it into the 1320 Declaration of Arbroath – Scotland's claim of right to be a nation in the wake of William Wallace's 'Braveheart' saga. It means, of course, that the mythological mother of the Scottish nation was . . . black.[2]

Whatever his ancient ancestry, Finlay the fisherman thought in the language of Eden, spoke very little in any tongue, and had more difficulty than most in working the land because of a birth defect that had caused his feet to be badly malformed. But in a boat, Finlay became a different person. His disability was transformed into a powerful ability at the oars and an electric twinkle came to eyes as dark as the depths were deep. He owned two boats. One was large and blue with clinker-built overlapping boards, like many a working boat around the coast of Scotland. This he used for transporting sheep, and for deep-water fishing 3 miles out to sea on a prolific underwater pinnacle called The Carranoch. He always promised to take me out there when I was old enough and could sustain the protracted haul on the oars. The other boat was sleek, long, low and jet-black from ancestral coatings of Archangel tar. Many years later, in Ireland, I realised that this craft was like the currochs of the County Galway Aran islands. My mother nicknamed it 'Hiawatha' because it looked for all the world like a big canoe.

The best time for fishing in our area was an hour either side of the high or low tide, but when there was no cold easterly touch in the wind. Finlay and I would put to sea with me at the oars, him seated in the stern. He would say nothing, but he'd watch my every movement, and signal for a little adjustment on this oar or that. Like most Lewismen in those days, Finlay couldn't swim. Tradition had it that this was kinder: if you fell in the water when under sail in a storm, or when out alone, it was said that swimming only prolonged the suffering. In any case, the sea had a claim to her own. What this meant in practice was that you had to be *able* in the boat. An 'able-bodied seaman', as they'd say (and it was always men in those days – women were considered unlucky in working boats!). So you'd not want to lose an oar, not under any circumstance. And you had to know all the tricks: how to tack diagonally to the wind to make grudging headway; how to hug the shore in a storm (because even the tiniest shelter could make the difference between rowing forward and blowing backwards); and how to drift the boat to a side wind, so that you arrived at your destination even though pointing a different way.

From Finlay's village of Ranish it was just a fifteen-minute haul on the oars to reach the fishing spot off Grimashadar Point, beneath the croft of a local bard, Torcuil MacRath. There we'd let down our lines, each with two or three mussel-baited hooks. You soon knew if fish were present. They usually were. Within a minute or two you'd feel them nibbling at the bait. When a good tug came, you'd strike the line upwards and haul in 6 fathoms – 12 metres, near enough. We'd talk in fathoms, you see, because that is the natural measure; that is what represents the complete cycle of one arm and then the other pulling in line, almost a metre at a time. I can still hear the 2/2-time rhythmic drawl of that coarse cord coming over the boat's gunwale, spurting out a jet of water as it pressed the worn wood. It is not for nothing that my school-friend, the poet Ian Stephen, calls one of his works 'Fathoms and Metres'.

Often Finlay and I would catch two at a time – haddock or cod if we were lucky. And sweet eating they were, normally between half a pound and one-and-a-half pounds in weight. We'd fill the bucket. That was enough for ourselves and the neighbours. Then we'd up anchor and pull for home.

Sometimes there would be no fish. After about three minutes, Finlay of the few words would look at me solemnly and say, 'Very dead.' He'd stay for another half-hour just to satisfy me, but if such a pronouncement was made, rarely would we catch anything. If conditions were right, the fish would either be there in sufficient numbers for instant success or there'd be none that day. That's the way it is with creatures that go about in shoals.

As I grew into my early teens I was allowed to put to sea alone. At first my mother would be anxious, especially on windy days when white horses rose up on wave crests, indicating a gusty Force 5 wind. 'Don't worry,' my father would tell her. 'There'll be at least three telescopes trained on him, and if there's any problem, the boys'll be right out.'

And that was the way of it. The simple activity of a youth going fishing connected in with the human ecology of the whole village. The mussels might have been gathered by Norah along with other shellfish like cockles and razorfish on the low tide a couple of days earlier. The old men were unpaid coastguards. Everybody had a useful role. I remember one day when the wind got up so much that I was hardly able to haul for home. I rode at anchor for a while, but eventually elected to make a break for fear it would freshen further. My main worry was not that I might get blown on to rocks or out to sea; rather, that the old men would see I'd misjudged the conditions. I would then suffer the ignominy of needing to be rescued, thereby entering the village's litany of amusing events for the rest of my days!

Whenever I came back with a good catch, I'd share it out as I cycled home the 5 miles through Ranish, Crossbost and Leurbost villages. This was the late 1960s and even then few people had fridges; still fewer freezers. There was just no demand for them. Neither was there money to buy such hardware. If you had a supply of something perishable, you shared. When your neighbours had a surplus, you received. People's 'deep freezes' were, in effect, the village itself – with the advantage that what you got was always fresh and there was no need for nuclear power stations or defrost disaster insurance policies.

The closeness of the link between fishing and eating was why locals often referred to the fish as being 'sweet'. It does taste that way straight out of the loch when it curls like a still-living thing in the frying pan, but it loses these qualities within hours. And because the economy was based on sharing, I'd sometimes go fishing and come back not just with haddock, but also with eggs or a pat of butter – butter that tasted so strong that the flavour would roll around in your mouth for half the morning after breakfast. I suppose most modern palates would have dismissed it as rancid! Modern palates, however, may not be the most discerning frame of reference within which to judge the quality of a local diet. In 1940 the Medical Research Council published a study entitled *Dental Disease in the Island of Lewis*. It concluded: 'The teeth of the inhabitants are markedly superior in their freedom from disease to those of the inhabitants of most parts of Britain.' Among country schoolchildren in Lewis, 28 per cent were free from dental decay, compared with only 6.3 per cent on the neighbouring Highland mainland, and 1.9 per cent in London.[3]

I now understand that the society I was privileged to be a part of in those days was based upon an economy of mutuality, reciprocity and exchange. These qualities mattered to us at least as much as cash transactions did. The social thinker Ivan Illich has called such a system 'the vernacular economy'.[4] This is, he says, like our vernacular, or mother tongue. It is a way of doing and being that is learned, effortlessly, through the culture. Often we do not realise what we have it until it goes. However, it would seem to me that if such principles can be communicated afresh, they could be of value to community groups everywhere that are trying to develop what E. F. Schumacher called 'economics as if people mattered'.[5] Allow me, therefore, to explore the economic workings of what I have just described.

In the Hebridean vernacular economy, people understood themselves to be responsible for one another. Everyone was their brother's and sister's keeper. Let me unpack the three faces of this, and then a fourth. At the deepest level of care is *mutuality*. As the owner of a fishing boat, let's say, I will give you fish simply because I have plenty and you have need. It would be nice if you could give me some eggs in return, but only if you're able so to do. If you can't, because you are too sick, too old, or just a bit feckless, somebody else will see that I have eggs. The fact that I have a need will get around, because gossip is the oil of oral culture. It lubricates relationships and we slander its character when we, the children of written truth, unthinkingly predicate it with the adjective 'malicious'.

Now, my giving you fish comes from a sense of obligation, because we are mutually part of the community. Likewise your giving me eggs. And nobody keeps a formal score of things because the village economy is centred around seeing that everybody has sufficient. In this system sufficiency is the measure of prosperity. Surplus is for sharing before trading, and the joy is in the giving, not the accumulating. Our 'poverty', if it is that, is a dignified *frugality*, not the degrading destitution of economies where an elite harbours all the resources to profit from artificially maintained scarcities.[6]

Let's move on now to the second pillar of the vernacular economy: *reciprocity*. Here I catch the fish and you, let's say, still produce eggs. I agree to give you fish *if* you keep me in eggs. However, in this conditionality we measure only the function and not the degree of our sharing. If the fishing is bad, you still give me eggs. If the hens are moulting and therefore not laying well,

I still give you fish. What we see here is a communal division of labour system. It differs from mutuality only insofar as it makes explicit that there are no free lunches and everybody must play their part. Usually, in a vernacular society, relationships will be reciprocal when people are fit and of an economically active age, but mutuality comes into play as a safety net when they are unable to care for themselves. In Scotland folklorists have called this the 'Highland welfare state'.[7] And we might note, in passing, that many of the older British co-operative insurance companies called themselves 'mutual societies' – at least, they did before privatisation became all the rage.

The third vernacular pillar – and we're starting to see a spectrum of economic understanding emerge here – is *exchange* or *barter*. Here the principles of measurement that lie behind cash economies drop into place. In a barter system, I give you, say, one fish in exchange for three eggs. In other words, goods and services have a *price* fixed in terms of other goods and services. Goodwill is no longer the primary driving mechanism, but we are still sufficiently connected to each other for the economy to be personalised. The immediacy of exchange means that, most of the time, we can see where our produce is coming from and we know who makes it. This helps to maintain norms of social and ecological justice.

The problem with barter is its rigidity. If I have fish to trade but I don't want your eggs, we cannot do business. That is where, fourthly, *cash* enters the equation. It lubricates between supply and demand for goods and services. Money is, at its most primitive, just an accounting system. It records our obligations to one another using banknotes and other bills of exchange as IOUs. These are given legitimacy, normally, by a government bank in which people have *confidence*. That confidence demands *faith*. The focus of such faith, however, has moved away from an immediate relationship with a home community and a local place.

In the twentieth century Lewis underwent an economic transition such as more 'developed' parts of the world had experienced much earlier in history. The island shifted along the spectrum of mutuality, reciprocity and exchange, headlong into the cash economy. Once surpluses were shared and this yielded goodwill. Mutual dependency was the glue that facilitated social cohesion. Now, because money (unlike fish and eggs) does not rot, it can be invested, yielding interest, a dividend or capital gains. Money thereby takes on second-order characteristics over and above its primary accounting role: it makes money out of itself. This has the effect of shifting benefit away from the community and towards individuals. It assists the concentration of wealth, and that leads to an increasing rigidity in access to resources for the majority.

Whereas the vernacular economy is necessarily mindful of the human and biological processes by which goods and services come into being, the new way – capitalism – reduces human labour and nature's providence to figures on the London or Tokyo stock exchanges. It hammers whole ways of life into speculative chips, drip-feeding a casino economy. Such is the essence of neo-liberal globalisation: competition subsumes the co-operative relationship. Government is forced out of the economy, but money then takes its place as king and it cares little for community or environment. Plutocracy – government by the rich – yields inevitably to oligarchy – government by the few. Reverence falls by the wayside, having become an irrelevance. People know that something is wrong. But it's hard to see what it is, and the world goes on, after a fashion.

It would have been around 1970 that the fishing started to change in the Hebrides. I was coming up to fifteen years old and it was a very sudden thing; disturbingly sudden. We'd put to sea and find ourselves catching nothing, without apparent reason. The tide would be normal. There'd be no hint of east in the wind. Just nothing. Very dead, as Finlay would say. Conditions would be like that for about two weeks, and then the fish would come back in. And then: nothing again. So, very dead. Why?

At first we were nonplussed. This had never happened before in people's memory. Then people started to notice the reason. Torcuil MacRath, with his croft so close to the fishing point, tells me that he was one of the first to see it. Now and again a boat would come in at night, with its navigation lights turned off, and would illegally trawl the sea loch. In one fell swoop our fish would be gone.

At first this seemed incomprehensible. You just didn't do that sort of thing. You respected the 3-mile limit. There was a taboo – and the law. Why was nobody reporting these boats to the fishery protection vessels? Why were the skippers not put behind bars?

There was talk in the villages about dropping old cars into the sea to snag their nets. But it never happened. As the inshore fishing became more and more pointless over the course of just a year or two, the reason why nobody acted dawned with what, for me in my naivety, was a gentle horror. These were *our* boats: not east-coasters, not the marauding Spaniards, but local trawlers. There was nothing anybody could or would do.

Many years later I saw a similar thing in the Solomon Islands. It was 1989. I was investigating the logging of tropical rainforests and we travelled all day by canoe through the South Pacific Ocean, off Malaita Island. A baited line trailed out behind. By evening, it had hooked just one little garfish. That night we ate canned tuna. It came from the Taiwanese trawlers whose lights glittered prettily out at sea.

Polycarp, my guide, sat on a wooden bus-stop bench. He casually took out a knife and cut a long groove. Finding a hard stick, he then rubbed vigorously to and fro, blowing gently, until some shavings glowed with sufficient fire to light his cigarette. It was a year ago, he explained, that the coastal fisheries had collapsed. The Taiwanese had started coming in to net just off the coral reefs. They were after baitfish for commercial tuna operations. A few politicians in Honolulu got rich on the licensing backhanders. But for village people it had meant a shift from catching their own food to having to buy it. Only out of habit did they still navigate their canoes with a lured line hanging out the back.

And where did they acquire the money to buy tinned tuna, I asked? No problem. That came from Kayuchem, the Taiwanese logging company that paid poverty wages and a royalty of one dollar per tree – a forest giant for which the company would receive on average a thousand dollars.

Around us played naked brown children with distended bellies. A nutritionist explained to me that infant malnutrition normally declined as soon as the children developed teeth hard enough to crack the protein-rich *Terminalia brassia* nuts. But now this tree was all but logged out. Even crabs and shrimps were scarce, because logging had taken place right down to the shoreline, where tangled roots had previously maintained a sheltered nursery environment. Capital-intensive production methods had usurped ecology and human community. The ecosystem of place had started to unravel.

It is when the capacity of a place to sustain itself becomes ruptured that the human mind is forced to reflect upon ecology. Only then do most of us consider the interconnections between plants and animals and their environment. Ecology teaches that you cannot damage one part of a system without causing knock-on effects elsewhere. If there is no respect and no limitation, there is, in the end, no thing – nothing. But what is so remarkable and disturbing is how easily we all collude in ecocide – what the scholar Carolyn Merchant calls 'the death of nature'. Usually we do so without even realising it. 'Father, forgive them . . .'

Let me give a personal example. At the same time that I used to go fishing with Finlay, I also spent many a Saturday with a retired English couple who lived in the neighbouring village of Ceos or Keose. Stella and Ted Sills had been colonial farmers in Kenya until the Mau Mau drove them out. Ted had a noble-savage view of the black man and lamented how degenerate 'he' had now become. They were always 'he' in Ted's view! The idea that colonisation might have been responsible for this would hardly have entered his mind. His ideas were obviously rather right wing, but that all went over my head because what mattered to me was not his politics, but the kindness that he and Stella showed me – and their six-berth yacht. Weather permitting, we'd put out each Saturday in the *Pegasus* on Loch Erisort, the next sea loch south of Leurbost. With us would be two or three scallop divers from Stornoway led by Angus F. MacLeod, a fine man.

My job was to row a boat all morning. I had to follow the plastic buoy attached by a long cord to the divers' scallop bags 10 fathoms down. Whenever one of them surfaced and gave the thumbs-up sign, I'd haul up a harvest of beautiful shells the size of a man's spread hand. The limiting factor in all this was how hard I could row. If I could hold steady for a couple of hours, then the men could work. If the winds and tides were too much for me, we'd have to go home. In retrospect, it was remarkable that the whole operation revolved around the fledgeling strength of a boy not yet in his teens. And yet this was typical in such a community. We children contributed to the world of work as soon as we were able, and we felt great as a result. There was rarely any question of our suffering from low self-esteem. Our worth was in our work, and all of us could see and value this. Indeed, our worth lay in our capacity to relate to *reality* – to the social and the natural environments. Years later I would come across a passage by the Apache philosopher V. F. Cordova. She expresses this idea perfectly, but in a Native American context.

Many years ago I watched my daughter and her 'Anglo' friend take their infant sons out for their first springtime. My daughter set her eight- or nine-month-old son on to a barely greening lawn. She introduced him to the grass, encouraging him to touch it, even taste it. She pointed out the temperature, the breeze, the sky and clouds. The other mother came differently prepared for her son's encounter with the world. She brought a blanket, which she spread out for her son. She brought toys as distractions and she did not *join* her son so much as *hovered* over him in a protective manner: not allowing him to crawl away from the blanket; not allowing him to grasp at the grass ('dirty'). My daughter introduced her son to the world he lived in; the other mother introduced her son to a potentially dangerous 'environment'. The Anglo child's world consisted of his toys, his blanket, his mother, his artificial setting; the world 'out there' was alien. He ended his excursion in his mother's arms. My grandson ended his when his mother chased after him as he explored his new surroundings. 'This is the way it is done,' I thought. 'This is why we are different.' We discourage competitiveness and encourage co-operativeness; we frown on selfish behaviour and encourage perceptiveness of the other; we correct by offering alternatives rather than through threat of punishment or admonitions; we encourage laughter and camaraderie – there is no one 'out there' waiting to 'get us.' We transmit these values through loaning our attitudes to our children.[8]

So there I would be, working unpaid every Saturday to help haul the scallops in, and loving every moment of it. Now, from time to time in the village you'd hear mutterings about overfishing. Some people seemed to have a downer on new-fangled technology like diving. Well, personally I never paid much attention to such talk. There always seemed to be plenty of scallops when we went out.

It was not until I started writing this book that I learned otherwise. I perchanced to open the *Stornoway Gazette* and there, in the nostalgia column, was the following story, reprinted from 25 March 1972:

> Lewis District Council are to make recommendations to the Scottish Secretary to have skin diving for scallops made illegal.
>
> Councillor Donald J. Mackay, Lochs, said that Islanders at one time could get scallops in inshore waters, but these areas were now cleaned up completely by skin divers, mostly from England, although some were from Lewis.
>
> He said: 'We used to keep a few for ourselves and give the rest to neighbours, but these skin divers are making a trade of it.
>
> 'In one day last week, they took 520 scallops as well as several lobsters out of Loch Erisort.'

At the time I had been virtually unaware of this controversy, yet I'd evidently played my small part in it. The proposed legislation was never passed. What's more, many of the divers have now lost their livelihoods. These days most scallops are dredged. Powerful little boats trawl up and down the coast, twenty-four hours a day, seven days a week in some areas, dragging behind them heavy contraptions that plough up the seabed with rows of 6-inch metal spikes. Almost irrespective of their maturity, the scallops get caught up in the devouring bags following on behind.

I can remember the first time that we were out on Loch Erisort when 'Angus F' dived on a spot that had been dredged with such an instrument of maritime torture. He came up, shocked, saying that a great gouge of death had been scored through the muddy bottom. Arms had been torn off starfish, claws ripped from crabs, and all manner of broken shells and dug-up worms lay dead or writhing. Such a fishing technique has been likened to picking apples by running a combine harvester through the orchard. Trouble is, there's nobody down there to witness it, nobody to protest. And if anybody raised a voice, they'd probably only be told that they're obstructing progress. They'd be left, an unheard Cassandra, like Councillor Donald J. Mackay was. Unheard by people like me.

The crazy thing is that sensible, sensitive and productive resource-management policies could so easily be put in place. In shallow waters these might allow only the traditional method of scooping scallops up with a long pole after spotting them through a glass-bottomed bucket. This would restore opportunities to the old men and the children. Diving could be restricted to deeper waters, and dredging, in my opinion, should be banned outright. That way, the habitat of worms and other creatures could recover and, because these help to feed fish, the catches would improve.

Today, in both the Hebrides and the Solomon Islands, hardly any of the fish consumed has been self-caught. Most is purchased. Processing factories in

Stornoway sometimes even import from the mainland! The fish from our waters are as likely to be landed in Vigo in Northern Spain as in Mallaig in the West Highlands. And yet, in terms of our Gross National Product (GNP), we are better off. In the days when people like me caught enough for the pot, we had a socially supported initiation ritual into adulthood. But we were classed as poor because nothing went through the cash economy. Now it is different. We buy fish, and it counts as economic activity. We buy fuel oil for the boats instead of using our muscles to row, and again, it measures as economic activity. Meanwhile, young people get drunk, inject drugs, fight, smash windows and otherwise create some sort of rite of passage, no matter how perverse. This too adds to GNP. Repairs to vandalised shop fronts also count as 'wealth' in national accounting. So do the hospital casualty services, and the alcohol consumed, and the policing and court time.

Accordingly, the use of GNP to measure wellbeing is an astonishingly crude yardstick of national accounting. It reflects the triumph of the cash economy in the years following the end of the Second World War – the triumph of quantity over quality. The alternative economist Wolfgang Sachs sees it as part of a 'collective hallucination', induced by an engineering approach to human development.[9] The consequences are rather splendidly illustrated in this tale that was passed around on the Internet.

An experienced economist and an inexperienced economist are walking down the road. They come across a pile of dog dirt on the pavement.

Says the experienced economist to his inexperienced friend: 'See that? You eat that dirt, and I'll give you $20,000.'

So the inexperienced economist runs through his brain the cost–benefit equations that he'd learned from the experienced economist. He figures that it's worth eating, gets down on his hands and knees, does the necessary, then collects his money.

Continuing on their way, the pair go a little further and almost step in the same again. This time the inexperienced economist says: 'Now, if *you* eat this dirt I'll give *you* $20,000.'

The experienced economist runs the cost–benefit optimisation equations through his brain. Because they're the same equations as he'd taught the inexperienced economist, he arrives at precisely the same conclusion. Accordingly, he too gets down on his hands and knees and, well, allow me to be discreet.

He gets up, takes a handkerchief to his chin, collects his money, and the pair walk on.

After a while, the inexperienced economist, being the student, starts to think.

'Listen,' he says to his mentor. 'We've both spent $20,000 but each of us still has the same as we started with. We've both eaten shit, yet I don't see us being any better off.'

'Well, that's where you're wrong,' comes the reply. 'You see, we've just upped the GNP by $40,000!'

The point is that mainstream economics, financial economics, is a social and psychological construction. We see its shortfalls where it clashes head-on with ecological economics – with the kind of economics that takes as its frame of reference the real world of nature. Yet that reality, our reality, I must admit, had its cruelties too.

The news came in a letter from my father when I was out teaching in Papua New Guinea. Aye, the news came – and all that I have now is a piece of the prow of *Hiawatha*, hanging by a silver cord from my wall.

Crippled Finlay, wise, kindly, of few or no words; elder who taught a small boy how to handle a small boat in big weather. I remember your promise never met, Finlay, to take me fishing far out there, beyond our normal haunt, in the big blue boat – to The Carranoch! The submerged reef was a kind of initiation rite to all us youngsters aspiring to a place in the tough world of men. Three miles easting of Lewis, just north of the 58th parallel.

Broken promise, broken fingernails. Finlay, alone on the water. Cramped grip on tarry keel. Scraped down beneath Loch Grimashadar. Goodbye, dear friend.

And I shall always slightly fear the beauty of that sea loch now, the cruel sea, the shadow side of nature that we can but accept, accept, and like the next wave, accept.

'Very dead,' as you would say on those rare days we let down baited lines 6 fathoms but to no avail. Very dead was how the divers found you, under the whelming tide, Archangel tar beneath your splintered nails. Very dead, dear Finlay, in all but memory of your brightness setting on the western wave.

4. Celtic Ecology

What we were experiencing with our inshore fisheries in the 1970s was much more than just the selfishness of a few local lads. It was culture change. The Highlands and Islands Development Board had introduced a capital grants and loan scheme to enable modernisation of the fishing fleet. New steel-built trawlers were starting to appear in Stornoway harbour, and very impressive they looked too. Most boats were now equipped with echo sounders as the electronic technology became cheap. This enabled accurate charting both of rocky reefs on the seabed and of fish shoals.

To walk around Stornoway harbour was to view a fishing-technology theme park. The old skills, and with them, the time-inculcated sense of responsibility towards place, were losing sway. Boats were increasingly crewed by relatively inexperienced young men who took their bearings not from tradition, but from technology. For many, fishing was a way to service both the bank loan and the fancy new car or house. Fewer and fewer people still saw it as a way of life to be honoured. If fish could be found close inshore and if you're only living for today, why not go after them? In any case, at that time Britain was entering the European Common Fisheries Policy. Boats from anywhere in the Common Market would soon have access to our waters. The skippers reckoned they might as well grab all they could before the big free-for-all began. The incentive to respect nature was disappearing and the ecology of place was therefore unravelling. To understand these processes more usefully we must explore some of the principles of ecological science.

The word 'ecology' derives from the Greek word for household. It was first defined as 'the science of communities' by an American scientist, Victor Shelford, in 1913.[1] Growing up on an island makes it very difficult to be unaware of ecology, and ecologists like nothing better than an island where they can study, in relative simplicity, how different species interact. For an ecologist, the word 'island' is used in a special way. It refers to any ecosystem that is isolated from the wider world. For example, it might be an island of the right kind of trees for a particular caterpillar to feed on. It might be a part of the seabed protected by reefs where the scallop dredgers can't get in. Or a national park where hunting is forbidden so there's plenty of game to support big cats, wolves and bears.

To an ecologist, an island can also be a *remnant* of something that was once much bigger. Such ecological islands are havens for remaining wildlife. But as human activities expand, so forests are cut down, seas are overfished, and ecosystems shrink, first to islands, and then to wasteland. Nature, being a complex web, is fragile. Everything interconnects. If species start dying out, the diversity of life – biodiversity – declines. The scale at which this is happening in today's world reveals the degree to which human impact is proving disastrous for other species. Some 73 per cent of the world's large mammals have become extinct since the end of the last ice age just 10,000 years ago. One-fifth of the world's birds have vanished in the past 2000 years: instead of some 11,000 species, there are now only 9040.[2] In Britain, a 1998 report to the Government's Joint Nature Conservation Committee shows that, as a result of habitat loss and the use of agricultural biocides – pesticides, herbicides, fungicides and other chemicals that kill life – the previous twenty-five years saw 'common' birds like turtle doves decline by 69 per cent, yellow wagtails by 74 per cent, grey partridges by 86 per cent and tree sparrows by 95 per cent.[3]

The fragile species and the ones found nowhere else in the world are the first to disappear when nature's three-billion-year-old process of evolution comes under pressure. Two per cent of the world's natural forests, 150,000 square kilometres, are felled each year in an evolutionary holocaust.[4] I have seen it happen. I have heard the tropical forest fall silent after the clearfell operations. And, as was demonstrated in the example from the Solomon Islands, I have seen the parallel process of human culture disintegrating as the satisfaction of greed displaces the fulfilment of sufficiency in need.

Often the knock-on effects of damaging nature are far greater than would at first seem apparent. Take the destruction of 'keystone species'. The keystone is the tapered block that completes an arch above a doorway. If that goes, other stones resting on it also tumble. The evolutionary biologist E. O. Wilson says: 'The loss of a keystone species is like a drill accidentally striking a power line. It causes lights to go out all over.'[5] The American alligator is an example of a keystone species. In the Florida Everglades it digs deep depressions known as 'gator holes' which collect fresh water during dry spells. These provide refuge for all kinds of other animals, birds, fish, insects, plants, tiny worms and microbes. If the alligator got completely shot out by hunters, some of these other creatures would go locally extinct along with it. Their extinction would be complete, global, if they happened to exist nowhere else on Earth – if they were endemic to that area.

As plants and animals – flora and fauna – get squeezed into ever-smaller island ecosystems all over the world, the web of life starts to collapse. A golden eagle, for example, needs up to 100 square kilometres of hunting territory capable of supporting prey in order to survive. England is now down to its last breeding pair of golden eagles. They live in the Lake District, which has become a remnant island of suitable habitat.

For the renowned English botanist Oliver Rackham, native species are what maintain the distinctive feel of a place. 'I am specially concerned,' he says, 'with the loss of meaning. The landscape is a record of our roots . . . . Every oak or alder planted in Cambridge (traditionally a city of willows, ashes, elms and cherry-plums) erodes the difference between Cambridge and other places. Part of the value of the native lime tree lies in the meaning embodied in its mysterious natural distribution; it is devalued by being made into a universal tree.'[6]

Both computer models and actual ecological surveys suggest that when an area loses 90 per cent of its native forest, at least 50 per cent of its species are wiped out.[7] Calculations can be made of global extinction rates by using scientific information such as satellite imagery to analyse habitat loss. This is the origin of E. O. Wilson's much-quoted estimate that seventy-four species become extinct each day.[8] By contrast, in a situation without human interference, the expected 'background' naturally occurring extinction rate, based on observations from the fossil record, would be only about one species every year.[9] Even allowing that the fossil record documents only a small proportion of what has actually happened, it is indisputable that humankind has accelerated the extinction rate many times over. For example, it is thought that the maximum background extinction rate among the world's 4000 or so living mammals should be only one in 400 years, and among birds, one in 200 years.[10] What's more, with so many habitats around the world being reduced to wasteland, the opportunity for new evolution is diminished. It's like expecting industry to innovate new products during a war when the factories keep getting bombed.

Extinction is a crime against all time. It makes the world a poorer place, forever. The process is not new in human history. It has happened whenever there has been a period of major human change. The arrival of people in Australia 50,000 years ago, and in the Americas 11,000 years ago, coincided with large-scale extinctions of hunted species. It is important to remember this because, in rightly valuing the wisdom of indigenous peoples, we must not idealise them and thereby subject our readily maligned postmodern selves to unrealistic comparisons. The harmony with nature that we have come to associate with settled indigenous peoples has been in part a *learned* harmony. It has been kept in place by technological limitations, by totemistic respect for other life and by taboos against disrespect. But the fact that some societies *have* managed to achieve ecological harmony in the past is important to us today. It offers hope, showing that sustainable ways of life can, indeed, be compatible with human wellbeing.

I have already mentioned how, as children growing up on Lewis, our attitude towards nature could be somewhat cavalier. Closer examination hints at a discontinuity between the approach of our post-war generation and that of the old people. I first became aware of this not on Lewis, but on the Aran Islands off the west coast of Ireland, where the native people are also Gaelic Celts. The similarities are remarkable in all but religion – they being Catholic, whereas we were Protestant.

One of the islands' priests, Fr Dara Molloy, pointed out to me how a deep respect for one another and an intense reverence for nature are woven into the very language of many of the people. Concepts like blessing and providence are innate. God is presumed to be immanent in the world where daily life goes on. When people say 'God bless you', or 'God willing', they mean something that ought not be dismissed as superstition or treated on the same level as the routine 'Have a nice day' you might hear in a McDonald's hamburger joint. Community conflicts, of course, take place, but the majority of these get pushed aside or are forgiven out of necessity the next time a demanding common task arises, or at an island dance. Says Dara: 'The structure of certain Irish dances makes it impossible not to come face to face with everybody else on the floor at some time in the evening. Then it's harder to maintain a feud after you've been dancing together!'

In many rural parts of Ireland wells, groves, archaeological sites and mountains are still considered holy. This is true to a much lesser extent in Protestant Scotland. Here, the religious Reformation of 1560 swept aside many such beliefs. However, what I have found is that after becoming sensitised to seeing these things in Ireland, it is easier to see in Hebridean culture the truncated taproots of what had previously escaped notice.

A good family friend of ours was the late Dr Donald Murray of Back and, latterly, Crossbost. He was a remarkable man of the most profound sensitivity, intelligence and independence of mind; born in a Lewis blackhouse, he became a physician and travelled the world, carrying out medical practice in rural Nepal. As a boy he'd go shopping to Stornoway by foot, just a dozen miles away, once a year. Those were the days when a Stornoway merchant would order a hundred pairs of ladies' shoes without specifying colour or style, because fashion had not yet been invented. Anything not produced on the island was a luxury: as Donald used to put it, 'An orange was for Christmas.'

'In the old days,' he'd tell us as we sat around my mother's hearth, 'people were ecological without knowing that they were so or why they were so.' They would carefully re-lay surface turf after cutting out the underlying peat for fuel. Three wise men were chosen by the village to ensure that this was properly done. Nowadays, of course, there is no such inspection process, and so there is much shoddy cutting of the peats. The living layer of surface turf, full of heather, grasses and insect life, often gets thrown down in any old haphazard way. This makes the ground lumpy and boggy. Erosion can then get a grip on the land, making an ugly scar of oozing black mud. It blocks renewed peat formation and cannot support grazing animals or nesting birds.

'The interesting thing,' Donald would conclude, 'is that when we used to do things right we never questioned why we did them so. It had to go wrong before we could understand why the old folk's ways were right. The challenge of today is to become ecologists once again, but this time to be so consciously. We have to understand the "why" and not just follow the "how" of ecology.'

Visiting the Isle of Lewis in 1695, Martin Martin wrote that up until the time of the Reformation, churches and sanctuaries were held in 'greater veneration'. Nature was more honoured. A cup of ale would be poured into the sea to thank the sea god, Shony, for providing seaweed. This was accompanied by the words: 'Shony, I give you this cup of ale, hoping that you'll be so kind as to send us plenty of sea-ware for enriching our ground for the ensuing year.'[11] However, such veneration did not die out with the Reformation. In a history of the Hebrides published in 1919, W. C. MacKenzie says:

> Veneration! That was at the root of the religion of the Lewis people of old, alike when they were pagans, Roman Catholics, Episcopalians, and Presbyterians . . . . When the people of Lewis were first baptised as Christians, mainly, it is to be assumed, through the instrumentality of the Columban Church, the new creed was grafted on the old. The graft of Christianity upon paganism produced a nondescript fruit, which was neither Christian nor heathen. The names of the deities were changed, but the essence of the old creed remained unaltered. The policy of the mediaeval Roman Church was not to destroy, but to assimilate . . . . Veneration is to religion what sap is to a tree. In mediaeval and post-mediaeval times, the people of Lewis were profoundly religious, in the sense that they were *deeply reverential*.[12]

What, one may ask, were the markings of this 'nondescript fruit . . . neither Christian nor heathen' – the 'Elder Faith' as it is sometimes called, with Christianity grafted to it?

There are many hints in Scottish and Irish Gaelic literature. In my view, these reveal a profound indigenous green consciousness that speaks even to modern times. We find it recorded *par excellence* in Alexander Carmichael's *Carmina Gadelica*, a collection of prayers, blessings and songs collected from the Hebrides in the nineteenth century. Tessa Ransford of the Scottish Poetry Library refers to Carmichael's anthology as 'the Parnassian Spring of poetry in Scotland'. A leading Gaelic scholar calls it 'a treasure house . . . a marvellous and unrepeatable achievement'.[13] Material in a similar vein is found in Adomnán's *Life of Saint Columba*, as we have already seen in discussing the Vision of Ethne. This dates to about 796.[14] Pushing time even further back, we have the 'Song of Amergin', said to be the first ever composed in Ireland. Douglas Hyde, who was professor of Irish at University College, Dublin, in the early twentieth century, describes the song as, 'noticeable for its curious pantheistic strain which reminds one strangely of the East'. The bard Amergin supposedly chanted it as the first ancestors of the modern Irish people stepped ashore from the sea:

> I am the wind which breathes upon the sea,
> I am the wave of the ocean,
> I am the murmur of the billows,
> I am the ox of the seven combats,
> I am the vulture upon the rock,
> I am a beam of the sun,
> I am the fairest of plants,
> I am a wild boar in valour,
> I am a salmon in the water,
> I am a lake in the plain,
> I am a word of science,
> I am the point of the lance in battle,
> I am the God who creates in the head the fire.
> Who is it who throws light into the meeting on the mountain?
> Who announces the ages of the moon?
> Who teaches the place where couches the sun?[15]

Indeed, green spiritual consciousness pours from all the Celtic creative forms. Like a visual representation of the music itself, Celtic art is based on circularity, on the curve and the spiral, more than on regimented squares and angularity.[16] Knotwork and vinework patterns interlaced on ancient Pictish stones and in later sacred books graphically illustrate the interconnectedness of all things. In the *Book of Kells*, which was probably started on Iona and then taken to Ireland during the late first millennium, flowing foliage represents Jesus's metaphor of the 'Vine of Life' from John 15. Interconnection is represented as the very spirit of Christ, incarnate in this world, alive today as in all time, animating every person and all of nature.

Evidence of green consciousness also abounds in anthologies such as Professor Jackson's *Celtic Miscellany* and his *Studies in Early Celtic Nature Poetry*. In another wonderful collection, the great German scholar Kuno Meyer describes this body of material, which was written down from the seventh century onwards, as 'impressionist . . . like the Japanese'. He says:

> These poems occupy a unique position in the literature of the world. To seek out and watch and love Nature, in its tiniest phenomena as in its grandest, was given to no people so early and so fully as to the Celt. Many hundreds of Gaelic and Welsh poems testify to this fact.[17]

Professor Jackson notes that the Irish tales 'are inclined to desert the natural and possible for the impossible and supernatural'. In so doing, he goes on to imply, the mundane is humorously raised to the level of the gods.[18] Perhaps it is with such an eye that we might view that genre of nature tradition known as faerie lore. Inconvenient though it might be for the strait-laced Christian fundamentalist and the secular rational scholar alike, the tradition gives the realm of faerie a very serious place in its worldview. Marion MacNeill's study *The Silver Bough* is one source. Documenting Scottish Highland beliefs in 1822, W. Grant Stewart provided several chapters sporting venerable titles like 'Of the Fairies as a Community – Their Political Principles and Ingenious Habits'.[19] They like to be taken seriously! And from the south-west of England, W. Evans-Wentz (of *The Tibetan Book of the Dead* fame) recorded beliefs similar to the Irish and Scots in his memorable nineteenth-century study *The Fairy Faith of Celtic Lands*.

In the southern Highlands of Scotland in 1691, the Rev. Robert Kirk set the faeries in full biblical context in *The Secret Commonwealth of Faeries, Elves and Fauns*. Kirk, who also translated the first Gaelic Bible, was concerned to show that such traditions were not at odds with Christianity. While some have sought to dismiss his treatise as just 'an isolated phenomenon', folklorists accept that it aggregates widespread peasant beliefs of the time.[20] For example, we can find a lovely resonance with Kirk in the memoirs of Elizabeth Grant of Rothiemurchus. Writing between 1797 and 1827, she observed:

> Our mountains were full of fairy legends, old clan tales, forebodings, prophecies, and other superstitions, quite as much beloved as in the Bible. The Shorter Catechism and the fairy stories were mixed up together to form the innermost faith of the Highlander, a much gayer and less metaphysical character than his Saxon-tainted countryman.[21]

There are also many songs and poems from the bardic tradition of the Highland–Irish continuum that express green consciousness. Those of Duncan Ban MacIntyre in the eighteenth century are the best-known Scottish examples.[22] Some poems and songs are British-wide. These include variants on 'Tam Linn' and 'Thomas the Rhymer', closely connected in England with Robin Hood and lore about 'the Greenwood'.[23] Such themes also seem to find expression in the enigmatic 'Green Man' imagery of English ecclesiastical architecture. And while we're on the subject of Merrie England, we might remember that Rudyard Kipling represents his *Puck of Pook's Hill* as England's last faerie, emerged from out the magic hill.[24] And for what purpose? To reconnect the children with their cultural history!

The Elder Faiths appear to have dovetailed with Christianity; they held sway in parts of Ireland at least until the Great Famine. Estimated regular attendance at mass in Ireland was little more than 30 per cent before that holocaust, rising to over 90 per cent in 1850, by which time starvation had run its devastating five-year course. Estyn Evans, an expert on the significance of place and belonging, suggests that the people 'were to find a new identity in the Catholic faith'.[25] During the famine Irish food was all the time being dispatched under armed colonial guard to England. But the common people lacked an adequate political analysis of this and were inclined, according to Evans, to conclude that nature had let them down. Today, as the Irish church begins to lose its grip, secular materialism seems to be taking over. Even holy Ireland is succumbing to that late-modern sickness characterised by the great Hebridean scholar John MacInnes as a plight in which 'the Gaelic world has suffered, and continues to suffer, a reduction in "the natural emotions". People nowadays are less hospitable, less kind to each other, less generous, more materialistic, and altogether less "spiritual".'[26]

What can we glean of the Elder Faiths from the literature? They were, or so it would appear, substantially animistic. They expressed a personified worldview where nature was filled with soul – the sea, for instance, with its 'god' in Shony. In my view this was clearly a shamanistic culture. A shaman, to use the word in its generalised rather than its culturally specific sense, is one who steps outside of his or her society's normal framework of reality and enters an *imaginal* or 'spirit' world. From this vantage point any sicknesses of the culture or of an individual can more clearly be seen. The shaman can then step back into normality and address the people's problems as healer, poet or prophet.[27]

Of all the ancient material that illuminates what might be thought of as a Celtic shamanism, I love best of all the translation of *Sweeney Astray* by Seamus Heaney. This is based upon a twelfth-century Irish manuscript, but the story is rooted in the seventh century. Suibhne or Sweeney is a seventh-century 'king, saint and holy fool' sent 'mad' in battle by a cleric's curse. This shamanic craziness (or *geilt* in Irish Gaelic) transforms him by both 'curse and miracle' into a bird. He flies off on a magical journey, falling in love with nature and becoming a poet of what we would now call 'deep ecology': the idea that the human self is ultimately grounded in nature – the 'ecological self'.

Interestingly, Sweeney has no problem reconciling such 'paganism' with a belief in Christ. But he staunchly challenges the efforts being made by career clerics to set up an institutional church. 'I perched for rest,' Sweeney's bird self says, 'and imagined cuckoos calling across water, the Bann cuckoo, calling sweeter than church bells that whinge and grind.'[28]

Flying around Ireland and the west of Scotland, he roosts on Ailsa Craig, a massive rock in the Irish Sea otherwise known as 'Paddy's Milestone', and undertakes six weeks of contemplation in the cave of St Donan on the Isle of Eigg (pronounced 'egg'). He proclaims:

From lonely cliff tops, the stag bells and makes the whole glen shake and re-echo. I am ravished. Unearthly sweetness shakes my breast. O Christ, the loving and the sinless, hear my prayer, attend, O Christ, and let nothing separate us. Blend me forever in your sweetness . . .

I prefer the squeal of badgers in their sett to the tally-ho of the morning hunt; I prefer the re-echoing belling of a stag among the peaks to that arrogant horn . . .

Though you think sweet, yonder in your church, the gentle talk of your students, sweeter I think the splendid talking the wolves make in Glenn Bolcain. Though you like the fat and meat which are eaten in the drinking halls, I like better to eat a head of clean water-cress in a place without sorrow.[29]

As Seamus Heaney says in his introduction, one importance of this text is the light it sheds on the dynamic between Christianity and the Elder Faith. The former, at its best, emphasises forgiveness and, therefore, what it takes to build community and social cohesion. The latter, at its best, illuminates God in nature. Woven together with myth and metaphor, these two beliefs combine to create what is most distinctive in Celtic Christianity – community and nature in a triune confluence with God.

However, while such nature religion is distinctive in Celtic Christianity, we must not think it unique. A similar understanding is apparent in the preaching of St Francis of Assisi. The interesting thing is that when the southern Hebrides (where most of the *Carmina Gadelica* was gathered) was re-evangelised in the spiritual vacuum experienced after the Reformation, it was by Irish Franciscan missionaries, and it was in these Roman Catholic enclaves that the nature-religion traditions persisted the longest.[30]

In material like the Sweeney text we are faced with a mindset that is very different from the Greek rational and empirical framework which has become the mainstream of western thought. Indeed, the worldview of many indigenous cultures is not based on linear logic at all. It is, first and foremost, mythological. Reality is 'mythopoesis' – an interesting word, combining the prefix 'myth' and the Greek origin of the word poetry – *poesis* – which literally means 'the making'.

Mythopoesis is therefore about the construction of reality from story. Equally, as those great English mythical writers like C. S. Lewis and J. R. R. Tolkien so richly understood, it puts the storyteller in 'the capacity of a "sub-creator", thus fulfilling God's purpose' in recounting 'true myth'.[31] The so-called 'primitive,' 'primal' or 'archaic' mind, and even that of the odd Oxbridge professor, moves in a world of story. As we have seen, where you come from, who you are and what your destiny proves to be are all linked within that story, which is nothing less than the story of the world's creation, of the human and animal forebears, and of the world's destiny. The creation myth of the book of Genesis was so believable in times gone by precisely because, in this metaphorical way of looking at life, it seems profoundly true.

It reflects the poetic arising of reality that is 'the Creation'. It reflects a God who is the cosmogenetic poet, and who, as we see in the Old Testament and other sacred books from around the world, causes the prophets to speak in poetry whenever they get really inspired.

That is what makes this profound understanding of story, this *mythos* or mythological framework of reality, the domain of the bards, of the shamans and of the medicine women and men.[32] They hold the soul of any culture, including, variously, its history and genealogy. The outward formal expression may take the form of institutional religion, but as every prophet knows, religion requires continual reformation to prevent ossification, and that reformation comes from periodic reimmersion into God's creative fire.

Genealogy – our earclippings – is therefore about much more than mere gene sequences. It is also about relationship and embeddedness. It is about the social context in which genetic expression takes place – 'nurture' as well as 'nature'. That's important to understand: we may not be able to change the hardware of our brains very easily, but we can work on the software. That's what cultural evolution is all about.

In the year 2000 Lord Parekh published a landmark report called *The Future of Multi-Ethnic Britain*. Courageously, it directly addresses these matters. The top priority listed by his eminent commission seeking to tackle racism was to recognise that 'Britain is a recent creation, and that colonialism and empire were integral to its making'. If Britain is, instead, to become 'a community of communities . . . at ease with its place within world society and with its own internal differences', then we must, according to Parekh, engage in 'rethinking the national story'. The report quotes a Nigerian-British writer to demonstrate just how vital story is to the practical business of forging a humane national politics.

'Stories,' writes Ben Okri, 'are the secret reservoir of values: change the stories individuals and nations live by and tell themselves and you change the individuals and nations.' He continues: 'Nations and peoples are largely the stories they feed themselves. If they tell themselves stories that are lies, they will suffer the future consequences of those lies. If they tell themselves stories that face their own truths, they will free their histories for future flowerings.'[33]

Because we are all interconnected, living with one another means getting to know one another's stories. It means understanding one another not just on the surface, but from the inside out. That means listening with an ear of love tuned to nothing less than beauty. It means listening for truth – including the tough truth that always flows from stories that require confession, forgiveness and redemption. And what is this 'past' that is the stuff of story but a wave on eternity's ocean. And what are we today but its surf-tossed leading edge. That is a thrilling place in which to be alive.

5. By the Cold and Religious

Well, the Hebridean world of the 1960s was far from that of Sweeney. Education was seen as the big answer to living on the outer (some would say utter) edge of the world. Our teachers, parents and everybody else were proud that Lewis was said to send more students to university per head of the population than any other part of Britain. However, there was also a cultural downside to this.

Education meant acquiring the ability to 'get on' and thereby 'get out' – out into the 'big wide world'. 'Get on, get on!' was repeated to us like a mantra in school. I can remember one teacher, who presumably meant well, saying that because I daydreamed a lot, I would never get on – I'd 'just fall by the wayside'. Quite where the wayside led to, and wherefore its fearsome properties, was never explained. Indeed, today most of my best ideas start as daydreams; and as for the wayside, I find it to be a perfect remnant haven of biodiversity.

I grew up in a conservative and fundamentalist culture. In both primary and secondary school we had to learn whole chapters of the Bible by heart. As one of my friends from the village put it recently, 'Many of our teachers were halfway between the minister and the policeman.' Each morning, classes started with a mass recital of the question-and-answer doctrinal responses from the 1647 *Westminster Shorter Catechism*, the creed of Scots Presbyterianism. I still remember Question No. 1: 'What is the chief end of man?' The reply was: 'Man's chief end is to glorify God and enjoy Him forever.' And maybe I was daydreaming and missed it, but I can't remember anyone ever explaining to us infants what a 'chief end' actually was. Indeed, I can remember, when I was very young, wondering whether it had something to do with a person's 'rear end', and, as I got older, noticing that the part of a car's crankshaft to which the pistons transmit their power is called the 'big end'. Maybe that got close to it; after all, a 'chief end' is that which drives everything else around. It is concerned with fundamental values.

All the emphasis was placed on the first part of the prescription – the glorification of God. We were taught much about austere worship, and about our sinfulness, but little about the *enjoyment* side of the equation. Sometimes us boys would dig out certain parts of the Bible, like passages from the Song of Solomon – those parts, often disguised with heavy metaphor in the King James Version, that are replete with a richly erotic and joyous spirituality. Lines like Chapter 5:4, which, in modern translation, stripped of the rich poetry with which King James cloaked it, reads: 'My beloved thrust his hand into the opening, and my inmost being yearned for him' – and the context makes it abundantly clear what 'the opening' in question was! If we were feeling brave, we might ask a teacher about the meaning of such lines. The response was always something like, 'Now put that away, and get on with what you're meant to be learning, or I'll give you something to put a smile on the other side of your face!' In retrospect, maybe what perplexed us was that, actually, we were being taught bad theology – a dispassionate theology. The whole point of the glorification of God is to maximise the *enjoyment*, the warm intimacy, and that's why Solomon's song uses the full-blown sexual metaphor that it does.

As for my more general school performance, I had struggled to read and had a bad memory for rote learning. Sometimes we had to write out whole chapters of the Bible several times as a punishment. At other times kids were thrashed for not knowing their religion. This punishment was undertaken with the tawse – a thick leather strap with two fingers of fizzing fire. The more sadistic teachers carried theirs around like a holstered gun under the jacket. They'd pull it out at the least provocation and, with a thunderous crack, thwack it down on a desk to scare us. It was not used only for religious instruction, of course. There was a wide range of sins for which our outstretched trembling hands could be strapped 'for our own good'. But when belting was used as a scriptural aid, I can remember feeling particular resentment. Frankly, it was spiritual abuse of children. It has left some people I know quite unable to open a Bible and ascertain for their now-adult selves whether there is anything worth digging for there. Such is the control-freak inquisitional tendency that has, too often and rightly, given religion a bad name.

Years later it felt like a defiant liberation to play, at full volume, Pink Floyd's album *The Wall*, proclaiming with outrageous grammatical imprecision that the kids don't need no education. And I laughed at the way in which the teacher's sneering voice in the song was given a Scottish accent as he tells the kids, like generation upon generation of his type: 'Do it again! Do it again!' And I delighted in a subsequent Pink Floyd album, *The Final Cut*, especially the line about being taken in hand by the cold and religious – the latter-day Pharisees – and being made to feel bad while being shown the things of life that were, supposedly, good.

With the notable exception of some wonderful teachers who were our saving grace, our education, then, was not informed by what would today be called a 'child-centred' approach. Rather, it was about forcing round pegs into square holes. Only a few wise eyes have been able to see through these holes and speak out against the conditioning we experienced. I particularly admire Canon Angus John MacQueen of the Isle of Barra in the southern Hebrides. 'All we want,' says this controversial Roman Catholic parish priest, in a wickedly sweeping generalisation for which I, for one, absolve him utterly,

> All we want is the privilege of remaining poor and being crofters. Crofting is about poverty with dignity. If you stand on your own four or eight acres, you are monarch of all you survey, and it gives you a natural dignity which you are without the moment you walk on to the mainland. Education now in the Hebrides is rubbish. These schools should be in the middle of England. The 80 per cent of them who want to be fishermen should be encouraged to do what they want. But the younger people now want to get on. Education has ruined them, and made parents ambitious for their children to get on, when they should be enjoying life. I don't blame them for wanting to get on, but I feel more at home with the lad or the girl who leaves school at 16 and becomes a fisherman or whatever. For those who have to go through the rough world of colleges and university, it's very unbalancing. So many of them are packing in halfway through their courses. *A Hebridean will find a quality of life, or else become an alcoholic or a drug addict. He will cave in completely.*[1]

MacQueen would have found much to share with an American friend I made in later life, the psychotherapist Jane Middleton-Moz. Jane is white, but grew up adopted into a Native American family. Now much of her work is with the victims of sexual abuse by clergy in the mainstream churches, and with the children of alcoholics on 'Indian' reservations.[2]

'We have to face the reality of cultural trauma,' she told me. 'We have to understand that these unresolved historical remnants break out as lateral violence – violence that goes sideways, against friends, family and the self, because it cannot resolve itself vertically. It cannot deal with the real cause of the problem – the cause that's pressing down from on top – the burden of a tragic history set in place and often held in place by powerful interests.' These things knock on from one generation to another. They constitute intergenerational cultural trauma. They replicate themselves in sensitivities and insensitivities alike, just as the children of alcoholics often become alcoholics, or the abused become abusers. Loss of cultural meaning is why so many native peoples drink or take drugs or take their own lives. Often they blame themselves because they have internalised victim-blaming. Really, the fault lies with a cultural denial and disempowerment imposed by historical circumstances from the outside.

'Do you see that school?' Torcuil MacRath, the bard of Grimashadar, asks me, voice heightened, finger pointing accusatively up the hill outside.

It was down off the end of Torcuil's croft that I used to drop anchor when fishing with Finlay Montgomery all those years ago. But now it was the 1990s. There were no longer wild whitefish to be caught in Loch Grimashader. None. And this wiry-framed retired oil-rig welder is in his seventies, a one-time patient of my father, living alone in the utmost simplicity. It was poverty by any other standard: a house unpainted in a generation; and there we are, huddled around a peat fire, with no central heating. But every stick of furniture is saturated in the history of who has sat there before. And this man works surrounded by shelves of books replete in history and culture as he bashes out, on an electric typewriter, a river of stories 'for the next generation'.

Here is a man with no aversion to learning. Indeed, here is perhaps the most learned man in the village. And I had gone to hear his latest bardic song. It was inspired, he says, by watching a TV programme about Native Americans.

Our education system, and its integral connection with religion, had its origins in the reign of King James VI (1567–1625). His era is important, and not just for Scots. It laid the foundations for what historians call the 'modern' era, and it contains the roots of those ideologies that we now associate with 'globalisation'.

The infant James's mother, Mary, Queen of Scots, had been imprisoned by Elizabeth I and then executed because, as a Catholic, she was a threat to England's Protestant succession. The motherless boy was subsequently raised a solid Protestant by a succession of regents, all of whom died from either natural causes, murder or execution. His education was trusted to a learned but cruel tutor, George Buchanan, who 'methodically thrashed and overworked him'.[3]

When the childless 'Virgin Queen' Elizabeth passed away in 1603, James was the nearest in line who could be trusted to uphold Protestant principles. He was therefore invited to constitute a 'United Kingdom' of both the Scottish and the English crowns. So it was that he went off down to London with much pomp and circumstance, only once ever to come home again. One can imagine that 'home' might not have meant very much to him.

The new kingdom of James the First (as he was now numbered) was symbolised by the 'Union Jack'. A 'jack' is both an old naval name for a flag and, as 'Jacques', the French form of James – hence 'Jacobites' for supporters of the Stuart line. Aspiring to be a 'universall King', James wanted absolute control over both spiritual and temporal power. He wrote a book on witchcraft called *Demonology* and took a personal interest in the persecution of witches. He had the Bible translated into English, thereby giving us the 'Authorised' or 'King James Version' of 1611 which, to this day, connoisseurs consider to be 'the noblest monument of English prose'. Its telling dedication starts: 'To the most High and Mighty Prince James, by the Grace of God, King of Great Britain, France and Ireland, Defender of the Faith, Etc'.

By the end of his reign, James had established 'plantations' or colonies in New England, Virginia, Bermuda, Newfoundland, Guyana, the East Indies and India. As we can see in the powerful children's movie *Pocahontas*, the British had begun to build the empire upon which the sun would never set.

'These *Red Indians*, if that is what you would call them,' Torcuil continues, gazing directly into my eyes, monitoring every unconscious flicker as he tells me about the television programme that has made such an impact on him. 'They said that their culture is dying. They said it's because the Circle, the Sacred Hoop, has been broken.'

Long pauses punctuate every statement. This is not snappy soundbite culture; this is where meaning lies more between the words than in them.

'Well, I'll tell you this, Alastair. I'll tell you this, my boy! It's the same for us. It's the same for the Gael. At least, that's what I think. Because when I heard them on the television, those Indians, I understood instantly what they meant.'

And then he sings his song in Gaelic. He translates a verse for me into the English:

> The Circle is broken and I cannot raise a tune
> The faeries have left and they will not return
> When the faeries danced on the land the Circle was whole
> And then you could raise a tune

'But do you see that school?' the bard repeats . . .

The Reformation of 1560 hitched the Protestant cause to Scottish nationhood. Its values owed much to the Swiss-based French reformer, John Calvin, and his followers – some of whom put out a hard line.[4] King James himself was not a Protestant of the Presbyterian variety. He believed in having bishops rather than church democracy since he wanted to be head of the church himself. Nevertheless, Calvin's magisterial *Institutes of the Christian Religion* of 1536 shaped much of the theology of James's era.

To understand the origins of modernism in Western thought as it was disseminated through the British Empire, it is instructive to understand something of Calvin's thought. There is much about his schema that was liberating for his era, and the Presbyterianism or bottom–up church government that developed as a result has, with justification, caused his *Institutes* to be described as 'the seedbed of democracy'. Calvin's aim, after all, was to free the soul from the increasingly corrupt, superstitious and oligarchic strictures of the late-medieval Roman church. However, his rigidly reasoned application of logic to the metaphorical poetry and music of Scripture led to ossification, and he probably did not always foresee the consequences of the forces of the mind that he was liberating.

In particular, Calvin argued that the medieval Catholic Church's injunction on lending money at interest – usury – could be 'accommodated' into the Christian framework. The Jews, after all, were already doing it, so why couldn't the Christians likewise permit moneylending and thus claim greater economic autonomy? However, this widened the conceptual door to the possibility of becoming a capitalist – one whose sole contribution to industry might be the provision of capital, upon which a return would be expected.[5] So it was that 'the Great Transformation' of modern times became morally acceptable, as the Western world rapidly shifted from a peasant and land-based system to an industrial and largely urban-based economy.[6] Newly invented engines of mercantile empire – so-called joint-stock corporations – drove this forward with their Crown-granted trade monopolies over colonial territory to provide returns on private shareholder capital. The system was pioneered during James's reign by the East India Company, which ran a whole subcontinent as its corporate backyard.[7] And because it represented a group of people – shareholders – the corporation became accepted as being a 'fictitious person' in British company law. As a legal entity, it curiously started to acquire 'human' characteristics, having both rights and obligations.

In nineteenth-century England further legislation was passed to give investors 'limited liability' towards their corporate obligations. This meant that in the event of a company collapsing, shareholders would lose no more than the value of their investment. They could live to invest another day. An individual could be put into prison for polluting, poisoning and murdering; but not so shareholders. They were to be protected by a legal membrane: limited liability meant limited responsibility.[8] Originally, this was all under state control. When the Great Indian Mutiny came about because the East India Company had been throwing its weight around too much, the British state was able to dissolve the corporation. It could manage the genie it had set loose. That is not so nowadays. If a multinational runs into trouble in one part of the world today, it simply shifts operations elsewhere. Union Carbide after the Bhopal disaster is a case in point. The Indian subsidiary could be let go, and years later the American parent company would still successfully be denying compensation to thousands of the maimed, blinded and bereaved.[9]

The acceptability of early capitalism was, according to some influential analyses, helped along not only by Calvin's loosening of the constraints on moneylending, but also by his ideas on the predestination of the human soul. 'Our salvation flows from God's free mercy,' he wrote, 'freely offered to some while others are barred from access to it. Eternal life is foreordained for some, and eternal damnation for others.'[10] Max Weber has famously argued that this 'double predestination' – predestination for either Heaven or Hell – gave impetus to the 'Protestant work ethic'.[11] Gratification in the investor, he argued, is 'deferred': both in waiting for the next world and in saving up surplus cash during this one. We can see from this that accumulation thereby substitutes for the spiritual presence of providential waiting on 'daily bread'. Trust is placed in the bank, as well as, of course, in God! Those who are materially blessed in this world might then imagine that their success has been a sign of 'justification' before the Lord. Prosperity was seen as evidence of God's blessing and gave the rich 'assurance' that they were among the elect – the saved. Those who suffered were, by implication, seen as the damned. Calvin himself would never have made such a glib formulation. It would have been unscriptural. But it is easy to see how those who wanted both insurance in this world and assurance for the next could thus adapt his ideas. Conservative religion and acquisitive political economy tend to be closely linked; both are rooted in existential insecurity.

While the new religion allowed the economy to be set free by sanctifying capital, two other major factors were required to facilitate the full emergence of future globalisation: control over land and sea (as the source of resources and basis of communications), and the development of technology (with which to acquire leverage of power). Scientific reason melded to religious rectitude thereby made the emergent British Empire unlike any previous efforts at world domination. It gave competitive advantage in navigation, in industrial production, in war and in presumed moral righteousness. Francis Bacon, Lord Chancellor to King James until he was imprisoned for taking bribes, gives a telling insight into the seamier sides of the ideology behind this. Bacon is often lauded as the 'greatest of the moderns' and 'the father of modern science'.[12] Twentieth-century scholars of military espionage have also suggested that the principles of 'simulation and dissimulation', as used in warfare, have their origins in Bacon's essays. Today's feminist philosophers, however, see his 'malestream' mindset, advancing the new mainstream of Western thought, as epitomising the exploitation of nature represented by the 'burning times' era of the torture and persecution of the 'nature people' – the so-called 'witches'.[13] Credited with coining the phrase 'Knowledge is power', Bacon carefully wrapped his ideas in Christian sweet-talk, but developed a chilling instrumentalist technocracy. One of his works is revealingly called *The Masculine Birth of Time*. In another, *The New Atlantis*, published in 1605, he foresaw a scientific utopia with flying machines, submarines and climate control, complete with the brave new biotechnological vision of

> . . . parks and inclosures of all sorts of beasts and birds, which we use not only for view or rareness, but likewise for dissections and trials; that thereby we may take light what may be wrought upon the body of man . . . . We try also all poisons and other medicines upon them, as well of chirurgery [vivisection] as physic. By art likewise, we make them greater or taller than their kind is; and contrariwise dwarf

them, and stay their growth: we make them more fruitful and bearing than their kind is; and contrariwise barren and not generative . . . . We make them also by art greater much than their nature . . .[14]

Technological development contributed directly to the rise of sea power. With the Royal Navy as 'the Senior Service' and slave routes to defend, the nascent British Empire by the late seventeenth century had claimed its edge in world trade. Starting with the Navigation Act of 1660, the Empire was closed to foreign shipping. This, in the words of Christopher Hill, 'realized a Baconian vision towards which men had long been groping: that state control could stimulate material progress'.[15]

It is, however, changes in landed power that I would most like to focus on here. The Scotland of King James provides an instructive case study of how privatisation of common land came about.

In 1597 an act of the Scottish Parliament ordered everyone who claimed land to produce title deeds. However, the traditional tenure system of heritable trusteeship, known in Gaelic as *dúthchas*,[16] was usually oral – spoken but not written down. Title deeds were held in the bards' memories as clan history rather than as legal papers in a city lawyer's safe. In any case, nobody could really 'own' the land, because the Bible, in Leviticus 25:23, states that it belongs to God. The Crown's demand for title deeds was, therefore, an act of intimidation. Those who lacked written title could be sorted out with it, but only if they affirmed loyalty to the Crown, which, in a feudal system, theoretically delegated most property rights on behalf of God. The effect of James's measure would have been to strengthen property title, rather than the duties of heritable trusteeship, as the controlling factor in future social development. Similar measures were taking place all over Europe. Indeed, in England the process of enclosure had started to deprive the common people of their lands in earnest under Henry VIII as far back as 1530, and by 1780, it had virtually all been stitched up by the powers that be.[17]

The Hebrides at the start of James's reign had a greater affinity with Norway than with the Lowland-based Scottish Crown.[18] A cultural continuum connected the Gaels of Scotland and Ireland. The bards, or tribal poets, as learned ambassadors, could move freely across territories, enjoying 'a kind of diplomatic immunity' even in times of warfare. 'The person of a poet was sacred.'[19] And with few roads, the sea was their highway. This made Ireland seem considerably closer than Edinburgh.

James therefore set about breaking the unity of Gaelic-speaking peoples so that by dividing he might better rule. His 'Plantation' of Ulster used mainly poor Scots Protestants to settle Irish land. In so doing, he wronged the indigenous Catholic Irish and wrongfooted the poor Scots Protestants. The Gaelic continuum was divided by a Protestant buffer zone; Britain today is left with its troubled 'province', Northern Ireland, and the killing has continued into the twenty-first century.

But in Scotland, James's approach was subtler. The name of the game here was 'pacification' through 'civilisation' – colonisation from the inside of the culture. In the *Basilicon Doron*, written around 1598, James had described the mainland Highlanders as 'barbarous for the most parte, and yet mixed with some shewe of ciuilitie'. But even such a 'show of civility' was totally lacking in Hebrideans, who he described as 'attulerlie barbares' (utterly barbarous).[20] This was not a tolerable situation. So it was that in 1598 James launched his own proto-Thatcherite privatisation initiative. He granted a charter to English-speaking 'gentlemen' from Fife in Lowland Scotland to colonise the Isles of Lewis, Rona and Trotternish in Skye with law-abiding Protestants. It was to be a test run for an imperial policy that would shortly afterwards be exercised with greater effect elsewhere, especially in Ulster.

James aimed to wrest from the indigenous islanders control of both arable land and the potentially valuable Hebridean herring fishing industry. However, the indigenous culture was stronger than he had bargained for. An uprising led by Neil Macleod sent the so-called 'Fife Adventurers' packing. Tradition has it that Macleod was eventually captured, but only after the womenfolk and relatives of his followers were placed on an ocean rock and left to drown as the tide rose, not being rescued until the 'rebels' surrendered their fort. Macleod was duly hanged in April 1613 in Edinburgh, his head 'strukin frome his body, and affixit and set upone ane priket'. Happily, we are assured that he died 'verie Christianlie'.[21]

But it was in 1608, five years after he had created the United Kingdom, that James embarked upon his most notorious measure of forced pacification. He commissioned Andrew, Lord Stewart of Ochiltree, to take a ship to the Isle of Mull in the Inner Hebrides, where a dozen of the most powerful clan chiefs happened to be gathered. Ochiltree and the 'silver tongued' Andrew Knox, Bishop of the Isles, persuaded the chiefs to come on board by pretending that they were to be delivered of a goodly sermon. But the bishop betrayed them, the ship upped anchor, and they were kidnapped, taken down to the Lowlands to be separately jailed in the castles of Dumbarton, Blackness and Stirling. Here the chiefs were held for ten months and not released until they agreed to go to the sacred isle of Iona in 1609 and sign the Statutes of Iona.[22] It may be significant that this was the resting place of the 'black stones', upon which any oath made 'was decisive in all controversies'. Macdonald, King of the Isles, had once 'delivered the rights of their land to his vassals' using the Iona stones 'instead of his Great Seal', and swearing never to revoke his decree.[23] Evidently that was to be no more.

Through the lens of the Statutes of Iona we can see how the early British state was cemented together by a process that the historian Michael Hechter calls 'internal colonisation'. Troublesome areas like the Highlands were made into 'an internal colony within the very core of [the] world system'.[24] James clearly understood that if he was to control the people politically, he had to take control of their indigenous religious and poetic structures and replace them with his own worldview. This called for education.

Accordingly, two of the Statutes of Iona impacted directly on the bardic tradition that had carried the indigenous knowledge base.[25] Restraints were placed on the hospitality necessary for the maintenance of bardic retinues, and it was bluntly decreed that itinerant bards would 'be tane and put in suir fensment and keiping in the stokis, and thaireafter to be debarit furth of the countrey with all guidlie expeditioun . . .'. In modern English, that means they would be detained, encased in the stocks, kicked out of the area and debarred from coming back.

But it was Article VI of the Statutes that probably caused the greatest cultural dismemberment. This decreed that the traditional leadership had to have their eldest sons educated in the English language. This, of course, meant sending those who would inherit away to England or the Lowlands. The effect was to alienate them from their own culture. Following a MacDonald rebellion in 1616, a further education act made the policy of cultural genocide against the Celtic world quite explicit. James decreed that traditional leaders were to send all children, not just the first-born, away to English-language schools at the tender age of nine. Nobody in the Isles unable to speak, read and write in English was to be allowed to inherit property or to tenant Crown Lands.[26] The Act required that

> . . . the true [Protestant] religion be advanced and established in all parts of this kingdom, and that all his Majesty's subjects, especially the youth, be exercised and trained up in civility, godliness, knowledge and learning, that the vulgar English tongue be universally planted, and the Irish [i.e. Gaelic] language, which is one of the chief and principal causes of the continuance of barbarity and incivility among the inhabitants of the Isles and the Highlands, may be abolished and removed . . . [thus] in every parish . . . a school shall be established.[27]

The steady onward progress of modernisation was to find its most famous expression in 1776 when the Scots economist Adam Smith published *The Wealth of Nations*. In Smith's worldview the 'invisible hand' of the market becomes, as we might see it, the secularised working through of God's providence.[28] Not surprisingly for one of the 'imperial Scots', community for Smith is a community of interests, one that understands power differentials to be 'natural'. His introduction to Book One says that the work is about 'The Causes of Improvement in the Productive Powers of Labour, and of the Order According to Which its Produce is Naturally Distributed Among the

Different Ranks of the People'.[29] And he goes on to say that slavery, although a backward system because of surly inefficiency, is nonetheless justified if it can efficiently generate wealth for owners. This, he opines, will rarely be the case, except in sugar and tobacco plantations where 'the number of Negroes accordingly is much greater, in proportion to that of whites'.[30]

The process of modernisation of the Scottish Highlands rolled on relentlessly for three hundred years. Finally, in 1872, it reached a symbolic zenith with the passing of the national Education Act. This made a de-Gaelicised education compulsory for all children.[31] The 'Scots Enlightenment' ideas of Smith and a few other elite thinkers were now canonised and taught as our mainstream Protestant heritage. Religious instruction and collective daily acts of worship were made compulsory in schools. Corporal punishment – which had had little place in traditional 'ceilidh-house' education[32] – became routine, continuing in state schools right through into the 1980s, when it was abolished under pressure from European human-rights legislation. In short, the Baconian vision of modernity that James had championed was complete.

Well, in all but the papering-over of its cracks.

'Do you see that school?' repeats Torcuil MacRath, the bard of Grimashadar, for a third time, as he builds up the tension, rising in full declamation to the planned thunderclap of his dénouement. And I sit, auspiciously, on his grandmother's chair, by the shimmering peat embers, whisky glass long since drained, both of us too engrossed even to notice.

Torcuil had been a pupil in that school between the two world wars. He was left-handed. To force him into the uniformity of using his right hand, the teacher would physically tie down the left to the desk with string.

It was commonplace in those days for children to be punished for speaking Gaelic in the playground. In some schools they had to hang a spoon round their neck. This could only be got rid of by informing on some other poor kid, who in turn inherited it. Whoever had the spoon at the end of the day got sent home with a thrashing.

He told me that the Grimashadar village school was built on top of a *Sithean*, a faerie hill. Some would say that this was a place where nature should have been left to itself. But such was not the main cause of Torcuil's complaint.

'That school . . .' said this man, voice trembling with emotion now; this man who had once faced Hitler's forces in the Royal Navy and risked his life fighting for freedom. 'That school . . . *was a concentration camp!*'

And I'm older now – still living in Leurbost and going to school in Stornoway, but a teenager now. And it was 1972, I remember, and I'd gone camping with my friend down in South Harris.

We all knew him by the unflattering nickname 'Cabbage'; 'Cabbie' for short. Our school, the Nicolson Institute, had been kind in many ways. It equipped us well to exercise choice in the world that lay ahead. And it had allowed some of us to use a spare classroom to make a natural history museum. My own passion was for collecting and exhibiting stones.

So here's me and Cabbie, camping by the foot of the highest mountain in South Harris, Mount Roineabhal. In Gaelic, 'bh' is pronounced 'v', so the name makes a pleasing sound to roll like a malt whisky round the tongue – Roi-nya-val.

We've got an ex-Army Geiger counter with us and we've hit it lucky. The very spot where we pitch the tent is by a pegmatite outcrop in which there's a pocket of rusty tar-black metallic mineral. The Geiger counter is hardly necessary for verification. We've found pitchblende – uranium ore. It's clear from the shell-like fracture pattern when you break it, and the distinctive yellow coating from gummite, a highly oxidised derivative – in plain language, uranium rust.

When pressed right up against our find, the Geiger counter shoots nearly off the scale. These are gamma rays coming mostly from radium, a breakdown product of uranium. Yippee! Eldorado! The danger to health is no greater than for any uranium prospector, which, after all, is what we like to think of ourselves as being. So just for the boyish hell of it, we hack out as much as we can. To us sons of the atomic age, this is better than striking gold. You'd have thought we were going to make the Hebridean atom bomb, or at least Stornoway's contribution to the Manhattan Project.

That night we discuss the geological significance of the find in the manner that only boys, being great authorities on such matters, could do. Uranium is not uncommon in ancient pegmatites. However, the rock here is insufficiently abundant for commercial exploitation. Pity. We'd all learned from our physics textbooks that the future lies in nuclear power. Imagine if we could have had a bit of the action right here! But there might be consolation. Other commercial prospects are apparent. Most of Mount Roineabhal is made of anorthosite – a rare calcium aluminium silicate feldspar. It is hard and dense with a range of industrial uses, the most humdrum of which is as an excellent road stone.

The next night I'm out and disguising my age at the bar of the Rodel Hotel. 'Rum-and-coke please' – sweet, fizzy and effective. I'm chatting with some of the unemployed men propping up the bar. All agree: it would be great for them if an anorthosite quarry could open up. There used to be a small one operating between the wars. It left a pockmark on the side of Roineabhal, a white scar that's small, but still clearly visible. Quite a few men were employed there. Couldn't the same happen again?

The idea gains energy in my mind. I resolve that, once back home, I'll type a letter to the Highlands and Islands Development Board urging government action. Indeed, I'll even point out that I would *love* to work in such a quarry. After all, I was soon going to Aberdeen University, where for four years, in old-school Scots generalist fashion, alongside physics, geography, psychology and philosophy, I'd be studying geology.

The next day Cabbie and I climb Roineabhal. It is the first time we've been up something that really feels like a mountain. You start from the road and scramble over heathery hillocks and great tumbled mossy boulders. Soon you're into one of numerous little valleys with xylophonic streams that make a tinkling music with their water's fall. As the slope rises more steeply, you encounter a series of naked rocky ridges, each stripped by ice-age glaciers that retreated some 10,000 years earlier – just a moment ago in geological time. At last, approaching the summit, vegetation becomes scant, even where thin soil has managed to form. The plants are alpine and this creates an otherworldly air. Right at the top is a stone cairn, around which a low wall gives shelter from almost constant wind. And beyond, the full majesty of the Hebrides.

To the south is the island-studded Sound of Harris, North Uist and Berneray. To the east is Skye and the Inner Hebrides. You can't quite see Eigg. To the north is Lewis, and at night, far above, dance the *aurora borealis*, or Northern Lights. In Gaelic this iridescent curtain flowing over clear winter skies is personified as *Fir-chlisme*, 'the men of the tricks', the leaping, darting ones. And out to the west surges the great Atlantic. It's amazing to think that there's nothing between us and America: the great America, with its Wild West, Red Indians, and whole mountains full of gold and uranium.

I'm surprised how struck I am by the beauty from the top. Growing up on Lewis and Harris, you take beauty so much for granted that you rarely bother to notice. But that's the point about mountains: they take you out of your normal perceptual framework. Such are the qualities of stone. Says contemporary American writer Susan Griffin:

> It is said that the close study of stone will reveal traces of fires suffered thousands of years ago . . . . I am beginning to believe that we know everything, that all history, including the history of each family, is part of us, such that, when we hear any secret revealed our lives are made suddenly clearer to us . . . . Perhaps we are like stones; our own history and the history of the world is embedded in us, we hold a sorrow deep within and cannot weep until that history is sung.[33]

The Rev. Alastair MacLean of Daviot had words for the panorama that radiates from oceanic mountains like Roineabhal. He wrote about a similar vantage point in *Hebridean Altars*, a wonderful collection of Celtic anecdotes from 1937. Indeed, the reverend gentleman could easily have been writing about our vantage point that day – only we at that age would have missed the point of his spiritual vocabulary. We'd have been more interested in *The Guns of*

Navarone or one of those other war stories by his son of the same name. For we boys were capable of seeing but a fraction of what actually lay before our senses. Susan Griffin's insight would have been way beyond the spectral range of our consciousness. We lacked the grounding in our own culture that would have been necessary to weave the weft of heart's perception to the warp of what actually lay before our eyes. But with the colouring of retrospect, like a graphic artist retouching an old black-and-white photograph, the Rev. MacLean's account can substitute for how we, too, could have described that experience. Here, then, is MacLean describing a panoramic Hebridean mountain. Imagine him up there; imagine it is on Roineabhal, if you will. And like me with Cabbie, he's with his good friend, John of the Cattle of Mull.

We sat together, under the shadow of a rock, each of us, in his own way, worshipping the glory that is the Hebrides .... Above us, and between the blue of the sky and the brown of the Earth, floated the wonder veil, the veil of the purple light. On the day of the year that was clearest and most still the folk who had come from the Hebrides to the Upper Land leant out over the golden sills and, for the space of an hour, saw everything as it once had been. Their old homes. Little ones at play. Roses blushing in the gardens. Men drinking deep from wayside wells. Lovers with misty eyes wandering through a hazel wood whose other name is Eden. It was a sight, however, that was ill for peace of mind – as things beyond your reach mostly are. So the Good One, who knows what is best for everyone, gave the veil of the purple light to His four archangels, bidding them spread it well between the blue of the sky and the brown of the Earth. And this His servitors do. And there is such a depth of purple in it that the Upper Folk cannot see the Isles. And nowadays are well content. 'What the eye does not see,' says the Gaelic proverb, 'the heart will not desire.'

That day, when we both drank our fill from Beauty's chalice, I was a lad in my teens. My companion was a cattle-dealer. He was of Mull. A soft-spoken kind of man. Quick of pride. A treasure-chest of ancient wisdoms and songs and tales .... He it was who taught me that, in his essence, a man is a spirit, and that the essence of spirit is truth and beauty and love. The legend of the veil of the purple light was his story, as was the reason why the King of the Elements made the Hebrides ...

'These islands,' he breathed, with a gesture towards the North, 'aye, 'tis myself that is as fond of them as a mother of her baby-child, and, mind you, they are the great favourites with the Good One above us as well.'

'Indeed,' said I.

'Yes,' he went on, 'or rather, as I should say, the greatest favourites of all. Now,' he raised his forefinger impressively, 'listen to what I am telling you. The Good One made the Hebrides on the eighth day.'

'The eighth day!' I cried, 'but the Bible . . .'

He waved his hand for silence. 'The Bible is a grand book entirely, and the stories of Samson and the other noble heroes in it are warming to the heart. But, mark you, lad, a man who writes a large book cannot mind everything and' – he hummed a little at this point – 'and, like enough, the decent man forgot about the Islands being made the eighth day. But they were, and this was the way of it. The world was finished and the Good One was mighty tired and took a rest and, while He was resting, He thought, "Well, I have let my earth-children see the power of my mind, in rock and mountain and tree and wind and flower. And I have shown them the likeness of my mind, for I have made theirs like my own. And I have shown them the love of my mind, for I have made them happy. But halt," says the Good One to Himself, "I have not shown them the beauty of my mind." So the next day, and that was the eighth day, He takes up a handful of jewels and opens a window in the sky and throws them down into the sea. And those jewels are the Hebrides. I had the story of it from my father's father,' he went on. 'An extra fine man, and terrible strong for the truth.'[34]

On one of the ice-polished ridges traversing Roineabhal, Cabbie and I chance upon a mineral-rich vein of rock. I strike with my geological hammer – not the sort of thing you'd do these days, but this was those days. It opens. To my astonishment, inside rests a perfect crystal of tourmaline. The stone – for this is a gemstone, modest but resplendent – shines jet black. Its facets flash light for the first time since the mountain gestated in the world's womb two billion years previously.[35]

The crystal is triangular. It protrudes an inch from the bedrock. A natural triquetra, and it resonates to this day in my mind. It brings up images of triple-swirl symbols: on ancient Pictish slab stones at Meigle, on the Christ page in the Book of Kells, and carved in weathered sandstone at Iona Abbey's north gate. The sacred Celtic three. The poetic 'triple Goddess' of Robert Graves's maiden, mother, crone.[36] The Hindu triad of life, death and rebirth. The Christian trinity of Father, Child and Holy Spirit's woman-spirit rising.

The three-sided black crystal shines to this day, a memory in my hand. It spirals from out my mind, down the summit of Mount Roineabhal. I do not recall what happened to that stone. It exists now only as a reminiscence. But once it rested solid in my palm. It filled me with delight and does so yet.

And somewhere, high up over Roineabhal, golden eagles soar. But either Cabbie and I missed them that day, or they missed us in our boyish insignificance.

6. The Admiral's Birthday Surprise

As I became older and stronger, my skill at the oars of a boat developed into a marketable commodity. So it was that from my mid-teens through to my early twenties – some eight years in all – I found myself taking summer work as a ghillie on local estates.

Ghillie is the Gaelic word for servant. It applies particularly to outdoor service at sporting lodges and especially to handling the boat from which guests fish for salmon. It can also involve being the 'pony boy' who goes out with the stalkers and brings the stag's carcase back on the saddle of a horse.

To see the hunting and shooting country life close-up is to see through a window into the mores of those who run the Western world. Among the visitors to the Soval and Eisken estates where I variously worked, there was, for example, Mr Rodway, who told me that he owned twenty-nine companies in South Africa, including schools and gold mines. I once asked him about apartheid, and while I forget his precise answer, I think he considered it a necessary eventuality.

Then there was a chairman of Cartier, the French diamond merchants. He returned each year with a different glamorous 'secretary'. We ghillies were bemused by the Parisian fashions; Lewis sheep had never before seen the like. But at least it showed what happens to Harris Tweed when it left the island.

I remember making an expedition with packhorses to a remote mountain loch with Major Coates of Kenya. He rolled out his catalogue of bagged elephant, rhino and lions, telling me: 'You see, Alastair, I'm what you might genuinely call one of the last of the great white hunters. The last,' he insisted, with an air of self-revulsion, 'because most of Africa's game has been shot. Shot out, I'm afraid to tell you, by people like me! And that's why I'm a conservationist now.'

Then there was Colonel 'Tishy' Benson. A tear came to my eye when I read his obituary in the *Daily Telegraph* on St George's Day 1999: his avid bravery; his refusal to reminisce about the sickening circumstances among Rommel's tanks that earned him high decoration; his uncanny ability to command the loyalty of the other ranks. True enough, he always pleaded poverty when it came to paying our tips, but we'd have done anything for him nonetheless. He was a lovely man.

And, finally, dear old Captain Bumford. He had suffered in the trenches of the First World War. This, he assured me, was what had left him with gout, and as such he was deserving of sympathy. 'You're young, Alastair,' he'd say to me on days when no salmon had swirled at his fly. 'You won't tell the others if I slip just a little worm on to my hook.'

These men moved in worlds that were completely alien to ours. And yet, here they were, on hill or loch with us, spending two weeks each year on the Isle of Lewis. In a curious way, we became their peers for that time. And I would have to admit that we felt dignified by their presence. It was an honour to work with such giants, not least because the majority of them had a strong and, at times, unexpected personal sense of honour.

In my boyish way, of course, I used to enjoy ferreting out real-life war stories from those who had seen active service. However, these were rarely told with the bravado for which one hoped. I remember once, while out on Loch Valtos, asking a General Sir Harry Williams, I think his name was, about the greatest heroism he had seen in action. To my disappointment, he said that it had been the work of conscientious objectors in the Friends' Ambulance Brigade who had attended the wounded of both sides on the front line. Others among them volunteered for bomb disposal to save lives. Such was my first introduction to Quaker pacifism and to the possibility that to die for one's country can require greater courage than to kill for it.

There was another time – it was at Eisken – and I was out on the hill as pony boy to the head stalker, Tommy MacRae. The year was 1976 and the 'gun' that day was a tall, angular Englishman, Commander Bray. Since Tommy was a person of great dignity and knowledge, I was deeply privileged to be his apprentice. Once the herd of deer had been spotted, my role entailed remaining about a mile behind and minding the pony. I'd watch the stalkers' progress through binoculars. Usually they took two or three hours to creep within range. Sometimes I'd get very cold lying in wait, or I'd be eaten by midges. Midges, after all, are the Highlands' secret weapon. They keep tourist numbers down. My only consolation, waiting and watching, was the sure knowledge that my compatriots were probably colder and itchier than I, as they crawled camouflaged in brown tweeds on all fours through thickly oozing peat hags.

On this particular day I could make out clearly both Tommy and the 'gun' not too far off. They were after a fine stag with a good head; not quite a twelve-pointed 'Royal', but a decent set of antlers nonetheless with which to grace some southern drawing-room. When they got within a couple of hundred paces, the Commander took aim. The stag flinched and the distance-softened sound of the shot followed. But as I watched, the beast started to stagger away. He was only wounded. A second shot thudded out, devoid of any echo on the wide-open heather-clad moor. Only then did the Commander's handsome quarry fall.

The next day this same dismal performance was repeated. I was further away, hiding in a hollow. The gun went off but, as sometimes happened, I'd lost sight of the beast; it blended in so well with its environment. This left me unsure whether it was safe to break cover. The procedure when this happened was not to advance until Tommy had gathered a little heap of heather and set it ablaze. I'd watch for the smoke signals, as in a papal election, and thereby know when I could advance without disturbing a hunt still in progress or, for that matter, entering the line of fire between the gun and a panicking wounded beast.

But on this occasion no puff of smoke followed the first shot. There was a long wait and then a second report, after which I saw the puffs of smoke. Evidently, the animal had been hit but had run some distance before being finished off.

On arriving to load up the carcase, I was surprised to find the Commander sitting on a tussock of dry grass, looking as if he himself were the wounded party. His face was ashen. I could see that something within him had died. Without any ado, he told me straight that his 'nerve' had gone. After spoiling the first shot, he had trembled so much that he was forced to hand the .303 rifle over to Tommy. It had been the head stalker, and not the guest, who had dispatched the final slug of lead.

What a sense of responsibility Tommy had! His was a real respect for the creatures of which his job involved necessary culling. Once he spent all night out with his dog hunting down a wounded beast to put it out of its misery. He told me that you usually find them cowed in a peat hag, or sometimes standing neck-deep out in a loch, haemorrhaging into the brown water. He reckoned this was a desperate last-ditch attempt to put his dog off the dripping blood's scent.

All three of us walked back silently that botched day. It was like coming home from a funeral without the anticipation of a good wake. On arrival at the Lodge, the Commander entered the tackroom, where the day's exploits were always shared over glasses of whisky. He solemnly announced to everybody that he forthwith disqualified himself from shooting. He could not justify what he was doing if, for two days running, he had been unable to make a clean kill. Henceforth he would spend his time more peaceably – fishing on the loch.

To this day, I really respect that man's courage: his willingness to be vulnerable. It taught me more about genuine humility than I have learned from many a more obvious spiritual teacher.

Most of the time, of course, there was no such sombre sobriety about the job. My favourite story was the occasion that Tommy and I ended up drinking whisky by the side of Loch Eisken with me in my birthday suit – 'the full monty' as they say – alongside an admiral of the British Navy whose birthday it just happened to be.

On this occasion we had left Sandy, the experienced horse, behind, and were training a young Icelandic pony, Freya. I had set off early in the morning to ride her the 5 miles along a dramatic winding track to the head of the sea fjord, Loch Shell. Tommy and the Admiral followed on in an open boat powered by a 5-horsepower Seagull. When we met up together, there was no sign of any deer, so we walked on in a posse, through the hauntingly beautiful and utterly remote Loch Shell valley, passing a cluster of stone ruins. Behind us, and southwards, were the slopes of Uisenis rising steeply up from ocean cliffs. There lay the crashed remains of a Second World War bomber that had failed, one fateful night, to make it safely into Stornoway. More than thirty years on, it still felt like a disaster that had just happened: the airmen's rain-soaked flying boots; the scattered unspent ammunition; the broken navigational instruments.

I had asked several times about the ruined buildings that we passed through, but I'd never been able to get an answer. 'They're just something from the old days,' Tommy would say. That was strange. They, like the air crash, looked old and yet so recent. And the raised-bed agricultural system of *feannagan* or 'lazybeds' around them showed that the land had been actively cultivated. Neither was it ancient cultivation, because these were straight *feannagan*. You can tell the older, pre-Reformation ones, so I've been told, because they snake sinuously down the slopes. This was to put the Devil off. In those more superstitious days, it was believed that he could only walk in straight lines.[1] 'Where have you come from?' God asks Satan in the opening chapter of Job. 'From going to and fro on the earth,' Satan replies, 'and from walking up and down on it.' The straight, post-Reformation *feannagan* probably owe less to a reduced fear of the Devil than to the practicalities of title deeds. Wherever you see straight lines in countryside, suspect the markings of a lawyer's pen. So who knows, maybe the Devil had ridden into this remote valley after all.

The path rose steeply and we climbed on up by the deep waterfall pools where, on hot days, I'd tether the pony and bathe on my way home. Still no sign of the 'cattle of the faeries', as deer are known in folk tradition. Eventually, Tommy concluded that they must be over the other side of the Ben Mor – over the top of the mountain that, viewed from Achmore, halfway between Leurbost and the Calanais stones, lines up perfectly with Eisken's woman-shaped Sleeping Beauty Mountain, becoming her great pregnant belly.

And so we slogged hard up through a mountain saddle, rising at last over the rounded Ben Mor. It was getting on for mid-afternoon before we sighted the herd. We all hoped that the kill would be quick. The route back was going to be rough and very slow. Neither the horse nor I knew that distant ground, and even Tommy rarely walked these far-flung parts.

A storm was building now – a late summer storm. The clouds blackened and heaved with brooding gravity. From on high we looked down on the neighbouring Loch Seaforth and, beyond it, the haunting hills of Harris. Once the Lordship of the Isles had rested its seat somewhere on these shores. Of course, it had been all very well for King James to call the Hebrideans 'utterly barbarous'. But frankly, to borrow from Milton, his criticism was partly a case of 'they who have put out the people's eyes reproach them for their blindness'. In the Hebridean oral tradition the Lordship is remembered as something of a cultured golden age, or at least, as close to that as any patriarchal warrior society is ever likely to get. Until the second half of the fifteenth century, the Hebrides and parts of west Scotland had been controlled from Norway. James IV, an earlier Stuart king who married Margaret Tudor, had wished to bring the Lordship into accountability to the Scottish Crown. He particularly resented its tendency to intrigue with the English.[2] When the Lordship fell into a period of infighting and its Council of the Isles was no longer able to ensure good order, James took the opportunity of forfeiting it. The feudal system was formally imposed from 1493 – very late, as European history goes. This, of course, led to resentment, the result being a prolonged period of bloodthirsty instability that James VI was later able to use to justify his ill opinion of the Hebrideans. Clan power became scattered and sometimes despotic. As John Lorne Campbell puts it, 'the Scottish Crown had at last succeeded in shooting down the eagle, but had thereby only let loose a flock of kestrels'.[3]

The investiture ceremony for the Lordship of the Isles is telling for its combined Christian, druidical and bardic elements. Hugh MacDonald, the seventeenth-century historian of the MacDonalds of Sleat on Skye, recounts that

> At this ceremony [involving] the Bishop of Argyll, the Bishop of the Isles, and seven priests ... there was a square stone, seven or eight feet long, and the tract of a man's foot cut thereon, upon which he [the new Lord] stood, denoting that he should walk in the footsteps and uprightness of his predecessors, and that he was installed by right of his possessions. He was clothed in a white habit, to shew his innocence and integrity of heart, that he would be a light to his people, and maintain the true religion. The white apparel did afterwards belong to the poet by right. Then he was to receive a white rod in his hand, intimating that he had power to rule, not with tyranny and partiality, but with discretion and sincerity. Then he received his forefathers' sword. ... When they were dismissed, the Lord of the Isles feasted them for a week thereafter; gave liberally to the monks, poets, bards and musicians.[4]

From the earliest recorded times up until the advent of James's early-modern era, the Highlands and the Celtic world in general were steeped in a mythopoetic culture. People's very sense of who they were, what their human worth

was and what values they espoused was transmitted through legendary genealogy, myth, poetry, the pibroch (*piobaireachd*) of classical bagpipe-playing and
harp-accompanied song. In this sense their mindsets were very different from
those schooled in Greek rationalism. They had more in common with the
Hebrew metaphoric mind than with mainstream Europe's self-proclaimed
'Enlightenment' or 'Age of Reason'.

Central to cultural maintenance were the bardic schools, the indigenous universities of life. Their curricula probably encompassed all matters pertaining to
the soul of the people. In ancient times this had been the provenance of the
druids. Bards can be looked on as the druids' Christianised medieval succes-
sors. In the nineteenth century the bardic ethos found prophetic expression
through *na Daoine* – 'the Men' – and the evangelical revival that led up to the
1843 church Disruption. The connecting principle between druid, bard and
evangelical preacher alike was sensitivity to poetics. As the great Celtic scholar
Raghnall MacilleDhuibh puts it, 'Poetry and prophecy went hand in hand . . . .
The highest and most important function of poetry was prophecy . . . . Both
poetry and prophecy required a heightened spiritual awareness.'[5]

The highest order of bards were the learned *filidh*, trained in accredited
bardic schools of literary quality, of which there were perhaps four still flour-
ishing in Scottish Gaeldom by the accession of James VI.[6] Lower orders,
known as the *cliar sheanchain*, ranked all the way down to itinerant storytellers
and buskers. These were seen by the Lowland authorities as being no different from beggars and vagabonds. The effect of the Statute of Iona limiting
hospitality was to target mainly the *filidh* and their retinues, while the Statute
threatening exile was probably aimed at the *cliar sheanchain*. Large-scale hospitality was essential to bardic retinues because, familes included, they could
number forty to sixty persons.[7] As Professor Hyde put it, 'As the bards lived
to please, so they had to please to live'.[8]

It is difficult to say how direct a consequence the Statutes of Iona had.
They certainly aimed to promote a cash economy and thus operate 'against the
solidarity and continuity of Highland culture'.[9] Specific court prosecutions
under the Statutes are recorded.[10] And yet the seventeenth century was certainly not bereft of bardic output.[11] In the absence of very much historical
research, we are probably safest to look on the Statutes as indicators of the
prevailing political climate rather than being the direct cause of changes that
followed. However, given that the Statutes suggest that bardic power was some
kind of threat to James's colonising plans, and given that these plans were in
many ways a template for how the biggest empire the world has ever seen
would be constructed, we should, while still in our vantage point on the Ben
Mor, survey in some detail what the bards represented at this turning point
in world history. The insights that Highland and Irish culture can reveal may
then be seen to have resonance and relevance far beyond the Celtic world.

The bards were 'to a large extent the political brains behind the Highland chiefs' military strength, and probably the authorities were right to be afraid of them'.[12] Edmund Spenser, advising the English authorities on Irish colonial policy in the late sixteenth century, warned:

> But these Irish Bardes are for the most part of another minde, and so farre from instructing yong men in morall discipline, that they themselves doe more deserve to bee sharpely disciplined; for they seldome use to choose themselves the doings of good men for the arguments of their poems, but whomsoever they finde to be most licentious of life, most bolde and lawlesse in his doings, most dangerous and desperate in all parts of disobedience and rebellious disposition, him they praise to the people, and to yong men make an example to follow . . . tending for the most part to the hurt of the English.[13]

The Celtic bards held together a society 'dependent for its stability just as much upon the might of the word as upon the might of the sword'.[14] They maintained a 'poetic map' of social and geographical relations,[15] and helped uphold social order by their use of 'panegyric' – eulogistic praise poetry – or, if necessary, a cutting-down-to-size satire. Bards thereby had the power effectively to bless or curse. 'To satirize an enemy was to destroy him and thus, again, to save the tribe,' say Morton Bloomfield and Charles Dunn in *The Role of the Poet in Early Societies*, their fascinating cross-cultural study. 'A satire could cause a king to waste away; it could cause a victim to melt; it could raise blotches on his face.' But equally, 'it could recoil on the satirist himself, if he uttered an undeserved satire, and at the least raise blotches on his face or even cause his death'.[16] There is a striking parallel, certainly in its punitive aspects, with the role that I have seen played by sorcerers exerting traditional social control in Papua New Guinea.[17] In a mythopoetic society poetic justice ultimately keeps things under control.

The bards' praise poetry had a distinct structure, something that John MacInnes – one of the greatest living authorities on Gaelic culture – calls the 'panegyric code'. This amounted to a set of cultural norms that expressed principles of right relationship. It encoded a traditional psychology that deeply interlocked people, place and divinity – the Celtic triumvirate of community, nature and God. And it set high standards of kindness, bravery, conviviality and ecological awareness that the chiefs were expected to live up to, having been praised in prior anticipation.[18] Such poetry was central to underpinning the vernacular economics of mutuality and reciprocity that has been called the 'Highland welfare state'.[19] As an elegy to Murdo MacFarlane puts it, he having been the bard of Melbost, Lewis, who died in 1982: 'Yes, a mind extraordinary,/A Gaelic poetic mind,/One that cherished the underdog.'[20]

Johnson and Boswell, visiting Scotland in 1773, supposed that the Hebridean bardic tradition, what they called that 'dawn of intelligence', had died out almost a lifetime earlier.[21] While this was unduly pessimistic, it is true that its supporting social structures, such as the bardic schools, had certainly attenuated. I know of only two contemporarily documented accounts of the bardic schools. Daniel Corkery, the great Irish authority of the early twentieth century, says that this dearth is to be expected because the institution was too familiar for early writers to bother describing.[22]

One of these accounts, recorded on the Isle of Skye by Martin Martin in around 1695, is particularly fascinating because it contains distinctive shamanistic or yogic elements. Martin tells how the bards would compose their works by lying on their backs for a day in a darkened room, with their woven woollen plaids or mantles wrapped around their heads, eyes covered, and a stone on their bellies. This latter feature would probably have affected respiration – something that is today recognised as being capable of producing dramatically altered states of consciousness akin to the effects of psychedelic agents like LSD or magic mushrooms.[23] Indeed, it is possible that psychoactive mushrooms were employed (perhaps even by St Columba, according to Professor O'Cathain's analysis of the folklore surrounding his life).[24] Martin Martin additionally remarks on how bards in the chief's circle were held in higher esteem than doctors of medicine, that they had taken over the oratorical function of the druids, and that 'by the force of their eloquence [they] had a powerful ascendant over the greatest men in their time'.[25] John MacInnes states that some sources 'suggest that the bard might act in other capacities also, such as those of shaman or seer [and] achieve mystic vision and engage in divination'.

The bards' period of training is said to have covered seven years: 'It is obvious that the Bardic Schools had a severe academic discipline.' Of the typical product of these schools it has been said that:

> He [sic] was, in fact, a professor of literature and a man of letters . . . . He discharged . . . the function of the modern journalist . . . a public figure, a chronicler, a political essayist, a keen and satirical observer of his fellow countrymen. At an earlier period he had been regarded as a dealer in magic, a weaver of spells and incantations, who could blast his enemies by the venom of his verse . . . . He might be a poet too if, in addition to his training, he was gifted with the indefinable power, the true magic, of poetry.[26]

In its shamanistic attributes, elements of the Celtic tradition would not be strange to other primal peoples, such as some Native Americans. For example, in Ulster, *tigh n' alluis* or sweat lodges were used to prepare a man or woman for the *dercad,* an act of meditation, by which Irish mystics would attempt to achieve a state of *sitcháin* or peace.[27] The Gaelic word for peace, incidentally, is the same as that for *faerie.* Another shamanic dimension is that in Highland dream lore differing animal totems represent the various clans. These were used both for poetic allusion and the interpretation of omens.[28] For instance, the totem of my own clan, Mackintosh, is the wildcat. This gives rise to the clan motto: 'Touch not the cat bot (but) a glove', meaning that if you mess with the Mackintosh the gauntlet will be thrown down and you'll have a fight on your hands! The totem of the Mathesons is the bear; the deer symbolises MacKenzie; and so on.[29]

Often a taboo, known as a *geist* or *geasa*, protected such totem animals. For instance, the Irish hero Cuchulainn, whose name means 'hound of Culann', was forbidden to eat the flesh of dog. He met his end after being caught in a situation where he had to transgress this.[30] To the present day, some tradition bearers still take totemistic omens very seriously. One example is John MacInnes's reflections on deer as the 'cattle' of the faerie world. As such, they symbolise *wildness*, in contrast to the settled control of civilised ordinary cattle in the village. 'I remember very vividly, when I was a little boy,' John says, 'seeing a wild hind grazing within the confines of the *baile* (village). Those who could read the signs realised that the natural order was being over-turned . . . . Not very long after that the Second World War began. That sighting, *that metaphor of order invaded by the wild*, helped those who witnessed it *to arrange their experience*.'[31]

Far away by the western tip of Loch Seaforth was the white lodge of the Aline Estate, North Harris. It is strange how often sporting lodges are painted brilliant white. It makes them look neat and pretty, but reminiscent, somehow, of proverbial whitened sepulchres.

The herd grazed restlessly. Tommy hurried: the deer would move off once the expectant heavens opened. I stayed back alone beneath the skyline, waiting, hiding, in pre-emptive exhaustion.

The Admiral fired from a longer range than would be normal. He was a good shot, and within a few minutes, the little puff of heather smoke signalled for Freya and me to advance.

By the time I got to them, the 'gralloching', as removing the innards is called, was already complete. Bloody intestines reddened the heather, a good meal for a lucky crow or hawk. After a quick wee dram from the Admiral's flask, we hoisted the warm carcase onto Freya's saddle, strapped it tight with leather belts to ensure the antlers could not jab her flank, and with the deed done, we made off.

Then the sky ripped open.

There is a tradition that bards were born, not made, and very often a male bard would stress that the gift had come down through his mother's family line.[32] Some would seem to have had supernatural powers of the 'second sight'.[33] Indeed, Ronald Black, in his outstanding collection and commentary on the twentieth-century bards, refers to, 'that foreknowledge which is the special gift of those devoted both to prayer and to poetry'.[34] Inspiration was often associated with what we would today think of as 'liminal' or threshold states of consciousness – those places mediating between this and the 'otherworld'. Faerie hills are one such liminal place: an entrance – an *en-trance* – into the realm of magic that is the realm of *poesis*.[35]

This otherworld, partaking as it does of the eternal, provides a deeper perspective on reality than the temporal world of normality. Normality proceeds from the mythopoetic rather than the other way round. The mythopoetic is more fundamental. I think that this is terribly important: it is why, ultimately, the true bard does not just compose poetry. Rather, she or he is gripped by it at the gut level of cultural genesis. Poetics makes the bard. As such, to be a poet is an outrageous calling, not a judicious career move. The bard at most *invokes* awareness or opens up consciousness to that which is already present in mythopoesis. As such, the bard mediates between consciousness and the Jungian collective unconscious. This is why Scotland's greatest modern bard, Hugh MacDiarmid, was able to say: 'We must return to the ancient classical Gaelic poets. For in them the inestimable treasure is wholly in contact with the inner surface of the unconscious'.[36]

The sky rips open like this on Lewis only in early autumn, but when it does, nature sets loose a naked assault of icy white firestone. Huge melting hail pellets fired down on us with shotgun-like ferocity. We couldn't look up. Their relentless drumming on our oilskin hoods made conversation futile.

We trudged drearily on. The Eisken river was already in flash flood as we reached the headwaters. We followed down the bank until we came, at last, to the loch. There, a mile by the crow's flight on the other side, stood the Lodge.

Once safely back home there, the Admiral would go for a stiff dram in the tackroom and then on to dine. Tommy and I would flay the carcass in the larder and heave it up to the rafters with a pulley, there to await the butcher's collection. Tommy would also pull out the stag's 'tusks', the two ivory-like side-teeth, which fetch a good price as material for cuff-links. Then we'd feed the horses, grab a quick bite to eat for ourselves, and get to bed by about ten, ready to rise at dawn the next day.

That's what we'd do once we got home, but we weren't there yet.

John MacInnes describes a Uist poet who would say that when composing, his mind was 'away in the Hill'. This, the faerie world, is 'a metaphor for the imagination'.[37] The 'Hill' is the potentially superconscious realm of what is normally unconscious, what has either been buried away or has never yet come fully into being. We would do well here to distinguish between that which is 'imaginary', and therefore unreal, and that which is 'imaginal', and therefore beyond the normal bounds of consciousness – but not necessarily any less 'real' because of it. Poetics speaks to a deeper stratum of reality than does the trance of semi-sleepwalking awareness that, most of the time, passes for being awake.[38]

Another revealing account in MacInnes's extensive repertoire tells how the accomplished female bard, Maighread Ni Lachainn, would 'see' her poems running along the green turfs that formed the intersection of wall and roof in her blackhouse.[39] These have walls up to 6 feet or 2 metres thick, lined with turf on top where the wall meets the pitched thatched roof. If we allow Ni Lachainn's image to be illuminated by principles gained from the under-standing of shamanism in other cultures, the vision could well be equated with a class of liminal experience whereby the sky or Heaven (roof) is brought into connection with the mortal realm that is the Earth (wall). Such is the point where creative experience takes place.

There is nothing exceptional about such accounts from the Celtic tradition when seen in shamanic and bardic terms. For example, the Sufi mystic Inayat Khan tells of a very great Persian poet who, on entering into a certain mood, 'used to make circles around a pillar which stood in the middle of his house. Then he would begin to speak, and people would write down what he said, and it would be perfect poetry.'[40] The modern-day English storyteller Leo Sofer gives a similar sense of images flowing through the psyche of one who is in tune with the otherworld. He recounts how, after a spiritual awakening, 'I began to see vivid fairy-tale scenes in my mind's eye which, as I described them, unfolded with a life of their own. I was being *told* a story!'[41]

As we have seen, Celtic society was 'dependent for its stability just as much upon the might of the word as upon the might of the sword'. The bard's greatest gift lay in 'wisdom and eloquence joined together'.[42] What was spoken always had to be true. If it was not, it could rebound with malevolent effect. The bard who failed to speak with the 'tongue of truth' (such as was given to Thomas the Rhymer after his seven years away with the Faerie Queen) would face sickness or even death should truth be betrayed. As such, poetics is a sacred art. Its effectiveness depended (as it still depends) upon respect for truth. As Morton Bloomfield and Charles Dunn put it: 'If early literature was not true, its magic would not work. The continuing dispute between history and poetry is based on the claim, unacceptable to the historians, that what the poets write is true.'[43]

To the poet, historical truth could not be separated from representation in the language of metaphor. As such, it is a qualitative reality rather than a black-and-white absolute. History, to the mythopoetic mind, was not just lit-eral; more importantly, it was also a very psychological and spiritual reality. Not to see this was to miss the crucial point of psychohistory: that history lives in us and that our lives are historically moulded. Not to see it was to get trapped in the head and lose the heart. It was to lay out the warp of history but neglect the deft weaving of its weft. To the bard, then, the bare bones of historical fact had to be fleshed out with illustrative meaning. In this way not just the truth but also the whole truth would be told. And in this way, too, a people knew who they were and what they stood for.

We can see, then, that legendary tales which to the modern mind exaggerate accomplishments – like Cuchulainn destroying twelve chariots with his bare hands in just one day – are, in fact, attempts to convey an accuracy that captures the truth of archetypal potency. Monsters, demons and angelic presences are therefore literal presences, used as metaphors of psychodynamic reality. Our modern psychology might talk of the Jungian shadow, the Freudian id and cognitive structures. It might recognise that these can be 'socially constructed' and 'role modelled'. As such, it might be accepted that psychodynamic forces are both personal and interpersonal – they are both specific to us and they have a kind of life of their own. But to the primal mythopoetic mind, all this could be expressed plainly through motifs in story, as, for example, with the Devil personified as Satan. To such a mind, nature itself has a life beyond the one-eyed seeing that allows perception only of its mundane facets. Such, then, is the Celtic 'otherworld', existing not necessarily as some distant Eden or *Tir nan Og* beyond the western wave, but interpenetrating the world all around us if, as Jesus often said, we have but eyes to see and ears to hear.

Tommy, the Admiral and myself, with the pony in tow, started to edge our way around Loch Eisken. The usual track was flooded in places, so progress was going to be unduly slow. With 2 miles remaining, it would take another hour at this rate. Suddenly Freya decided otherwise.

With a jerk of her head the reins were whipped out of my hand, and she bolted into the water. The swollen river had made it unusually deep right by the edge. Freya struck out and headed straight for the Lodge. She was going home by what looked to her to be the short way.

The Admiral looked at Tommy. Tommy looked at me. And I had nobody else down the line to look towards. I mentioned earlier that there are moments of initiation that life in a place like Lewis offers to the young man, usually quite unexpected moments. Here was one.

So I looked at the horse. Rapidly, the hollow stag's carcase was filling with water. Freya was sinking lower and lower under the fast-increasing drag. You could sense her panic, yet she swam on, well out into the depths.

There was only one recourse: I had to try and get the saddle off her and guide her to safety. I wrenched off my oilskins and the layers of sweaters. Trousers too, and never mind the niceties of concealing the full monty. I pulled my flensing knife from its sheath, gripped it between my teeth, and with a strangely objective sense of melodramatic surreality, dived into the foaming head of the loch.

Tommy shouted after me. It was something about trying to avoid cutting the saddle straps and something about avoiding the pony's legs. Later, he explained that when a horse swims, its legs extend out, so you can easily get a nasty underwater kick.

I swam a lot in those days. I regularly went down up to 3 fathoms with just flippers, a mask and snorkel, holding my breath for more than a minute at a time to gather scallops, seek lobster pots broken free in a storm or to disentangle boat moorings. So I was fit. Never been fitter. Pressing hard on the water, stroke after stroke, I was soon level with the horse. Only then did it fully sink in that I didn't actually know how to handle the situation. Exactly how do you approach an animal in panic when it is so low in the water that only the eyes and nostrils are showing?

Then suddenly she stopped. Freya stopped swimming! She moved around slowly. She was walking! It took a few moments to realise what was happening. She had hit the salmon lie – the sandbank that leads out from the point at the loch's head and extends into the middle of the water.

Any half-decent ghillie always knows what's under the loch. You chart it carefully. You're told about the rough underwater contours by the old men, but do the fine-tuning yourself. On the bright sunny days, those flat calm sunny days when there's no hope of catching anything, but the guest still insists on being out there anyway, just in case – these are the days that you fill in the mental map. Every so often you slip the oar from the rowlock and press it down to feel for the bottom. Four to 7 feet, a couple of metres, is ideal for a salmon lie and this was what Freya had inadvertently struck. Of course, I knew the direction it ran in. Together, we waded nervously back to safety. A long gush of bloody water streamed from the carcase as the horse finally heaved herself up onto the shore like some beaching two-headed antlered monster.

The Admiral stood beaming on the bank. His job had once been to command the British fleet in the North Atlantic. He looked like he was presiding over the bridge of an aircraft carrier and was about to give me the Military Cross, or better, for having just single-handedly saved the entire war effort. Rarely in a distinguished naval career can an officer have enjoyed a more proud moment. As for Tommy, he didn't quite know where to look, because I had nothing on. But Tommy knew that he'd done a good job, because I'd done a good job, and that's what that sort of camaraderie is about. That's the reward of a real mentoring relationship.

The silver hipflask was opened. I drew long and deep. It was the best wee dram ever. It was also the worst thing you can do when your body has shut down the peripheral blood vessels to conserve heat. Dizzy, and with speech slurred from the early stages of hypothermia, I dragged some clothes back on and ran for the Lodge. I didn't stop. I just knew I had to get back – had to get warm.

There is a special kind of coldness that you feel when you're not just shivering, but when your body temperature has actually fallen below the threshold of safety. Yes, it gets into bones that are 'chilled to the marrow', but also, the flesh clinging to them feels like cold dead meat. When it's like that you know that your reserves are running out. So that was why I ran and ran non-stop. In a blood-pounding daze, I stumbled into the Lodge kitchen and collapsed speechless on to the flagstone floor. My whole body immediately seized up into the most terrible cramps. Every muscle knotted. Astonished housemaids rushed to administer hot presses, stretches and massage. There was something about calling the doctor for the doctor's son. As for me, I just lay there, and as the spasm gradually passed, I yelled and groaned like only half the man I'd supposedly proven myself to be.

So much for pride coming before a fall. So much for whisky. So much for the young male ego. But what a tale! What manifold layers of meaning! What happy times!

7. Such Happy Times

'They were such happy times, the old days,' Captain Audley Archdale of Eisken would tell me, when we were out together on hill or loch. He was late-middle-aged, white-haired and balding, of medium height, decidedly portly, yet fit. Over the laird's trademark checked cotton shirt and green shoulder-padded military-style jumper he wore a worn Barbour jacket. A natural, welcoming smile was never far away as he bumbled and brooded about his business, enjoying nothing better than being sidetracked into unfathomable conversations about ghosts, UFOs, or whether or not there is life after death.

We liked each other, Audley and I. He'd been an Army officer during the Second World War and often envied, in a very generous way, my opportunity for higher education. 'I only had a year at Cambridge,' he'd say nostalgically, 'and that was in preparation to be cannon fodder.' In the Army of his youth, a commission was almost automatic for someone from his social background.

Eisken had been left to Audley when his aunt, Miss Jessie Thorneycroft, passed away. On accession he immediately raised staff wages to at least the agricultural minimum, plus tips. As lairds go, this made him popular. But within a few years Audley would run out of money, forcing him to sell Eisken to an Anglo-Norman businessman. He in turn would stay for a few years before selling out to a Swiss banker, who passed it on to an international sportsmen's syndicate. But for as long as Audley was there, the halcyon days of the British old guard remained a residual reality. How strange it was that, in this remotest corner of the Outer Hebrides, I thereby found it possible to gain an insight into the forces that had formed our modern times.

'Yes, they were happy days then, when I first came up here in 1935,' he'd tell me. 'I was just fifteen, you know.'

'That was at the end of my great-aunt Mrs Platt's time,' he continued. 'She was the proprietor before my Aunt Jessie. There was a staff of fifty then. And do you know . . . once a year they'd all go out for a picnic! Everybody was invited from the lowest to the highest. On that day they'd all be equals.'

What made this fact exceptional could still be read between the lines of a redoubtable notice headed 'Rules for Servants'. While these no longer applied, they remained, for old time's sake, inscribed on the Lodge's tackroom wall where rows of guns and rods were arrayed on racks. Rank, everywhere, had been the controlling factor. Indoor and outdoor servants were demarcated to the point of enforced incommunicado. Unauthorised liaisons between servant classes would bring about dismissal. And sex, of course, did not exist; but everywhere it strained and heaved under the regulations.

'There were no children here in those days, of course,' Audley continued, pulling gently at his handlebar moustache. 'Allowing me to come at just fifteen was exceptional. The family always said, "No sneezles or measles!" You see, people were here to shoot and fish and enjoy themselves. They didn't want *children* running around. Yes, they were such happy days in Mrs Platt's time.'

I listened, but beneath the semblance of good order, right conduct and due process, something was not quite fitting together.

'What are these ruins *really*, Tommy?' I asked again one day when walking through the vacant presence of the glen at Loch Shell.

'Just something from the old days.' And he went very quiet. It felt inopportune to enquire again.

My curiosity soon subsided in the swell of other events – how readily the immediacy of life pulls us away from the wider context! I'm sure, had I pushed him, Tommy would have told the story if he knew it. He was not a secretive man; only reserved, like most loyal servants of the privileged. It is true that segregation between servant groups was no longer practised at Eisken, but renunciation of 'tasteless' talk was certainly an implicit part of the job contract. 'Discretion, Jeeves, discretion.' After all, how could dutiful servants like Tommy or myself look their superiors in the eye if, all the time, we were deconstructing the scene behind the master's back? There had to be some unspoken collusion, some community of interest.

That is why it was many years before the question of the Loch Shell ruins came up again. 'Twenty years for the truth, I had to wait.' But to crack it, I had to go 12,000 miles, to the furthest corner of the Earth.

You see, the more that I had got on and got out into the world after leaving Lewis, the more I became aware of how industrial economy was, everywhere, usurping community. It's true that I probably had a particular sensitivity to this, with community running so strongly in my blood. But you can imagine my delight when I discovered that, as far back as 1897, the French sociologist Emile Durkheim had given a name to the symptom of my unease. He called it *anomie* or anomy.[1] According to Robert M. MacIver, who made his name fighting for academic freedom during the McCarthy era after emigrating from a Lewis village to America,

Anomy signifies the state of mind of one who has been pulled up from his moral roots, who has no longer any standards but only disconnected urges, who has no longer any sense of continuity, of folk, of obligation. The anomic man has become spiritually sterile, responsive only to himself, responsible to no one. He derides the value of other men. His only faith is the philosophy of denial. He lives on the thin line of sensation between no future and no past.[2]

So it was that while spending four years working in the South Pacific, over two periods in the late seventies and the mid-eighties, I first started to make the connections between what had, for example, disrupted our Hebridean fisheries, and the same anomic condition worldwide. I had done a financial MBA at Edinburgh University and had learned the workings of monied power from the inside out. Now I was playing a lead role in developing the Pacific Regional Sustainable Forestry Programme. In due course it featured in the Government's 1990 environmental White Paper, showing off the best of British abroad.[3] The programme helped village people in Papua New Guinea, the Solomon Isles and Vanuatu (the New Hebrides) to regain control over their own rainforests. It helped them to develop an economically viable alternative to large-scale corporate logging practices. The key was to use small-scale, low-impact portable sawmills within a sustainable forest-management plan to produce certified 'ecotimber'.[4]

I can remember sitting down with a Papua New Guinean woman who went by the somewhat European name of Miriam Layton. I was asking about her people's relationship to the forest. But she turned all my questions around. 'How much of Scotland is covered by trees?' she wondered. 'And how much tribal land does your family have?'

My answers were singularly unimpressive. I had to admit that, once upon a time, more than half of Scotland had been covered by birch, hazel, rowan, ash, oak and pine. By the early 1600s, 90 per cent of it had gone, leaving just 5 per cent of the land area covered by native forest.[5] Then, over the past 400 years, even this has been reduced to just 1 per cent of the land area. Most of the forest that we now see comprises introduced commercial species like the Sitka spruce. Climate change, commercial felling to fuel the Industrial Revolution and intensive grazing have all conspired to leave Scotland a 'wet desert'. And as for our 'tribal lands', well, we have none, of course! In Papua New Guinea 98 per cent of the land continues to be owned by village people. Even in Brazil, which has one of the worst patterns of land ownership in Latin America, fully 1 per cent of the people own 45 per cent of the land. But in Scotland, at the turn of the new millennium, just a thousand owners controlled nearly two-thirds of the private land. These owners represent one-fiftieth of 1 per cent of the nation's population, and even at that, many of them are absentees living outwith Scotland.[6]

The proprietors claim, of course, to be the people who 'understand what is best for the countryside'. They 'conserve our national heritage' by opening their stately homes to the public. And they 'pump £30 million [or is it £130 million? The figure fluctuates] a year into the Scottish economy from blood-sports'. We ought to be grateful, ought we not?

'Yes,' replied the wizened Miriam. 'And Papua New Guineans should be grateful on the same basis. Grateful to those who hand out sweeties to stop us crying while they strip away everything that's precious.'

'We could never understand why they would come up here in their Rolls-Royce motor cars, make such a hue and cry about it all, and be so cruel in the way they would catch a salmon,' my old crofter friend Dr Donald Murray would say when we'd talk about life at places like Eisken.

'After all,' he continued, 'we would all gladly take a fish from loch, river or fathoms of ocean. But the object was to get it into the pot as quickly as possible.' There was only one exception to such efficiency. 'Sometimes us boys would go out on a Sunday, and we'd catch a salmon lying under the river bank by tickling it. You know – you gently massage under the belly, move your hand slowly down to the tail, and before he knows what's happened, you've whipped him up and he's out on the bank! Well, our parents wouldn't let us bring a fish back on the Sabbath day. Oh, no! So what we did was to slip a noose of string around his tail and we'd tie the other end to a wooden peg that we'd drive into the ground. We could then place the salmon safely back and alive into the river. That way the Sabbath stayed intact. The killing didn't happen . . . 'till after school on Monday!'

'Then what was the problem,' I asked, 'with the gentry's way of doing things?'

'Well, it was the notion of playing it for sport. That was what we found such a strange idea. Of course, I'd have to admit that it was an idea that was not without the power to become infectious; but to us in those days, who were seeing the whole carry-on with fresh eyes and for the first time, it certainly seemed like a cruel way of doing things. Very cruel. To us, you see, it summed up the whole business of landlordism. I mean, the salmon that we would peg with a stake was a necessity. It was our diet. But these people were not coming up here because they needed to eat. For them the chase and the killing itself was the pleasure and point of it all.'

It is said that one of the Hardy brothers, famous for manufacturing the world's best rods, always wore a black tie 'out of respect for the fish' when he'd have a day on the river. But what sort of 'respect' is involved in such a one-sided power relationship? Sport anglers will talk as if the quarry is pitched equally against them. Yet their situation is, frankly, a far cry from the profound spiritual dignity of the life-upholding hunt revealed in, say, Hemingway's *The Old Man and the Sea*. To the old people of the Hebrides, catching a fish, felling a deer or drawing milk from the udders of a cow meant participation in nothing less than God's providence. It was a blessing received; not a boast to be claimed.[7] Hardy was right to think in terms of respect, but what is respect, after all, but *re*, meaning to do something again, and *spect* as in the words *spectacles* or *spectate*. It means to look at something or somebody again, which is to say, more deeply. True respect therefore gets beneath the surface of things. It opens the door to veneration, to reverence.

The kill, of course, can be equally cruel whether for food or for sport. The difference is how it affects us – what it says about us. It is easy to hide behind talk of 'light tackle giving the fish a chance' – a justification that I often heard when out on the loch – but it is hard to avoid the bottom-line conclusion that recreational killing, for its own sake, is a socially accepted expression of sadism. As a Canadian fisheries biologist puts it:

> It is . . . the degree to which hooked fish express their pain and suffering, for which sporting fish are valued. The erratic and rapid swimming, the twisting of the body, the jumping out of the water, and so on are all behaviours of fish associated with fear, pain and suffering. These behaviours are a direct result of being hooked. The use of sophisticated and specialized tackle types, fishing rods of various sizes, lines of different thicknesses, and reels to match them is designed to derive the utmost pleasure from the struggle of hooked fish. Indeed, all fish are classified by anglers into those that struggle well when hooked, i.e. game fish, and those that do not.[8]

As I gained an insight into the psychodynamics of the sporting estate while growing up, I observed that the most penetrating comment on the recreational kill often comes from the rod's or gun's own words. For some, like Audley Archdale, sport was just a way to be out amid nature, justified by the need to cull but with minimal intervention. For others, it was a jocular kill, a form of entertainment, where success entailed excess. Take, for example, a half-page feature headed 'Dressed to Kill' in the *Sunday Times* of 10 January 1999. Here, Jeremy Clarkson tries to describe an executives' pheasant shoot in a humorous tone. Instead, he comes over like a schoolboy pulling the wings off flies. Subtitled 'Fashion Shoot' because of the social requirement to wear Harris Tweed, drive a Range Rover, and stomp about in wellie boots that 'cost at least £180', Clarkson closes his article by admiring 250 dead birds hanging from a trailer. He casually muses:

> Ordinarily, you will go home with a couple of birds, but because you haven't got the faintest idea of how to pluck them, they will eventually get thrown away.
>
> Morally reprehensible? Oh yes, but when you're out there on a chilly day with a bellyful of sloe gin and you blow a high bird clean out of the sky with a single shot, it awakens the hunter-gatherer that lurks in all men.

And when you watch the pheasant cascade into power lines, sending up a shower of sparks and blotting out the electricity supply to a whole valley, it almost – almost – makes up for that ludicrous need for tweed.

'LOADED lairds and lovely LASSIES; SUNNY Scots and holiday PICTS: why we love our Highland playgrounds,' proclaims an off-guard but by no means off-colour edition of the high-society magazine *Harpers & Queen* from 1992. The name of the game, it seems, is more than just natural resource management and the cull. It is, as the society photographs in such magazines amply confirm, a bonding and courtship ritual for the masters of the universe:

> The international social set hang up their party boots at the end of July and depart for caiques off the Turkish coast, villas in the South of France or huge yachts in Sardinia. But not the Old Guard British – there's only one choice for them: the Highlands .... There's nothing like Scotland in August for sheer expenditure of physical energy; the grouse moor, the deer and the salmon river claim the chaps during the day, who then heave a lot of whisky down, change into kilt (if they qualify), evening tails (if they don't) and go reeling until dawn with wind-burnt girls adept at quick changes from muddy tweeds to ballgowns and tartan sashes. There's ... nothing like Scotland for stalking the biggest social game.[9]

'So how's it going these days?' I asked Tommy MacRae, on revisiting Eisken in 1998 to get a feel for the state of play. The old man was retired now, but still rippling with muscular power and dignity. He was busy helping a stalker haul a boat from the loch.

The place looked well kept. The present incumbent, an international financier called Nicolas Oppenheim, evidently had a sporran as deep as his love of the place.

'Well,' answered the stalker, 'it's not the same as when you were here.'

'You mean, Oppenheim's no good?' I asked.

'Oh, no. It's not his fault,' said the stalker, speaking as if for Tommy. 'It's the type of people who go in for this sort of thing these days. They just want a kill and then back to the Lodge as quickly as possible. You'll even be just getting up on a stag when the mobile phone goes off! They'll leave it switched on because they'll be more interested in a commodity deal in Zurich, or something like that. There's just not the respect. Not the same respect.'

An article in *Tatler* in September 1996 acknowledged that the popularity of 'field sports' had indeed spoiled things for such olde-worlde purists.[10] But apparently this had its plus sides. 'Never in the history of sporting conflict have so many started shooting what was once shot by so few,' it proclaimed, as it lined up a gallery of marriageable 'hot shots' under forty. The number of punters taking up the sport had tripled in the past twenty years, we are told.

But that's democracy, and democracy is needed to protect hunting interests. Modern-day shooting, more a matter of farming the kill than culling overspill, 'depends on a meritocracy based neither on money nor status but on skill'. And a table provided a graphic illustration of the progress of the said democracy:

1976	1986	1996
Farmers, landed gentry, grandees	Farmers, landed gentry, Masters of the Universe, Saudi princes, Japanese businessmen, a handful of rock stars	Farmers, landed gentry, Masters of the Universe, Saudi princes, Japanese businessmen, all rock stars, film directors, publishers, accountants, fashion designers, builders, architects, solicitors, teachers, style gurus, interior designers, chefs, etc. . . .

Shooting had become the chic 'sport which defines who you think you are', *Tatler* tittled on, revealing how the Duke of Westminster once bagged an escapee parrot by mistake, advertising boxes of Godiva chocolate shotgun cartridges 'to ward off hunger pangs before lunch' (£11 for twenty), and illustrating the sport's social utility by inviting readers to consider an imaginary (meritocratic) exchange between two wives:

Woman A: 'Can you come to dinner next Thursday?'

Woman B: 'Darling, we'd love to, but sadly we're shooting at Holkham that day.'

Woman A is now jolly impressed: Woman B knows someone frightfully grand well enough to be asked to do things with them, *and* her husband is either important enough to take a day off midweek or rich enough not to work.

Concludes the sagacious *Tatler*, 'This interest is not confined to the rich'. On the modern shoot, 'People of all ages, sexes and backgrounds mix together'. After all, in preparation for her wedding in a secluded millionaire's castle to a man parading in the Mackintosh kilt (Ritchie being a sept, or sub-clan), even the pop icon Madonna, late in the year 2000, was laying down her sporting virginity on the Highland moors. The *Daily Mail* reported: 'Madonna has been learning to shoot, and walking on land once owned by the Dukes of Sutherland, who happen to be cousins of Ritchie.'[11]

And meanwhile, at the opposite end of the social spectrum? Well, *Tatler*'s final words say it all: 'A quiet word of praise from a loader who has never flown first-class makes the day of an international businessman.'

8. Gunboats and the Old Man of Eisken

It was not until the late 1980s, nearly twenty years after first starting work as a ghillie, that I came round to reading James Hunter's landmark text *The Making of the Crofting Community*.[1] It blew my mind. It set Dr Murray's unease about sporting mores in a context wider by far than either fish or pheasant.

I had always been given to understand that the Highland Clearances were a regretful necessity. True, the eighteenth- and nineteenth-century peasantry, like my four-times-great-grandparents in Strathconon, may have been forced off the land to make way for sheep ranches and, later, sporting estates. But this, we were taught, was an economic necessity. The lairds did their best for a godforsaken place and people. Even my father had maintained that the Clearances hardly touched Lewis.

But this was not so. And here, at last, was the key to the Loch Shell ruins. It lay folded in Hunter's scholarly discussion of a nineteenth-century sportsman's guide which said, with a most disarming air of innocence, that nowhere, beyond Eisken, was there 'a more attractive sporting place'.[2]

Hunter documents how, in 1817, the whole of Lewis became the possession of one man from the south: Lord Seaforth, otherwise known as Mr Stewart Mackenzie – later to become Governor of Ceylon. He wrote that his pressing concern was with 'the population and how it is to be disposed of'.

It was time, he said, 'to pave the way for the grand improvement of the introduction of mutton in lieu of man'. Accordingly, 'Whatever grounds are from their nature and situation peculiarly fitted for sheep pasture must be so arranged that the present occupiers may be removed to allotments which are for that purpose to be laid out for them'. The evicted tenants 'must and ought to be content with whatever land we can give them'.[3]

During the 1820s and 1830s, 160 families were forced off their ancestral lands in the Pairc (Park) area of Lewis, this becoming Eisken Estate. I have heard that the Loch Shell ruins may have been an inn. It haunts me to think that music and stories might once have filled that glen.

Scores of those displaced in the Pairc Clearances are recorded to have petitioned the Colonial Department requesting assisted passages to Canada. Some resettled in my home village of Leurbost. Others ended up in the designated neighbouring township of Balallan. Indeed, it was in this apartheid-like concept of 'townships' that many of our present-day crofting villages had their origins. That is why, even today, the perceptive visitor will note that the bulk of the population live on the poorest land: native reservations by any other name.

In 1844 Lord Seaforth's Lewis estate was sold by his widow to Sir James Matheson. Matheson's Hong Kong-based company, Jardine Matheson, is one of the biggest in Asia to this day, now running joint ventures with Bacardi-Martini, Caterpillar, Securicor, IKEA and Taco Bell. It boasts of penetrating China with the Pizza Hut franchise in 1994.[4] But what the multinational's present-day website doesn't tell you is that its revered co-founder started up the business (and built Stornoway Castle) with profits from the Chinese Opium Wars. In *Sybil*, Disraeli called him 'a dreadful man, richer than Croesus, one MacDrug, fresh from Canton with a million in opium in each pocket'.[5]

After her husband's death in 1878, Lady Jane Matheson assumed proprietorship of all Lewis. It was she who, as we have seen earlier, took measures to conserve the Calanais Stones, and she who sublet Eisken as a hunting and fishing estate. Sheep had gone out of fashion. The ending of the Napoleonic Wars and the reduced demand for troopers' coats, cheap fleece imports from Australia, and constantly improving breeds from agricultural innovation had devastated the wool market. A new use had to be found for the land. That use was sport. So it was that all over the Highlands in the 1880s sporting estates were set up and castles built to provide the Industrial Revolution's *nouveau riche* with trappings just like those of old-moneyed landed power.

It was against such a scenic backdrop that Joseph Arthur Platt, an English industrialist, took the Eisken lease from Lady Matheson. An ironmaster, smelting and casting textile-manufacturing equipment, he was evidently quite a decent sort in his own way. Some of the family fortune was donated to provide machinery for modernising the island's Harris Tweed production. It was Joseph's wife and Audley's great-aunt, Mrs Jessie Platt, who organised the famous staff picnics in those 'happy times' of nostalgic memory. She was widowed in 1910, bought out the estate's freehold in 1924, and died at the Lodge in 1934. That was how Eisken came to Audley's aunt, Miss Jessie Thorneycroft. And that, too, is a typical family history of one of the great Highland sporting estates.[6]

A hard-working entrepreneur, judiciously applied philanthropy, a penchant for both big smoke and heather glen – it is easy to see how the likes of Great Uncle Jo must have felt justified, if not necessarily in the word's full theological sense of 'before the Lord', then certainly, in the reasonableness of his presumption to enjoy his property, exclusively, 10 miles down Eisken's winding road to secluded privacy.

However, the displaced crofters of Pairc had a different take on history. 'Foxes have holes and birds have nests,' says a Scripture passage.[7] And damn it, even the bloody sheep have their folds. But the crofters, like the Son of Man himself, were left without place to adequately rest their heads, destitute; and all so that the *Bodach Isgein* – the 'Old Man of Eisken' as they called him – could come a-hunting on vacation. Verily indeed, 'justification' was lacking on both scores.

So it was that on 22 November 1887, between 200 and 700 hungry and impoverished residents of Balallan, Leurbost and surrounding townships set out for Eisken on a hunting raid. They carried some fifty rifles. These, according to an uncorroborated report by the County Mayo land reformer Michael Davitt, had come from Ireland.[8] The resulting act of civil disobedience became immortalised as the 'Pairc Deer Raid'. The Rev. Donald MacCallum, a Church of Scotland minister of rare radical credentials, takes up the story in his bardic testimony, reproduced here courtesy of Professor Meek's translation:

> We rose early in the morning
> driven by some desperation –
> to bring down, with sharp aim,
> the deer from the mountain tops . . .

> We are certainly not robbers,
> as lying statements claim;
> we are, in truth, brave people
> being ruined by poverty.[9]

Joseph Platt was away on business in England at the time. The avarice of he and his social class, said the reverend bard, had left the Hebrides empty of all 'but little fairies/without guile or hatred/who neither plant nor reap':

> 'My rule extends
> over all that I see,'
> said the Old Man of Eishken,
> 'both peatland and hill.'
> That he spoke the truth
> has broken my heart,
> and has caused this country
> to shiver with chill.[10]

On seeing that the Gaelic-speaking raiders were intent on something that was not-quite-the-usual-annual-picnic, Mrs Platt personally accosted them. With a most piquant courtesy, they looked her blankly and replied, 'My lady, we have no English.'

Over three days the crofters killed perhaps as many as 200 deer with which to feed what the Sheriff of Ross-shire himself was to grant were 'their starving families'.[11] The response from the Government in London was to send in a gunboat loaded with Royal Scots and Marines, as it did with Skye a few years earlier in order to suppress rent strikes. Six ringleaders were shipped off to the law courts in Edinburgh, later to be acquitted. A kind of peace, though possibly not the picnics, resumed.

How, we must ask, could subjects of the crown have been reduced to such a plight? Well, we saw earlier that the Highland policy of King James had triggered off gunboat diplomacy in a domestic context with the kidnapping of the Highland chiefs in 1608. If we fast-forward to 1707, we arrive at the full realisation of his political vision: the Union of the Scottish and English Parliaments, which made the concept of a Great Britain complete. For the English, who were at war with Catholic France, the Union slammed the door on Scotland's 'Auld Alliance' or *entente cordiale*. It blocked the way for future military alliances that could, for example, have given invading French ships access to Scottish ports. For the Scottish merchants and lairds who dominated the nation's undemocratic Parliament at the time, the Union gave 'full freedom and intercourse of trade and navigation' in England's vast and expanding colonial markets.[12] On top of that, some of the Scots parliamentarians were bribed. As Robert Burns famously put it, 'We were bought and sold for English gold/Such a parcel of rogues in a nation'.[13]

To the common people of Scotland, the Union was 'a bad thing'. Rioting broke out. The English spy Daniel Defoe, of *Robinson Crusoe* fame, reported that he 'never saw a nation so universally wild'.[14] Even the Union's ardent supporters admitted that over three-quarters of the population opposed it.[15] 'Britishness was superimposed over an array of internal differences in response to contact with the Other, and above all in response to conflict with the Other,' writes Linda Colley. As such, 'Britain was an invention forged above all by war . . . . They defined themselves as Protestants struggling for survival against the world's foremost Catholic power. They defined themselves against the French as they imagined them to be, superstitious, militarist, decadent and unfree.'[16] It is to this history, of course, that we must look to understand more recent British ambivalence to increasing political union with Europe and especially with France.

Soon, revolt was in the air. A Jacobite uprising of 1715 failed. Then, on 23 July 1745, the Jacobite 'Young Pretender', Prince Charles Edward Stuart or 'Bonnie Prince Charlie', secretly landed from France in the Outer Hebrides and quickly rallied an army at Genfinnan near Fort William on the Scottish mainland. To the clans, he probably symbolised neither Catholicism nor France, but rather a symbolic alternative to the brave new Hanoverian world imposed by the spurned Treaty of Union.

With remarkable rapidity and ease, Charles's peasant army won control of most of Scotland. The Jacobites then pressed on into England and reached Derby, 127 miles from London. Here they ran short of supplies and made what was probably intended to be a tactical retreat, hoping that the French would carry out a pincer invasion movement on England's southern front. However, the French, whose fleet was prone to being scattered by 'Protestant winds' at all the wrong moments, had gone soft on the idea of dominating England and failed to turn up. The English were therefore freed to redeploy their forces, and the following year they dispatched King George II's portly young son the Duke of Cumberland northwards in pursuit of Charles's troops.

Cumberland, whose forces, incidentally, included a great many loyalist Scots, defeated the Highlanders on 16 April 1746 at Culloden near Inverness. It was the last battle to take place on mainland British soil. His 7000 men suffered sixty casualties, while the Highlanders' ill-equipped, mostly untrained, hungry, cold and poorly led force of 5000 lost at least a third of its men.

Charles fled. At one point he dressed as a maid and was rowed across the water by Flora MacDonald, which inspired the song 'Over the Sea to Skye'. The romantic story is rather spoiled by the fact that Flora later went to America and became a slave owner. The human condition has its vicissitudes. However, despite an incredible £30,000 price on the Prince's head, the Highland people never betrayed him. Five months later a French frigate safely picked him up. But meanwhile, the 'butcher' Cumberland was sending troops far into the Gaelic heartlands under orders to harry, burn and kill men, women and children alike in a campaign of reprisal that echoed the barbarity of the final Elizabethan conquest of Ireland at Kinsale in 1601.[17] On the distant western island of Canna, for example, women were forced to flee to the caves when marines from the Royal Navy's *Commodore* landed with authorisation to rape. Bishop Robert Forbes records of Canna, in notes transcribed from eyewitness accounts, that a fifty-year-old woman was unable to leave the house in time, being constrained by a late pregnancy. She managed to escape as troops 'fettered her husband in order to quench their concupiscence on his spouse', but she died after hiding in a bog all night and aborting. On neighbouring Eigg, Hanoverian atrocities included thirty-eight men being taken on board a man-of-war and dispatched to white slavery in Jamaica, half of them dying in passage. Bishop Forbes reported: 'The most of them were marryed men, leaving throng families behind them. They [the soldiers] slaughtered all of their cattle, pillaged all their houses ere they left the isle, and ravished a girl or two.'[18]

Intent on preventing further uprisings, a final solution to pacifying the clans became the British state's immediate post-Culloden priority. Jacobite clan chiefs were dispossessed of their lands. In 1747 an Act of Proscription was passed which, along with the related Disarming Act, forbade freedom of assembly, banned the carrying of arms and outlawed wearing the tartan, kilt or plaid under pain of being 'liable to be transported to any of His Majesty's plantations beyond the sea, for seven years'.[19] The full plaided kilt – 'a spiritual garment in which you walk two feet taller'[20] – was replaced by the trousers. Shirt, suit and tie as normally unconscious symbols of acquiescence to the new world order would, of course, duly follow, with even tribal body scent being standardised, in the fullness of time, with the advent of deodorants – natural body scent being something that turns to objectionable odour, of course, only when we are in stressful circumstances, not at ease with our condition.

The Act of Proscription was not repealed until 1782, by which time the remnant symbols of 'noble savagery' could be safely repackaged into a short-bread-tin mélange of British identity. Here, Highlanders took their place beneath the Crown of Empire, caricatured by 'loyalty, royalty, Balmorality and tartanry'.[21] The internal colonisation of the British Isles was complete, achieved substantially by inner colonisation – colonisation of the soul. Those reluctant to join the project were perforce subordinated to the client status of a patron establishment for whose civilising ways they were expected to be grateful. The world became the oyster of the Mathesons, the Platts and their ilk, and, except for only occasional domestic duties, the gunboats could concentrate on overseas action, putting the 'Great' into a British presence that painted a quarter of the world map red.

9. Voice of Complicity

Between Culloden's final showdown in 1746 and the dawn of the twentieth century, probably some half a million Scottish Highlanders were forced off their land.[1] The old clan leaders had valued land for the number of people it could support, but the new breed of owners – some indigenous, but Anglicised through James's educational measures; others with no cultural connection to the place whatsoever – were products of Enlightenment thought. To many of them, economy and its new breeds of sheep came before people. You had to 'be realistic' in the face of economic exigencies more and more determined by a frame of reference that Empire rendered not local, but global.

The circumstances of the population's dispatch in the consequent Highland Clearances were often brutal. In the Uists, which lie just to the south of Mount Roineabhal on Harris, the Clearances took place so recently as to have been captured in photographs.[2] Here is one first-hand account, collected from Catherine MacPhee in the late nineteenth century:

Many a thing have I seen in my own day and generation. Many a thing, O Mary Mother of the black sorrow! I have seen the townships swept, and the big hold-ings being made of them, the people being driven out of the countryside to the streets of Glasgow and to the wilds of Canada, such of them as did not die of hunger and plague and smallpox while going across the ocean. I have seen the women putting the children in the carts which were being sent from Benbecula and the Iochdar to Loch Boisdale, while their husbands lay bound in the pen and were weeping beside them, without power to give them a helping hand, though the women themselves were crying aloud and their little children wailing like to break their hearts. I have seen the big strong men, the champions of the countryside, the stalwarts of the world, being bound on Loch Boisdale quay and cast into the ship as would be done to a batch of horses or cattle in the boat, the bailiffs and the ground-officers and the constables and the policemen gathered behind them in pursuit of them. The God of life and He only knows all the loathsome work of men on that day.[3]

'I had heard some rumours of these intentions but did not realise that they were in process of being carried into effect,' wrote Sir Archibald Geikie, the great British geologist, of the Boreraig and Suishnish clearances in autumn 1853.

> As I drew nearer I could see that the minister with his wife and daughters had come out to meet the people and bid them all farewell. It was a miscellaneous gathering of at least three generations of crofters. There were old men and women, too feeble to walk, who were placed in carts; the younger members of the community on foot were carrying their bundles of clothes and household effects, while the children, with looks of alarm, walked alongside . . . . Everyone was in tears . . . . When they set forth once more, a cry of grief went up to Heaven, the long plaintive wail, like a funeral coronach, was resumed, and . . . the sound seemed to re-echo through the whole wide valley of Strath in one prolonged note of desolation.[4]

The introduction of intensive sheep ranching had consequences that were ecological as well as social. A number of contemporary accounts refer to the loss of biodiversity, especially woodland. As Daniel Corkery said of the Irish bards' perspective, 'the downfall of the Gaelic [culture and] the downfall of the woods – these two went together in their verses'.[5] To ignore such poetic evidence would be unscholarly, uncultured and unacceptable. It is, of course, a coincidence, but an interesting one, that Scotland's last wolf was shot in 1743 – a significant local species extinction just three years before Culloden signified the full force of cultural genocide.[6] Writing about the introduction of sheep ranching to the area around Loch Maree, the Scots herbal physician Dr John Mackenzie had this to say about ecocide in his memoirs:

> It was in as lovely a spot in a wild Highland glen as any lover of country scenery could desire to see. I mean then, for then no sheep vermin had got hoof in it, as ere long they did. Then only cattle ever bit a blade of grass there, and the consequence was that the braes and wooded hillocks were a perfect jungle of every kind of loveable shrubs and wild flowers, especially orchids – some, of the *Epipactis* tribe, being everywhere a lovely drug that I often got many thanks for sending to botanic gardens in the South. The milk cows never troubled their heads to force through this flowery jungle, laced up with heaps of honeysuckle and crowds of seedling hazel and other native trees and shrubs. Till my Father's death in 1826, no sheep's hoof defiled the glen unless passing through it to the larder. But very soon after, an offer of a trifling rent for sheep pasturing let these horrid brutes into the glen, and every wild flower, and every young seedling bush or tree was eaten into the ground, so that an offer of a thousand pounds would not find one of my loved wild flowers or a young shrub from seed – nothing but a bare lot of poles, whose very

leaves were all eaten up the instant one of them appeared. Those who remembered the wooded glen of 1826, and now looked at it, would never believe it was the same place – unless seen from a distance, for the sheep could not eat up the beautiful wild hills.[7]

The options open to the vanquished human population were dismal. They could emigrate to the colonies, especially North America and Australia: there the oppressed too easily became the oppressors of other native peoples. They could join the loyal Highland regiments of the British state and advance the Empire: this, at least superficially, allowed some warrior-like semblance of 'manliness' to be maintained in a one-time warrior culture.[8] Or they could turn to waged labour in the Industrial Revolution. Many of the Highlanders' descendants live in poverty in British cities to this day; only the memory of more dignified origins remains. The poet Duncan MacLaren writes of such 'intergenerational poverty' in his hometown near Glasgow, where unemployment in the 1980s reached 30 per cent after the shipyards closed:

> Bruach Chluaidh. Bidh bruadar air uair agam 's tu nad eilean air bhog eadar Ceann Bharraidh agus Nèimh . . . Clydebank . . . I sometimes dream that you are an island afloat between Barra Head and the end of Heaven and that the only speech on the tongues of your people is the language of the Hebrides and the mists would put a poultice on your stinking houses and it wouldn't be vomit on the street but bog-cotton and your rusty river would be a dark-green sea. And, in the faces of your people, the wrinkles of their misery would only be the lash of wind and waves and your grinding poverty would somehow be diminished . . . agus thigeadh lughdachadh air do bhochdainn chràidh.[9]

Events like the Clearances had, of course, taken place over much of Europe, but usually further back in time. In the Roman world vast farms called lati-fundia were carved out for colonists – often slaves who had won their freedom by fighting in the legions. A colonia or colony was a detachment of soldiers who were rewarded with land to keep order among the vanquished, and remit taxes back to the metropolitan hub and conscripts to the frontier. Ironically, Roman latifundia tenants may, at times, have been better off than under British rule. For example, Article XI of the Statutes of Emperor Fredrick threatened 'imperial punishment' for any citizen 'found so bold as to dare to interfere with, swize, or carry away' either the peasants themselves or anything belonging to them.[10]

The only reason why the Scottish Highlands and Islands offer such a vivid window into the process of cultural genocide is that events there took place so recently in history. By contrast, enclosure (privatisation of common land) in England started with the Statute of Merton way back in 1235. This spoke of the need to 'approve' or improve land to extract a greater rent. Things really got moving under Henry VIII and Elizabeth I, and by 1592, Bishop Latimer was testifying that 'The rich . . . say their land is their own and they turn [the poor] out of their shrouds like mice. Thousands in England beg now from door to door which have kept honest houses.'[11] The 1601 Elizabethan Statute of Charitable Uses, which still sets the framework of British and Commonwealth charitable law, was originally intended mainly to alleviate social problems caused by landless itinerants. The older poor laws had been rendered inadequate. The final land grab of the early eighteenth century saw the passing of some 4000 Private Acts of Enclosure, culminating in the General Enclosure Act of 1845. By 1876, the process of depriving the 'commoners' of England was so complete that the New Domesday Book calculated just 0.6 of 1 per cent of the English population owned 98.5 per cent of the land.[12] Three-quarters of this larceny had taken place as early as 1700.[13]

If it is the case that many English people today take landed power for granted and even admire 'their' aristocracy, some explanation might lie in the fact that, as folk singer Dick Gaughan reminds us, 'It is easy to forget that England is the most colonised nation in history'. High land prices (which we all pay for in rents and mortgages) are really no more than a tax by the rich on the poor. And whereas most people will pay income tax, national insurance and VAT on their leisure activities, the rich employ armies of chartered accountants to show that their estates are 'businesses' and therefore tax-deductible. You can bet that the Land Rover from which the pheasant shoot takes place has usually been put through the books. Said a nineteenth-century wag:

> Men of England, wherefore plough
> For the lords who lay ye low?
> Wherefore weave with toil and care
> The rich robes your tyrants wear?[14]

After giving talks about the Highland Clearances, I am often approached by English people who feel confused about their national identity and ask what they can do. I simply suggest that they dig where they stand, and recover their own suppressed but very wonderful traditions. People like William Morris, William Blake, and the seventeenth-century radical movements – the Levellers, Diggers, Ranters, early Quakers, *et al.* – represent a rich taproot of indigenous English social and ecological alternative values. As Christopher Hill demonstrates in books like *The World Turned Upside Down*, English radicals urged a breaking-up of the class system by 'levelling' formalised distinctions of rank. They fought the 'wage slavery' of landed power on grounds of being 'no man's Lord and no man's servant'. Gerard Winstanley, who would have loved the modern-day direct activist's motto 'Break the laws like bread', had his own, which was: 'Work together; eat bread together.' He told the squires of England:

> The power of enclosing land and owning property was brought into the creation by your ancestors by the sword; which first did murder their fellow creatures, men, and after plunder or steal away their land, and left this land successively to you, their children. And therefore, though you did not kill or thieve, yet you hold that cursed thing in your hand by the power of the sword; and so you justify the wicked deeds of your fathers, and that sin of your fathers shall be visited upon the head of you and your children to the third and fourth generation, and longer too, till your bloody and thieving power be rooted out of the land . . . . True freedom lies in the free enjoyment of the Earth.[15]

Just as England can salvage wonderful material like this from a chequered past, so can any country – Scotland and Ireland have got it down to a fine art! Perhaps this is the big challenge of our times: to both heal nationhood and build a healing nationhood. And remember: no place is more sacred, and no peoples more worthy of honour, than those that have made beauty blossom anew out of desecration.

When the radical English historian John Prebble first popularised the history of the Highland Clearances in 1969, he met with derision from the academic establishment.[16] The Historiographer Royal for Scotland, Professor Gordon Donaldson of Edinburgh University, objected in the strongest possible terms. 'I am sixty-eight now,' he promulgated, 'and until recently had hardly heard of the Highland Clearances. The thing has been blown out of proportion.'[17] Other apologists had long been making out that the landlords had acted out of kindness.[18] The Clearances were made inevitable by overcrowding: the result, according to George Rainy, laird of the Isle of Raasay, 'of reckless, improvident and early marriages entered into without the slightest forethought of future consequences'.[19]

What went unsaid was that while the population was certainly rising, as it was all over Europe during the modern era, the people were simultaneously being pushed on to marginal land in the name of a calculated economic rationale. In 1815 Patrick Sellar, legal agent or 'factor' for the Sutherland Estates, articulated this policy as follows:

> Lord and Lady Stafford were pleased *humanely*, to order a new arrangement of this Country. That the interior should be possessed by Cheviot [sheep] Shepherds and

the people brought down to the coast and placed there in lotts under the size of three arable acres, sufficient for the maintenance of an industrious family, but pinched enough to cause them turn their attention to the fishing [i.e. waged labour]. I presume to say that the proprietors *humanely* ordered this arrangement, because, it surely was a most benevolent action, to put these barbarous hordes into a position where they could better Associate together, apply to industry, educate their children, and advance in civilisation.[20]

Within a century, Lord Delamere was applying identical justification on his 150,000 acres of Kenya. The peasantry, he said, needed to be deprived of their tribal lands to stimulate economic development. 'If . . . every native is to be a landholder of a sufficient area on which to establish himself,' Delamere told the Native Labour Commission of 1912–13, 'then the question of obtaining a satisfactory labour supply will never be settled.'[21]

As late as 1960, J. L. Sadie put it very clearly in the *Economic Journal*:

Economic development of an underdeveloped people by themselves is not compatible with the maintenance of their traditional customs and mores. A break with the latter is prerequisite to economic progress. What is needed is a revolution in the totality of social, cultural and religious institutions and habits, and thus in their psychological attitude, their philosophy and way of life. What is, therefore, required amounts in reality to social disorganization. Unhappiness and discontentment in the sense of wanting more than is obtainable at any moment is to be generated. The suffering and dislocation that may be caused in the process may be objectionable, but it appears to be the price that has to be paid for economic development: the condition of economic progress.[22]

Such a mindset, writ large across the world as the touchstone of modernism, was to carve deep wounds into the psyche of indigenous peoples. Hehaka Sapa or Black Elk of the Oglala Sioux said that the 'Wasichus', or white oppressors, 'have made little islands for us . . . and always these islands are becoming smaller, for around them surges the gnawing flood of the Wasichu; and it is dirty with lies and greed . . .'.[23] 'Alas,' wrote a Maya prophet of the conquistador colonisers: 'They came to make our flowers wither so that only their flower might live.' And of the 22 million Aztecs alive in 1519 when Hernán Cortez entered Mexico, only a million remained by 1600.[24] The Wasichu, suggests Native North American poet Leslie Marmon Silko, sees no life; he sees only objects. Yet he fears an objectified world, and so seeks to destroy it. He steals the people's rivers and mountains, jerking their mouths from their Mother. And so the people starve.[25]

Analysing French colonial power in twentieth-century Algeria, the Caribbean psychiatrist and liberation fighter Frantz Fanon described the colonial psychodynamic of cultural undermining as 'inferiorisation'.[26] Edward Said saw the same phenomenon in his native Palestine,[27] as did Daniel Corkery in Ireland under the British yoke.[28] And writing from modern Brazil, Paulo Freire wrote powerfully of 'cultural invasion'. 'In this phenomenon,' he said,

> the invaders penetrate the cultural context of another group, and ignoring the potential of the latter, they impose their own view of the world upon those they invade and inhibit the creativity of the invaded by curbing their expression . . . . Cultural invasion is thus always an act of violence against the persons of the invaded culture, who lose their originality . . . . [It] leads to the cultural inauthenticity of those who are invaded; they begin to respond to the values, the standards, and the goals of the invaders . . . . It is essential that those who are invaded come to see their reality with the outlook of the invaders rather than their own; for the more they mimic the invaders, the more stable the position of the latter becomes . . . . It is essential that those invaded become convinced of their intrinsic inferiority.[29]

So there we have it. History gets pushed aside as 'just something from the old days'. A culture of silence takes hold, and that silence is, of course, the voice of complicity; the voice of all of us who are afraid to stir from the spell of what Professor Donald Meek calls 'heavy doses of cultural anaesthesia . . . to blot out the hardships of the past'.[30]

It is as if memory itself has fallen into a deep pool of forgetfulness, and somebody has put up a sign that says 'NO FISHING'. And I'm feeling puzzled and angry, and I'm wondering how the hell that order was enforced.

It finally came to a head on the Ullapool ferry to Stornoway. I had sat myself down beside Calum Macleod, a retired teacher. He lived just over the road from Finlay Montgomery's place.

At school we had called him 'Cicero' because he taught Classics. Greek and Roman culture were, of course, part of the educational package in this far-flung outpost of the Empire. Unlike Celtic studies, Classics was deemed to 'improve the mind'. It would help us to 'get on'.

A teacher more gentle, warm and wise than Cicero would be hard to imagine. It so happened that I had a copy of Hunter's book with me, and I turned on the inquisition.

'But why didn't you people teach us this stuff too?' I demanded, waving the book and speaking in an almost accusatory tone. But I didn't need to worry. Cicero knew exactly what I meant and was sympathetic.

'Ah, well . . .' he replied, signalling a conversational deepening of psychological depth. 'You see, it was not in the curriculum. And in any case, *we were ashamed of it.*'

Shortly afterwards I met Jock Mackenzie, an old schoolfriend from Keose, where we used to go scallop diving in the *Pegasus*. I'd done shift work with him in the seaweed-processing factory when not out on the loch or hill.

'Jock,' I said. 'Did you know about this stuff? Cicero says they were *ashamed* of it! Am I the only one who missed it all?'

In the back of my mind I was wondering if it was because I had an English mother. Maybe people had just been too polite?

'No – me too,' Jock replied. 'I only found out recently. And I've been asking the boys about it too. Some knew. Most didn't know much. It was just never spoken about.'

My old schoolmate from Leurbost days, John 'Rusty' Macdonald – the village blacksmith – had the same story. Writing in the parish's historical journal, *Dusgadh*, he said: 'When I was in school, history was usually about the antics of Attila the Hun and Henry the Eighth or the sanctified version of the British Empire. Where was our own history?'[31]

Where indeed? And, of course, by now we all knew the answer. But as Runrig, the folk-rock group from Skye, put it, we'd had to wait twenty years.

Fichead Bliadhna
(Twenty Years)

Freedom of the moor
Freedom of the hill
And then to school
At the end of a summer
Children, five years of age
Without many words of English

Here is your book
Here is your pen
Study hard
That's what they told me
And you will rise up in the world
You will achieve

I learnt many things
The English language
The poetry of England
The music of Germany
The history of Spain
And even that was a misleading history

Then on to further education
Following education, more education
Like puppets
On the end of a string
Our heads filled with a sort of learning
And I did rise in the world
I found my suit
I found my shirt
I found a place in the eyes of men
Well away from the freedom of the moor

But why did they keep
Our history from us?
I'll tell you – they are frightened
In case the children of Gaeldom awaken
With searching
And penetrating questions
Twenty years for the truth
I had to wait
I had to search
Twenty years of deceit
They denied me knowledge of myself[32]

10. Echoes Down the Glen of Landed Power

Looking back, the guests on our Hebridean sporting estates demonstrated it all so very well. Ordinary, otherwise nice people get carried along in mindsets that are bigger than they are. On a one-to-one basis, a profound humanity was very often evident. But set in the wider social frameworks of military, corporate, political and even religious power, it was equally evident that underneath the ermine, chequebook and charm lay a basic willingness, if necessary, to use the most awesome violence to maintain privilege and keep control. Self-defence is one thing, but a 'better dead than red' ferocious readiness to take out everybody else with you is quite another. The gunboats might no longer have been visible on the horizon, but they continued to lurk beneath the surface, and patrolled the globe with massively magnified menace. 'There is no doubt that when you went to sea [on routine duty], you went to war,' says Commander Jeffrey Tall, captain from 1989 to 1991 of the nuclear submarine, HMS *Repulse*.[1] And this is not just Britain. Mutually Assured Destruction – MAD – equally underpins the nuclear defence strategies of, among others, France, America, Russia and China.

Probably the most psychologically perceptive work on the Scottish land question is *As An Fhearann: From the Land*.[2] It was published in 1986 to celebrate the centenary of Parliament's passing of the first Crofting Act. Embarrassed by criticism in the London press and pressured by crofters who had recently acquired the right to vote, the Government in 1883 set up a commission of inquiry under Lord Napier.[3] This found that conditions were, indeed, outrageous. The consequent legislation granted heritable security of tenure and controlled rents to those fortunate enough to live in designated crofting zones. As a result, a way of life was preserved. An ecological island of remnant human culture was secured, albeit on a reservation basis.

In among the *As An Fhearann* essays is a picture by Murdo MacLeod of Shawbost, Lewis – the same photographer whose work appears on the jacket and in the plate section of this book. It is called 'Archie watching television' and it shows a boy glued vacuously to the box, receiving impressions from . . . where? In the photomontage 'Reagan at Callanish', also by Murdo, former US president Ronald Reagan peers from a TV screen among the 5000-year-old Calanais Stones. It brings to mind Alice Walker's words:

> No one can watch the Wasichu anymore
> He is always penetrating a people whose country is too small for him . . .
> Regardless
> He has filled our every face with his window
> Our every window with his face.[4]

Another page shows a formation of bombers on an exercise at Stornoway's NATO airbase. And elsewhere, General Curtis le May is pictured shooting deer in the Scottish Highlands in 1967. The icy caption reads: 'General le May was Commander in Chief of the USAF when the atomic bomb was dropped on Hiroshima.'

And so it is that my mind drifts back to 1977. It is my seventh and last summer at Eisken. I am in the boat on the high loch, fishing with the Admiral's wife, a year after the famous birthday-suit incident.

We're talking about war. I'm no longer angling for the gory stories. In fact I'm questioning them – the whole damnable thing.

She's a little unclear as to where I'm coming from. I never used to trouble her peace. But I think I do now. She casts out a line for rhetorical reassurance.

'There isn't very much violence in our society these days, is there, Alastair?' It's a statement, not a question.

High up above us on the mountain, her husband, the Admiral of the Senior Service who once controlled the sea lanes of the North Atlantic during the Cold War, is stalking deer.

I simply look this good woman through the eyes and into the heart. I raise a finger, and I point it gently, but precisely, upwards, past where the eagles nest.

Some time later, the Admiral's shot blasts through our lengthening silence. It echoes down the glen and over the haunting ruins at Loch Shell. It reverberates through our minds and far out beyond that lovely spot.

'It all goes back to Culloden,' people will often say about the dysfunctions of modern Scotland – the apathy, the disempowerment, the sectarianism, the bigotry, the funny handshakes, the drugs and booze and smokes, the highest West European incidence of heart disease, the broken-heartedness, the blaming of the English, the not blaming of the English enough, the propensity to shoot ourselves in the foot. Aye, people from Highlands and Lowlands alike will these days often say, 'It all goes back to Culloden.'

Robert Burns, Scotland's national bard, wrote his two-verse 'Strathallan's Lament' in 1767, just twenty-one years after the battle. In this poem he stands in the shoes of the 5th Viscount Strathallan, whose father had been slain by Cumberland's vanquishing troops. Burns portrays an emotionally vacant new world order; one in which neither the savage beauty of nature nor the soft conviviality of human community (the 'busy haunts of base mankind') can any longer bring solace. Even the young Strathallan's capacity for perception is altered: no more can he see the world as it was before.

> Thickest night, surround my dwelling!
>   Howling tempests, o'er me rave!
> Turbid torrents wintry-swelling,
>   Roaring by my lonely cave!
> Crystal streamlets gently flowing,
>   Busy haunts of base mankind,
> Western breezes softly blowing,
>   Suit not my distracted mind.
>
> In the cause of Right engaged,
>   Wrongs injurious to redress,
> Honour's war we strongly waged,
>   But the heavens deny'd success.
> Ruin's wheel has driven o'er us;
>   Not a hope that dare attend,
> The wide world is all before us,
>   But a world without a friend.[5]

And Burns, as we know from his other work, was all too aware of what he meant by the 'wide world' before Strathallan: it was the emerging colonial marketplace; a mindset in which return on capital replaces conviviality in community.

Burns knew that the old vernacular ways had finally been crushed. As a Gaelic Jeremiah writing around 1770 about Culloden would cry out, 'My mind will not aspire to music/My heart is full of sadness . . ./Godliness has been conquered/And justice will not return again to our land.'[6] As the prophet Joel observed of the vanquished Hebrews: 'Has such a thing happened in your days, or in the days of your ancestors? Tell your children of it, and let your children tell their children . . . joy withers away among the people.'[7] And as the land-reform campaigner John Murdoch wrote in the *Highlander* newspaper in 1875, after the Clearances had hammered the last nails into Culloden's coffin:

We have to record a terrible fact that . . . a craven, cowed, snivelling population has taken the place of the men of former days. In Lewis, in the Uists, in Barra, in Islay, in Applecross and so forth, the great body of the people seem to be penetrated by fear. There is one great, dark cloud hanging over them in which there seem to be terrible forms of devouring landlords, tormenting factors and ubiquitous ground-officers. People complain; but it is under their breaths and under such a feeling of depression that the complaint is never meant to reach the ear of landlord or factor. We ask for particulars, we take out a notebook to record the facts; but this strikes a deeper terror. 'For any sake do not mention what I say to you,' says the complainer. 'Why?' We naturally ask. 'Because the factor might blame me for it.'[8]

And mark that this is not just Scotland, dear reader. This is the world, planet Earth, dug from where you agreed to stand with me. It seemed a little parochial at first, did it not? I worried that I might lose you! Well, now you can see the wider relevance.

But please, let us persist a little longer. We have not yet passed unharmed through Nebuchadnezzar's furnace.[9] We cannot yet quite see the path that leads beyond, and touch the joy, and laugh, as we most certainly will do before the covers of this book are closed.

When Conrad's Marlow eventually arrived at the heart of 'darkest' Africa in search of Mr Kurtz, he found a tyrant brutally ruling over a personal fiefdom. Kurtz had become a man who 'lacked restraint in the gratification of his various lusts' because there was 'something wanting in him'. Was he capable of seeing his own degeneration? 'I think the knowledge came to him at last,' Marlow recounted,

– only at the very last. But the wilderness had found him out early, and had taken on him a terrible vengeance for the fantastic invasion. I think it had whispered to him things about himself which he did not know, things of which he had no conception till he took counsel with this great solitude – and the whisper had proved irresistibly fascinating. It echoed loudly within him because *he was hollow at the core*.[10]

'We penetrated deeper and deeper into the heart of darkness,' wrote Conrad, menacingly, as it slowly dawned on Marlow that the 'darkness' of Africa was none other than the projected shadow of imperialism itself; a system constructed primarily, 'to tear treasure out of the bowels of the land . . . with no more moral purpose at the back of it than there is in burglars breaking into a safe'. In the end, Kurtz's corruption was so great that he destroyed himself and 'ruined the district' for other ivory traders. The colony itself suffered meltdown.

Kurtz is an extreme example, certainly. That is the novelist's prerogative. But perhaps there is a little of him in us all, and there lies the fascination that he holds. 'Do you know where wars come from?' asks Anthony de Mello, the

Indian Jesuit. 'They come from projecting outside of us the conflict that is inside. Show me an individual in whom there is no inner self-conflict and I'll show you an individual in whom there is no violence.'[11]

In *To Have or to Be?* Erich Fromm suggests that when we substitute outward power for inner presence of being, we act out of the delusion that it is possible to 'have' in order to 'be'.[12] The human self that is not centred inevitably collapses into being self-centred. The ghillie's day on a sporting estate is filled with snippets of discourse that demonstrate such substitution of money for love in human relationships.

'Who *is* he?' '*Is* he *anybody*?' one guest might ask another, as they head off to the loch.

'Oh, he's *quite somebody*,' comes the reply. 'He's . . .' such and such a company, title, spouse, connection or landed property. And of course, if 'he' happens to drop down a rung or two in life, then he's 'ruined'. It's as if a person's possessions are their being.

Disproportionate and unaccountable power, then, is not healthy. It merely bolsters an artificial sense of *being somebody*. It carries its price to pay. The more a man or woman builds themselves up in a community, the more others feel put down. The trouble is that the person in power rarely sees that in marshalling their assets and *expecting* honour, they're only playing out their own inadequacies. In a world of real need, outward riches thereby betray inner poverty. The flashy car, boat or aeroplane amplifies the impression of power, of solidity, of reality. But the soul ossifies, and the environment pays, and a culture of envy, fear and dissatisfaction develops based on acquisitive addiction to the all-consuming thrill of speed or the chase or the boardroom takeover. In the lotus-eating economy that results for the few, the majority, with a deficit of outward power, slog daily in factories making toys for the rich, instead of building homesteads for the poor. Their labour is degraded by the unacceptability of lives rendered futile.

This is why economic power to which justice is not germane is always a form of violence and why such an economic system is, in theological language, idolatrous. 'Whose head is this, and whose title?' asked Jesus when the Pharisees enquired about paying imperial taxes.[13] They had showed him a coin, a silver denarius. The head was the Emperor's; his title, 'TIBERIUS CAESAR, SON OF THE DIVINE AUGUSTUS, AUGUSTUS'.[14] Before famously replying 'Render unto Caesar what is Caesar's', Jesus sidestepped the small question and threw back the big one. He asked them, in effect, 'In whose economy do you place your confidence? Is it that of Caesar, who sets himself up as an imperial god, or that of God, whose passion is for the widow, the orphan and the poor?'

And that's the problem with both old-style imperialism and modern corporate globalisation: both serve money before love. The real ethical question of our times, then, is not which of biotechnology, organic agriculture, the motor car, heart transplants, fair trade or computers are, in themselves, 'a good thing'. That is a meaningless question. The real question is, rather, how and why and who and what do these things *serve*? Do they free the spirit and feed the hungry? Do they honour the diversity of life on Earth? Or do they, somewhere or for somebody or something, mean enslavement?

Quaint though it may seem, we must push further this question of idol-atry – the question of what happens if we worship any god other than love.

11. World Without a Friend

In the Highland bardic tradition Mammon, the personification of wealth, is an evil master who, Jesus suggested, could not be served alongside God.[1] He sits enthroned by the sea, a golden scallop shell overflowing with jewels on his knee.

'Will you, darling, please pass me back that beautiful ruby that's just fallen out,' he says to Donald, who has come from the village seeking a bit of retail therapy with which to salve a crack in his heart – his broken-heartedness. Donald obliges.

'Yes, thank you; that one was the heart of Callum the Grasper, my previous visitor. You see, darling, I will make you rich, very rich – but first you must leave me your heart.'

Well, Donald finds his shirt and his suit and goes to America and becomes very rich, rich as a powerful laird. But his life is blighted by emptiness, depression and insomnia.

Three physicians are consulted. The first prescribes medicine. The second, travel. And the third, hunting and feasting. None of these works. At length, he goes again in desperation to see Mammon and ask for his heart back.

As the Rev. Donald MacCallum, bard of the Pairc Deer Raid, puts it in an epic poem about Donald's return to simple fishing life in the village: his heart is salved (that is to say, he finds 'salvation') only when 'all his riches have *melted in his generosity like snow*'.[2] God repairs the crack in his heart and thereafter keeps it next to God's own.

There was nothing unusually 'bad' about Donald, who, after all, in the eyes of the world had 'made good'. He just got swept away in a mindset bigger than he'd bargained for. He met with unanticipated emergent properties – things that appear only as their scale and context becomes bigger. The point is that we're all sleepwalkers, says Charles T. Tart, one of the world's leading researchers into human consciousness.[3] Powerful forces construct social reality – parenting, schooling, television, advertising, dress code, corporate ethos, military drill. They're all, Tart suggests, variations on hypnosis. Mostly we walk around in a semi-trance. We want what we're conditioned to want. We're like the hypnotised subject who happily eats an onion thinking it to be an apple. We only believe the onion's an apple, Tart says, because we've built a mutually reinforcing sense of reality with one another. This is known as *consensual reality*, or consensus trance reality. It's what makes a football result seem important, what drives fashion, and causes the day to be spoiled by make-believe tragedy in a soap opera. The implication is that we're all living a dream, a myth, and that if we don't persist and insist on what C. G. Jung called 'individuation' – if we don't start living our *own* dream and being authentic to our *own* deepest calling – then life itself will be sucked away by the energy vampires of consciousness. Jung surmises: 'The individual who is not anchored in God can offer no resistance on his own resources to the physical and moral blandishments of the world.'[4]

Consensus trance reality seduces us with something that falls short of the fullest possible spiritual presence. It offers only a half-baked reality, and that's what's perilous, because when you bite deep into the apple, you find that the worm's been there. As Miriam Layton of Papua New Guinea told me, it's like 'those who hand out sweeties to stop us crying while they strip away everything that's precious'. Put another way, Ronald E. Shor, writing in the *American Journal of Psychotherapy*, defines hypnosis as

> ... *a contraction of the usual frame of reference*. When this occurs there is a consequent forgetting of the situation as a whole, and a loss of the internal alertness to the whole universe of other considerations which usually fills our waking minds . . . . A good hypnotic subject may be defined as a person who has the ability to give up voluntarily his usual reality-orientation to a considerable extent, and who can concurrently build up a new special orientation to reality which temporarily becomes the only possible reality for him . . .[5]

Developing that idea further, I think it could be said that hypnosis is the ability of one person to focus the attention of another; to shape the reality of another by drawing their sense of presence into a particular constellation of reality. This may represent a 'contraction of the usual frame of reference', but it can also, as with therapeutic hypnosis, represent an expansion or transformation of a person's previously constrictive or even pathological self-image and worldview.

When we become engrossed in a book, captivated by a film or entranced in dance, or even when we daydream while looking out of a window, we are, in this broad sense, 'hypnotised'. In their study of the bardic tradition, Bloomfield and Dunn speak of 'verbal magic and the hypnotically fascinating manipulations of word'.[6] What seems to be happening is that the loudness of wider reality gets turned down, and that to which we give our attention is correspondingly turned up. This is the focusing function of consciousness, but psychologically it also entails a realignment or retuning of reality. Indeed, the essence of story, poetry and music is to achieve just this, ideally leaving a willing and delighted audience 'spellbound'. Such can be the dynamics of complete presence in going with the flow: sheer enjoyment, even ecstasy. But it is one thing for this to happen in a context in which the participant chooses it, or requests it, and does so for their own pleasure; quite another when it is used, covertly, to exploit.

My point is one that would not surprise a Papua New Guinean sorcerer or a medicine man or woman. It is that hypnosis, or whatever we like to call it, may be far more prevalent in the modern world than many would think. One researcher remarks that most consultants in today's business world 'would deny using hypnosis, not knowing *that all techniques involving imagination are hypnosis*'.[7] The relevance to our discussion of the bardic tradition will be obvious. These are things that perhaps we need to understand if we are to be honest, and therefore accountable, responsible and most deeply effective as poets, writers, artists or whatever, and maybe even as creative scientists and managers. This is why, as we have seen, truth must be kept at such a premium when working at a psychodynamic level; indeed, it ought to be nothing short of the work of healing based on love.

But when powerful emotions such as fear, guilt, hate, love and sex are engaged, as in advertising or political demagoguery, the potential to sculpt the imagination carves out whole new worlds replete with artificial meaning. Celtic storytellers knew this: they referred to 'the glamour', a spell cast upon the eyes by witches or bad faeries that made the worthless seem attractive.[8] The most powerful genre of modern advertising aims to cast a similar spell, having drawn on the psychological insights of figures like Jung, Freud and Adler – insights originally meant for healing, not marketing.

'*L'âme. Au coeur de tout ce que nous créons aujourd'hui* [Soul – at the heart of all that we create today],' says one French advert for Mercedes-Benz sports cars. 'Stir your soul,' says a similar British ad in 2001 for Alfa Romeo cars. '*Telle est la vie. Tel est vivre. Commencez à vivre* [Such is life. Such is it to be alive. Start living],' continues the Mercedes brochure.[9] The 1950s 'depth boys' school developed psychological marketing techniques to keep American corporations busy after the end of the Second World War threatened to rob them of an ever-expanding market. One of the depth boys said: 'Basically, what you are trying to do is create an illogical situation. You want the customer to *fall in love* with your product and have a profound brand loyalty when actually content may be very similar to hundreds of competing brands.'[10]

Here we see the core dynamic of consumerism – the notion that it is necessary 'to have' in order 'to be'. And that dynamic is, like all violence, like all sublimated expressions of domination or war, an *erotic* dysfunction. Love is displaced from things that are living on to a mere branded product. Eros is hijacked and perverted; it is a rape rather than love-making. The erotic, as Audre Lorde brilliantly points out, is about much more than sexuality alone.[11] It is 'the personification of love in all its aspects . . . the passions of love, in its deepest meanings.' It is the bridge connecting our inner, psychological and spiritual nature with the outer, social and political expressions of life in this world. Eros, says Lorde, is nothing other than the full extension of *feeling*: it is how we feel with our hearts what it's like truly to be alive, and start living.

It follows from Lorde's definition that the opposite of the erotic is pornography. Pornography, she accordingly says, 'emphasises sensation without feeling'. It is the 'world without a friend' of a heart violated and cauterised, violating and cauterising. Thus, at the root of domination is an inability to feel; erotic dysfunction. Like 'galloping consumption' (as tuberculosis used to be called), consumerism ultimately makes you cough and spit. It mainlines you to the drip-feed credit line of usury addiction. Its cup can never be full, not even when overflowing. Mercedes' next model will always leave you dissatisfied, wanting more and willing to get that next job to 'work your ass off' for it.

It may be, then, that mainstream Western culture has fallen victim to 'voodoo economics' to an extent much more wide-ranging than has been acknowledged. Indeed, I have discussed parts of this analysis with Haiti's leading sociologist and indigenous expert on voodoo, Laënnec Hurbon of the Université Quisqueya, Port-au-Prince.[12] We concluded that while the West has distorted and caricatured real contemporary voodoo – that post-slavery Caribbean synthesis of African animistic religions – it may have fallen victim to its own brand of voodoo in consumerism's culmination of the Baconian project – the idolatry of rationalistic conquest and control. How ironic it would be if the reforms of King James, the man in whose name 'witches' were burned alive at the stake,[13] had played a not insignificant role in setting loose a global system of emergent properties that, for many of the exploited indigenous peoples of this world, has been experienced, very frankly, as the white man's 'black magic'.

Mammon is the symbolic name of these properties – emergent from the veneration, or worship, of money. In a biography of John Maynard Keynes, interestingly subtitled 'The Economist as Saviour', Lord Skidelsky makes telling reference to 'Keynes's sense that, at some level too deep to be captured by mathematics, "love of money" as an end, not a means, is the root of the world's economic problems'.[14] There we have it: these are things that go 'too deep to be captured' by the accepted tools of the Western mind. That is why we need cross-cultural and transdisciplinary analysis, and perhaps we need to use afresh some of the ancients' ways of knowing.

It was 'Mammon', then, that conducted the Clearances, and what led up to them, and what follows in residual structures of landed power today. And because a false god has no reality, because he is just a mirage, he must 'keep up appearances'. That means persuasive glossy brochures, yes, but ultimately what these all seek to construct is *control*. Mammon is a control freak. He must get richer, exponentially, compound interest, sustained growth, or else collapse into a crater-like bankruptcy of the soul. If he's not puffing and steaming and growing; if he's not always getting bigger and better, newly revamped, then he's dying, he's losing market share – and so he must keep eating up life. He must keep sucking all attention in to himself because he requires total spiritual presence – worship. '*Vous. Le composant le plus essentiel de tous nos véhicules* [You. The most essential component of all our vehicles],' concludes the Mercedes ad, revealing it all.

That's Mammon, ruler of the world. He merely asks us 'to be realistic', to appreciate all that he does for us. He merely asks that the collection plate be passed round to feed his Great Economy. He merely asks that we sing from a common hymn sheet. And as Marlow said of that song, or the realisation that it gives rise to: 'It echoed loudly within him because *he was hollow at the core.*'

Emergent properties are characteristics not evident at a small scale. However, as the scale at which a system works increases, characteristics evolve that may be qualitatively different and greater than the apparent sum of all the tiny parts. For example, the enormous biodiversity of a coral reef is partly an emergent property of billions of microscopic polyps. Similarly, at the human level, hamlets emerge out of families, and cities out of hamlets. As such a change of scale comes about, little seeds of good or evil barely visible at an earlier stage can unfold in quite unforeseen ways. In the absence of consciousness, awareness, mindfulness, it is possible for an expression of evil to emerge where there may have been no original intent to implant it. This danger is inherent in social systems, but, if we understand the degree of unintentionality that can be involved, it can also be a basis for hoping that forces seemingly beyond our power can be confronted and even transformed.

There is a passage in John Steinbeck's *The Grapes of Wrath* that is unsurpassed as an illustration of how emergent properties can lead to structural oppression.

> The owners of the land came onto the land, or more often a spokesman for the owners came . . . . Some of the owners' men were kind because they hated what they had to do, and some of them were angry because they hated to be cruel, and some of them were cold because they had long ago found that one could not be an owner unless one were cold. And all of them were caught in something larger than themselves . . . . The owner men explained the workings and the thinkings of the monster that was stronger than they were . . . . You see, a bank or a company . . . those creatures don't breathe air, don't eat side-meat. They breathe profits; they eat the interest on money. If they don't get it, they die the way you die without air, without side-meat. It is a sad thing, but it is so. It is just so . . . . When the monster stops growing, it dies. It can't stay one size . . . . We're sorry. It's not us. It's the monster. The bank isn't like a man.
>
> Yes, but the bank is only made of men [said the tenants].

No, you're wrong there – quite wrong there. The bank is something else than men. It happens that every man in a bank hates what the bank does, and yet the bank does it. The bank is something more than men, I tell you. It's the monster. Men made it, but they can't control it.[15]

What is sometimes called 'the system', or, more explicitly, 'the Domination System',[16] then, is an emergent property of ordinary human failings and commonplace darkness. The 'monster' is created bit by bit by individuals, but its emergent properties transcend us all. This, perhaps, is what our forebears meant by 'the Devil'. There need be no great mystery, superstition or even anything of the supernatural about it. The flaws in our nature that allow such emergence – that, indeed, make it inevitable – are so commonplace as to pass normally unremarked. Theologians of a more antiquated age called these human tendencies 'original sin'. Today we might see in it what Hannah Arendt, in her study of Nazi war crimes, called 'the banality of evil'[17] – the horror in which we are all unwittingly or only half-wittingly caught up as a matter of everyday experience. Indeed, it is awareness of this very banality that has caused vocabulary like 'evil' to lose much of its meaning in the modern age. The expression seems too extreme for something that is, when reduced to its component parts, so very ordinary.

In the aftermath of the Nazi Holocaust and while the Vietnam War was still taking place, a number of social psychologists undertook experiments that tried to shed greater light on human darkness. Two of these are of profound importance in understanding the analysis and methodology that I am unfolding in this book. In the first experiment Philip Zimbardo divided a group of ordinary American volunteers at random. He set them up to be either 'prisoners' or 'guards' in a make-believe 'jail' in the basement of Stanford University. The researchers were shocked at how quickly the volunteers fell into role and conformed to group stereotypes. The 'Stanford Prison experiment' got out of hand. It had to be terminated prematurely. Zimbardo summarised his observations as follows:

Within what was a surprisingly short period of time, we witnessed a sample of normal, healthy American college students fractionate into a group of prison guards who seemed to derive pleasure from insulting, threatening, humiliating and de-humanising . . . . The typical prisoner syndrome was one of passivity, dependency, depression, helplessness and self-depreciation. Prisoner participation in the social reality which the guards had structured for them lent increasing validity to it and, as the prisoners became resigned to their treatment over time, many acted in ways to justify their fate at the hands of the guards, adopting attitudes and behaviour which helped to sanction their victimisation. Most dramatic and distressing to us was the observation of the ease with which sadistic behaviour could be elicited in individuals who were not 'sadistic types' and the frequency with which acute emotional breakdowns could occur in men selected precisely for their emotional stability . . . . Our results . . . [demonstrate] that evil acts are not necessarily the deeds of evil men, but may be attributable to powerful social forces . . . . The inherently pathological characteristics of the prison situation itself . . . were a *sufficient* condition to produce aberrant, anti-social behaviour. The use of power was self-aggrandising and self-perpetuating.[18]

In an even more controversial experiment, now replicated cross-culturally in various parts of the world, Stanley Milgram of Yale University examined the role of blind obedience as the 'dispositional cement that binds men to systems of authority'. He was staggered to find that 65 per cent of volunteers could be persuaded to administer what they believed was a dangerous electric shock to punish a victim – who, unknown to them, was just an actor and was not really being shocked at all. Most people, the experiments suggest, can easily be broken down and persuaded to participate in dehumanising others. The 'banality of evil' is laid bare. When confronted with their actions, many participants in the 'obedience experiments' justified themselves by blaming the victim. They said things like: 'He was so stupid and stubborn, he deserved to get shocked.' Milgram surmised:

The essence of obedience consists in the fact that a person comes to view himself as the instrument for carrying out another person's wishes, and he therefore no longer regards himself as responsible for his actions . . . . [He] sees himself not as a person acting in a morally accountable way but as the agent of external author-ity . . . . Unable to defy the authority of the experimenter, they attribute all responsibility to him. It is the old story of 'just doing one's duty' that was heard time and time again at Nuremberg. But it would be wrong to think of this as a thin alibi concocted for the occasion. Rather, it is a fundamental mode of thinking for a great many people *once they are locked into a subordinate position* in a structure of authority. The disappearance of a sense of authority is the most far-reaching con-sequence of submission to authority. Although a person acting under authority performs actions that seem to violate standards of conscience, it would not be true to say that he loses his moral sense. Instead it acquires a radically different focus. He does not respond with a moral sentiment to the actions he performs. Rather, his moral concern now shifts to consideration of how well he is living up to the expec-tations that the authority has of him. In wartime, a soldier does not ask whether it is good or bad to bomb a hamlet; he does not experience shame or guilt in the destruction of a village: rather he feels pride or shame depending on how well he has performed the mission assigned to him.[19]

Or, as a steely-eyed brigadier once told me in the officers' mess at a NATO establishment – a man who, when I pushed him, reluctantly admitted to having killed (he protested that I was not asking him a fair question, but I insisted) – the ethics of armed combat boil down 'to doing a good job'.

The 1986 disaster at Union Carbide's Bhopal plant in India released methyl isocynate into the air, injuring some 200,000 people and killing 2000. The process by which full corporate liability was dodged is revealing. Immediately after the disaster, the chairman of the board, Warren M. Anderson, was so upset that he told the media he would spend the rest of his life attempting to make amends. One year later, he was quoted in *Business Week* saying that he had 'over-reacted', and was now prepared to lead the company in its legal fight to minimise payment of damages.[20] Many of the injured remain uncompensated to this day.

What had gone on in this man's mind? Zimbardo's and Milgram's studies perhaps shed some light on the process. For a moment, the shock of the tragedy had perhaps shifted Mr Anderson out of his usual role. He spoke from his heart. Quickly, however, the pressures he was subject to in his role re-established their hold over him. Obedience to peer and shareholder authority, which is the rudder of advanced capitalism, resumed its hypnotic para-mountcy. This is socially possible because the structure of corporations means that the diffusion of responsibility is ingrained. Shareholders appoint people like Mr Anderson, but their only real interest and feedback mechanism is the share price and dividend yield. But of course, limited corporate liability allows for limited shareholder responsibility. If Mr Anderson doesn't serve the monster with all his heart, the company's stock value will slide. Investors will sell and the company will then have difficulty raising fresh capital, because investors don't put up money to compensate poor Indians. If a spiral of decline in stock value sets in, the company becomes vulnerable to a predatory takeover by another corporation. Mr Anderson would then get fired, any resid-ual scruples would be scuppered, and the remainder of the company might get asset-stripped or re-established under a new trading name. A glance through the business pages of any newspaper shows that this kind of corporate predatoriness goes on every day. It is the stuff of high finance and it marks the distinction between what I refer to in this book as 'advanced capitalism', and old-style 'family' or new-style 'community' entrepreneurship. The problem is not with entrepreneurship *per se*; it is with irresponsibility and emergent properties that militate against being able to act responsibly.

Studies of the 'authoritarian personality' suggest probable links between the need to dominate others and the 'loss of soul' in early childhood. If this is true, it is very important. It suggests that resolving the ills of the world must start in the nursery. In his remarkable song 'Working Class Hero', John Lennon sets out the case. He starts by recounting the effect of love denied at a tender age – the child made to feel small from birth onwards, receiving insufficient parental attention, and the pain that builds up and smothers the capacity to feel.

Lennon moves on to the double-bind of the 'damned if you do; damned if you don't' Catch 22 situations that destroy self-confidence and implant inferiorisation – the hurt and the hitting, the being hated if clever and despised if a fool, and being driven crazy with having to jump through all their hoops. Then there are the 'bread and circuses' social narcotics of religion, sex and television that maintain apathy and sculpt the psyche of a pliant, consumer populace. We're no better, Lennon concludes, than 'fuckin' peasants' – but ones who, nonetheless, think ourselves clever, classless and free.

And finally, there's the comfortable complacency of those who, in order to get on, have gotten out; those whose mores have unquestioningly become part of society's structural violence. These are the people who find 'room at the top', a nice house on the hill, because they've learned how to smile as they kill. They're the social class to which the working class hero is supposed to aspire. Lennon's song closes by seeming to recommend himself as the role model to follow in order to become such a hero.

I'd always thought this was a rather cryptic ending. But on finishing this book, I phoned up the company that handles copyright permissions for Lennon's estate – I was hoping to be able to quote the lyric in full. It is, after all, readily accessible on the Internet. However, I was told that a 'non-negotiable' payment of £350 is always required for use! Evidently, the capacity to recognise issues of social justice does not necessarily correlate with living out the beliefs this capacity implies – or, at least, with the heirs to one's estate so doing.[21]

The danger to society of a dysfunctional childhood derives, of course, less from the poor than from the rich. There is an asymmetry here. The poor might take out their frustrations on others in a relatively confined family or neighbourhood context. The rich, however, can magnify their dysfunction through the lens of position, power and money. Political biographies yield many examples. One is Alan Clark, the late defence procurement minister.

Clark (a Highland laird, of course) says how his father, Lord Kenneth Clark of *Civilisation* fame, was 'better at conveying things without expressing them than anyone I've ever met. He made me feel inadequate intellectually.' He said that his days at Eton, England's most elite private school, were 'an early introduction to human cruelty, treachery, and extreme physical hardship . . . the equivalent of three years in jail'.[22] In 1992 Clark had to resign his cabinet post for having been, as he put it, 'economical with the *actualité*' over the Arms to Iraq scandal. In short, he was one of the men who had armed Saddam Hussein. And Saddam Hussein, incidentally, was himself reportedly beaten by a cruel uncle as a boy.

Prison psychiatrists Bob Johnson in England and James Gillegan in the United States maintain that it is precisely these types of background that they invariably discover in psychopathic criminals.[23] However, the flog-them-and-hang-them brigade mostly don't want to know. Probably it touches on too many unresolved home truths. Indeed, Johnson had to quit his post at Parkhurst Prison because his outstandingly successful work was made eventually impossible by Michael Howard, a discipline-obsessed Home Secretary spawned by the Thatcher regime.[24]

In her studies of why people do terrible things to each other, the Swiss child psychologist Alice Miller describes child rearing based on fear and emotional absence as a 'poisonous pedagogy' resulting in 'soul murder'. 'A child,' she says, 'responds to and learns both tenderness and cruelty from the very beginning.'[25] Where the child has been traumatised or emotionally abandoned, and not allowed to express her anger or grief, or not loved for herself (as distinct from being loved for her performance), then the patterning scores deeply. The capacity to relate to others with *empathy*, with feeling, through Eros, is impaired. Miller maintains that this syndrome is illustrated by every senior member of the Third Reich about whom a detailed childhood history is known. As writers like Erich Fromm and Wilhelm Reich have similarly shown, such syndromes typify the 'body of authority' that is fascism.[26]

'Violence,' says James Gillegan of Harvard University, writing from his experience of directing the psychiatric services of the Massachusetts prison system, 'is the ultimate means of communicating the absence of love by the person inflicting the violence . . . . The self cannot survive without love. The self starved of love dies. That is how violence can cause the death of the self even when it does not kill the body.'[27]

Like life, however, death cannot be compartmentalised. If the remains are swept down into the dungeon or the cellar, sooner or later an odour creeps back up the stairs. After a while it pervades the living room, and after a little time longer, neighbours start to notice that 'something doesn't smell right' about that family, or person, or situation. And that's the trouble with worshipping Mammon. He smells. It can be a very tangible smell – one that spawns a vast deodorant and perfume industry to mask what our bodies are actually trying to tell us. For at the core of domination – at the core of colonialism, landed power, and any abuse that causes others to suffer – is necrophilia: the love of morbidity, the honouring of and seeking honour through death.

Sigmund Freud saw this late and last in his work: 'I have lately developed a view,' he wrote in 1920, speaking of what later was called 'Thanatos' after the Greek god of death, 'according to [which] we have to distinguish two classes of instincts, one of which, the sexual instincts or Eros, is by far the more conspicuous and accessible to study . . . . The second class of instincts was not so easy to point to; in the end we came to recognize sadism as its representative.'[28] But it was Erich Fromm who really opened the can of worms. We are looking, he wrote, at a syndrome that

. . . can be described as the passionate attraction to all that is dead, decayed, putrid, sickly; it is the passion to transform that which is alive into something unalive; to destroy for the sake of destruction; the exclusive interest in all that is purely *mechanical*. It is the passion to tear apart living structures.

Fromm and the Frankfurt School of which he was a part[29] saw necrophilia as the bottom line of domination, the driving dynamic that destroys both community and environment. It converts, he said, the 'world of life' into

> ... a world of 'no-life'; persons have become 'nonpersons,' a world of death. Death is no longer symbolically expressed by unpleasant-smelling faeces or corpses. Its symbols are now clean, shining machines; men are not attracted to smelly-toilets, but to structures of aluminium and glass. But the reality behind this antiseptic façade becomes increasingly visible. Man, in the name of progress, is transforming the world into a stinking and poisonous place (and this is not symbolic). He pollutes the air, the water, the soil, the animals – and himself. He is doing this to a degree that has made it doubtful whether the earth will still be liveable within a hundred years from now. He knows the facts, but in spite of many protesters, those in charge go on in the pursuit of technical 'progress' and are willing to sacrifice all life in the worship of their idol. In earlier times men also sacrificed their children or war prisoners, but never before in history has man been willing to sacrifice all life to the Moloch – his own and that of all his descendants.[30]

So now we can see the fire. It starts as a feeling of warmth in the hip pocket – just a little bit of Mammon. But then it starts to burn, and you realise that if you don't take it out it may make a hole, and you'll lose it. So you place it before you, and then you see that what you've got is actually a little stone statue. It's hollow – '*hollow at the core*'. Hollow and hot, because a fire burns inside; and you peer in, and he leers, and grows, and it's no longer this little statue before you, but you're before it, and prostrate, and this is Moloch – that fire-filled Old Testament stone idol into whose burning arms the ancient Israelites sacrificed their children, yes, their little ones, hoping to be repaid in what? In economic prosperity![31] You can have wealth if you honour Mammon, and you can keep Mammon only if you worship Moloch.

And Moloch, of course, can be invoked. Moloch can indeed be rendered visible. His Old Testament theology can actually be rendered postmodern, and that is part of the bardic function for our times.

Mary McCann composed 'Working for Moloch' after reading the work of Adrienne Rich.

> the cleaners are scrubbing the Institute lavatories
> because women are supposed to do that
>
> the girls are typing in the Institute offices
> because women are dedicated and careful

the women are assembling printed circuits
because women are good at delicate work
and women's eyes are expendable

the young men are doing their PhDs
because young men are obedient and ambitious
and someone wants warheads
laser rangefinders
hunt and destroy capabilities
multichannel night seeking radar
and science is neutral

back home the wives of the PhD students are having babies
because women are maternal and loving
and who else can have children but women?

at the top of the tower the old men and the middle aged men
and sometimes one woman professor
meet to form plans, cadge funds and run the place
because obedient young men turn into obedient old men
and it's all for the good of the country
and defence funds are good for science
and science is neutral
and no one notices Moloch

the women bring them
clean toilets
cups of coffee
typescripts
micro circuits oh so neatly assembled
and children

and it's hard to see Moloch because he is both far away
                                        and everywhere
and no one asks to whom they are all obedient

and they say, 'Who's Moloch? Never heard of him'
as out in the dark Moloch belches
and grows redder and redder
and fatter and fatter
as he eats the children[32]

12. Seeds of Fire

We're all implicated in the state of the world, but we need not remain trapped by this. We need not remain powerless. We may not be able to change much, but we can at least work on the Zen of personal integrity. And we can start with choices. As God told Moses: 'See, I have set before you today life and prosperity, death and adversity . . . *I have set before you life and death*, blessings and curses. *Choose life* so that you and your descendants may live.'[1]

'Choosing life' does not mean turning our backs on modern medicine, technology, industry, genetics, mathematics, rationality, and so on. Quite the contrary: these things can be gifts. Rather, it is a refusal to pretend that any of them are 'neutral' or 'value-free'. Everything that we allow to shape the values in our lives, everything that we use to demonstrate what we stand for – these things can be described as our 'gods'. Spiritual unfolding is a matter not of denying our gods, but of owning up to them – 'confessing' them – and figuring out whether they sit comfortably with those deepest understandings of God consistent with our highest possible hopes and aspirations.

The question is not whether to have a god – with or without the capital 'G' and with or without 'dess' on the end – but whether we're open to the god that's big enough to give life. As Jung said, 'You can take away a man's gods, but only to give him others in return.'[2] Maybe, like Abraham, we actually need to haggle with God or with what we think God is. Like Abraham did, maybe we have to throw out the challenges: 'Far be it from you to do such a thing, to slay the righteous with the wicked,' Abraham said, as if in rebuke of God. And at the end of the day, God agreed not to destroy the city if just ten decent people could be found in it.[3] Jeremiah scored even better: he beat God down to just one righteous person![4] That says something, metaphorically of course, about the premium God places on the integrity of the individual. In our fledgeling integrity we might even give God hope. We maybe encourage God, metaphorically of course, to try a little harder!

The human search for God, then, is the age-old search for meaning in life – to find a life worth living. And really, there's just so much to be living for:

such scope for massive transformation of this world if we could only pull it off. That's why it's worth the trying. That's why we shouldn't give in and lie down before the idols. Just consider, for example, what a life-long framework for, let's say, a spiritually rich, holistic education might look like: it might start with soil structure and why the biochemistry of organic farming sustains biodiversity, and go on to look at how biodiversity equates with an optimal balance of arable crops and animal stock, and that with animal welfare and human health; with awareness of energy alternatives that would mitigate dangers of global warming and keep the old and poor from being cold; with ecological restoration including computer modelling of new techniques and evolutionary processes; with maximising economic linkages and multipliers at bioregional, national and global levels; with business structures that harmonise enterprise with accountability and co-operation; with an economics of 'Fair Trade'; with ecological architecture and clean, efficient public transport systems; with the spiritual ability to see anew why all life is providential; with healing skills based on advanced scientific and spiritual principles; with knowing the roots of artistic creativity and inspiration; with poetics and story, and learning how to listen to one another; with a participatory politics of empowerment; with awareness of the psychology of prejudice and the resolution of conflict; with a nonviolent civic-defence strategy and taking away the causes that give rise to war; with cherishing human life from cradle to grave; with extending the erotic into all of life, including sexual love; with the kids having fun and playing in treehouses; with the discovery of beauty as the touchstone of what is good; in short, with the building of *community* as right relationship between soil, soul and society, powered up by the passion of the heart, steered by the reason of the head, and then applied by the skilled technique of the hand. And remember: this is not a pipe dream. Humankind is already well on the way towards understanding most of these principles. It's just a matter of linking them up and applying them.[5]

That's what joined-up thinking is all about. That's what you get when you refute the politics of death and embrace *free love* – yes, because only love freely given is worth having. It alone transcends the politics of control. The God of love tolerates evil because life and death are set before us as a *choice*. Anything less – any scenario where death was not a freely choosable option – would be the forced love of the control freak. As such, free love is the utter antithesis of idolatry, because idolatry demands hypnotic shutting-down; unconscionable obedience; death.

So there we have it. As activists or potential activists for social and ecological justice, as women and men who would build community, we must not despair to the point of incapacitation at the state of the world. That means we must refuse to lose sight of that different fire, beyond the flames of Moloch. 'I came to bring fire to the earth,' said Jesus, on good Zoroastrian form; a

Jesus speaking of the incandescence of love: 'and how I wish it were already kindled!'.[6]

In my experience it is not possible to engage fully with the world without a growing understanding of spirituality. Yes, we can run from God, but we cannot run away. If we do, we're like the two fleas on the back of a collie. One day the first turns to the second and says, 'You know, I don't think that I believe in the dog anymore.'

Such is our relationship to God. Spirituality is interconnection, and that's hard to see because, like Moloch, it's everywhere. It's like looking at the back of a hand. Normally, we're only aware of ourselves as separate entities, like the distinct nails on each finger. But as we enter into that wrestling-match engagement with love in the company of others, we slide down the finger. The psycho-spiritual distance between each finger gets less. Ultimately, we arrive at the body of the hand and look upwards. We then see that each finger, each life, is a part of the whole. Well, that's God-consciousness. We are, as Jesus said, all branches on the vine of life; as St Paul says, 'members one of another' in the Body of Christ.[7] I'm expressing these things in a Christian framework because that's what's most relevant to where I'm digging from culturally. But equally, the same thing can be said from within any faith based on love: we are also all parts of the 'Body of Islam'; expressions of the 'Buddha nature'; children of the Goddess, or, in the Sanskrit of Hinduism, *Tat tvam asi* – 'That thou art' – meaning individual soul (Atman) is ultimately at one with universal soul (Brahma).

The Norwegian philosopher Arne Naess calls such sensitivity to the inter-connectedness of all things 'deep ecology'. The ultimate human self is, he suggests, the 'ecological self'. Self-realisation – the full expression of who we are – means starting to feel ourselves as part of everything. The Australian rainforest activist John Seed says:

Once we have . . . 'fallen in love outwards', once we have experienced the fierce joy of life that attends extending our identity into nature, once we realize that the nature within and the nature without are continuous, then we too may share and manifest the exquisite beauty and effortless grace associated with the *natural* world.[8]

Such spirituality is not *pantheism* – the idea that God *is* nature. That would be idolatrous: it would limit God to the immanent material reality of our senses and deny the possibility of transcendence. Rather, it is pan*en*theism, God as *present* in nature.

Jesus put it like this: Heaven is not to be found up there or over here or at some time God-knows-when, but 'within', in the here-and-now religion of the present moment.[9] Buddha would have slapped her hands with glee at such enlightenment: 'What is the sound of one hand clapping?' Ah! Heaven. This, then, is 'liberation theology' – theology that liberates both the human spirit and theology itself from the strictures into which the control freaks, and especially our own internal control freaks, have locked it up.

The practical tactics that I use in my own activism have been hugely influenced by Walter Wink, an American liberation theologian. Spirituality, he says, is the *interiority* of a person, an institution, a nation or any thing. This interiority shapes the flow of *power*. All power ultimately comes from God, but expressed through human agency in this world that power is invariably 'fallen': it falls short of the higher, God-given vocation that is its true potential. Structures of fallen power participate in what Wink calls 'the myth of redemptive violence': the idea that violence can itself control violence; that fire can be used to put out fire. Redemptive violence is the perpetuating mechanism of the Domination System. How can we change that?

What Wink does is to suggest a three-part model for transforming the fallen Powers that Be: *naming* the Powers, *unmasking* the Powers and *engaging* the Powers.[10]

Naming the Powers recognises the spiritual truth that giving something a name makes the invisible manifest. It puts a handle on things, which, incidentally, is why the Powers, sometimes with justification, may fiercely resent 'being labelled'. The Powers that Be, Wink argues, are not sitting up in the sky like old-style demons and gods, but are resident within – where they've always been. Names like Mammon and Moloch (we could add a few others too, like the Golden Calf) help to make them visible.

Having named them and thereby rendered them perceptible, we can, secondly, move on to *unmasking* the Powers. That is, we can unpack their psychospiritual effects on life. The Domination System dominates through the sanctioning of violence. It inculcates a fear that leaves us senseless, complicit. Unmasking this takes the greatest courage and perseverance. But doing so can be very powerful, as the Rev. MacCallum's bardic exposure of Mammon with his shell of jewels or Mary McCann's poem about Moloch demonstrate so well.

Only when they have been named and unmasked can we start *engaging* the Powers. Engagement is a process of wrestling – seeking not to destroy, but to challenge (and accept being challenged) and to uplift. As Wink says: 'The Powers are good. The Powers are fallen. The Powers must be redeemed.'[11] Engagement, then, is about action for transformation. It is not about terminal destruction. The Powers do have a rightful and necessary place in life. But when power ceases to be predicated on service, when it ceases to be carried lightly and held responsibly and accountably, its fallen nature shows. That's the corruption, and the role of redemption is to catch such fallen-crestedness and draw it back to its higher, God-given vocation. Such, of course, is the theology of nonviolence and forgiveness that underlies South Africa's Truth and Reconciliation Commission.

Liberation theology therefore pushes us, as activists, into new ways of seeing and being. When we understand the ills of the world to be essentially spiritual, the level of being at which we find the front line of engagement with reality shifts. This can be quite uncomfortable, particularly for those of us coming from backgrounds that are secular or where we underwent spiritual abuse at the hands of the cold and religious. Wink, however, is unrelenting in naming the tools needed for our kit. For example, he says:

> Those who pray do so not because they believe certain intellectual propositions about the value of prayer, but simply because the struggle to be human in the face of suprahuman Powers requires it. The act of praying is itself one of the indispensable means by which we engage the Powers. It is, in fact, that engagement at its most fundamental level, where their secret spell over us is broken and we are re-established in a bit more of that freedom which is our birthright and potential. Prayer is . . . the interior battlefield where the decisive victory is first won, before engagement in the outer world is even attempted. If we have not undergone that inner liberation, whereby the individual strands of the nets in which we are caught are severed, one by one, our activism may merely reflect one or another counter-ideology of some counter-Power. We may simply be caught up in a new collective passion, and fail to discover the transcendent possibilities of God pressing for realization here and now. Unprotected by prayer, our social activism runs the danger of becoming self-justifying good works, as our inner resources atrophy, the wells of love run dry, and we are slowly changed into the likeness of the Beast.[12]

Action for transformation, then, starts with becoming truly aware of how we feel: within ourselves, in our communities and in relation to nature. It faces up to the reality of disease – the spiritual dis-eases of disequilibria, stunted growth and cancerous growth. Rather than pushing away or masking existential pain with consumption or addictions, it recognises its value. The pain is the mantra. It is the signal that points us to where healing is called for. That's why we need to feel it, to go into it, to see where it's coming from and to find what it asks of us. Healing then becomes a process of re-creation, opening up the channels of creativity.[13] And creativity is nothing less than the renewal of *eros*; the cutting edge of *poesis*; the literal unfolding of reality on the rolling crest of time in the ongoing process of God's creation through all eternity.

This is what makes spiritual activism so compelling. It brings alive the feminist principle that 'the personal is the political'. It lights up the darkness so that the blind see, the lame walk and even the dead rise. In other words, the simple act of becoming truly aware of reality can cause miracles. It can set loose *magic*. Says Starhawk about this:

Magic is another word that makes people uneasy, so I use it deliberately, because the words we are comfortable with, the words that sound acceptable, rational, scientific, and intellectually sound, are comfortable precisely because they are the language of estrangement.

Magic, she continues, 'encompasses political action, which is aimed at changing consciousness and thereby causing change'. It is '*the art of changing consciousness at will*'.

Magic can be very prosaic. A leaflet, a lawsuit, a demonstration, or a strike can change consciousness .... Those techniques, like any techniques, can be taught in hierarchical structures or misused in attempts to gain power-over. But their essence is inherently antihierarchical. As a means of gaining power-over, magic is not very effective – hence its association with self-deception, illusion, and charlatanry in our society. Magical techniques are effective for and based upon the calling forth of power-from-within, because magic is the psychology/technology of immanence, of the understanding that everything is connected.[14]

The function of the shaman or bard, as we have seen, is to step outside of consensus trance reality, observe the psychodynamics of individual or social disease, and then step back in to protest for change. 'Protest' – now there's another uncomfortable word! It comes from the Latin *protestari*, meaning 'to testify for something'. As such, work of social and ecological witness is necessarily about protest. Theologically speaking, this makes it *prophetic*.

'Prophecy': another uncomfortable word! Let's go into the meaning of that too. The Greek origin of 'prophecy' is 'to interpret', or 'to speak on behalf of'. Old man Moses insisted that prophecy should be a norm, not the exception: 'Would God that all the Lord's people were prophets, and that the Lord would put his spirit upon them!'[15] he thundered in the wilderness, desperately struggling with dissenting elements among his own people while leading them to a land 'flowing with milk and honey'. As protesting activists often necessarily working alone, as Audre Lorde says, 'perversely, with no extraordinary power', we might observe that the prophet's prime task was frequently 'to gather the remnant' – the scattered community of the true people of God. Elijah thought that there was no one left. He went and sat under a solitary tree on Mount Horeb and asked to die. But an angel came saying, 'Get up and eat', because he was going to need strength for the work ahead. And a great wind came, then an earthquake, followed by fire, and finally, 'a sound of sheer silence' – and God told him to get back down the mountain, because there were still 7000 of the remnant who he hadn't noticed, but who were waiting to be united.[16]

And maybe that's still how it is today. Maybe the 'prophetic' task for our times is to find the remnant community of activists who care – the bleeding hearts and the artists; the scientists and the practical people – and to gather ourselves into movements. Maybe the name of the game is to identify remnant islands of both human culture and natural ecology, and to nurture them: to help them find the angelic manna that will rebuild their strength, even for those on the verge of death. I always remember an Indian ecologist telling how they'd fenced off an area of land long overgrazed, and to the villagers' amazement, a great many trees long thought locally extinct started to sprout again. The remnant taproots were still there under the ground. With pressure of grazing removed, new life could be regenerated. You see, that's the reality of prophetic ecology, and the reality can be every bit as thrilling as the metaphor.

Of course, the Domination System doesn't like to have prophets railing against it. They undermine the credibility of the collective hallucination or consensus trance. Stanley Milgram's later electric-shock experiments are of very great interest in this regard. He went on to find that willingness to go the whole way varied directly with the *perceived legitimacy of the authority figure conducting the experiment*, and with the degree to which the person administering the 'shocks' felt close to or distanced from the victim.

Compliance fell away dramatically if the scientist controlling the experiment was not wearing a white coat, or if the events took place in a seedy downtown building rather than the university, or if the victim's hand had to be physically placed on a metal plate before applying the voltage (thereby creating a sense of closeness). Most striking of all was the outcome when two white-coated experimenters were in charge, but one started protesting that the experiment should be stopped: the compliance rate fell right away to *zero*! This is a very powerful finding for the activist to note. It suggests why authoritarian regimes cannot tolerate dissent: it cracks their spell of consent. That is why fascist systems have to be totalitarian, all-embracing: they have to have undivided obedience from their subjects. From this we can see why Gandhi discovered that *satyagraha* – the truth force – was more powerful than the sword. It cuts sharper – and nobody gets irreversibly cut up either.

It is at this point, as we've begun to see, that much of the biblical prophetic material, perhaps to our embarrassment, can become powerfully magnetic for the activist. Often those crusty characters of old also felt uncomfortable about their role. They tried the same excuses for inaction that we try. Jeremiah protested to God that he was 'only a boy'.[17] He was put in the stocks and down a well for his alleged treachery in preaching against the nation's tyranny. He accused God of making him a laughing stock: 'For whenever I speak, I must cry out, "Violence and destruction!"' he says, realising that people would think his behaviour over the top. And why did he do this? Because 'there is something like a burning fire shut up in my bones [and] I am weary with holding it in'. In what has been described as the most blasphemous part of the Bible, Jeremiah uses a metaphor of rape in depiction of God's insistence that he be a protester: 'O Lord you have enticed me . . . you have overpowered me . . . Cursed be the day on which I was born!' he says. 'Why did I come forth from the womb to see toil and sorrow, and spend my days in shame?'[18]

Then there was Isaiah. Isaiah, the greatest of the Old Testament's composite prophetic figures, told God that he was an unworthy servant. He was 'a man of unclean lips'. Well, that didn't seem to bother God, but one does wonder what the ladies serving tea and cakes in the temple hall would have said if he walked by spouting off, especially since we're told that he 'walked naked and barefoot for three years as a sign and a portent'![19]

As for Moses, he felt disabled, complaining, 'I have never been eloquent . . . I am slow of speech and slow of tongue'.[20] There was also the great biblical ecologist, Ezekiel, who had to be fortified first with a remarkable shamanic vision of totemic creatures and crystal (disconcertingly 'New Age'!), and then with the courage not to be afraid 'of their words, though briers and thorns surround you and you live among scorpions'.[21]

Elijah's work was so badly paid that ravens, as well as the Angel, had to feed him on his travels.[22] Rather interestingly, Elijah's successor, Elisha, seems to have been one of the few to relish his calling. He asks Elijah if he might inherit *a double dose* of his power. When the old man dies, Elisha finds that this is granted. Sure enough, Elijah's mantle remains magical. Elisha tries it out by dividing the waters of the River Jordan. With his feet still dry, he then makes off to ascend Mount Carmel. But as he passes through a village, the children tease him about a bald patch in his hair. And then, in a passage about which not many sermons are preached, we see this double dose of shamanic power rush to the prophet's head. Elisha's male ego is affronted. He turns round and curses the children in the name of the Lord. Two she-bears obligingly come out of the woods. They tear apart two and forty of the little miscreants. And so, verily and perhaps merrily, Elisha continues on his way, apparently without remorse.[23]

So there's another thing that we fear. We fear the whole process getting out of hand. Can we handle it? Where might it all end? Won't people think we're peculiar, and then there'll be no way back on to strait-street? We also fear that if we engage the Powers it might be for the wrong motives. It may just be ego; indeed, we know ourselves, and so we realise that to some extent it *will* be ego! Also, it may be that the corporation, or the Government, or 'the system', or whatever it is represents an unresolved complex with a parent or some other authority figure from childhood. There's nothing really wrong with the world – we're just projecting our own crap out on to it! Well, that is where discernment, self-criticism and the tools of psychospiritual healing and growth must be brought to bear. Maybe we do need to take more time out and allow the shit to compost into a rich soil from which new life can emerge. Or maybe not. Maybe it just means that activism has to be an iterative process: one of working on ourselves simultaneously with working in the world; a continuous process of experimental action and critical reflection.

At the one extreme, then, we think we're not good enough to testify for a better world. At the other, we fear going crazy, screwing up, failing, being crucified or ego-tripping our way to the madhouse. However, if we are really called to bear witness to a concern, it will not usually leave us resting long in comfortable complacency. The archetypal forces that tossed the reluctant Jonah out of his boat and into the belly of the whale are a symbolic case in point.[24] When summoned by the deep inner self ('the Lord', as the Bible's antiquated feudal language would have it), our narrow little egos are not our own. The common task of the prophet, shaman and bard, then, is to get out and help to constellate an alternate reality. The deeper the *poesis* this draws upon, the deeper it draws from the wells of Creation, the more our work will make poetry, music and magic, and the more closely it will accord with love.

'Constellate' – now there's another cracker of a word for the toolkit. *Con* as in congregate, and *stella* as in star: 'to group meaningfully together', like a pattern of stars. The Celtic bards understood that 'conscientisation' – the deepening of both consciousness and conscience together[25] – is a spiritual process. It constellates the energies of a specific passion: something that W. B. Yeats called 'fire in the head'.[26]

The fire in the head is an inner fire – not the outward shine of Mammon; not even the spluttering coke-stoked glow of Moloch. It's a fire that wakes you up at night and penetrates your darkest spaces, burns off the psychological crap, freeing energy and inspiration to attempt the otherwise unthinkable.

The nuns of St Bridgit nursed this sacred fire. It is what gives life radiance, what makes the sun and other stars go round, what shimmers in reflection from the sword that guards the pathway back to Eden.[27] It is the origin of *poesis* – the silver nectar of the Tree of Life – the very passion of Creation.

'Now the bardic schools were the seat of that passion,' writes Professor Corkery in his classic study of how Ireland kept its spirit alive in the face of colonisation. 'In them was the flame nursed, fed, distributed – "*siolta teine*" – "seeds of fire".'[28]

As Scotland's Kenneth White, until recently professor of twentieth-century poetics at the Sorbonne, writes:

                    for the question is always
                        how
                out of all the chances and changes
              to select
        the features of real significance
                        so as to make
          of the welter
                    a world that will last
      and how to order
                the signs and symbols
          so they will continue
                to form new patterns
            developing into
            new harmonic wholes
                so to keep life alive
          in complexity
                    and complicity
                        with all of being –
                there is only poetry[29]

It's twenty years on, twenty years since my last stint on the sporting estates.
A phone call comes out of the blue.

'Alastair? Alastair, how are you? It's Audley! Remember? The Captain!
Audley Archdale!'

My astonishment was all the greater because I had just finished drafting the
passages in this book about Eisken.

'We *must* meet, Alastair. I'd *love* to see you again. I've seen you on *television* talking about land ownership. *Can't* understand where you're coming
from! *Frightfully* erudite-sounding! But it would be *so lovely* to meet again.'

We met over a coffee: the Captain with his military whiskers; me with my
stereotypical beard in counterpoint. Genuine warmth rolled between us.

The Captain peeled back the lapel of his jacket and revealed a small button
badge. It carried a blue cross and the letters 'NFSH'.

'Do you know what that means?' he asked.

'No,' I replied.

'It means something terribly important to me, Alastair. A lot of different
things have happened since you last knew me.'

'Yes, but did you know . . .' I pressed him. 'Did you know about the ruins
at Loch Shell . . . the Pairc Deer Raid . . . the Clearances?'

'Oh, yes,' he told me. 'But remember, these things were always less black
and white than people present them as being. Remember that, won't you? Do
remember it.'

I felt uncomfortable. I don't think this dear old man fully realised the gravity of what I was pushing him on.

'We've still got all the press cuttings in the family archives,' he added.

'So what do you think about them?' I asked.

'I don't know,' he said. 'Remember, Alastair – I've told you before – I didn't have the education you've had. I don't know all the facts.'

'But didn't you ever reflect that . . . well . . . underneath those happy times of your great-aunt, the annual picnics and everything, there was real suffering? Injustice was going on.'

'I don't know, Alastair,' he sighed. 'What I loved was the sound of the rivers and the smell of the heather. There's nothing else like it *anywhere* on Earth . . . But look. I must tell you what this badge means. It's what's taken me forward. It's changed my life.'

The letters stood for National Federation of Spiritual Healers.

Now, I do not want to enter into a discussion here about the validity or otherwise of spiritual healing, or describe how Audley got involved with it. Simply allow me, with gratitude for his assistance in the writing of these sensitive chapters, to rest my discussion of the erstwhile laird of Eisken at this point. As Audley said, things are seldom black and white, and a resplendent human being like him serves to remind the campaigning reformer, I think, of the importance of trying to go 'heavy on the issues, but gentle on the people'.

So that means we don't forget the issues.

It is 1994, and I am on the Isle of Skye. By this time I'm postgraduate teaching director at the Centre for Human Ecology in the Division of Biological Sciences, Faculty of Science and Engineering, University of Edinburgh. I have taken my class – a dozen human ecology MSc students – to a village that was cleared in the nineteenth century.

We hear from our guide about an old woman who had been evicted from her house at the start of winter. They took the roof off it to prevent her living there. She made herself a hut down on the beach. Her neighbours were dispatched across the Atlantic. By the time spring came, the old woman had died alone.

> *Anns an adhar dhubh-ghorm ud,*
> *airde na siorraidheachd os ar cionn . . .*
> In that blue–black sky,
> as high above us as eternity,
> a star was winking at us,
> answering the leaping flames of fire
> in the rafters of my father's house,
> that year we thatched the house with snowflakes.

And that too was the year
they hauled the old woman out on to the dung-heap,
to demonstrate how knowledgeable they were in Scripture,
for the birds of the air had nests
(and the sheep had folds)
though she had no place in which to lay down her head.

O Strathnaver and Strath of Kildonan,
it is little wonder that the heather should bloom on your slopes,
hiding the wounds that Patrick Sellar, and such as he, made,
just as time and time again I have seen a pious woman
who has suffered the sorrow of this world,
with the peace of God shining from her eyes.
... *is sith Dhe 'na suilean.*[30]

We walk through the rock-piled ruins of the large village, stop, and drink from a murmuring stream. I lean over stones polished smooth with generations of past use, look into the water, and feel the *holiness* of this place.

It's like looking into the tender vulnerability of a child's face, or being deeply present with a loved one, or the haunting glimpse of some anonymous refugee on a television bulletin when you feel yourself melting into the love of who you intuit them to be. It's that kind of mélange – stillness, sadness and beauty – and the terrible loveliness in the face of one prematurely deceased. That, anyway, is how I feel it. That is my experience; my testimony.

Some powerful inner urge compels me to remove my boots. I walk on, barefoot, a little apart from the rest of the group. Others sense and respect my wish to be alone. Stillness. Silently I pay homage to this place.

The empty windows. Gaping doorways. The hollow homely walls in this monumental gentle spot. In my mind there are echoes of the vacant Eisken glen, and as I stand, lines from 'Beinn Shianta', a poem written in 1830 by a Morvern doctor, John MacLachlan, come to me.

Many are the poor bothies destroyed on every side,
Each one only a grey outline on the green grass;

And many a roofless dwelling
A heap of stones beside the bubbling spring;

Where the fire and the children were,
There the rushes grow highest.[31]

And to think of such events within touching distance of history, and to walk barefoot, and to realise that you're not thinking, but *reverberating*; that your mind is now resounding to the power of having paid heed, paying heed to an old, old passage:

> Put off thy shoes from off thy feet,
> for the place whereon thou standest is holy ground.[32]

And to find that the cringe factor of its Old Testament source dissipates. For what other words could express this?

When you go barefoot, you feel the touch of the ground. Some of the rivulets are warm to the step. They've flowed long on sun-warmed surfaces. Others are icy; freshly sourced in the spring. They're the ones to drink from. And you tread on the Earth so much more gently barefoot. You don't dig in as with hard-heeled boots when stepping down the slopes; you softly contour your toes and grip the land, like an embrace. You lean forwards rather than backwards; you see better what lies beneath your feet. You pass, unharming, over emerald sod and yellow-flowering tormentil with its golden mandala-shaped petals. You realise, afresh, why we evolved toes, their function in giving balance. You experience a harmony of body, soil and soul. You become more . . . incarnate.

I walk on like this for two or three miles. Not far away, the high Cuillin rise. We walk on, all of us, until, to our amazement, three eagles ascend and wheel over the mountains' silhouette. They draw us back, together, into a space that now is different; different now, as we too lift and soar on eagle wings.

PART TWO

The French Revolution on Eigg and the Gravel-pit of Europe

13. Well of the Holy Women

It was in autumn 1990 that Tom Forsyth first came to see me. A crofter from the West Highland community of Scoraig, he was originally of Fife coal-mining stock. A fine, strong, white-haired man he was, of mystical and sometimes outrageous disposition. Tom was then just coming up to his six-tieth year. He looked like the American poet Walt Whitman and quietly walked the Whitmanesque talk: 'Urge and urge and urge/Always the procreant urge of the world.'[1] He loved living things, and his once barren and windswept croft, now planted with trees, teemed with all manner of wild flowers, birdlife and little critters.

Tom had suffered enough of landlordism. He was sick of Scotland's feudal system, which had endured since the eleventh century. He'd seen too much of ordinary folks needing the big man's permission to plant a few trees; to shoot something for the pot; to extend a house. Rarely a week went by in rural Scotland without some story emerging of a laird pulling down a home because he didn't want people living near 'his' river, charging fees for the ancient right of cutting peat as winter fuel, or blocking walkers' access to a remote but beautiful glen. Landlordism at Scoraig, however, had followed a pattern of benign neglect. That was useful. It had allowed the crofters to experiment with greater freedom than most places enjoyed. They'd been able to live unfettered. They'd been able to show that, in the words of Montesquieu quoted by de Tocqueville in *L'Ancien Régime*, 'The soil is pro-ductive less by reason of its natural fertility than because the people tilling it are free.'[2]

So it was that Scoraig's population had steadily increased and folks who otherwise never could have dreamed of having homes of their own had built comfortable houses, often from materials thrown out in skips. In its earlier days the inhabitants had rejected opportunities for both mains electricity and a main road. People got on and off the remote peninsula by boat across Little Loch Broom. Most of their electrical power came from homemade windmills. They also had their own secondary school – the smallest in Britain. In general, when the place was working well, which had to be most of the time for sheer survival's sake, it effused a homespun, confident and resolutely anarchistic dignity.

But Tom Forsyth was not content to live out his days warming his toes from logs he had once pressed into the ground as saplings. The plain fact was that he had an obsession, and the object of this obsession was an island: Eigg, 'the garden of the Hebrides'. It pained him to see islanders struggling under an ownership regime that, like so many in rural Scotland, was felt to be oppressive. 'If only they had the freedom to do what we've done,' he'd say, 'think what they could demonstrate to themselves, to Scotland and to the world.' But what made Tom's musings different from most pipe dreams was a serendipitous encounter; one that pushed him to think big. It had happened back in 1974. He had perchanced, as can be the wont of Scoraig folks who love subverting stereotypes about themselves, to attend a banquet at Lennoxlove, the baronial hall of the Duchess of Hamilton. While sipping champagne, feeling not at all ill at ease among the powerful and titled, Tom found himself drawn into conversation with Lady Ursula Burton. So he told her that Eigg was coming up for sale.

'Well,' said her ladyship, with the supreme confidence of a social class for whom money has always been just a form of energy that can be switched on and off at will, 'why don't we form a trust and buy it out?'

'That was the moment of conception of the Isle of Eigg Trust,' Tom would later say. 'And who would believe it all started at a baronial banquet!' What made it even more ironic is that Lady Ursula was the wife of Lord Burton, named by Andy Wightman in the *Sunday Times* as one of the top ten Scottish lairds whose actions have contributed most to the public demand for land reform![3] It would seem, however, that while Lady Ursula moved in her husband's world, she was not stuck in it. Renowned as a spiritual director and remembered through the legacy of the Coach House retreat centre near Inverness, she was a woman of rare sensitivity. Her depth of inner vision, it is said, touched on the prophetic.

Vision and visions were qualities Eigg had never lacked. The island's oral tradition tells that in the mid-nineteenth century a very strange and ominous apparition had been witnessed. Tradition bearer Duncan MacKay told it like this:

Two Laig herdsmen were working in the hills one day when the figure of a man appeared suddenly to one of them. He could see him perfectly well, but his companion could not see anybody there at all. The herdsman soon realised that he could only see the stranger if he stood still in the same position, otherwise the figure would vanish if he moved or if he sat down at all. Then he saw something else behind the man, a flock of sheep coming down from the hills. He knew then for certain that the apparition was the *tabhaisg* [the ghostly double] of someone who would appear for real one day.[4]

In 1828 the island had fallen into private ownership when the old clan system finally crumbled. What survived of the house of Clanranald had become as degenerate and Anglicised as most other chieftainships in the crushing aftermath of Culloden. To clear his gambling debts, Ranald MacDonald, chief of Clanranald, sold the land he had previously held in trust for the people for £15,000 to Dr Hugh Macpherson, formerly a surgeon in the Indian Medical Services and then a professor of Hebrew, theology and Greek at Kings College, Aberdeen. Shortly afterwards, Angus Òg, who held a 'tack' (a traditional type of sub-lease) on the lands of Laig and Grulin, took up a commission in the 11th regiment of Wisconsin, but he died from injuries sustained in the Civil War. Dr Macpherson accordingly advertised the pastures at a commercial rent. A farmer from the Scottish Borders took the lease, but he did not care for 'swarms of poor crofters unable to pay their rents'. Without further ado the fourteen families of Grulin were given notice to quit at Martinmas 1852. 'Our proprietor was like plenty of proprietors in the Highlands at the time,' said another Eigg tradition bearer, Hugh MacKinnon, 'and this did not trouble his conscience very greatly. It was just a case of telling the poor crofters who were in Grulin that they would have to clear out, and there was nothing else for it [but to] take themselves off to America.'[5]

In June 1853 eleven of these families were shipped to Nova Scotia. They arrived dressed in rags and close to starvation. Little more was ever heard of them, though from time to time Canadians have arrived on Eigg claiming to be their descendants. The emigrants who survived those first winters are thought to have been assisted by the Mi'Kmaq native people. Only three of the cleared families managed to stay behind, including that of Alistair MacKinnon, who settled elsewhere on Eigg. One of his sisters never recovered from the trauma. She took herself up to some high cliffs and leapt into the waves.

The new tenant of Laig was Stephen Stewart. Such was the fertility of Grulin's arable slopes that in the first two years all his sheep had lambs, making a handsome profit. To the islanders, of course, he was the very man whose *tabhaisg* had been seen in the vision of Angus Òg's herdsman. Strathallan's 'world without a friend' had arrived.

In 1896 the Macpherson family sold Eigg to one Robert Thomson. He had started life as the Far East correspondent of *The Times* and made his money as an international arms dealer, supplying hardware for revolutions and uprisings in Peru, Chile, Afghanistan and China. He celebrated the Japanese victory over the Russian Navy in 1904 by building a huge bonfire on the Sgurr, Eigg's highest point; the warships had been supplied by him.[6]

In 1917 Thomson sold the island on to Sir William Petersen, a wealthy London ship owner who boasted that his fiery temper derived from his Danish Viking ancestry. He built a wooden platform from which to address

Eigg's tenants in a regal manner. As he drove past in the island's first car, boys and girls had to line up on either side of the road respectively, standing to attention. Behind his back, however, the bardic tradition had its revenge. Satirical Gaelic verse about Petersen was composed for singing at ceilidh parties. To this day it remains a source of amusement.

After Petersen died, his daughters, who had used Eigg as an extension of their Derby-winning racehorse stable, sold the island, in 1925. Once again the price was £15,000, and this time it went to one of their father's friends, the Moor Line shipping magnate and government minister Walter Runciman, the 1st Viscount Runciman of Doxford.

Lord Runciman ushered in a golden age during which staff were well looked after, houses improved and agriculture flourished. Woodcock wintered in profusion on Eigg, and, according to the shooting log, 611 birds were bagged in one year.[7] Runciman's second son, Sir Steven, inherited the island and used its luxurious Italianate lodge as a *pied-à-terre* for writing his unsurpassed three-volume epic *A History of the Crusades*. (These Christian holy wars were, he concluded, 'nothing more than a long act of intolerance in the name of God, which is a sin against the Holy Ghost'.) Sir Steven was connected with the Bloomsbury Group and therefore mixed with such company as John Maynard Keynes, Lytton Strachey and Virginia Woolf; his first pupil at Trinity, Cambridge, was the spy, Guy Burgess, who he remembered for both his brilliance and his dirty fingernails. As a boy, Sir Steven was able to read French at three, Latin at six, Greek at seven and Russian at eleven. These precocious gifts heralded his fascination with the Orthodox Church, which, together with an honorary position in Syria as a whirling dervish, contributed towards a 1987 tribute on Channel 4 called *Sir Steven Runciman: Bridge to the East*.[8]

In 1966 Sir Steven, desiring a more accessible country retreat, sold Eigg for £82,000 to Captain Robert Evans, a Welsh-cum-Shropshire landowner. Evans was too old to spend much time on the island and, in 1971, made a handsome profit selling it on to Commander Bernard Farnham-Smith for £120,000.

The Cockney-accented Farnham-Smith wanted Eigg as an out-of-sight and out-of-mind base for his charity, the Anglyn Trust, which specialised in helping 'difficult' children from wealthy families who had run into the buffers at public school. However, the Commander soon started cutting wages and messing about with islanders' household tenancies. Discontent set in and newspaper investigations revealed that the only commandership heroics that Farnham-Smith had ever conducted were not with the Navy in China, as he had boasted, but as a commander of the London Fire Brigade! With his credibility duly doused, the wet-squib firefighter placed Eigg back on the market in 1974 – which happened to be the point at which Tom Forsyth was living it up with Lady Burton at Lennoxlove.

The following year the island went under the hammer for £274,000. The new laird was Keith Schellenberg, the millionaire heir to a knacker's yard that boiled up bones for wartime aeroplane glue; also a successful car dealer, power-boat racer, amateur aviator, vintage-car collector, Liberal Party candidate (with professed Tory leanings), Olympic bobsleigher, captain of Kaiser Bill's steam yacht across the North Sea and, according to the *Daily Express*, the inventor of that most English of winter sports, ice cricket.

Legend has it that the day Keith Schellenberg bought Eigg he found himself accidentally locked in a room high inside Udny Castle, the stately pile of his then wife, the Honourable Margaret de Hauteville Udny-Hamilton. There was to be a blind auction, with interested parties invited to submit sealed bids, and the high-noon deadline was drawing near. Schellenberg knew that the state-run Highlands and Islands Development Board were planning to pitch in against him, hoping to bring the island into experimental public ownership and arrest the miserable decline that had taken place since the halcyon days of Runciman, and he was determined not to be defeated. He later said he had bought Eigg specifically to stop the HIDB in its tracks. He deplored the 'rotten' tide of socialism that state land ownership represented. He felt duty bound to stick his finger in the dyke, for Britain's sake.

So it was that the great man abseiled out of a window and down the castle walls, roared off down country lanes like a dirt-snorting dragon and, some say, completed the triathlon by hurling his envelope like a javelin on to the desk of an astonished lawyer. His offer topped that of the HIDB by £70,000. Schellenberg then went on to astonish Eigg's population by making his debut arrival in a self-piloted private plane. He landed on a steeply sloping field and told Angus MacKinnon to look after the aircraft. Under no circumstances was a particular button to be touched. But the button somehow got pressed, and Schellenberg's flying chariot lurched to a heroic end on the rocks. As Eigg's historian, Camille Dressler records, 'the new ownership had started with a bang'.[9]

'You must be able to guess: it's Mr Toad,' commented one of his friends to a high-society journalist. 'First it's a canary-coloured caravan and then it's a motor car . . . poop, poop and all that. I mean, Keith actually wears those round goggles and he's always arriving in places with a lot of noise and clouds of dust.'[10]

Life at the Big House, Eigg Lodge, retained a calculated 1920s character. 'We spent our days as if we were Somerset Maugham characters, sunbathing or playing croquet on the manicured lawn,' recalled one guest. 'We piled on to the running board of the stately 1927 Rolls and made our way leisurely to jewelled beaches for long, lazy picnics or midnight games of moonlit hockey and football.'[11]

Much about Schellenberg was harmless; indeed endearing in an eccentric way. As a vegetarian, he had, unusually for a laird, allowed no hunting over his ground. And as lairds went, he was better than many. Early on he opened up opportunities for incomers, causing the population to rise from thirty-nine to sixty. He could express a visionary humanitarianism, saying, for example: 'It is necessary for people working under oppressive urban conditions to have a place where they can restore their fundamental values.'[12] He tried to be kind and wanted to be popular. The only problem was that he never recognised how the spectacles of wealth and power tinted his vision.

In consequence, many employees experienced him as an idiosyncratic autocrat.[13] After getting off to a great start, relationships would sour. People felt that their hopes had been built up and then dashed. They had invested in a major change in life, then the rug was pulled from beneath their feet and they were left stranded. One couple told me that when they first came to Eigg, Schellenberg had been a father figure to them. 'But as we grew more confident in ourselves and wanted to be less dependent on him,' they said, 'it was as if he started to reject us. It was like we got cast in the role of his rebellious children.' Indeed, much of the reason for the sharp rise in Eigg's population for which Schellenberg often claimed credit was its high staff turnover. Those who did not want to leave the lovely island after a catastrophic bust-up simply moved over to the crofting village of Cleadale, where, protected by crofting law and helped by indigenous islanders, they could run cottage industries without the laird being able to do much to touch them. The days had gone when the laird would walk into a house without knocking and lift the pan lid to check if they were cooking anything of his. However, other control structures remained in place, as they did right across feudal Scotland. If people acted out of order, they or their nearest and dearest could lose their jobs, find their leases were not renewed, suffer consequential loss of certain state benefits, or be required to pay huge sums to lawyers in order to obtain the estate's signature for some trifling planning or licensing matter.[14]

If law was the outward form of this domination system, its inner structures were psychological. A *Harpers & Queen* article carried a revealing photograph of Mr Schellenberg's many sporting trophies. Above them hangs a handmade map of the Eigg, as if the island itself is another trophy. This marks even the sites of houses from which people had been evicted in the Clearances. Embroidered underneath the map are the telling words: 'The supreme happiness of life is the conviction that we are loved.'[15] And there you have it. Often lairds let slip their desperate need to be loved, but this is hitched to a sense of self entangled with property as a code for power over others. It is as if the power of love has been replaced with the love of power in order to keep control of the love; in order not to risk losing it. As such, the archetypal laird often acts like a spoiled child. Each car, plane, racehorse, boat and house is an assertion of 'being somebody' of consequence and demonstrating it through judiciously applied largesse. 'The conviction that we are loved' is thereby displaced into proprietorial control. It amplifies the empty rattle of a hollowed-out soul and attracts the applause only of sycophants.

One only need talk with some of Keith Schellenberg's former employees to find various of these points illustrated. Writing in *Scotland on Sunday*, Stewart Hennessey profiles the laird as follows:

> Arrogant and lucky is how Schellenberg, fairly, describes himself. However, he's also a romantic and his love of the island has an enthusiasm and innocence about it. The ex-rugby player, bob-sleigher and vintage car collector and racer has an irresistible passion for life. He exudes boyish charm. How do you tell someone more than twice your age that they're a charming but spoiled brat?[16]

Hennessey goes on to interview Duncan Devlin. Devlin gave up his teaching job and moved to Eigg in 1975 with his wife and three children to run the estate's craft shop and guesthouse. Devlin, according to the report, soon found that bills went unpaid and the house was left with only polythene for window panes. 'I felt like I was going to be part of the team,' he said. '*Team* was one of Schellenberg's favourite words, but he was always captain.' Such team spirit, Devlin went on, divided the island into an out-group and the Schellenbergian in-group:

> His people intimidated us. He was a great guy so you must be a rat for being against him. That was the poison put about; when he needed someone you jumped. You felt like you weren't your own person. It seems dramatic but you felt defiled. On an island of 60 people, passing someone on the road without them saying hello, as if you weren't there, it was horrible and tense. And his people were always round the house. I remember that the mere sight of the blue transit van they went about in just made us all jump.

Schellenberg eventually served Devlin with an eviction notice. Brother Graeme and Brother George of the Anglican Order of St Augustine were, at the same time, evicted from the old farm they had set up as a micro-monastery.[17] But Duncan Devlin fought back, taking out and winning court actions for breach of contract and harassment. Schellenberg denied this to Hennessey in the *Scotland on Sunday* interview; that is, until he was shown the documented evidence.

In a drafty house battered by Hebridean gales and not allowed to fell firewood, the Devlins maintain they were frozen out. Schellenberg just shrugged it off. His defence was that Devlin 'simply occupied somewhere which was needed for someone else. That's as far as it goes. Maybe because he was from

Glasgow he couldn't cope with the life. He simply wasn't up to the job.' Hennessey's piece in *Scotland on Sunday* concluded:

> Maybe this is the way Schellenberg sees it; maybe he is oblivious to what the family . . . went through. He laps up the aesthetics of the remote, sparse island but is completely naive about the harshness of living there and, by his own admission, 'ordinary' life.
>
> Schellenberg refers to his Border terrier Horace as a 'friend' and discusses his relationship with the dog lovingly and in detail. It is a sensitive sentiment but he adds that people 'will *always* give you trouble in the end'.
>
> His other 'old friends' which are discussed warmly are vintage cars and boats. I spent several hours with him. He never mentioned any human friends.

It was to my office at Edinburgh University's Centre for Human Ecology that Tom Forsyth came that day in autumn 1990, sixteen years after the banquet at Lennoxlove. Until recently I'd been business advisor to the Iona Community, and its then leader, the Rev. John Harvey, had sent Tom in my direction. 'He used to run the Community's youth camps in George MacLeod's days, back in the 1950s,' John told me on the phone. 'He wants to start up some kind of a trust to buy Eigg. Not got any money. I know it sounds crazy, but I said I'd give him fifty or a hundred quid if he gets it going. He's not a crank. Did a lot to get Scoraig up and going again after it had become depopulated in the 1960s. I'd say you should give him some time.'

So Tom came. He explained that he was joined in his prospective venture by Liz Lyon, a Glasgow artist, and Bob Harris, a farmer from Lochwinnoch. Liz had originally visited Eigg as a guest of the Schellenbergs, but her growing awareness of the condition of the common people marred the comfort that Keith and Margaret lavishly provided. Bob, as well as having a big sheep farm outside Glasgow, was the leader of his local community council and a poet. All three of them understood and deplored the insidious interplay of land and power. They wanted, Tom told me, to stir up a happening – something that would challenge the established order and demonstrate that life could be different. But they lacked certain skills. That was why John Harvey had put them on to me. So would I, Tom wondered, become the fourth founding trustee of an 'Isle of Eigg Trust'?

At the time, I had never visited Eigg. Tom's idea felt like something out of a fairy story – unrealistic and magical in equal measure. He assured me that a number of islanders had quietly given him the green light. Mairi Kirk, in particular, had provided substantial hospitality and moral support. People were desperate for change. The trouble was, he said, that most of them were simply not in a position openly to state their views with any hope of getting anywhere. Many had a justified fear of victimisation. And others, to be frank, were understandably dubious about the idea of a trust. Their only previous experience of such a thing had been Farnham-Smith's Anglyn Trust, which (not unlike the landlord system as a whole) had merely served to dump on them the casualties of public-school education. How were they to know that our Trust would be any better? Might it not be just a tax dodge? Or a seductive front behind which we concealed an intention to become the lairds of misrule ourselves?

The Trust's role, Tom said, was initially going to be uncomfortable. It had to assume a mandate of *advocacy* on behalf of that majority of islanders who, he believed, privately wanted reform. It had to kick-start a process that would break the spell of consent that landlordism had enjoyed. It had to create a new constellation of possibility.

Now, in community work the assumption of having an implicit mandate is always dangerous, normally misguided and usually ends in tears. If I'd followed my academic instincts, I'd have said, 'No, thank you, but I'll publish a good paper out of what you're doing!' However, I had found out enough about Eigg to see that it fitted the pattern of rural disempowerment elsewhere, not just in Highland Scotland but in much of the world. And like John Harvey had said, something about Tom's analysis came across as an idea the star of which was rising. Maybe, I thought to myself, external advocacy sometimes has to precede grassroots empowerment. Sometimes folks just need a hand to get out of a hole. And maybe this might dislodge more than just the normally absentee occupant of Eigg Lodge; maybe it would trigger a political debate in Scotland about the whole mindset of landlordism.

After all, look at how Milgram had observed his subjects' compliance rapidly collapsing when authority came under question. It was true that in the late twentieth century Scottish lairds could no longer have their vassals flogged, or sold into white slavery as happened in the eighteenth century on Skye. Most of feudalism's overt abuses had now ceased. But the remainder represented unaccountable control over other people's lives and a steady transfer of wealth from poor to rich in rent or fees. Echoes of Culloden and the Clearances were still reverberating through the Scottish psyche, even in the cities, where people suffered from an often-fractured sense of identity and their feelings of powerlessness led them to accept poor governance as a norm. Taking on landlordism by setting up an Isle of Eigg Trust, then, would be a symbolic work. It would send out signals aimed at a wider transformation, connected as it was to a sense of belonging and the human 'claim of right' – the right to freedom. It would mean naming and unmasking a system that held its spell intact only so long as nobody stepped behind the scenes and saw that this great huffing and puffing Wizard of Oz was really just a pathetic little old man pulling well-connected levers of power. The authority structures that held it all in place might resemble a fortress; and in certain ways, some of which were not to be underestimated, they were a fortress. But in other ways they were just eggshell. Yet as long as that eggshell remained painted with iron bars, it could imprison oppressor and oppressed alike in roles as moribund as in any prison of Dr Zimbardo's making.

Cracking Eigg, if we were to do it, was therefore going to mean engaging power, and not just Schellenberg's power but the whole corpus of landed interests that could be expected to rally behind his front line. It would mean drawing presumed authority structures into question and helping to build an exciting and sustainable alternative. And that needed a 'big picture'. As Tom repeatedly said, it needed *vision* to lift the debate beyond negativity and to accept confrontation but not get stuck there. It needed to make connections in many people's minds, so that even far away from Eigg headlines would be made and passion for change aroused. In short, we had to try and repoliticise an agenda that was, at that time, below the threshold of most people's social consciousness. We had to shake people out of a meek acceptance of the Powers that Be, out of the consensus trance zone and into the transformative fire of indignation. We had to attempt something that, especially if by any fluke it were to be achieved, would have national and even international ram- ifications. So how could this be done, Tom and I wondered? How could it be done starting with zero resources except the reality of the situation and our- selves? What could be achieved with only a belief that hope is even more infectious than gloom, and that life's capacity to heal outstrips the potential for hurt?

A starting point lay, it seemed to us, in not underestimating the potential strength of the situation. If the first rule of strategy is to assess the arrayed forces, distinguishing real iron bars from eggshell, the second rule is to study the ground upon which those forces are positioned, distinguishing relevant from irrelevant context. In other words, appraise first the set and then the set- ting. I knew from my work in human ecology that 'state of the world' issues were of growing concern in people's hearts. Recognising such dynamics is important. It gives you your first advantage, because people still trapped in their heads miss these subtleties. It gives you the advantage of moving in a direction that builds motivation. While analysis using the head can show you what the powers look like, their outward forms, discernment using the heart shows their inner strengths and weaknesses. This is because the heart is an organ of vision. Its perceptual faculties can help us to change the hearts of others.

And that leads on to a third rule of strategy: look at the stars. Figure out the constellations taking shape in the really big picture. Get the setting not just into local perspective, but also out into the global scheme of things. Let the small picture blur, reorganise and re-emerge in relation to the big picture. Let yourself hear the old myths and also the new ones coming forward. Discern, then navigate. Never be so vain as to expect to reach the stars, but do set your course by them. That way, even when on a small scale things seem to be going wrong, when you're losing the battles, life and what is life-giving will be on your side because you're onside with it, and you'll invariably end up winning the war.

Connecting a specific situation to its much wider context in this way is very empowering. I call it the activist's amplifier. Just look, for example, at the iconic significance of the Scottish land question. Look at how a local situation on a tiny Scottish island can connect in with many people's situations around the world – if not directly, then certainly by metaphor or empathy. Consider estates on which dozens or hundreds or thousands of people live being traded on world markets to individuals or corporations whose sole qualification is their wealth, and whose prime motivation is power and status; folks being dangled insecurely on short leases, or short job contracts, because the ease of getting rid of them increases utility, disposability and, therefore, market value; folks who feel defiled because Big Brother, the Wasichu, 'is always penetrating a people whose country is too small for him'. Are these not familiar themes everywhere? A fresh energy of solidarity is released when such 'little local difficulties' are globally contextualised. This is what becomes apparent when you stand your ground, dig resolutely where you stand, and keep your eyes open.

And just look at what, in the case of landlordism, the alternative could be. With community ownership, security and commonwealth could become the core values rather than profit and domination. Rents and other revenues could support infrastructure rather than subsidising the idle mores of the rich. People could recover an authentic sense of connection with place and therefore have a framework in which to cultivate responsibility. They might learn again how to work out the full meaning of relationship with one another without the mediation of an imposed authority figure. Respect and even reverence might, just possibly, come back into the way of things. After all, how else did co-operative cultures of the past get their acts together? We know that these cultures can work, given half a chance, and some of us have actually experienced them working.

As I talked with Tom, these were the kind of thoughts that we shared. Maybe the ancient Greeks were on to something when they spoke of *kairos*, the turning point in coming time that heralds *metanoia*, a transformation in human consciousness. Yes, it sounds heady and idealistic, but remember, this was in a Scotland gradually powering up for political devolution, and precisely such theological concepts as *kairos* and *metanoia* were being openly advanced by some of devolution's foremost theorists.[18] So, yes, I told Tom, I would participate in his experiment, half-baked and idealistic though it might appear. Indeed, it was more than just that: it was outrageous and perhaps a lost cause

from the start. But then, if we only do what we're sure will succeed, we condemn ourselves to very boring lives; and worse than that, if we only fight the
battles we're sure we'll win, we generally find ourselves standing on the same
conservatively safe side as the oppressor.

So it was that I stepped into the breach of the Isle of Eigg Trust and became
a founding trustee. Amusingly, I did so thinking about the karma yoga of the
Bhagavad Gita – the Indian philosophy of doing work independently of the
anticipated outcome. As Kipling surmised, triumph and disaster are but two
impostors. By letting go of control and neither craving the 'good' nor running
demented from the 'bad' that comes our way, 'karma' loses its grip and, just
maybe, serendipity is set free. The possibility of providence is permitted, for
that's all we're left with to fall back on. And maybe that's enough for miracles
to happen.

Some island it was, 3 miles long by 2 miles wide, this 7500-acre 'jewel in
the heart of the Hebrides'. Runciman's 1966 sales brochure had lovingly
called it 'a perfectly secluded island of the Old World, the very beautiful island
of Eigg'. Famous visitors included the violinist Yehudi Menuhin, who eulo-
gised Scotland's traditional musicians (of which Eigg had more than its share)
as 'those who will give our civilisation voice, spirit and shape'.[19]

It is in this living crucible, on the south coast, at the ruined village of
Grulin, that Tom Forsyth commences work with his *amncara*, or soul-friend,
Djini. All around is high bracken – the sure sign of neglected pasture.
Standing just above are the geometric stone walls of the derelict homes of
those who once lived in this most beautiful of places.

In the middle of the village is a dank muddy hollow, a place where cattle
drink and churn the soil and feed on watercress. To any casual passer-by it
would look like a marshy trickle. Not so to Tom and Djini. They know this
to be where waters resurge, waters that have percolated down through the
organ-pipe flumes of the Sgurr's basaltic columns. This, indeed, is the ancient
and venerable Well of the Holy Women. To clean it out, to rebuild its stone
walls, to let it run clear – this is a labour of reverence.

The high Sgurr rises up immediately behind to the north. Eagles sortie,
undaunted as the couple work, in and out of their eyrie. Beyond the Sgurr lies
the Loch of the Big Women, and further on yet there are stunning views of the
jagged Cuillins on Skye. Eastwards, over snow-tipped waves, is Ben Nevis,
Scotland's highest mountain. To the west, far beyond Rum and Canna, lie the
Outer Hebridean liturgy of Mingulay, Vatersay, Barra, Eriskay, South Uist,
North Uist, Berneray, Pabbay, Killegray, Ensay, Taransay, Scalpay, Scarp,
Bernera, Harris and, of course, Lewis. To the south is the massive volcanic landmass of Mull; the dark island largely empty since the Duke of Argyll did his
worst, but beaming off its westernmost point is the spiritual lighthouse of Iona.

All these islands and all these lives. So many stories to be told and to be heard. Such presence and presences.

In 1874 one of the most powerful bardic works of the Clearances was written by Iain Mac a' Ghobhainn, John Smith, of Earshader on the Isle of Lewis. Called *Spiorad a' Charthannais* (The Spirit of Kindliness), it directly addresses the Holy Spirit – the Holy Ghost, as a more antiquated language would call it. Smith puts the troubles of the world down to a simple but profound cause: the departure of 'kindliness'. That is what lets the Domination System loose. That is why joy has withered from the faces of the people. Translated from the Gaelic, he writes:

> O gentle Spirit of graciousness!
> If you lived in our midst,
> you would give healing and release
> to people withering with wounds;
> you would inspire the hearts of widows
> to sing with joyful strain,
> and you would not leave them heartlessly
> in the dark prison of their pain . . .
> But I fear that you have left us
> and fled to heaven above;
> our people have grown in wickedness
> without the presence of your love.[20]

Smith goes on to abominate how spiritual teachings have been twisted to serve vainglorious ends, especially by the churches. He lampoons the 'preachy sermoniser'

> who shouts aloud with strength –
> that we are cursed if we heed not
> his creed – the one that's best . . .
> That surly, gloomy Christian
> who meditates with zeal,
> who assumes a holy countenance
> like a prophet in a trance,
> who makes a terrible slaughter
> of all horror in his breast . . .
> Christianity has become
> like the monster of many heads . . .

He recounts the Clearances in their full biblical-epic proportions: the emigrant ships, the mountain 'bens' and valley glens emptied to make way first for

sheep and then for deer. He tells, too, of young men drafted to fight at
Waterloo: 'Their sons were on the battlefield/to save a heartless land'. Back
home their homes were being burned like coal, their old folks turned out. 'As
Britain was rejoicing,' he writes, her ruling class

> . . . reckoned as but brittle threads
> the tight and loving cords
> that bound these freemen's noble hearts
> to the high land of the hills.
> The grief they suffered brought them death
> although they suffered long,
> tormented by the cold world
> which had no warmth for them.

Finally, he rounds on the men of property, his bardic declamation fully
unsheathed – the Jeremiad of God flashing:

> O tremble midst your pleasures,
> you oppressor, hard and strong!
> What pain or death can justly be
> your reward for people's wrongs?
> The sorrowful sights of widows
> are what inflates your wealth;
> every cup of wine you drink
> is filled with tears of dearth.

The lords of the land, the princes of the church and the mongers of war will
all be levelled in due course. In the grave, Smith tells the laird grown fat on
oppression, 'the crawling worm will praise you, for the tastiness of your
flesh'.

The Spirit of Kindliness, *Spiorad a' Charthannais*, was forced out of the
world, he says, by 'the skin of surly selfishness': '*Nothing I know can pierce it
but the arrow of the Lord.*'

People had evidently lived here at Grulin since prehistoric times. Fragments
of flint are present in the clay that Tom and Djini scoop out from the
hollow. All day long they labour, then evening comes and clear water runs.

Cattle had long since knocked in the original stone surroundings. Nobody
had fixed them. By the next day, a new foundation is laid, deep in the
ground.

On the third day everything is restored. Tom and Djini cup their hands and
drink. Honoured again is the Well of the Holy Women. Gratitude flows.

In due course a holy woman will come from Ireland, the spirit of Tara, the green Goddess, compassion incarnate.[21] She will baptise Tom and Djini's lovechild, Ise Maeve. Ise is a Scots Gaelic word that means 'herself', and Maeve, or Mebd, was the legendary Irish queen of Connacht.

The well is now a deep, resurging, limpid pool. At this place you can lie among wild flowers and gaze on to shimmering pebbles below. Blue and white dapples down from above, and when you look into that pool, you see yourself.

'When you look into that pool you see your Self,' Tom says, adding that it would be 'quaint' to find another face reflected – a *tabhaisg* – looking in over your shoulder; the face of one of the old folks who were here before.

And I'm intrigued. Who were the 'Holy Women' and the men that are said once to have embraced contemplative lives here at Grulin in humble stone cells? And who were the 'Big Woman', both in the name of the loch and in the island's ancient Gaelic name, *Eilean nan Ban Mhor* – the Island of the Big Women?[22]

There's a cave down at the shore. It faces south, towards Iona, towards Ireland. Tom found it one day after scrambling under a steep cliff. Old Angus MacKinnon is not aware of it having any name. It lies more or less beneath the Well of the Holy Women; beneath the village. It sets me thinking about Suibhne, or Sweeney, the seventh-century Irish shamanic prince. Remember him? The one who became a bird, fell in love with nature, ate only watercress, and roosted for six weeks in a cave belonging to St Donan on Eigg.[23] Nobody on Eigg today has ever heard of a St Donan's Cave. But I like to weave together, in the mantle-fabric of my mind, ancient associations between the big women and the holy women, and between two men: Donan, who found God in the community that is his church; and Sweeney, who found God in the community that is nature.

Is this not a bit pagan, I hear my more conservative friends from back home asking. Well, let's think about what that might mean. The word 'pagan' originally meant 'country dweller'. The pagan religions were often just the folk faiths, the nature religions of the countryside. They were not necessarily idolatrous, like, say, the emperor worship of Rome. Even St Paul understood that! In Acts 17 he co-opts the 'unknown god' of the Athenians as a teaching aid for Christ, as well as appealing to the spiritual authority of two 'pagan' poets – Epimenedes the Cretan and Aratus the Cilician.[24] But the Roman church that developed after Emperor Constantine's conversion was not very rural or sympathetic to indigenous mores in its urbane 'city of God' vision of a 'Holy Roman Empire'. At the Synod of Whitby in 664, Rome declared the Celtic Church of Columba and Donan to be heretical. A monopolistic institutional dogma then set about trying to colonise the soul of all God's people, and, as the Inquisition would show, there would be times when it would tolerate few communities of contesting discourse. There are scholars today who play down the Synod of Whitby – it was, as my Papua New Guinean friends would so delightfully say, 'something nothing'. Just a storm in a teacup over the correct date for Easter and the right shape for a tonsure (a monk's haircut). Well, set that in the context of Milgram's work on authority, and the way that authority has its markers or shibboleths, and what seem like trivial points of principle often emerge as significant codifications of power.

In the sixth century St Donan had reputedly brought Christianity to Eigg and made it the hub of his missionary work in the Highlands and Islands. By the seventh century, Eigg had a population of 150 – almost three times what it was under Schellenberg. The place was a hive of spiritual activity with Donan, so it is said, in competition for soul-saving territory with Columba of Iona. Maybe it's unseemly for holy men to be in rivalry, but if you look into virtually any spiritual community, you'll see that nobody fights like saints. This is the difficult bit of making community: it means allowing natural human conflict to surface, revealing it, addressing it – continuously naming, unmasking, engaging.

Whereas Columba died the death of a white martyr, collapsing 'weary with age' before the altar of his church on Iona, Donan and his community died as red martyrs, supposedly after celebrating mass in the year 617. One legend has it that a mainland-based Pictish queen had taken offence at something Donan did and sent over her Amazonian warriors, perhaps 'Big Women' of the Scáthach tendency, to sort him out. Or maybe, as other sources suggest, invading Vikings perpetrated the massacre. The Norse to whom they were related, after all, so intermingled in this area that for a time they were the controlling power. Or maybe patriarchal clerics had a vested interest in fingering a local matriarchy for feminist crimes against the church. Who knows. Whatever happened, the Norse settled in Lewis and Harris in such large numbers that those islands became known (and remain known in the Gaelic-speaking world to this day) as *Innse Gall* – the 'land of the stranger', *gall* meaning 'strangers' or 'incomers'. Such was the scale of the infusion that by the ninth century, the people of the Outer Hebrides became known as the Gall-Gael – the 'strange' or 'foreign' Gaels, the Gaels being the original heartland people. It is by one of those ironies of history that, today, *Innse Gall* with its population of 22,000 comprises the highest density of native Gaelic speakers in the world. The stranger, it seems, became fully fostered into the heartland; place has assimilated its people. As a disgruntled Edmund Spenser wrote, around 1589, about the English difficulty in planting Ireland with their own colonists: 'I heard, that any English there should bee worse then the Irish: Lord, how quickely doth that countrey alter mens natures!'[25] And perhaps in the Gall-Gael we have a metaphor that can help to reconcile ethnic conflict between in-groups and out-groups in modern times. Perhaps place itself can be a defining and uniting principle.[26]

It seemed to me, as it seemed to Tom, and to Djini, that when you unblock a well you symbolically unblock ancient sources that come from very deep down. As Tom said, 'When you look into that pool, you see your Self.' And gazing into the Well of the Holy Women, as I subsequently did, I thought about Donan and Suibhne, the big and the holy women, the incomer and the outgoer, the Christian and the pagan. I thought of how, towards the end of his life, Sweeney, the deep ecologist, unites pre- and post-Christian traditions like a mantle of two fabrics scintillating on both sides. And I asked myself: do we have to accept the forcing-apart of the in-group and the out-group, the Christian and the non-Christian, the human world and wild nature? Is not ultimate reality neither Yin nor Yang, but Tao? And is that not what Celtic spirituality codifies, if not at all times in its varied history, then certainly in the direction that its inner fire has moved it towards among diverse peoples today? Such is the direction of a world re-enchanted; of soil and soul venerated together as the building blocks of society in constant renewal; the higher unity of nature, God and community.

14. The Mountain Behind the Mountain

Around the same time as the Eigg campaign was taking off, I happened to catch a television news story about plans to construct a 'superquarry' on Mount Roineabhal on the Isle of Harris. Ian Wilson, a Scottish businessman, had procured the mineral rights at some half-dozen key deep-water locations where ocean meets mountain. These were either in designated National Scenic Areas like south Harris, or other Scottish locations recognised as being of outstanding natural beauty.

In June 1991 Wilson came to see me and the other staff at the Centre for Human Ecology. It was natural that Wilson would value the support of an environmental think-tank such as the CHE. The quarry, he told us, would represent 'sustainable development'. It could be sustained for hundreds of years by gradually working its way back through the mountains of south Harris. Thirty-six tons of powerful explosive each week would slowly reduce the place to rubble. That would be acceptable because Harris was so rocky that 'it already looks like a moonscape'. The aggregate – stone chips – would be exported by ship to south-east England, continental Europe and perhaps as far away as America. When the quarry reached full production, 10 or even 20 million tons of stone would be extracted each year. This would serve needs such as road-building and the erection of coastal defences if predictions that the sea level would rise due to global warming proved correct.

A conventional large quarry in Britain extracts about 200,000 tons of stone a year.[1] What Mr Wilson was proposing was, therefore, some fifty times bigger than anything within the current experience of most British people; it was many hundreds of times bigger than the scale of what constitutes a quarry in the experience of most natives of Harris. The hole left behind, he said, would possibly be the largest in the world. As he described it, albeit with a degree of enthusiastic hyperbole, it would have affected an area of some 3 square miles. And yes, he said in reply to my disarmingly innocent question, it could be used for dumping waste into afterwards – but that was certainly not in the initial planning application and it would be imprudent to raise any such possibility at such an early stage.

The idea was that the mountain would be gouged out from immediately below its 1500-foot (500-metre) summit down to far below sea level. A natural rock wall would be left in place to hold back the water during the quarry's working life. At the end of sixty years this would then be blasted and flooded by way of environmental restoration. A new sea loch would thereby be created – a 'man-made marina for passing yachts' (provided, of course, that they had 300-foot anchor ropes with which to reach the bottom!). Tourists would come to view such a feat of technology; they would make up for the ones who might otherwise have come to walk the hills. Mountaineers could practise on the artificial crags rising to six times the height of the White Cliffs of Dover. Rare plants might take root there, birds would find even more nesting ledges than previously on such a rocky island, and crofters would turn the surrounding land green with trees grown on once-barren soil that had been 'remineralised'.

'Remineralised?' I asked.

'Yes: by getting rid of the dust from the quarry by mixing it together with silt from the River Elbe in Germany.' For if Wilson's vision was not stifled by people of small mind, part of the package that would make all this into cost-effective 'sustainable development' was that aggregate-carrying ships would be backloaded with sludge dredged from Europe's navigation channels. This would turn the existing Harris 'moonscape' into a beautiful man-made garden. Also, 'satellite quarries' would enable the cost-effective shipping-out of other mineral deposits in the Hebrides, thereby enhancing the economics. All in all, a 'crofting enterprise zone' buzzing with quarry-stimulated business would provide a reforested, revitalised, prosperous and sustainable future.

Wilson's scheme was in many ways impressive. After all, we in the CHE had been talking a lot about the need for industry and environmental agencies to put their heads together. We were anxious to explore the middle ground between the business-as-usual approach to industry and the 'ecofreak' view that all industry should be stopped and humankind revert to low-population hunter-gatherer tribal societies. It seemed to us that as we all used corporate products, we all had a duty to help corporations to behave responsibly.

'Given that we have to have quarries, is this not the way to go?' Wilson quite reasonably asked. But one of our number was not impressed. Alesia Maltz was then dean of the College of the Atlantic in Maine in the United States. She specialised in the human ecology of tiny communities affected by massive developments. Here she was on an academic visit, and by pure chance, I'd asked if she wanted to sit in on our meeting. She was a gentle, incisively insightful woman, potentially with much to teach us all. But Wilson hardly looked at her. All the eye contact was between the men. Evidently, a mere female professor hardly figured in the pecking order of a boys' power game.

That was useful, as it left Alesia free to read the body language. The more Wilson's vision unfolded, the more he relaxed, but something in me simultaneously tightened. I realised that I had to write down his key remarks. It might be important, later, to have an accurate summary. As I started scribbling, Alesia observed unease in this man, who, it later turned out, had left behind him a career path paved with the rubble of collapsed quarrying companies.[2] With a stroke of brilliance, she too picked up her pen and scribbled. Later we bent ourselves double laughing at this. 'I saw him looking at you, so I too started taking notes,' she told me. 'I figured that if we both did it, he'd just think, "They're academics; that's what academics do all the time."'

I had only just met Alesia that week. She was a colleague of a friend of the CHE's director, Ulrich Loening, and Ulrich duly offered her desk space. Ul had a gift for galvanising serendipity. He was a kindly and deeply inspirational man who'd often set up arrangements that caused major muddles for his colleagues to sort out. But sometimes – indeed, often – a sort of magic emerged. It was part of Ul's genius and what made the CHE such an exciting but totally unpredictable place. When Alesia walked in the door asking for the renowned Dr Loening, little did I suspect how closely we were destined to work together over the next few years.

'The silt from the Elbe,' I said to Wilson. 'If it's that good, why do the Germans not want to spread it on their own land?'

'Ah, well, it's a little bit . . . polluted,' he admitted. 'Nothing much – some oil and traces of heavy metals perhaps. But nothing to worry about. Nothing that would make it unsuitable for growing trees on Harris.'[3]

He went on to describe how, a number of years ago, he had gone to landowners and leased, in his own name, the mineral rights on all the best sites where mountains met deep water. 'Each of them now is a potential oil well,' he told us. 'I only need one of them to get approval and it will see me and my children all right for the rest of our days.'

Later, it emerged in the press that this 'father of the superquarry concept' had himself written a government report aimed at generating a favourable policy environment.[4] He warned in another report: 'Large forecasted future demand creates *environmental shock* . . . . The UK government [should therefore] press for coastal superquarry development to encourage exports and keep the UK self-sufficient in aggregates.'[5] In other words, the concept was to export the 'shock' from where affluent consumers live to the wild places that Wilson himself controlled. You make the unpalatable consequences of consumerism an 'externality' to the consumer's cost–benefit calculations, then what the eye doesn't see the heart won't grieve. In so doing, you overlook the fact that most of the proposed new sites are in designated areas of outstanding natural beauty. You overlook the fact that Britain's one existing superquarry at Glensanda has never operated much beyond half-capacity, and so the drive for more quarries is actually about corporate competition rather than real national need. You overlook the fact that if further capacity were really needed, there'd be plenty of space alongside Glensanda in what is now an already despoiled mountain range. And you overlook options like recycling old road stone instead of dumping it into landfill sites, producing building materials that are made to last rather than having inbuilt obsolescence, and developing a public transport policy that puts brakes on the road-building necessary to sustain the 'great car economy'.

The question that Wilson's scheme posed, then, was about much more than a hole in the ground. It was about the deadlock between an industrial society that makes things over and over again, and a natural world that was only made once. Indeed, it was a question about development and, specifically, the distinction between sustained development and sustainable development.

The point is that 'development' is a word that commercial interests have made virtually synonymous with sustained economic growth. It is one of those words that we need to reclaim, and we can do so by referring back to the etymology. This derives from *de* (to undo), and the Old French *voloper* – to envelop, as in our word 'envelope'. To *develop* is therefore to unfold, unroll or unfurl. The biological application, as in 'foetal development', embodies correct usage: the foetus develops in right relationship with its environment of the womb and the wider world in which the parents move. We can see, therefore, that *too little* development implies stunted growth – a condition of the poor; development in the *wrong place* means deformity – inequitable wealth distribution; and development *without limits* is a cancer that extracts life and brings death to the rest of the body – the planet. Properly used, then, the word 'development' means what one dictionary defines as 'a gradual unfolding; a fuller working out of the details of anything; growth from within'. Real community development – integral human development – should therefore be about enabling a community to become more fully itself. And that's the trouble with having a grand scheme imposed from the outside: it tends to permanently disrupt the very fabric of a place. As such, it ain't true development.

Listening to the silver-tongued Wilson, however, it was not immediately easy to judge whether his proposals were visionary, or just the green-wash coating of a cancerous mindset. He certainly had polished plausibility and a definite charm. In such situations, when you're trying to assess how genuine a person is, it often helps to treat the occasion like a job interview. Look to the past track record of achievement rather than the promises. My touchstone, then, was to ask myself what Wilson had ever done for the environment. How had he previously helped struggling communities?

'And the shipping side of all this?' I enquired, thinking of the closer-to-home jobs he might bring to Hebridean sailors. 'You obviously have past experience with the coastal bulk-cargo industry?'

'Oh, yes,' he acknowledged. 'First-hand, though you have to accept that more and more of that trade these days is going to foreign crews under flags of convenience. That's just the way it is now. But you know, I actually pioneered the shipping-in of coal from abroad. It was during the 1980s when the coalminers were holding Thatcher to ransom.'

'Ah ha . . . so you were behind the apartheid coal from South Africa! And the Columbian child-labour supplies!' I quipped, with a disarming laugh as if in jest.

'Well, I wouldn't say there was any child labour involved,' the would-be magnanimous quarry master replied. 'But they were certainly hairy times, those days. There was even one occasion when I got chased from a depot by flying pickets. No – I wasn't very popular with the miners!'

There were, indeed, many attractive features to Ian Wilson's vision. It would bring jobs and money to Harris. It would reduce pressure to create new quarries elsewhere or to extend existing ones in fragile areas. But it did not address the cultural impact of turning Harris into a company town. Or the environmental damage of making Harris into what one local crofter and lobster fisher, Norman MacLeod, dubbed 'the gravel-pit of Europe'. The scheme was based on the assumption that a car-based economy would keep booming and that more and more motorways were therefore needed. That was the most galling part. This was not about destroying a mountain in order to meet the basic needs of the poor for, say, decently built houses. It was not about a national economy of simple, dignified sufficiency. It was, rather, a symptom of our profligacy with nature's non-renewable resources. The Conservative British government at that time had neither an environmentally minded transport policy nor an energy policy worthy of the name. True, at one level it was busy talking the language of 'sustainable development' in the run-up to the Rio Earth Summit; but in other ways it had completely failed to take on board the implications of its international commitments to environmental protection.

That summer, I went up to Lewis and Harris to take soundings. I wanted to walk the mountain and talk with people to find out how they felt about it. Some sort of a lull before the storm was building up in my mind. It reminded me of the chemistry set I had when I was a boy. In it were white crystals of a compound called sodium thiosulphate. You had to melt them down in a test tube, then allow the clear liquid gently to cool. Strangely, it would remain liquid instead of solidifying. According to the instruction book, this was because the chemical 'wanted' to return to crystal form, but the molecules 'didn't know how'. In order to recrystallise, they needed a pattern from which to 'get the right idea'. So what you had to do was to take one tiny crystal of sodium thiosulphate and drop it in. This provided the necessary template. Instantly, the whole tubeful would set as a solid crystalline mass.

That was how the quarry and our relationship to the land seemed to me. It was like new environmental ways of seeing and being were out there, just waiting to crystallise into a meaningful pattern. Pulling them together needed more than just rational analysis. Academic insight alone was not up to the job. There also had to be magic: a constellating force that provided vision. Such higher vision had to be born of passion, of life, and so, in essence, it comprised *poesis* – the making and fresh upwelling of reality. It had to come out of the primal creativity, to partake of what I came to call 'poetic constellation'. Sociologists have used the word *autopoesis* similarly to describe an ordering of social reality that arises out of itself.[6] If we understand this as coming from the deepest grounding of reality, then maybe we can glimpse common ground with what John Smith eulogised as 'the arrow of the Lord'. The seeds of divine fire, the bardic *siolta teine*, are the spiritual equivalent of that sodium thiosulphate. *Poesis* is the crystallisation.

To me, then, being pierced by this arrow meant opening up neglected areas of spirituality – discovering what Fr Dara Molloy, a friend who is a radical Irish Gaelic-speaking priest, calls 'our Celtic Old Testament'. It would mean honouring God's presence in nature; mending our schism with the rest of Creation. It would mean recovering the feminine face of a gender-fragmented God and so mending a schism in the human heart. But actually doing this would require the naming, unmasking and engaging of some very considerable Powers. And being increasingly busy with the Eigg campaign, I did not welcome the idea of another cause célèbre on Harris. Also, the MSc degree in human ecology was taking off nicely, and I had been made responsible by the Faculty of Science and Engineering for developing and directing it. The feedback from students and examiners was good. If I sat pretty at Edinburgh University, and if I kept publishing several papers a year as I was doing, then I could be in line for a personal chair in human ecology within the next ten years. There was much to play for – and much to play safe for.

But then another of Ulrich's connections turned up. And thus I came to share my office with Orin Gelderloos, professor of biology and environmental studies at the University of Michigan-Dearborn in the United States. He had come to the CHE to write a book, *Eco-Theology: The Judeo-Christian Tradition and the Politics of Ecological Decision Making*.[7]

Orin and I chatted a lot. It had never much occurred to me before that Judaeo-Christian theology could be both so ecological and so political at the same time. I found myself reflecting, increasingly, on Celtic-cum-Franciscan insights about the unity of social and ecological justice. I found my appreciation of mystery deepening, and this included many different and even apparently contradictory church and non-church positions. As the mystics say of contradiction: 'The opposite of one great truth is another great truth.' In short, the mountain was starting to grow. It was becoming something more than just stone and heather, yet no more than what these things really mean. How can I explain that? Well, consider this passage by the Irish writer Fr Noel Dermot O'Donoghue, who is reflecting on Kathleen Raine's expression 'the mountain behind the mountain':

> The mountain behind or within the mountain is not the perfect or ideal mountain in some Platonic sense. Neither is it the mythical Mount of Parnassus on which the Muses dwell. Nor yet is it the Holy Mountain in which God reveals himself in theophany [a manifestation of God to people] or transfiguration [elevation to a spiritual state]. Each of these mountains belongs to its own mindset, its own world of imagination. The mountain of that kind of Celtic tradition to which Kathleen Raine belongs, and which nurtured the people from which I came, is neither an ideal nor a mythical mountain, nor is it exactly a holy or sacred mountain made sacred by theophany or transfiguration. No, it is a very ordinary, very physical, very material mountain, a place of sheep and kine [cattle], of peat, and of streams that one might fish in or bathe in on a summer's day. It is an elemental mountain, of earth and air and water and fire, of sun and moon and wind and rain. What makes it special for me and for the people from which I come is that it is a place of Presence and a place of presences. Only those who can perceive this in its ordinariness can encounter the mountain behind the mountain.[8]

And so I made further visits to Harris, and the more I walked Mount Roineabhal and spent time with the people living around it, the more the 'Presence and the presences' came alive. As near-forgotten fragments of history were fished from long-overgrown pools of local knowledge and told to me, I was starting to see what lay behind the mountain.

The most striking thing that I learned was that in pre-Reformation times, Mount Roineabhal had been in the parish of Kilbride – *Cill Bhrighde* – the church of St Bride. This had stretched from Harris right down to the southern Hebridean isles. The foundations of what is probably the old church dedicated to Bhrighde can still be seen in the village of Scarista, running under the walls of the present-day Church of Scotland building. Alongside is an ancient graveyard. Here, Jim Crawford, a local archaeologist, tells me he has found foliated grave slabs, one of which is from the medieval Iona school of carving.

It is fascinating how such simple facts dropped into a saturated solution of experience invite poetic ways of seeing. Stretching out from Scarista Bay on the west coast of Harris, a sandy and seaweedy bottom gives the Atlantic an unusually soft emerald quality. Moving further out still, a white maelstrom can be seen undulating beneath the waves at low tide. It surges like a great hand beckoning. This is *Bogha na Cille* – the Rock of the Church. A local tradition bearer told me that because the church was originally dedicated to Bhrighde, it remains her rock. And so I allow her name to resonate through my mind like a mantra – *Breeeee-jah*. It reminds me of *Jah*, the Rastafarian word for God. 'I feel strongly about the rock's presence,' said my informant, an island man of the most impeccable Presbyterian credentials. 'It is out of sight but still there, always reminding you of Bhrighde, the lady.'

St Bride, Bhrighde, Brigh, Brig, Bridey, Brigid or Bridgit – there are many variations of this Celticised and then Christianised name of the mother Goddess; she who possibly gave her name to the rivers Brigit, Braint and Brent in Ireland, Wales and England respectively, as well as to the Hebrides. According to folklore, each spring she would roll out the great green mantle that had kept her warm through winter and lay it over the Earth. Grasses would grow and the white cow, sacred to Bhrighde's name (and possibly linked to the Hindu tradition), would become rich with milk. So too would nursing mothers. The hibernating bear would awaken from her lair – this harks back to ancient times when bears last roamed the land. The serpent would emerge from her hole in the ground, her old skin shed – a symbol of rebirth. And the world would be filled with flowers.[9]

According to the Scottish tradition, Bhrighde grew up on Iona. One day the 'Evil One' espied her playing among the rocks down by the shore. But the oystercatcher saw him coming, and the bird concealed the little girl with seaweed. In those days all his feathers were black, but now he has a white cross on his back that is visible when his wings are spread. St Michael put it there in gratitude. And to this day, the oystercatcher roams the shore of places like Scarista. He calls the name of his beloved saint, reminding all with ears to hear that he is her servant, her ghillie. '*Ghille-ghille-ghille-ghille-Breeeee-jah*,' he plaintively cries, as if summoning her return from oceans crystal-green. '*Ghille-ghille-ghille-ghille-Breeeee-jah*.'[10]

What is a mountain actually for? That is the real question. Is the value of Roineabhal just a few pounds per ton for road stone? Is Eigg, as Keith Schellenberg once suggested to me, just 'a collector's item'? Or do these things have an intrinsic value? A value that perhaps testifies, ultimately, to the glory of God?

Just a few miles from Scarista, right at the foot of Roineabhal's southern slope, is St Clement's Church, a miniature Iona Abbey. Each time I was in the vicinity I'd be drawn to the belltower of this exquisite little sixteenth-century building. Halfway up the first flight of stairs a huge rock protrudes through the wall. The church sits on a sharp slope and this is actually bedrock protruding from the hill outside. Some believe it was once a pagan site – a place of, let's say with a little poetic licence, Celtic Old Testament veneration.

Often I'd go and sit there with my spine resting against this stone. If nobody was around, I'd pick up my penny whistle and play. Once a bus party arrived, and I was so carried away that I didn't notice until they were well on their way up the stairs. Embarrassed, I just carried on playing, as if in a trance, which I kind of was, pretending not to notice them. But then some of the tourists started throwing down coins. 'No, no!' I exclaimed, stopping in mid-flow and feeling even more embarrassed. 'I'm not busking!'

'Ever so sorry,' grinned a crimplene-clad blue-rinsed Englishwoman. 'We thought you'd been put on as part of the tour!'

Alone again – it could have been that occasion or one of several others – and I breathe into this most primitive of instruments. Music echoes hauntingly around the silent tower. Tunes not written by anybody arise, and I listen as they flow. 'The songs of the fiddle are on every tide, mixing peoples and cultures,' wrote Donnie Campbell of Eigg in one of his poems.[11] And I know that, buried in vaults under this church, are the MacCrimmons, hereditary pipers to the clan chiefs, 'a family which for sheer genius is quite unequalled in any branch of music'.[12] Their music is said to have come straight from faerie – from the hollow hill on which the first of the MacCrimmons had slept. He had answered wisely when a faerie woman asked him, 'Which wouldst thou prefer, skill without success or success without skill?' And in my imagination it feels like the spirit of the MacCrimmon is present with me here. It's as if I'm being taught the music of Avalon, *Tir nan Og*, the Celtic otherworld.

'This is to fortify and give comfort,' a voice says in my mind's ear. 'It's easy to make the music. Just watch nature and play what you see and hear. Play the waterfall, play the birdsong, play the beat of the butterfly's wings. That's the only score you need. That's faerie. That's the very creativity of God. Holy, Holy, Holy. *Breeeee-jah . . . Breeeee-jah . . . Breeeee-jah.*'

> . . . and this girl said
> the girl with love in her eyes
> 'You will accept it'
> and I said
> 'I will accept what?'
> and she said again in the same calm voice
> 'You will accept it
> accept the flood
> accept the calmness
> accept the otherworld people
> and accept human beings'[13]

And I maybe wander off down to the sea. Sometimes I have with me a drum. I made it myself and painted it rainbow colours in refusal to accept greyness after the Gulf War. And I sit, gazing out on some rocky kneecap over surf, mindful now of eagles on the mountains above; minded now by eagles soaring in my soul.

There's nothing but the pebble beach and surging Atlantic between here and those other native peoples in North America. And a rainbow medicine drum beats in four-four time. Is that my rhythm? Or do I hear it on the wind?

I listen deeper, westwards, and detect with inner ear the salutation gravely chanted. The wind is loud. The surf heaves and sighs. I trust that I am unheard by human ears and so join in with the sound of ancestors piped by MacCrimmon from up beneath that whelming tide.

'There's nothing strange about this,' I reassure myself. 'Nothing strange, if seen from within the Tradition.' Alexander Carmichael would have been familiar with the phenomenon. 'I have known,' he wrote,

> men and women of eighty, ninety, and a hundred years of age continue the practice of their lives in going from one to two miles to the seashore to join their voices with the voicing of the waves and their praises with the praises of the ceaseless sea . . . intoned in low tremulous unmeasured cadences like the moving and moaning, the soughing and the sighing, of the ever-murmuring sea on their own wild shores.[14]

Old Murdo MacLennan, he would have understood this too, I'm sure. And I feel myself reaching for connection with the forebears, with the cultural soul, with a legitimacy that explains what could only otherwise be madness. Aye, that is the question in this kind of activism, this kind of transgression. Do you allow yourself to be pushed, by inner forces, beyond the bounds of normal behaviour and experience? Do you enter that territory where, as Ben Okri puts it, 'All true artists suspect that if the world really knew what they were doing they would be punished'?[15] Or do you squash those promptings? Do you remain safe, but arguably among the dead – like those entombed residents of Gray's elegiac country churchyard, whose 'sober wishes never learn'd to stray . . . far from the madding crowd's ignoble strife'. And why? Because 'Along the cool sequester'd vale of life/They kept the noiseless tenor of their way'?[16] So do you play safe and be like them – perhaps like Job: simultaneously 'blameless and upright' and yet with 'no end to [his] iniquities'?[17] Or do you, as Tom Forsyth often advised me, 'go out on a limb . . . that's where the blossom grows'? And what makes for the blossom anyway? How can we be sure of it when we see it? How do we judge our effectiveness, especially when we're being audacious, following inspirational leadings into unknown territory like hyperlinks clicked in the unconscious psyche? Is there not a danger that we end up like the idiotic dog in a storm: the dog that has just lifted his leg against a mighty tree when it is struck by lightning. He hears the trunk crack, watches the tree crash down, and says, as the trickling pool of piddle is thrown up into spray by the wind: 'My goodness! Look what I just did!'

Aye, Murdo: you were a free spirit who understood these tensions. The story was told in your obituary of how you were asked by the Free Church to introduce English-language worship at Dunrobin. It was to serve the work-force, brought in from afar to build the wretched Duke of Sutherland's equally wretched castle. The old elders walked out of the church in protest. Maybe they were forgetting how the Syrophoenician woman had challenged Jesus when he initially denied her daughter healing on the grounds of where she came from. Maybe it was like that. But when the elders heard the beauty of the singing that came from inside, they, perhaps like Jesus recognising the faith of the distraught mother, filed back in, one by one.[18] Aye, Murdo: you knew the power of poetics. Thou of blessed memory, of whom it was written:

> The burst of swelling melody which arose was magnificent and overwhelming. His voice extended everywhere without any apparent effort. All heard, and all seemed to be fully qualified to join. Join they did, and as one wave after another of fast harmonious sound rolled upon the ears of those who listened ... the effect was such as music had never produced upon them before, so touching, so sweet, so passing sweet. Friends from the South who had not before heard the old church tunes with their beautiful and prolonged variations, looked at each other for an instant, as if to say that now, for the first time, they were listening to the sound of praise as it ought always to be heard. Their looks were those of surprise – soon changed to looks expressive of the deepest emotion. Tears filled many eyes. Not a few, unable or unwilling to resist the tumult of their feelings, bent their heads forward over the book-boards and wept, some audibly.[19]

I think that Murdo would have seen God's mountain behind that of the quarrymasters. And I think Alexander Carmichael would have seen that the arguments of economists, ecologists and sociologists alone had little hope of saving this mountain; and little hope of recovering land for the people. But poetics might. The bardic tradition just might. As Angus MacKinnon of Eigg said, 'Music and song, laddie, you must have that in you, or the island will lose its soul'.[20] Aye, the late and loved Angus, who once sat with me by the tea-room, staring at the ground, and telling me that God is in the little flowers.

Gazing out to sea from the south wall of St Clement's tower is a Sheila-na-gig, usually an early Celtic feature, a carved 'goddess' or 'saint' figure. She holds her back, as if protectively, to the mountain. The doors of her *eros* are fully open. Her arms cradle what looks like a baby seal. In Ireland, Bhrighde was said once to have been concealed from danger by being wrapped in seal-skin. I know of no such legend in the Hebrides, but my mind plays poetry with the image anyway. It pleases me to think that a Sheila-na-gig was also found in Kildonan churchyard on Eigg, and that a third is built into the wall of the old nunnery on Iona.

They say that the hills of the Hebrides were made by giant women long ago who fell asleep and turned to stone. Beautiful Roineabhal! All along the bays of east Harris you can see her long hair swept back at the summit. A two-billion-year-old youthful face gazes heavenwards. Breasts, belly, long legs, even two kneecaps, before feet softly touch the ocean where otters play by Lingerabay.

And now I remember the three-sided black crystal that I found here so many years before. It must have been lost or given away, enduring now only as a fragment of memory. But once I held it in my hand, even as Cabbie and I failed to see the eagles. And the crystal filled me with delight. Then it was just a stone. Now, it has grown, this seed-crystal of vision: this triquetra of maiden, mother, crone; life, death, rebirth; St Patrick, St Columba and Bhrighde, who I love.

Ian Wilson's intended means of delivering his conception was to team up with one of Britain's biggest multinational construction companies, Redland Aggregates plc. Their value on the stock exchange was some £4500 million – $7 billion.

Wilson believed that he could keep Redland under control. He would personally take care of ensuring that the planners put proper checks and balances in place. However, in the local press, I was starting to express alarm. Perhaps to appease this, Wilson duly turned up at a Centre for Human Ecology public lecture given by Alesia Maltz on 15 October 1991. When she had finished speaking, he rose from the floor and said:

> Quarries make bad neighbours . . . . The industry itself, the quarrying industry in the UK, if it could get off with raping the Highlands would do so. I mean, they are business people. But they are not going to get away with it . . .[21]

At this stage very few people seemed to be aware of the scale of what was proposed and the threat that it posed. Most of those who were starting to speak out around 1991–92 were what I'd call 'inside outsiders' to the island – incomers who had lived there for some time. Chief among these were the Johnsons, a family of meticulous researchers into environmental-planning law who had started the renowned Scarista House Hotel next door to the one-time church of Bhrighde, and the Callaghans, who had succeeded the Johnsons as proprietors there. Inside outsiders, of course, would not necessarily have to live permanently with any consequences of speaking out against something that, at that time, many people wanted to see happen. Few indigenous islanders – 'inside insiders' – spoke out in public. Norman MacLeod was a notable exception. As for me, my role was that of an 'outside insider' – that is, I had grown up and been educated in the Hebrides, but now lived away. My family had a decent track record of contribution to the place. Accordingly, I would receive a hearing that would be, at least, patient.

In so using that voice I came to rely greatly on the knowledge and insights of Ian Callaghan. He was about my own age and, by one of those spectacular ironies, had been a leading merchant banker before taking over Scarista House Hotel with his wife, Jane. One of his previous projects had been undertaking the financial engineering for the Channel Tunnel – a project that had drawn its aggregate from the superquarry at Glensanda. Ian's past business expertise had included the exploits of multinationals in Africa. He knew all about corporate sharp shooting and, furthermore, had done his university honours dissertation on wartime media manipulation.

'It's just like the American attitude in Vietnam,' he said to me one night, as we strategised over a bottle of malt whisky by the fire in the hotel library. 'The idea is that you have to have the quarry to save Harris.'

'What's that to do with Vietnam?' I asked.

'Well, you know the justification they gave,' he replied. 'They said: "We had to destroy the village in order to save it."'

Indeed, Redland's own figures showed that extracting 550 million tons of rock over the quarry's life would require 82,500 tonnes of powerful explosive.[22] A figure like this is meaningless to most people, especially when the existing level of explosive use for Lewis and Harris was less than 100 tons a year. This is where imagery helps to unmask the Powers. How could this best be illustrated? So I investigated the bombing of Hiroshima. It was equivalent to 13,000 tons of high explosive. Divide 82,500 by 13,000, and it turns out that Redland planned to drop the equivalent of six atom bombs on Roineabhal!

Obviously, Ian Wilson was not going to ignore the growing loose coalition that was starting to galvanise against his dream. But we were still a tiny minority. In 1991 perhaps 90 per cent of the people of Harris were thought to *favour* the development. Being desperately in need of jobs, some were saying things like, 'The quarry is our only salvation.' By early 1992, it looked to me as if our mini-campaign of letters in the press and speaking at public meetings might prove abortive. But suddenly, as happens so often with patience in such campaigns, the ground unexpectedly loosened. It became public knowledge that Wilson or Redland had superquarry designs on three other prospective sites: Carnish on Lewis, Kentallen near Glencoe and Durness in Sutherland. Local people in these areas contacted us for information and a furore got going. The smiling, confident Wilson suddenly showed a tetchy face. On 22 February 1992 the *Stornoway Gazette* ran as its headline 'Superquarry man hits at "scares"'. What I had written about possible waste dumping, based upon

Wilson's own remarks in the Centre for Human Ecology, was now, Wilson said, 'the worst form of scare-mongering' and 'deliberate mischief'. Our arguments, he believed, 'must be knocked on the head' so that the full benefit of Redland's potential investment could be won for Scotland.

This was interesting. Initially, the pro-quarry lobby had taken a benign 'let them have their say' approach to those of us on the other side. But now our arguments had demonstrated bite. We were succeeding in bringing on board powerful organisations like Friends of the Earth and the Government's own environment advisory agency, Scottish Natural Heritage. We were no longer a joke. Accordingly, both Wilson and one of his business associates wrote to my superiors at Edinburgh University complaining about the 'mendacious fanaticism' of 'our evangelical ecologist'.[23] The complaints bounced off. However, it did occur to me that if I had actually sighted two such letters, how many other quips had been made at dinners and cocktail parties? With the Eigg campaign also to consider, what glass doors and invisible tripwires might be going up in my way?

On 9 and 10 September 1992 Auslan Cramb, then environment correspondent to the *Scotsman*, ran a major two-part article on Mr Wilson and the quarry concept. It used dramatic graphics to show how, for instance, the depth of the hole would dwarf otherwise major landmarks like the Empire State Building and the Great Pyramid of Cheops. In an accompanying profile of Wilson, I was quoted as saying that I believed him to be 'a man with genuine vision, but one who does not always see the environmental and cultural side of what he is proposing'. Cramb himself judged Wilson more harshly: 'In conversation he is forceful, occasionally hectoring, and angry when his vision and the purity of his motives are questioned . . . . He explodes, "I have come up with the damn concept. Why should I try and justify it?"'

It was the first time that a national newspaper had exposed serious cracks in the rock face. Up until then, Wilson had promoted Scotland to potential investors as a quarry-friendly zone. The day after this exposé came out, I checked out Redland's share price on the London Stock Exchange. In one fell swoop, 8 per cent, or £160 million, had mysteriously been wiped off the market value of their shares. I do not know whether this sudden fluctuation was caused by the bad publicity, but it did stir the consideration that for some of us, what is at stake is a two-billion-year-old mountain and its human and ecological community. For others, it's millions of pounds and a project that Redland had made the flagship of its corporate strategy.

Up until this point, the Scottish Office – the British government's Scottish administration in the era before we got our own Parliament back – had staunchly resisted pressure for a public inquiry. The Western Isles Council had almost unanimously voted the proposal through the initial planning stages. But we'd now moved into a situation where phrases like 'the gravel-pit of

Europe' were starting to bite. Twice in public discussions I heard Wilson say that Ian Callaghan and I were the main 'troublemakers' in galvanising the pressure for a public inquiry. We knew that there were many others behind us, most of whom worked in less high-profile ways. But it was certainly encouraging to receive confirmation of effectiveness from the horse's mouth. It helped to mitigate our discomfort at standing up and speaking out.

By late 1992, newspaper editorials were warning that the superquarry 'could become the biggest environmental issue Scotland has faced for some time'. A breakthrough came on 10 September 1992 when the second part of the *Scotsman* exposé was accompanied by a leader headed 'Superquandary'. The goalposts of the debate had, at last, been widened from the local to the global. It said:

> In many ways the Western Isles Council is facing an impossible task in balancing environmental and cultural protection with the allure of jobs in a depressed area and the prospect of £500,000 a year in business rates. But there is a much wider debate. The lesson repeated time and again during the Earth Summit in Rio was that unplanned and uncontrolled business-as-usual policies have usually meant unsustainable development and led to the exhaustion of natural resources. Quarrying is moving to Scotland because it is finished elsewhere. So where does it end? Short-term thinking is always the enemy of the natural environment . . . . It is hard to resist the arguments which point towards a public inquiry.

And so the Secretary of State for Scotland did indeed 'call in' the planning application. The scene was set for what was to become the longest-running public inquiry in Scottish history.

15. Under Enemy Occupation

Meanwhile, what made the setting-up of the Isle of Eigg Trust so timely was that Keith Schellenberg had fallen under an order from Scotland's top judges in the Court of Session to sell up and divvy out the dosh. Or, as *Harpers & Queen* put it, 'Keith Schellenberg and his then wife Margaret bought Eigg jointly fifteen years ago. He *loved* Eigg. He nurtured it and coddled it and ran it like a private nature reserve. Though his marriage broke up, his little feudal kingdom didn't – until, that is, Margaret asked for her half back.'[1]

The Honourable Margaret de Hauteville Udny-Hamilton, now remarried and Mrs Williams, alleged that Schellenberg had mismanaged the island originally paid for with a substantial slice of her dowry. So it was that the Court of Session order tied Schellenberg's hands. 'Scotland's best-known English laird', as the media dubbed him, was now trussed up, an incapacitated Houdini unable to withdraw his precious asset from sale.

One of my old teachers from Leurbost days, John M. MacLeod of Balallan, had been actively recovering the history they had never been encouraged to teach us at school. He was now part of a committee planning to build a spectacular stone cairn to the Pairc deer raiders, to be erected, cheekily, at the start of the Eisken road.[2] This symbolism moved me and I sent John a donation. He sent a warm letter back. In the peculiar way that 'widow's mite' psychology can work – that is, a small gesture that triggers off a bigger process – it got me thinking and feeling deeper about what the raiders had done a century earlier. A passing remark in James Hunter's book jumped out. The raid, Hunter said, had been about more than just food. The perpetrators also hoped that 'the sporting value of Park forest would be so drastically reduced that its tenant would give it up, thus forcing Lady Matheson to [hand it] over to the crofters'.[3]

Hmm: market spoiling. Could the very presence of an Isle of Eigg Trust be a Sword of Damocles?

On learning of the Trust's establishment, Schellenberg said that it was all 'romantic gobbledegook and a recipe for total chaos'. He particularly attacked our suggestion that the population could be restored to something like half of pre-Clearance levels. Eigg, he said, was capable of supporting only three thousand sheep and three shepherds – and this, as one newspaper put it, from the 'exhibitionist whose ideal was to drive around the island in a vintage Rolls-Royce, the same man who boasted in an interview that under his ownership Eigg had kept its "slightly rundown . . . Hebridean feel"'.[4]

Shelter and Rural Forum described what that 'rundown feel' really felt like in a 1988 housing poverty report. Their survey showed that:

> Two-thirds of the community lived in below-standard housing or sub-standard cara-vans and it was the elderly members of the community who were worst off with 11 out of the 13 pensioner households living in seriously sub-standard accommodation. Most of their houses were uninsulated, severely affected by rising and penetrating damp and had no proper electricity supply. Some also had no water supply, so no baths or showers, no sinks and washhand basins and no WCs.[5]

With the rot so far advanced, many residents now feared that their commu-nity would die if it continued to be owned by celebrated playboy types. It was true that the laird was kind to the impeccably loyal, and he had not allowed recreational killing to govern wildlife management. But in other respects, most residents were either afraid to speak out about social conditions or had given up doing so in frustration at getting nowhere. Dr Hector MacLean, Eigg's retired physician who went everywhere in a kilt and tweed jacket, told me that landlordism had made island life 'like living under enemy occupation, except you're not allowed to shoot the buggers'. Eviction was an ever-present fear for those on short leases or with no tenure at all. Without security, people could not get grants or bank loans to improve their properties. That was a major reason why they'd deteriorated so badly. Even requests for a suitable site for a community rubbish dump had got nowhere. Most residents therefore had heaps of rat-infested garbage at the bottom of their crofts and gardens. In short, many of the people of Eigg were unable to access significant parts of the raft of civil assistance available to other British citizens. This, they felt, gave to Mrs Williams' allegations of 'mismanagement' an edge that cut beyond her own legal proceedings.

The selling price of Eigg in 1991 was touted at £3 million – twelve times what Schellenberg had paid for it in 1975. Land prices had rocketed during the years that Mrs Thatcher was prime minister. Wealth had shifted from poor to rich, and wealthy interests, many from outside of Scotland, were busy investing savings gained from monetarist tax cuts and new-wave entrepre-neurism. The attraction of Eigg to such people, usually men – women tend to become lairds by inheritance – was its seclusion. That was something, we fig-ured, that could be placed into question in seeking to precipitate a discount sale.

We also figured that if it did prove possible to knock a hole in the value of a flagship estate, a shudder would run through the whole landowning establishment. It might spur demand for land reform throughout Scotland. Our campaign therefore needed to look to the stars. Prominent in my mind was a famous passage from Rousseau's *Discourse on the Origin of Inequality*, written in 1754. Just as the Clearances were getting underway, he'd written:

> The first man who, having enclosed a piece of ground, bethought himself of saying 'This is mine', and found people simple enough to believe him, was the real founder of civil society. For how many crimes, wars, and murders, from how many horrors and misfortunes might not any one have saved mankind, by pulling up the stakes, or filling up the ditch, and crying to his fellows: 'Beware of listening to this impostor; you are undone if you once forget that the fruits of the Earth belong to us all, and the Earth itself to nobody.'[6]

So, exposing the heir to Rousseau's impostor was to be the name of our game. True, we would have to work with market forces to keep within the law. We would be trying to buy back what was, in effect, property stolen simply by having been declared property under historically lurid circumstances. But future campaigners elsewhere might find themselves in a more favourable political situation if Rousseau's stakes could once be pulled out and a few ditches filled up. It might become less necessary to raise outrageous sums of purchase money if land-reform legislation was ever brought about. Our wider game plan, then, was that if we could seed-crystallise the idea of community landownership in a modern Western European context, pressure for legislative reform in Scotland might become a political bandwagon. It would resonate with the growing need of people, everywhere, to recover a sense of identity, belonging and community values. This in turn would help constellate the responsibilities necessary to create right relationship with nature and one another. As such, the Isle of Eigg Trust might, just might, become a symbolic step towards addressing some of the global problems of our times.

Ironically, our strongest card in what we were to attempt was our knowledge that landed power would be unlikely to take us seriously. We'd have surprise on our side. After all, for a penniless trust to mount such a challenge would have seemed, at that time, too ridiculous for words. Scotland would never before have seen the likes. The closest thing to it would be the Stornoway Trust on Lewis, established in 1924 when the departing Lord Leverhulme gifted 64,000 acres to the people. Ironically, this democratic community land trust had worked so well that it mostly went unsung. It was an inspiration to us, but otherwise, in modern campaigning terms, what we were tackling was new territory.

Challenging landed power, in short, had to be about transforming the very fabric of social reality.[7] It needed to alter the co-ordinates by which reality was mapped and reset them – not according to power, greed and domination, but according to love, justice and freedom. My own knowledge of tactics came mainly from reading about popular struggles in Latin America. What struck me most was the way that liberation theology there provided legitimacy for people's claim of right to their place. The principles at play involved changing what sociologists Peter Berger and Thomas Luckmann call 'the social construction of reality'. It's a matter of developing 'plausibility structures' that give an alternative to what has previously constituted social power. It's a question of understanding symbolic actions towards this not as hollow gestures, but, in Jungian terms, as 'symbols of transformation'. At the deepest levels of the psyche this transformation has got to be cosmological. It has got to position the human person more meaningfully than before in relation to the universe. 'The ultimate legitimation for "correct" actions,' say Berger and Luckmann, is 'their "location" within a cosmological and anthropological frame of reference . . . the symbolic universe.'[8] In other words, it's about seeing ourselves in relation to the stars and to our full humanity. It's about snapping out of the consensual trance, of breaking out of Dr Zimbardo's prison roles, of having the courage to say 'no further' to Professor Milgram's authority. The issue of developing the courage to be, then, becomes a profoundly *spiritual* issue. That is why liberation theology, in its broadest sense,[9] was such an important underpinning, particularly given that Eigg, like Harris, was a nominally Christian cultural context. Let us, then, set aside any cringe factor (if we can) and succinctly unpack what liberation theology is about.

Gustavo Gutiérrez, the Peruvian Roman Catholic priest who pioneered modern liberation theology in the 1960s, describes liberation as a three-fold process. Firstly, he says, there is 'liberation from social situations of oppression and marginalization'. That is to say, liberation at levels that affect family, community and political and economic institutions. Next there is the need for 'personal transformation by which we live with profound inner freedom in the face of every kind of servitude'. This is psychological and spiritual development – liberation from our internal blockages, hang-ups and various uptightnesses.[10] And thirdly, there is what he calls liberation from 'sin'. What he means by this offputtingly loaded term, I think, is what Walter Wink would mean by complicity with the Powers. Ah ha! That relieves the cringe factor on 'sin' a bit.

Gutiérrez describes this level of liberation as that 'which attacks the deepest root of all servitude; for sin is the breaking of friendship with God and with other human beings'. Liberation, he concludes, 'gets to the very source of social injustice and other forms of human oppression and reconciles us with God and our fellow human beings'. It sets us free at social, psychological and spiritual levels of experience. 'Free for what?' Gutiérrez asks. 'Free to love,' he concludes, adding that 'to liberate' means 'to give life'.[11]

The Judaeo-Christian scriptural basis for all this is that Jesus said we should be living not just any old life, but 'life abundant' (John 10:10). This is not some transcendental pie-in-the-sky-when-you-die promise of deferred gratification, but a very practical concern. It starts with such outward necessities as having 'daily bread' (Matthew 6:11) in a this-worldly realm of God that is 'within' – in the here-and-now (Luke 17:21), and from there it develops the need for an inner life of living on more than just 'bread alone' (Matthew 4:4). But the sequence is important: before preaching, Jesus liked to see that the people were fed (Mark 8). That is why liberation theology lays great stress on the satisfaction of people's basic needs and why it is therefore a deeply political theology – concerned that the distribution of wealth should mirror just and loving relationship (Acts 2:44–45; 2 Corinthians 8:13–15).

Jesus (in my not uncontested view) did not see himself as the 'unique' Son of God in the way that so-called Christian fundamentalists suggest. On the contrary (if we are to get really fundamentalist about this), he implies that all who venerate God are divine children (John 10:34, based on Psalms 82:6). His mission is to help us transcend narrow egocentric understandings of self and come alive to that of God incarnated within (Galatians 2:20). This is what being 'born again' is really supposed to mean. It has nothing to do with rich men's right-wing tele-evangelism. It means, in fact, that we are to 'become participants of the divine nature' (2 Peter 1:4) – a passage that so astonished John Calvin that he remarked: 'It is, so to speak, a kind of deification.'[12] This, of course, is ground on which Hindu theologians can feel very comfortable. It conforms precisely with their own *Bhagavad Gita* and *Upanishads*, and if Christians can bring themselves to the watering-hole of these texts, they may come to understand the metaphysics of their own tradition more fully than is often the case.[13]

In launching his mission statement in the synagogue at Nazareth, Jesus placed primary emphasis on social and ecological justice (Luke 4:18–19). He does this by taking a reading from Isaiah 61, thereby linking Old Testament prophecy to his vocation. Consistent with the insight that 'God is love' (1 John 4:8) and concerned not with self-interested tribalism, but with the 'healing of the nations' (Revelation 22:2), Jesus's chosen reading is intriguingly selective. I find it telling that he proclaims good news for the poor, liberty to captives, healing of the blind, freedom for the oppressed and, rather pleasingly in some translations (actually, the King James Version), succour for the broken-hearted; but he misses out what Isaiah also said about enjoying the 'wealth of the nations' and having the 'sons of the alien' placed in subservient service (Isaiah 61:5–6). That is, he omits the unsound bits, choosing instead to highlight what liberationists call 'God's preferential option for the poor' (Luke 6;

Amos 5). Such a precedent of selectivity allows us to crunch on the fruit of the Bible and not have to chew the pips as well.

Liberation theology understands God as being revealed incrementally through history. The prophets announce a progressive liberation of the human construct of God.[14] The tribal patriarchal deity represented in some of the laws of Moses (for example, Deuteronomy 20–25) sanctioned rape, genocide and ethnic cleansing to an extent that makes Slobodan Milosevic look like the clown at a vicarage children's Christmas party (see Numbers 31; Joshua 6; Judges 21). As history progresses, however, the later Hebrew prophets progressively turn this world 'upside down' (Psalms 146:9, King James Version) until the old Mosaic Law, the Torah, is finally nailed to the cross of its own contradictions, fulfilled by being overturned by the law of love (Colossians 2:14; Matthew 5:38–48). Jesus noted that 'until now the kingdom of Heaven has suffered violence, and the violent take it by force' (Matthew 11:12). In other words, he understood his mission very specifically as a repudiation of the domination system. He says of the use of the sword, 'No more of this' (Luke 22:51).

Without a spiritually dynamic sense of history, then, we cannot understand the 'process theology' of continuous revelation in human evolution. We cannot understand the suffering of the world as being, as Jesus put it, 'but the beginning of the birth pangs' (Mark 13:8). Discovering a historical perspective therefore sheds spiritual meaning on time. This is vital in the cultural psychotherapeutic task of restoring grounding, vision and soul to us. Gutiérrez remarks how this is necessarily radical work:

> The history of humanity, as someone has said, has been 'written with a white hand.' History has been written from the viewpoint of the dominating sectors . . . . History's winners have sought to wipe out their victim's memory of the struggle, so as to be able to snatch from them one of their sources of energy and will in history: a source of rebellion. But rereading history means remaking history. It means repairing it from the bottom up. And so it will be a subversive history. History must be turned upside-down from the bottom, not from the top. What is criminal is not to be subversive, struggling against the capitalist system, but to continue being 'superversive' – bolstering and supporting the prevailing domination. It is in this subversive history that we can have a new faith experience, a new spirituality – a new proclamation of the gospel.[15]

Liberation theology accordingly places special emphasis on the need to contextualise biblical material in contemporary people's everyday lives. Thus the 'Mothers of the Disappeared', whose children were killed by the Argentinean junta, are portrayed in the art of Nobel Peace Prize winner Adolfo Pérez Esquivel as being the same as the women of Jesus's time who could do nothing but bring their powerful presences to the site of the Crucifixion – 'the spirituality of the foot of the cross'.[16] Similarly, images of Egypt and the Exodus have been used in contemporary land-rights struggles in Africa. And the legend of Noah's Ark has been used in North American schools to promulgate hermeneutical exegesis contextualised in the contemporary conservation of econiches conducive of megafaunal biodiversity . . .

You do have to watch it, though. As my friend Ian Ramsay said when making introductions at a party, 'This is Alastair, and his form of madness has a very specific symptom. The more excited he becomes, the longer the words get.'

16. Too Rough to Go Slow

It cost us about £3000 to register the Isle of Eigg Trust as a charitable organisation, to print a tastefully designed manifesto pamplet, and to call a press conference for the launch. Tom Forsyth covered most of the legal fees by building dry stone walls. Liz Lyon did us proud by paying for the manifesto and the press launch. To our horror, she booked it for Edinburgh's exclusive Balmoral Hotel, right at the heart of where all the journalists work. It made we three rural-rooted men squirm, but in retrospect it was the perfect tactic. It guaranteed immediate media attention because there was nothing more ridiculous than the poorest trust in town launching itself in the richest hotel. Sometimes when you have nothing else to draw on, you have to trade on humour. That establishes a bottom line of existence. You can move on to somewhere else from there.

We made an early Gandhian policy decision to be open with Mr Schellenberg. At all stages he was kept informed of our tactics and strategy. We therefore invited him to the Balmoral launch', set for 23 July 1991. He courteously replied, 'I appreciate a lot of your "woolly" sentiments and will do my best to be present.'[1]

The big man arrived a little late on the big day and sat at the back of a large room packed with wellwishers, reporters and television cameras. Surrounded by Tom, Liz and Bob Harris, I rose and opened the proceedings, delivering what felt like a formidable launch address. I laid out the history of Eigg and the stifling effects of landed power. My account was set in a context of Scottish history and the wider state of the world that would have made Sir Steven Runciman glow with pride. I concluded that if humankind is to have any hope of finding environmentally sustainable ways of life, we must rebuild community. That meant giving responsibility for their own place, planning and enterprise back to the people who actually live in an area.

A great round of applause rose up from all our supporters. It felt like history was being made. And I stood there, waiting for interested and intelligent questions from the press. But none came. Not one. Instead, the cameras spun round and zoomed in on . . . Schellenberg.

'Ah, um, excuse me a moment,' he muttered, rising slowly to his feet – but not, as it transpired, to the occasion. For, in a gesture that seemed calculated to hammer into focus how trivial he deemed our endeavours, he sweetly announced, 'I must just pop out and spend a penny.'

As Schellenberg shuffled off to the lavatory, the room collapsed in laughter. The seriousness of my speech lay tangled in the shreds of its own earnestness. With his maverick boyish charm, the laird had just stolen a march on us. He had revealed his ordinary, human nature and thereby blunted all my well-honed points about his extraordinary power. Mr Schellenberg, I was to learn, was an extremely clever communicator. When he spoke on the radio or television, he could be so persuasive that folks would sometimes say to me, 'Why have you chosen such a nice man with whom to tackle land ownership when there's so many real bad ones out there?' But listening to discussions of the same endearing broadcast in homes on Eigg was a different matter. 'Lies!' Maggie Fyffe or Colin Carr would exclaim. 'How could he say that when he just did such and such a thing to so-and-so.'

After spending his penny, Schellenberg assumed a commanding position before the cameras. He said that these grand ideas of ours were all very well. He truly wished us luck in attempting to pull them off. But we would 'not find one real Hebridean' willing to lend support. All the native Hebrideans wanted him to be their laird. They knew that if he wasn't there to see fair play, everybody would fight like cats in a bag. The clan needed a chief, as it were. 'So, I put out this challenge to you,' the big man concluded, firing at Tom, Liz, Bob and I on all cylinders. 'Find me *just one indigenous Hebridean supporter of your Trust*. Then somebody might take you seriously.'

Now, Schellenberg was accompanied wherever he went by his shaggy little pugnacious dog, Horace. All of a sudden it felt like Horace, with the sneering demeanour of a bespectacled private secretary, had just slithered out from under the podium and nipped the Isle of Eigg Trust on its Achilles heel. The truth was that only about a third of the residents of Eigg – some twenty people – were now indigenous Hebrideans. Another third were from elsewhere in Scotland, and the balance were mainly English incomers who had originally come to work there – mostly at the invitation of Schellenberg. And the Trust's big weakness was that it could not openly name its supporters. The situation was typified by one of the island's fishermen, who lived in a caravan because he could not get a house. (It was frightening, he said, in the middle of winter, when the gales were so strong that they had been known to lift caravans high into the air and dash them to smithereens on the rocks.) He slipped us a cash donation of £100, saying, 'This is so that what you're doing might work out. Me and others like me need it to work out. But don't tell anybody. I have to think about access and moorings for my boat. If "Schelly" finds out I gave you this, he'll make my life impossible.'

In the days that followed, it became clear that the Scottish media, at least, had taken the Trust's launch seriously. The *West Highland Free Press* asked: 'Will Schellenberg be the Last Emperor of Eigg?' But the English papers, perhaps less aware of landed issues, or perhaps protective of establishment plausibility structures, made a mockery of the whole thing. The old-guard *Daily Telegraph* set the tone. It described us, incredulously, as 'a group [who] admit they would like to see the law on land ownership changed and the concept of landlords abolished'.[2] Portraying land reform as a revolutionary notion and casting us as drop-outs suggested that even to challenge the sacred rights of property was larceny.

Immediately after the press launch, Schellenberg took us all out to lunch at Edinburgh University's staff club. It was a good-humoured affair. We asked if we could negotiate a buying price so that a fundraising target could be set. He warmly agreed to think about this, adding that he could afford to pay for the lunch 'in anticipation of you lot paying me a lot of money'. But he was shortly to change his mind about us. As soon as it sunk in that we were actually serious in our intentions, he told the press that he would never under any circumstances sell to a community trust.

Indeed, Schellenberg seemed to be one of those people who are incapable of distinguishing community from communism. In subsequent media debates he variously accused me of being a Marxist, a covertly aspiring laird, and even, during one rant in the BBC's Aberdeen studio, 'an IRA terrorist'. He would come out with some of the most remarkable interpretations of history. In a 1996 Channel 4 documentary called *Filthy Rich*, he told viewers that by forcing the crofters to move to the New World, the landlords of the past had done them a favour. Their descendants had prospered more than they would have if they'd stayed at home on marginal land. He made no mention of the lairds who had compounded the stresses of population growth by pushing the people on to such impoverished land in the first place. Neither did he spare a thought for those émigrés who died in passage to Nova Scotia under conditions that, in some cases, failed to meet even the regulations applying to British slave ships.[3] Nor did he speak of the men who drowned their despair in drink, or the women who, on arriving at far-flung destinations, had to sell their bodies to feed their children. He had probably never heard of the MacKinnon sister who threw her despairing body to the waves, or if he had, he'd probably have dismissed her as 'hysterical'.

In short, Schellenberg, like most lairds, had constructed a plausibility structure that sanctioned his own grip on power. His favourite activity and most extraordinary use of the island seemed to be the Eigg Games, whereby rich friends flew in to play war games with him. As teams of Hooray Henry types pelted each other with yellow tennis balls, and even when a Nazi flag was hung by his daughter from one of the Lodge windows as a joke, he appeared oblivious to the Hanoverian atrocities that had actually taken place on the soil over which they all pranced.

Once, I just made it by the skin of my teeth on to the ferry departing from Arisaig for Eigg. I leapt from the pier virtually into Schellenberg's arms, a bemused Tom Forsyth watching on and shaking his head at my always rushing around. Anyway, we got talking, keen to discover each other's business.

'Just going over for more of the Eigg Games?' I asked the laird.

'Ah, the Eigg Games,' he said. 'What a nice day for them. How about we play . . . General Franco against the crofters? And I'll be General Franco.'

I thought for a moment. With every intention of carrying on the good-natured banter, I quipped cheekily, 'Then I'll play Che Guevara.'

Instantly, his avuncular mood evaporated.

'We're not having any of those Islamic fundamentalist types round here!' he snorted.

I thought he was joking, but he shuffled off to a different part of the boat and didn't speak to me again.

Those who questioned his authority were 'hippies and drop-outs' whose 'well-organised conspiracy' had created 'a very serious law and order situation'.[4] Prospective buyers looking round the Lodge were reputedly told that as 'the crofting township is at the other end, they are far enough away not to be a nuisance'.[5] Writing in *Scotland on Sunday*, Dani Garavelli observed that 'Schellenberg's behaviour was that of someone who had been massively hurt and betrayed by his family. But this was not a family relationship. It was a feudal one based on superiority and inferiority.'[6]

'You've got an absolute creepiness about class,' he told me on the *Filthy Rich* programme. 'In the North of England you're as good as anybody and no better, and the idea, the whole business of the laird and all this, makes me shudder. You're producing all this rubbish. You're producing this sort of class, cringing business. People like me don't give a damn.'

Schellenberg's own assessment of the Isle of Eigg Trust was summed up in a letter that he wrote as if he was permanently resident on Eigg:

You are a thick skinned lot. Nobody that I know in the West Highlands has any confidence that you and your Group are anything more than a lot of publicity seeking windbags, who seek to justify themselves by fleecing their fellow man in the shape of the Taxpayer . . . . It is for those of us living and working on Eigg to try to find the best way forward without irrelevant, inexperienced, unwanted, outside interference . . . . But to turn to your new role. What I feel that you should be doing is taking on something worthwhile like . . . [the uninhabited island of] South Rona just north of Raasay, which has a number of habitable houses, a ruined village, including a school which I seem to remember still had a roof on . . . . It is not too far from your beloved Scoraig, so you could ship out colonists quite easily. I would be prepared to provide free transport for, say, two months, as well as up to 5 per cent of the purchase price if you raise the rest. Now doesn't that sound a bit more worthwhile than hanging around the journalists' bars in Rose Street hoping to get an invitation on to Radio Scotland? See you on South Rona.[7]

Often when I spoke with him, it was clear that he was genuinely confused and distressed as to why people did not appreciate what he gave to them. As Garavelli's article put it, 'He just couldn't seem to let go of the ungrateful, rebellious children, whom he believed would one day come to understand all he had done for them.' Like all who substitute charity for justice, he missed a crucial point, cogently made by Paulo Freire:

> In order to have the continued opportunity to express their 'generosity,' the oppressors must perpetuate injustice as well. An unjust social order is the permanent fount of this 'generosity', which is nourished by death, despair and poverty . . . . True generosity consists precisely in fighting to destroy the causes which nourish false charity. False charity constrains the fearful and subdued, the 'rejects of life', to extend their trembling hands.[8]

So it was that at times I'd feel sorry for this visibly ageing man with an island millstone round his neck to sell. He seemed to try in life – God, he seemed to try; but he kept crashing because he always needed to grab the steering wheel. He failed to perceive the suffocating strings that he attached to community relationships, or how evident it was that his island was little more than just another hobby. He confessed as much himself: 'Somehow it seemed more important to beat the Germans at Silverstone than to deal with a little Scottish island,' he told *Harpers & Queen*. 'The race put it all in perspective . . . I'm not worried if I don't win. I just don't want to lose.'[9]

I do not believe that people like Schellenberg are conscious of constructing reality to legitimise their power. This process is inevitable in a ruling class who, since childhood, have generally been emptied out from within themselves and are desperate for a world to fill the emptiness. Money lets them create a world of their own. For them, this is 'the real world', but for everybody else – for those whose lives are but props on their stage – the make-believe nature of such fairy-tale lives is obvious. The cardinal rule is that you don't name the game; you don't name the powers and thereby shatter their veneer. And if you don't play the game, your job, home, sanity and reputation may be at stake.

Your role, then, if looking at power from the underside, is to help 'keep up appearances'. Indeed, it is your role to prop up what Scott Peck calls 'the people of the lie' with their delusions of family, class, gender or racial superiority that justify privilege. Here mendacity lubricates 'normality'. It's not that the rich and powerful mean to lie; it's just that their reality is plastic. It can be moulded as much as money can buy. Agreements, memories and even histories become reconfigured in the mind as image defines reality rather than the other way round. Of course, we all do this (including the writers of books), but when those with power *over* others do it, they force their world on to their servitors – the ghillies, the housemaids, the waiters, and yes, the artists, accountants and lawyers too.

In such a world huge emphasis is placed on politeness: on having 'good manners'. You are part of 'the establishment' only if you 'know how to behave', if you 'know your place', if you know how to dress, speak and even eat 'properly'. It's a question, as the French sociologist Pierre Bourdieu says, of expressing the right 'taste'.[10] If things were otherwise, the rich would not be able to live with themselves. They need to believe their own story to keep in position the lens that focuses their own privilege. While some of this is just harmless ego posturing, much of it injures others. Victim-blaming, inferiorisation and even charity contribute to maintaining the edifice. All demarcate the boundary between the 'in group' of the elite, and the majority 'out group'. The poor are controlled by scapegoating if they are 'bad', or by patronisation if they are 'good'. The underlying sanction of punishment usually goes unspoken and thereby renders invisible the violence that keeps justice suppressed.

But the terrible price to be paid by the rich is to be untrue to one's own self. Mammon's only jewels are human hearts. Moloch is an empty stone god. That's the trouble with false gods: at the end of the day they let you down. Being death, they have no life of their own to share: only the transient proceeds of vampirism, sucked from other people's lives and from the Earth itself.

The false gods exist only as emergent properties of our own fears. We make the graven images, the idols. And if we let these reflections of our psychic shadow overcome us, if we let ourselves die spiritually, we will indeed find no God, no Heaven; because the god we were looking for was death, and death is, precisely, non-being.

Such are the dynamics of what in olden days was called 'Hell', the fire being only to warm an otherwise icy space, the brimstone only a suffocating smokescreen.

Tom Forsyth cut a quaint figure as he travelled around Britain drumming up support for the Trust over the months following its launch. Often he would fast for days, drinking just a little water. Sometimes he slept rough in woods and ditches wrapped only in woollen clothing hand-spun from his Scoraig sheep and on a mattress of yellow waterproof oilskins from his boat. This boat had been beautifully crafted to a traditional design by his Scoraig neighbour, Topher Dawson, in a workshop powered entirely from wind-generated electricity. Its name was *Wu Wei* – Chinese for 'action through no action'.

Wu Wei became a metaphor that necessarily expressed our approach in the early days of the Eigg Trust. I'd worry that we weren't doing enough quickly enough. Without being able to set a clear fundraising target, it seemed futile to try to raise money. We went through the motions of writing letters to donor organisations, but frankly, there was a fantasy element to it all. How can you raise serious finance for something that the owner has said you can't buy? 'Don't force it,' Tom would say to me. 'Just be mindfully present to the rightness of what it is we're attempting. Swing with opportunity as it arises, and wait at other times. It's the only way we can hope to go anywhere.'

'We've got no conventional resources,' Tom would continue. 'We'd wear ourselves out in no time if we beat our wings against the granite block of landlordism. So just flow around it for now, like a river. The times are getting right; opportunities will arise. Act effortlessly. Do only what feels good and gives you energy. And don't flinch from rising to the occasion, incisively, energetically, when the sand moves and the block starts to shift. That's the way of *Wu Wei*.'

And I thought of Hermann Hesse's *Siddhartha*: the monk who fell in love with the beautiful Kamala. Asked what he could do to be worthy of her, Siddhartha replied, 'I can think, I can wait, I can fast.' And asked what good fasting was, he spoke about himself, saying:

> It is of great value . . . . If a man has nothing to eat, fasting is the most intelligent thing he can do. If, for instance, Siddhartha had not learned to fast, he would have had to seek some kind of work today . . . for hunger would have driven him. But as it is, Siddhartha can wait calmly. He is not impatient, he is not in need, he can ward off hunger for a long time and laugh at it. Therefore fasting is useful.[11]

Tom often came down from Scoraig to the CHE. He worked with the students in building a magnificent elmwood table for the library, one that embodied the principles of human ecology in its beauty and design and in the timber, which was sustainably sourced from Ulrich's sawmill.

'It's not good enough to do your community-development work only at the grassroots,' he would tell us. 'So much of the grassroots are just at the level of spectator sport, television, cigarettes, drink and consumer culture. No, you've got to get down to the *taproots*.'

He'd draw an oak seedling on the blackboard. 'You see, its taproot is bigger than the growth above ground,' he'd say. 'Human culture's the same. The taproot of some trees remains even after the top has been shaved off by sheep. What we've got to do in the world, what we're trying to do on Eigg, is to graft on a scion, a new shoot, to that taproot. We've got to make for modern times new growth that's rooted in ancient spiritual bedrock.'

Then he'd pull from his pocket some winkles – a shell that is sacred to Bhrighde in the Irish tradition. He'd place them on the overhead projector. As their image was cast up, magnified, on to the wall, he'd say, 'Look: the spiral is central to life's growth processes. See how it starts so small, but exponentially builds a towering strength.'

All this was very reassuring to me, because the Eigg campaign at that time was running on little more than a trickle of widows' mites from people inspired by the newspaper reports. But there was that other factor: we also ran on poetry.

'You can't eat poetry!' a fellow academic once said to me. Well, maybe not, but with poetry you can, perhaps, get by with eating less. Indeed, just as the Isle of Eigg had an absentee laird, so the Isle of Eigg Trust had what, but for his passionate connection to his native land, we might have called an 'absentee bard'. This was Kenneth White, the Brittany-based Scots professor of poetry: 'in complexity/and complicity/with all of being – /there is only poetry'.

White was developing a field of understanding of what he called 'geopoetics'. It is 'in those rock-piles that the poetics lie,' he wrote, 'poetry, geography – *and a higher unity: geopoetics . . .*'.[12]

Here was Scotland's answer to Gary Snyder: pure Celtic Zen. White saw that flowing in stone and crystallised in the cry of a gull is the Greek *poesis*: reality constantly being made anew in *geo* – geology, the Earth. All four of us in the Isle of Eigg Trust felt this very strongly. We felt that we were being moved to take our stand not just by people in the community, but by the island itself; by Scotland and the Earth itself. Accordingly, in the Trust's manifesto Liz had quoted one of White's works, 'My Properties'.

> I'm a landowner myself after all –
> I've got twelve acres of white silence
> up at the back of my mind[13]

There were times that the media would ring and ask, 'How's it going? When are you going to poach Schellenberg's Eigg?' And I'd laugh to myself. I'd come out with some crisply quotable soundbite that would serve their immediate purposes. But what gave me confidence, what gave me a sense of being grounded and on the right path, was the feeling that at some spiritual level we already had the 7400 acres of white silence that is Eigg up at the back of our minds. But this was not a matter of being 'landowners'. We were more what I would call 'landholders': keeping the care of place in the palm of the hand – and an open hand, not a clenched fist.

Around the same time as the Eigg Trust was launched, White had published an article entitled 'A Shaman dancing on the Glacier' in *Artwork* magazine. Here he described his boyhood affinity with nature which, after reading

Mircea Eliade's classic *Shamanism: Archaic Techniques of Ecstasy*, he had come to realise was a magical relationship in an ancient tradition. Reflecting on the glaciers that had once crept down from Scotland's bleak Rannoch Moor, White felt that the 'companions of Finn' who had inhabited these lands after the ice had melted ten thousand years ago were, in fact, shamans. It was they, he suggested, who had constructed the mythopoesis of our early cultural reality. They articulated the taproot. 'I am suggesting,' he wrote, 'that we try and get back an earth-sense, a ground sense, and a freshness of the world such as those men, those Finn-men knew when they moved over an earth from which the ice had just recently receded. This is the dawn of geopoetics.'[14]

White's writings helped to legitimise the shamanic nature of what Eigg had drawn us into. Our work was, as Starhawk puts it, that of *changing consciousness at will*. It was a kind of magic, undertaken not with money at this stage, but with incantations of passion – with words – that came from a native ground-sense of place. We were crazy, all of us, very crazy – but not mad. There's a difference. It was an archetypal David-versus-Goliath situation. Schellenberg himself often said that it was 'pure soap opera'. But the more he reacted to the absurdity of our challenge, the more he became part of the show ('the Dirty Den of Eigg', as one media wag put it); the more fate advanced onwards as relentlessly as in a Greek drama. As such, the campaign was activist art. It was theatre played out on an island-sized stage with an audience that was national and, increasingly, global. Ours was the power of the jester who tweaks the whiskers of the king. As for me, I felt like a Socratic gadfly peskily zapping the rear end of a lumbering dinosaur. I knew that we couldn't hold back its cumbersome mass. But perhaps the distracting irritation would cause it not to notice the pit that lay in its path. Perhaps we could, after all, clear the land of monsters.

At one level, we who were running the Trust had to kid ourselves in the early days that a millionaire might read about Eigg in the papers and send the money with which we could make Schellenberg an offer he could not refuse. But at another, I believed that to succeed too early would actually have been the worst possible outcome. We might have procured the island, but the islanders would not have been sufficiently ready. They would not yet be in ownership of the process. Seven generations of demoralisation had left their mark. That was what had to be addressed first. In order to galvanise the process, it had been necessary for us to assume advocacy, standing up and standing out. But our real agenda now needed to be *empowerment*. This, we could feel, was latent in what was clearly a very special Hebridean community. You don't survive winters on Eigg and a series of eccentric landlords without inner stamina and a few tricks up your sleeve. But the islanders' time had not come quite yet. For now, we, as the outsiders, were being allowed by them to do the running.

great-great-grandparents, Murdo MacLennan, crofter, scribe and precentor, and Mary Gollan,
rounded by family at their golden-wedding celebrations in Jamestown, Strathpeffer, in 1896.

n MacGregor of Gearrannan at his loom, 1994. Harris Tweed, the 'green' fabric of the future, is
atural, hard-wearing, comfortable, warm and fashionable product of Hebridean crofts.

Waiting to bring home the kill with Sandy the horse as a pony boy and ghillie on Eisken Estate, Isle of Lewis 1976.

Tommy MacRae, head keeper of Eisk Estate, congratulates a paying 'gun' o felling a stag. Some guests would 'blo themselves, smearing their brows red triumphant celebration.

Tom Forsyth of Scoraig, founder of the
Isle of Eigg Trust, together with Djini
on Eigg after they had restored the Well
of the Holy Women.

Keith Schellenberg, laird of Eigg,
announcing a libel case against the
Guardian and *Sunday Times* in 1999.

The islanders debate whether they should take over the Eigg Trust, 1994. Clockwise from bel[o]
Caroline Read, Sheena Kean, John Chester, Marie Carr, Camille Dressler, Colin Carr, Maggie Fy[.
Lesley Riddoch and 'Sir' Maxwell MacLeod.

The Isle of Eigg Trust's community-elected board, 1994. From left: Barry Williams, Tom Fors[y]
(retiring), Fiona Cherry, Duncan Ferguson, Alastair McIntosh, Peggy Kirk, Dr Christopher Tia[.
and Katie MacKinnon.

...anders and supporters walk ashore under the prominent Sgurr of Eigg on 'Independence Day', ...June 1997, having supplanted absentee autocracy with local democracy.

...sonant with ancient sites like Calanais (see front-cover photograph), *Clach na Daoine* – the Stone ...the People – is decorated with Scotland's saltire flag to celebrate Eigg's community buy-out.

A computer-generated montage on an aerial photograph suggests how the Lafarge Redl superquarry on Mount Roineabhal would affect the National Scenic Area in South Harris.

With Sulian Stone Eagle Herney, Mi'Kmaq warrior chief and Sacred Pipe Carrier, before Mo Roineabhal on the eve of our public-inquiry testimony.

Mount Roineabhal from St Clement's Church at Rodel, Isle of Harris.

Lafarge vice presidents Philippe Hardouin, Gaëlle Monteiller and Michel Picard at Roineabhal during their fact-finding mission, January 2004.

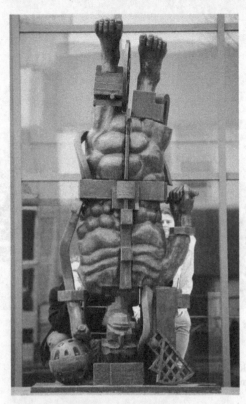

Egeria, by Sir Eduardo Paolozzi, commissioned to reflect 'the aspiration of those working within the new Michael Swann Building for research into biotechnology at the University o Edinburgh.

Members of the GalGael Trust trainir on the *Aileach*, an Irish–built birlinn, Hebridean version of which Colin MacLeod hopes to see built in Govan.

As 1991 yielded to autumn, the Trust was generating ever-increasing media interest in the land question. 'The debate on landownership was now kick-started back into life,' writes Camille Dressler in her history of Eigg. 'It encompassed a far larger problem than Eigg, but from that time on, Eigg would become one of the test cases in the crucial issue of land reform.'[15]

Among us trustees, however, indigestion from consuming too much poetry on an empty stomach and too few hard results was causing tension. Schellenberg's ex-wife, the Honourable Margaret de Hauteville Udny-Hamilton, was now married to Bill Williams – Liz Lyon's former husband and the millionaire owner of *Artwork*. Constant exposure to headlines like 'Scrambles over Eigg' had become a strain for the extended family. Liz diplomatically laid down her trusteeship but left us with her blessing. But other differences were also bubbling under. They surfaced at a trustees' meeting in October 1991.

'It's not tenable,' Bob said. 'We can't carry on like this any longer.'

'I'm with Bob,' I had to tell Tom.

It pained me curiously to disagree with him so strongly. This white-haired and grey-bearded weather-beaten figure had become something of a mentor to me. To those who did not notice and love the little wild flowers beneath their feet, or who released youthful energies revving up their motorbikes past his bothy home, he could be an angry, dour, unsociable and judgemental old goat – Saturn personified. But the underlying Tom was a man who insisted on nothing less than the absorption of his full presence into place and task. Like Siddhartha, he would fast, wait, and work what he wanted into being. He sought the enjoyment of God in the simplest of things, be it companionship with the blackbird living by his wood pile, the chopping of logs from trees that he had planted two decades previously, or sitting over a winter's fire burning the aromatic black peat that he had dug from a distant bog and brought around to the croft under sail in the *Wu Wei*.

Now I was challenging him about the Trust's direction and feeling almost impertinent in so doing. He was a true Quaker of the heart, often shaking visibly with emotion as powerful forces stirred his very gut. Sometimes it could be scary, kind of Plutonic. You'd wonder what might happen if the cauldron of his sturdy frame fissured under the pressure of his own metamorphic resolve.

'We have to ask them to come off the fence,' Bob said of Eigg's residents. 'The only way we'll do that is by giving them ownership and full control over what we do. Once that starts happening, then we should progressively withdraw from this self-appointed advocacy role.'

Tom shook his head doubtfully. 'I don't believe they're ready for it.'

'It's like the faeries in those old stories, Tom,' I countered. 'Our place is to arrive out of the blue and then disappear underground again. The majority of folk should be unsure whether they ever really saw us in the first place. The big work has to be done by them, not us, otherwise it will never be steadfast.'

The supernatural metaphor left me chuckling inside. Running through my mind was an image of us all – three full-grown men – as overgrown little-folk flying over Eigg, beards streaming in the wind, gossamer wings spreadeagled, and Tom in his wellie boots and bright-yellow oilskins flapping out behind.

'Keith keeps telling the press it's the greatest soap opera of all time,' added Bob. 'And he's right. That's what it takes to keep the land question in the public mind. But if we carry on like this we'll get ourselves miscast as laughing stocks. Your vision, Tom, the efforts of us all, will crumble to dust.'

'I still say they're not ready,' Tom replied. 'Look, a year ago they couldn't agree among themselves about some of the most basic things. It's fine for Alastair to talk about "intergenerational historical disempowerment" and other such fancy stuff, but with the amount of drinking that goes on –'

'Aye, you're right there,' Bob interjected. 'The media go up to meetings and all they notice is some folk needing to have a drink before they'll even open their mouths –'

'Which proves my point,' Tom resumed, 'not to mention all the smokes as well. I mean, when you hear some of the rubbish that's spoken –'

'Yes, Tom,' I cut in. 'But it's probably no worse than most other Highland communities. That, plus when the media turn up for a meeting everybody, including the village alcoholic, comes along too. You know how it is in a small community. Folks don't hide what happens behind closed doors like they do everywhere else.'

'All the same, it does play into Schelly's hands,' Bob said. 'The drink puts folk down then justifies keeping them down. Firewater and beads, I'd call it. Same as the Indians and Aborigines. If the pastor didn't get them, the bottle did – and that justified the pastor coming back to get them! Heavy drink toggled with heavy religion. What can you expect without a decent future to live for?'

'True enough,' I said. 'But Tom, it's not that we're suggesting abdicating from the Trust. What Bob and I are proposing is that we continue as we are, but simply ask the residents formally to endorse us. To forge ahead, we must get a mandate that stops people from knocking us.'

'And if they don't give it?' he asked.

'Then we're all wasting our time anyway,' Bob said.

'Look. You and Liz are the ones who've spent time on the island,' I said. 'You both reckon there's strong but silent support, right? Now, Bob and I are standing with you because we trust you on that, Tom. But the media don't know it. The public don't know it. Probably the folk on Eigg as a community don't even know it, because none of us have ever stood up there and openly asked them!'

'You see, to them we're just three bearded idealists,' Bob said. '"Father Christmas" I've heard they call you, Tom – aye, with not many presents in his sack either – and it's the "Three Wise Men" they're calling us too ... For God's sake, we've launched this Trust but never even had a meeting up there. They're suspicious, and too damned right. We've got to see ourselves in the context of all the sharpshooters they've had in the past. And we've got to remember that in the eyes of the media, Schellenberg's probably just as plausible as we are.'

Gradually, Tom came round to agree. It was not that we had won some sort of battle over him. What often happens in small groups like this is that each person takes up a position that represents some aspect of what others also feel. The group as a whole acts as an organism of different parts. The doubts that Tom articulated were things that we all shared at a certain level. The confidence Bob and I expressed was also present in Tom. By taking up different positions, we were able between us, perhaps unconsciously, to profile the issues more sharply.

It was therefore agreed to hold a public meeting on Eigg. All permanent residents would be invited. We'd explain ourselves fully, allow cross-examination, and suggest that they organised a vote of confidence (or otherwise) through secret ballot. If fewer than 50 per cent of the residents were with us, we'd fold the Trust up. But if we were given a mandate, we'd undertake not to make any major decision without the endorsement of the Residents' Association. That way they could stand safely back from our activities. They could avoid any danger of victimisation, but at the same time they'd have control over what was undertaken on their behalf.

As the campaign heated up, I'd often have to say or write something as spokesperson for the Trust that would leave my stomach rotating like a windmill. The stage of naming and unmasking the Powers was now shifting to that of engagement. I found myself experiencing what Walter Wink had described as 'the interior battlefield where the decisive victory is first won, before engagement in the outer world is even attempted'. Part of me thrived on it; part was troubled.

The Buddhists have a triple test of 'right speech'. They ask: Is it true? Is it necessary? And, is it kind? I never saw any problem with the first two criteria, but often wrestled with the last. To hold a mirror up to a laird, to a superquarry magnate-in-waiting or to university officials who were becoming increasingly edgy about the directions of applied human ecology within their prestigious science faculty – these can feel, superficially, like unkind things to do. And yet, 'Who will be the troubler of my peace?' Do we not need to hear the truth as others see it if we are to learn and grow? Is psychological honesty not vital to creating community? After all, Jesus never said not to have enemies; he only said we should love them.

Or is this just another version of the end justifying the means? Is it not what every fascist from the beginning of time has said to justify the adjective 'benign'?

'McIntosh! McIntosh!' came the voice from across the library table in the CHE one day. 'Will you stop all this nauseous wallowing in self-doubt!'

It was the Honourable Sir Maxwell MacLeod of Fuinary and the Isles.

'These guys just want you to think like that to blunt your teeth. They want you tied up, yapping while they suck the lifeblood of the poor. You only get the reactions you do because you're on to something. There's not enough people willing to use their position to say what you're saying, so go for it.'

Sir Maxwell MacLeod always called me 'McIntosh'. It was a hangover from his public-school days. His father, the Rev. Dr George MacLeod, Lord MacLeod of Fuinary, had rebuilt Iona Abbey. I remember that the first time I'd met old George was in Edinburgh's Waverley station. The big man ahead of me in the queue at the ticket office had an aristocratic Scots accent. I was curious, so leaned forward to squint at the name on his chequebook.

'Excuse me,' I said, 'but would you be Lord MacLeod, the anti-nuclear man?'

He turned round, slowly. And then raising both head and voice to the heavens, as if at the crescendo of a sermon (which, unbeknown to me, was precisely what it was about to become), he announced to the whole congregation of passengers: 'Yes. I most certainly am Lord MacLeod, the anti-nuclear man.'

Surprised ticket clerks stopped and stared. The spacious hall fell into a complete hush. A happening was happening. 'And have you heard the latest news?' the big man asked.

I shook my head, suddenly self-conscious.

'The Americans,' he told everybody, 'have just named their latest nuclear submarine Corpus Christi, the Body of Christ! Now, that is blasphemy.'

And he turned round to carry on buying his ticket.

George MacLeod had been decorated with the Military Cross for bravery in the First World War. On the ferry over to Iona, a journalist once quipped: 'Well, Lord MacLeod, it must be a great pleasure for you to come back every so often to such tranquil beauty.'

George, however, had made a career of engaging the Powers. 'No,' he answered stolidly. 'It feels like climbing back into the trenches.'

The Iona Community uses the wild goose as its logo. George had always maintained it to be a Celtic symbol of the Holy Spirit. Once, his biographer, Ron Ferguson, asked what his sources were. 'No idea,' he snapped. 'I probably made it up.'

That, of course, is precisely the gripe that the Celtosceptics have with contemporary Celtic spirituality. And you can see their point. At the same time, maybe they miss the point. Maybe the 'Holy Spirit' is a process of continuous revelation.[16] Maybe the Georges of this world are its prophets, whom they still persecute. When scholars like Professor Meek claim that later 'Celtic' sources (the quotation marks are his), like Carmichael's *Carmina Gadelica*, MacLean's *Hebridean Altars* and the prayers of George MacLeod, must be excluded from the canon of credibility because, 'they simply do not belong to . . . the more properly Celtic period before 1100',[17] then maybe, as I earlier suggested, they're missing the music, even the magic; and certainly, it seems to me, they're missing the self-evident spiritual testimony of wild geese calling in migratory formation – a heavenly music that drifts across the early winter landscape like brushstrokes blown through snow.

As for Maxwell MacLeod, he'd had a hard start being his father's son. However, when the old man died at ninety-six, Maxwell had the opportunity to develop into one of Scotland's most entertaining investigative journalists, packing away a small fortune from his newspaper cartoon strip *The Urban Crofter*.

'We need an expression for it,' I had said to him on our way back from the M77 anti-motorway protest in 1992. 'We need something that describes the way people mask their misery by going out shopping.'

He thought, for an unusually long time. 'How about,' he pondered, 'how about "retail therapy"?'

I was to use that expression many times in the years that followed. Finally, by 1999, it was even appearing in advertisements (including the one fronting up the website of *The Times* newspaper), all the more to promote consumer indulgence!

The day that old George died, Maxwell vowed never to use the inherited title. But the moment he got into a tight spot he reneged. Thereafter, friends called him 'Sir Maxwell': not as an honour, but as a nickname.

'Now, McIntosh,' Sir Maxwell said, as I fingered the contours of the elm table. 'Today you are going to buy me lunch. You see, I am as penniless as the Isle of Eigg Trust. But first, I am going to pay you for it. I'm going to tell you two of my father's stories, McIntosh, and you will remember and use these stories when you write a book.'

'Yes, Sir Maxwell. Go on then,' I replied.

'The first one,' he began, 'is about an old Scots missionary somewhere in the middle of Africa. Every year the people had a huge festival with all kinds of pagan goings-on. I needn't elaborate. You know how these things overexcite me. Anyhow, whenever such a ceremony began, the missionary would get out his soapbox, stand in front of the revelling masses, and preach the Word of God that they might repent.

'Now, this continued year after year. Eventually, there came a day when the missionary was struck down by malaria. That evening he heard the drumming start and he thought to himself, "I've been out there on my soapbox every year preaching in the name of the Lord. This time, just this once, I'll have to give it a miss. The Lord in His goodness will understand."

'So, McIntosh, the sickly servant of God is just going back to sleep when there's a knock on the door. Guess who's there? It's the village chief . . . all done up in his party togs. And the Chief says, "Ho there, Reverend! What's the matter with you? Why aren't you out there on your soapbox as usual, beating your Bible like one of our drums, and yelling about the lake of brimstone and fire?"

'And the missionary says, "Well, I don't see why you're so bothered. I happen to be a little bit sick this year. You're going to have to carry on without me."

'"But you can't do that to us, Reverend!" the Chief protested in open-mouthed disappointment. "You see, you're part of the ritual now!"'

'So you get my point, McIntosh?' Sir Maxwell concluded. 'You've got to keep it. Don't give in just because you get sniped at. Don't be upset because you're upsetting them. What you and the CHE are on about has got to be said. It needs to be spoken from a place like this. That's the very *idea* of a university – to make people think. Now, are you ready for my second story?'

'Go on,' I said. 'Make it snappy, then I'll take you for lunch.'

'No problem. It's very snappy. That's the whole point. It's about the same missionary. Somewhere right in the middle of Africa, he came upon a sign by a road that was so deeply potholed as to be almost impassable. It read: TOO ROUGH TO GO SLOW.'

I waited, expecting more. Sir Maxwell stared away blankly, watching birds nibbling nuts at the window. 'So?' I asked, 'Is that it?'

'That's it, McIntosh. You see, in the game you're playing you've got to put both feet on the accelerator. You've got to leap over the holes they dig in your path. Remember that story, McIntosh. Promise me you'll remember it. Your game's the same as that African road. Pussyfoot around and you'll get stuck forever. *It's too rough to go slow.*'

17. The Emperor's New Island

Mairi Kirk feeds us, then Tom, Bob and I get into her little red Land Rover to cross the island. The only place to hold the planned public meeting here on Eigg is the tea-room. Even that had to be arranged through the gracious offices of Mr Schellenberg. No bets as to whether he was reckoning on our endorsement or comeuppance!

I've neither made notes nor prepared a speech. I'll be winging it. But in my mind something archetypal is stirring. I start to feel distinctly strange. A profound calm has settled on me. Something almost visible is happening. It's as if a great door of history is opening up in my mind and I'm staring down through the corridors of time. I'm seeing everything converge on this place, at this moment, with these people.

To the west the Atlantic thunders. Mairi releases the handbrake. The vehicle rolls down the little hill past her house. We bump-start with a jerk.

In the crofting village of Cleadale a minibus and several cars are picking people up. All are heading for the tea-room. It looks like it's going to be a good turnout.

Mairi shifts the Land Rover into a lower gear. We grind steeply up the twisting single-track road. The island's central plateau opens out on top. And then a very strange thing indeed happens.

We're passing the highest spot in the middle of Eigg. It's just before the road drops down through the hazel wood. I'm crouched on the floor, uncomfortably, bouncing along in the back, and I start to become aware that a river is flowing into me. A river! It feels like all the ancient blocked-up wells and springs have broken free. They're merging and melding and the confluence is a torrential, silvery stream of light. I'm bathed, soothed, inwardly illuminated.

I become aware of what the stream is composed of: voices! A vast chorus of them. They're literally flowing out from the rocks and soil. They're coming from all around the Highlands. The Earth, the ground itself, is their source. These are the voices of the old people. The dead are with us. Dry bones have come back to life.[1]

The strange experience lasted about a minute; it faded as we came down through the wood on the other side of the island. I said nothing to the others. But as we walked into the tea-room that night, I felt swept along by an unstoppable confidence: an unshakeable knowledge that what we were doing was right; an entreaty to put aside self-doubt.

It felt like we were carrying what a voice in my mind called 'the mantle of Scottish history'. As they'd say in the movies, the force was with us. All we had to do was to follow the shaft of light; honour the voices; flow with the *Wu Wei*; walk the silver faerie path. In this I was not my own, and not on my own. In this, nevertheless, I was most deeply and joyfully rooted in myself.

Tom, Bob and I were warmly welcomed into the tea-room. People were excited. Children were playing under tables, dogs were yapping, and what appeared to be the entire population of Eigg from babies to octogenarians sat crammed on to chairs or piled up in corners.

As I got up to speak, a threefold approach to community empowerment came together in my head. It was straight out of liberation theology: a direct application of Paulo Freire's 'conscientisation' – that unity of conscience and consciousness which enables us to analyse and act upon the causes of oppression.

'What can we in Scotland do about landlordism?' I asked.

First, I suggest, we must re-member. We must remember in the way that those erecting cairns on Knoydart, or at the sites of land grabs in Lewis are presently helping us to do. As with personal psychological health, repression of a culture's past only turns anger and sadness inwards to deaden the soul. No cultural carcinogen is more powerful than oppression internalised to the point that a community blames itself alone for disempowerment, dysfunction and underachievement. So let us start by remembering. But let us do so mindful of the curative role which forgiveness must eventually play. Only forgiveness breaks the knock-on effects of oppression re-perpetuating itself.

Then we can engage in re-visioning. We must envision what our communities could become . . . sorting out the realistic from the fantasy and asking what kind of a people we want to be. Are our values primarily those of market forces, or do we stand for values to do with place, culture and relationship?

Finally, dare we re-claim? Can we, as in the words communicated by Moses in Leviticus 25, 'Proclaim the liberation of all the inhabitants of the land . . . a jubilee for you; each of you will return to his ancestral home . . . . Land must not be sold in perpetuity, for the land belongs to me'?[2]

Well, I'm told that I used too many big words. I'm told that the theology went over the heads of many and rubbed one or two up the wrong way, though, significantly, not the old people. But it was the atmosphere that did the real talking that night.

As we left the meeting, one of the most elderly indigenous women came up and fixed my eyes with hers. She spoke deliberately, croaking out each syllable. She said of Keith Schellenberg: 'Just help us to get rid of that man.'

During the following week the Isle of Eigg Residents' Association held a secret ballot. There was a 100 per cent turnout. A stunning 73 per cent voted in favour of the Trust's continued advocacy on their behalf. No longer could we be accused of having no mandate.

Doors now started to open everywhere. Skilled voluntary organisations gave support that helped islanders to develop their own vision. Campaigning BBC journalist Lesley Riddoch was so shocked at finding people frightened to speak out that she made a special point of encouraging them so to do. The local enterprise company provided £8000 for a feasibility study. Meanwhile, residents on another Scottish island, Gigha, consulted the Isle of Eigg Trust after their laird, the self-styled 'Baron of Gigha', Malcolm Potier, had collapsed into bankruptcy. His creditors wanted to maximise the island's value by offering vacant possession of properties. The press scooped pictures of doors freshly chalked with the letters, '*E II R – Evicted – 18 III 92*' (eviction in the name of Queen Elizabeth II).[3] This further helped to elevate land reform on to the national stage. On 4 June 1992 Ray Michie MP, speaking, she told me, as much for Eigg as for Gigha, said in the House of Commons:

> The assumption that [an] island and its way of life could be used simply as collateral in the affairs of a speculative property empire [is] offensive to anyone with even the most primary understanding of the need to maintain continuity in the rural economy, upon which much of our social stability depends. We shall never achieve a stable and equitable society in Scotland if this kind of market practice is allowed to prevail in the disposition of its land, perhaps its greatest asset . . . . Until a government has the courage to tackle the problem of feudal land ownership, it will remain a running sore and a cause of deep resentment and bitterness. The English had the good sense to get rid of their feudal system . . . in 1290. For us to retain in Scotland the titles of superior and vassal in this modern day and age beggars belief.

The Scottish Office Minister of State, Lord James Douglas-Hamilton, responded with complete abdication of governance:

> Highland land use has long been a particularly difficult and sensitive issue. Some appear to believe that all land in the Scottish highlands should be subject to a more or less compulsory purchase regime . . . . The Scottish Office is opposed to that approach. We believe that it is interventionist in character and that it assumes that corporate bodies are in a better position to determine how land should be used than

those directly involved [i.e. the lairds] . . . . [Any problem caused by land ownership] is essentially a private matter . . . best served by the removal of anti-competitive rules . . . . Ownership should be resolved within the framework of existing law. *Land ownership is not a matter on which I have a locus to intervene.* However persuasive the Hon. Lady is, I do not wish to adopt the mantle of paternalism in this matter.[4]

However, the local authority, the Highland Regional Council, took a very different line. Councillor Michael Foxley and his colleagues met with Tom, Bob and me. Afterwards, they signalled 'full political support'. An official wrote:

[The Council] determined to support the idea of community purchase and man-agement of the Isle of Eigg and would seek to assist this type of initiative by all available and practical means at its disposal . . . in collaboration with the Isle of Eigg Trust [as] the proponents of the initial concept.[5]

Announcement of a closing date for the sale of Eigg to comply with Mrs Williams' court order was now imminent. The island was being marketed through Savills, the top people's estate agent, but for some reason the usual bids from the seriously wealthy just didn't seem to be rolling in. It looked like market spoiling was working, for the expected closing date kept being moved back. Schellenberg was evidently in no hurry to clinch a deal with thin air.

Mischievously, I phoned up Savills to ask how it was all going. I said, quite truthfully, that I represented parties interested in buying the island – but not at the exorbitant asking price advertised. We were, I told the salesman, hoping that all the publicity surrounding the islanders' having backed the Trust might bring the price down. Was this, I wondered, a valid supposition? One Jamie Burges-Lumsden on the other end of the phone was very frank. He said:

This kind of thing could be done without – it causes buyers to be suspicious . . . because a buyer wants to be assured of having maximum control. Activity like this sets up a niggle in the back of the mind because future control could be compro-mised. . . . It worries private buyers and therefore could lower the price.[6]

Having now achieved the overt support with which to make a more credible fundraising pitch, we applied to the Government's National Heritage Memorial Fund. This was originally set up after the Second World War, sup-posedly to buy land for the people in just the way that we were attempting: but the upper echelons of the establishment under a Conservative government had now captured control of it. Our application was duly knocked back. Then, in early July 1992, the real bombshell dropped. A triple headline in the *West Highland Free Press*[7] summed it all up:

PARADISE LOST

Eigg back in the hands of Emperor Schellenberg:
Bitter blow to trust community stewardship dream

Astonishingly, and to the horror of most of his incensed vassals, Schellenberg had achieved the unthinkable. He had fulfilled the Court of Session requirement to sell the island, for the knock-down price of just under a million pounds. But the buyer was Cleveland and Highland Holdings – his very own private property company! Eigg had changed hands. The letter of the law (whereby a company is recognised as a distinct 'person' in its own right, and therefore separate from its owner, Schellenberg) had been adhered to. As an enthralled media put it, Schellenberg thereby became the first man ever to have 'sold and bought his own island'.

While initially disappointing, the dramatic effect of this was to galvanise a sea change in public consciousness. We had lost a battle, but it was only a tactical defeat. In public relations terms, and therefore in terms of carving out a political furrow, we were on a roll. And there was a further consolation. The *West Highland Free Press* also ran a smaller headline on its front page that day. It read: 'Assynt crofters forge ahead with estate buy-out bid'.

The North Lochinver Estate at Assynt had long been owned by the transnational meat baron Lord Edmund Hoyle Vesty. He had sold out to a Swedish investment company, but it had gone bankrupt. In a television programme on the subject, an Assynt community leader, Alan MacRae, identified the estate's history with that of Africans, Native Americans and Aboriginals. 'The land we stand on is in a sense the last stronghold of the native people,' he said. 'These lands really are the remnants of what the natives once possessed.'[8] This was great stuff. It was no longer only the Isle of Eigg Trust that was making links with native land rights worldwide. The ideas were catching on.

By December 1992 the Assynt crofters had raised £300,000, and, having driven the asking price down using similar market-spoiling tactics, they succeeded in bringing their land into community ownership. Later, Alan MacRae magnanimously told Tom and me: 'It's not widely realised that Assynt got its inspiration from Eigg. *That was the seed.*'[9] Similarly, Assynt crofter and academic Isabel MacPhail said that the inspiration of Eigg had 'raised again the issue of community ownership at a time when even the foremost proponents of the concept were in despair at the total lack of any progress'.[10] 'Really,' she went on to write in *The Crofter*, the newspaper of the Scottish Crofters' Union:

it is a bit like the end of colonial rule – gradually our imaginations are unchained. The rest takes a bit longer . . . . For me [it] has been a revelation. For the whole of my life people have been explaining Vesty's 'badness' to me: blocking development;

taking the mobile shop off the road (folk wanted to boycott his shops then, but where do you boycott to?); concentrating economic activity in his own hands ... and so on. And in all that time we never realised that if you point a TV camera at him, or give him a few column inches ... he'll do the job [of exposing the system] much better himself.[11]

Well, if Eigg had been the initial inspiration for Assynt, the people of Assynt certainly made a big contribution to Eigg. They helped us to refine our strategy, they affirmed the vision and visited Eigg to boost confidence at one of the low points. It was generous inter-community solidarity. But meanwhile, Schellenberg, on the face of things, was also full of magnanimity. After a debate between him and me on Lesley Riddoch's BBC show *Speaking Out*, he declared that he was going to meet with the islanders, hear their grievances, and commence a new relationship to be characterised by 'teambuilding'. Unconvinced, we dispatched him an open letter saying: 'Through wealth you may have re-won the legal title, but you can never own an island's soul.'[12] The Eigg Trust, we promised, would remain 'a trust-in-waiting'.

It took until April 1993 for Schellenberg's new face fully to reveal itself. One day Marie Carr, a daughter of the indigenous Kirk family, was presented with a lease for just two years on their farmhouse at Kildonan. Schellenberg's 'embarrassed' factor explained that this would give the family of seven time to move into her mother's farmhouse over at Laig, on the other side of the island. It marked the betrayal of what the Carrs had thought was a twenty-five-year tenancy agreement on Kildonan. 'It was as if our mother never existed,' said Marie's sister, Fiona Cherry, 'as if Laig was not her home at all, after thirty-six years there!'

Four months later, the Carrs came back from their first-ever family holiday to find that Schellenberg's men had removed the 450 lambs that Marie's husband, Colin, had reared and prepared for sale. Under the terms of an earlier agreement with Schellenberg, he had understood that these were meant to pay his wages. A little later, Colin saw his job as farm manager advertised in the newspapers, and a letter arrived, telling him not to go near estate livestock or machinery. In addition, Schellenberg talked about starting up his own wildlife trust to raise money for nature conservation. This caused the resident Scottish Wildlife Trust warden, John Chester, to fear for his future too.[13]

Early in the morning of 7 January 1994, flames were seen pouring from a garage down by the pier. Rapidly being reduced to a molten heap of scrap inside was the rare 1927 Phantom 1 Rolls-Royce shooting-brake with which a resurgent Schellenberg had earlier told the press he planned to make a 'triumphal tour of the island'.[14] As the *Sun* headline put it: 'Burnt Eigg Rolls'. The cause of the fire was never determined. However, heady and not always pleasant energies were starting to attach themselves to the land-reform cause, helped by the national politicians' complete abdication of governance on the matter. I was not the only one to receive a letter from the subsequently disbanded extreme patriotic group *Siol nan Gaidheal* – the Seed of the Gael – condemning us for working in ways that were inclusive of English incomers. 'Be careful, Mr McIntosh,' ended the letter from their 'Cultural Sub-Committee – National Security Department – Specified Aliens Section': 'Be careful, Mr McIntosh, that your accessible, inclusive, participative, tear-stained "idealism" doesn't trip you up.'[15]

There was a growing danger that passions might run out of control. On Eigg itself people were increasingly able to talk openly about events. However, many other Scottish communities suffering abuse were less fortunate. Anger often festers beneath outward peace and calm and this can create explosive tensions. After all, the whole nation can have a laugh when a laird like Mohamed Al Fayed claims to be 'well loved' on his 65,000-acre Highland estate and tells the *Daily Record*: 'I feel like your Lawrence of Arabia, in reverse. I am Mohamed of the Glen.'[16] But often only locals find out when a tenant farmer's lease is not renewed, or a family is evicted for not running out to open the gate for the laird's Range Rover, or a crofter is told to pay for seaweed gathered to fertilise a potato patch. Such events build up groundswells of anger. How it expresses itself and who takes up the cudgel can be unpredictable. The danger of extremist groups capitalising on frustration born of bad governance is very real. Such considerations made it all the more imperative that land reform be addressed at a political level. It was an issue not just for isolated little places like Eigg, but for the whole nation.

While Eigg residents protested their new-found faith in spontaneous combustion, Schellenberg, the English laird with a German name, blamed the fire on insurrection sown by revolutionary English incomers! He accused his former staff of stirring up revolt and thereby destroying the indigenous Hebridean way of life. He reckoned they got their inflammatory ideas from dancing at 'acid rock parties' and rolling their own cigarettes. This prompted a remarkable open letter signed by representatives from nearly every indigenous household on Eigg. It said:

> We, who have been born and brought up on the Isle of Eigg, would like to refute utterly the ludicrous allegations about the community here, made by Mr Keith Schellenberg . . .
>
> The island has a small but united population of local families and incomers who are between them struggling to develop a community with a long-term future against the apparent wishes of an owner who seems to want us to live in primitive conditions to satisfy his nostalgia for the 1920s. If the nature of the island has changed it could be said to have something to do with the fact that all of the local men working for the estate during Mr Schellenberg's first years of ownership have

left, taking their indigenous way of life with them. They and their families have found good jobs and a secure future across the water . . .

The incoming islanders play an active, caring part in the community. They help run the senior citizens' lunch club and meals on wheels, they drive the community minibus to enable those without transport to get to the shop or attend church, and have organised a Gaelic playgroup so that their offspring will have a chance of learning Gaelic in order to preserve the traditional culture of the island.

It is hard to see what could be and can be gained by painting such an inaccurate picture of an island community and we write to you to set the record straight.[17]

The emergence of strong indigenous leadership on Eigg was now apparent for all to see. People were overcoming their reservations about speaking out. In February 1994 Lesley Riddoch went to the island to broadcast her *Speaking Out* programme. Schellenberg was brought face to face with the community. Lesley later told me that 'getting everybody to start talking was the most difficult piece of radio I've ever done'. However, Schellenberg showed no inhibitions. Asked if he would not consider selling to the community, he replied, 'I would be pretty weak and wet if I did consider it.' The islanders, he said on air, in front of them all, were not sufficiently responsible to run their own affairs. The room erupted. A woman's voice cried out: 'In the past we've never had the chance to prove we were responsible people, we've never had the chance to do it.' For Camille Dressler, documenting Eigg's history, this programme was like the Road to Damascus. She later wrote me a letter, picking up on the ideas of Isabel MacPhail of Assynt, saying:

The anger which was released in the BBC *Speaking Out* programme really unchained minds. By being given for the first time the physical possibility of confronting Schellenberg, people were able to affirm their collective opposition. From that moment onwards his power was gone. His power was only resting on the fact that *he* had a voice and we had none. When the Trust arrived on the scene and told the islanders that it could be what *they* wanted it to be – then you became our voice, and that allowed us to find our own in time.[18]

By the early summer of 1994, that time had manifestly come. Tom, Bob and I accordingly, and gladly, offered to resign our roles. We wrote to the Residents' Committee formally offering to stand down and hand the Trust as a legal entity completely over to the islanders if they were ready to have it. But what might have been an easy decision for them was, in a final twist, made very hard.

The three of us went up to the island to have a community meeting in the tea-room. We had expected the process to be just a formality, but there had been further developments. As the meeting started, it was announced that

Schellenberg had phoned one of the women present the night before. He had allegedly asked for it to be made quietly known that if the islanders took over the Trust, he would refuse to sign papers granting permission for the construction of the old folks' sheltered housing.

I took a remarkable photograph of this meeting. Two features are striking. One is that the residents are gathered round a table overflowing with McEwans Export cans. As it happens, this was the last such formal gathering to be so lubricated. Thereafter it was decided that alcohol was no longer needed to loosen frozen tongues, and would be kept until after business was over. Secondly, the picture reveals an inner circle of women, surrounded by the men.

More and more it became apparent that the campaign on Eigg was being driven forward, in no small measure, by its womenfolk. Men were making most of the outward public statements, but women were central to the inner process of major decision-making. At parties and in the general banter of life, jokes were being cracked about the legendary 'Big Women' of Eigg having come back. It was a joke not without cultural antecedent. The great Scottish folklorist Hamish Henderson considers that in Celtic culture there is a 'hidden world of matriarchy . . . exercising power indirectly'. Colonisation, he believes, destroyed traditional male role models. 'It was the "women's world" which stood in with all its spirit, courage, and resilience, when the "man's world" faltered.'[19] Two of my students from the Centre for Human Ecology, Dan Morgan and Ayala Gill, undertook important fieldwork on Eigg. Dan enjoyed many a good party, contributed many ideas about participative democracy, and gained a PhD. Ayala undertook a much shorter MSc study but, interestingly, reported women agreeing: 'It's no longer the women who are disempowered here; it's the men.' The same has been said of many other parts of the world.

The conclusion of the tea-room meeting was unanimous. The old folks would never forgive the younger ones if they deferred to landed power. New ways forward had to be grasped. Accordingly, the island would warmly accept taking over full responsibility for its Trust. Elections would be organised forthwith.

The new trustees comprised equal numbers of women and men. Six of the eight places went to island residents;[20] half of these were native Gaelic speakers. One place went to Lesley Riddoch. I had also been asked to stand for election by the Residents' Association and was duly voted in to continue advocacy from the outside. Later, Maggie Fyffe was elected secretary, replacing the island's physician, Dr Chris Tiarks. After doing important and greatly appreciated pioneering work, he had decided to lay down his role in the wake of a threatening letter from Schellenberg's lawyer. Close liaison with the Isle of Eigg Residents' Association was ensured by such leading figures as Colin Carr, Mark Cherry and Karen Helliwell.

The handover of Trust deeds to the community took place on 16 July 1994. Fiona Cherry was appointed chair of the new board of trustees. Standing deliberately and symbolically just below the high-tide mark on the pier (this being outwith the laird's territorial domain), she read out the Trust's aims as drawn up by islanders on its new steering committee. These were:

> To secure the Island for Scottish and global heritage, to be run in the interests of the community allowing security of tenure and sustainable economic livelihood. To encourage continued growth of the cultural heritage and maintain and improve the built environment whilst conserving the ecology of this unique and beautiful island so that it may be enjoyed and shared by all.

Schellenberg declined an invitation to attend. The BBC broadcast him saying:

> I am not interested in supporting what I regard as a communist and childish takeover and certainly I see it as my duty for as long as I'm able to resist these daft efforts by some layabout publicity seekers.[21]
>
> I know there's been a lot of talk about a sort of commune there using funds from the taxpayers' estate; I mean, this seems to me completely like a return to 1797 [sic] and the French Revolution, but it doesn't do the wildlife any good . . . . Anybody coming in to the island would have to *co-operate* [his emphasis] with the islanders. Well, this is sort of shades of *Mein Kampf* and 'Come back Adolf, all is forgiven.'[22]

In an effort to repair the breach in the dyke, landed power pulled out its polished Purdies, only to shoot itself in the foot with both barrels. Debating with me on BBC Radio 5, Christopher Bourne-Arton, a council member of England's Country Landowners' Association (now euphemistically renamed The Country Land and Business Association), tried to defend the notion that the lower orders needed the patronage of their social betters. Seemingly confusing the community costs of running an estate with the cost of running a private sporting enterprise, he haughtily told the British people:

> Don't forget you need an awful lot of money to run a Highland estate . . . . You either own a Highland estate or you run three Ferraris, six racehorses and a couple of mistresses – I mean, the costs are much the same . . . . The Highland estate is never going to pay for itself. It is going to need constant capital input year after year. Who else is going to do that [but the wealthy]? Are you suggesting that we taxpayers should do that?[23]

All remained surprisingly peaceful in the weeks immediately afterwards. It looked as if Schellenberg had either been misinterpreted over his alleged threat to sabotage the old folks, or he had recanted. Indeed, it was not until

October that the time bomb went off. One morning both John Chester, the long-term resident warden of the Scottish Wildlife Trust, and the Carr family opened their mail to find a two-line letter from the lawyers. It ordered each of them to 'remove' by 31 December. Their homes, it seemed, were required for unspecified imperial purposes. As the Carrs had five children, these evictions would affect 12 per cent of the island's population. It looked like Christmas was going to be spent packing.

The timing of the letters was, from Schellenberg's point of view, impeccable. The news broke just a little too late for journalists to catch the weekend ferries. As that meant the newspapers couldn't get up-to-the-moment pictures, the story would be relegated to inside pages, somewhere among the slimming tips. However, Sir Maxwell, Lesley Riddoch and I could see that what he'd just scored was a colossal own goal. It couldn't be left to slip through the net unapplauded. So we pooled our resources and chartered a fishing boat over to the island. It cost £160. But we got the pictures delivered in the nick of time to the *Herald* and the *Scotsman*. Both ran the story as their page-three Monday-morning main hard-news story. Neither were the people of Eigg backward in coming forward to speak their minds. It was evident that if these eviction orders remained in place, it was not going to be easy to implement them.

The islanders were by now getting well into the stride of running their own Trust and using it as a soapbox. Schellenberg was still fulminating that he would never sell the island, but, unofficially, everybody knew that it remained on the market and was stuck there. Fundraising events and feasibility studies proceeded apace. T-shirts were printed, a logo designed, letterheads made up, and souvenirs promoting land reform were eagerly snapped up by well-wishing tourists in the shop.

Schellenberg carried on with his carry-on, like a naughty child, much heard but rarely seen. Really, Horace the dog spoke best to the situation. There he was, captured on Channel 4, yapping away in an open-topped vintage car and snapping impetuously at a pesky swarm of flies.

The Eigg islanders were now running a shadow-government-in-waiting. They no longer bothered asking the laird's permission to meet in the tea-room.

18. Stone Eagle to Fly In

'Can I speak to Sulian Stone Eagle Herney?' I ask, when the receiver lifts on the other side of the Atlantic.

'You got him,' says the cavernous voice in Canada. It's a confident tone, but there's a hesitancy; a gruff suspicion.

Some people call him straight Billy Herney. He'd been given that name at a white-run mission school. But like many native people, he prefers his Mi'Kmaq name – *Sulian* being the Mi'Kmaq for William. And 'Stone Eagle' is a special name – one, perhaps, to discover the meaning of.

'I'm phoning from Scotland. You won't know me, Mr Stone Eagle,' I say.

I'm not quite sure how to address him, but this application of 'mister' seems to carry due ceremonial weight. There's a certain collision-of-cultures humour about it too. Only later do I learn that, actually, this was *Warrior Chief* Sulian Stone Eagle Herney. Under the 1752 Treaty with the British, the Mi'Kmaq had retained sovereign territory rights. Accordingly, some of them have, since 1987, resurrected their warrior society, and its members had appointed Stone Eagle to be its paramount leader. By considerable paradox, and not without some reassurance for my own Quaker pacifism, the Grand Council of Chiefs (the Mi'Kmaqs' traditional governing body) had, in parallel, appointed him to oversee Sweat Lodge purification and healing ceremonies; he was also a Sacred Pipe Carrier, which gave him a spiritual role in maintaining community cohesion. These contrasts were, to say the least, intriguing.

'I was urged to contact you by Professor Alesia Maltz,' I say. 'Also, I spoke with your wife last month when I was doing a North American lecture tour. You weren't on Cape Breton at the time. But Leon Dubinsky took me to the cave on Kluscap, the sacred mountain. I got your wife's permission. Swam into it from a boat. Sat awhile there.'

'Who are you?' Stone Eagle asks, suspicion growing. 'What's your business?'

'I'm told that the late Grand Chief Donald Marshall put you in charge of stopping Kelly Rock from superquarrying Kluscap,' I say. 'Well, I'm one of the people fighting the same kind of development here in Scotland. I'm also working on native land rights in the Hebrides. Look, I know you don't know anything about me or our cause over here, but I'm calling to ask your help.'

'What do you know about me and who told it you?' he demands. He said later that he was running the permutations through his mind. Was I a private investigator from one of the corporations whose nose he got up? Or a New Age crank? Or a media set-up? Or a government spook?

'I know little more than what Alesia and Leon told me. That you direct the First Nations Environmental Network. You're involved with land rights all over Canada. That you witnessed armed conflict when serving under the Mohawk Warrior Society at Oka in 1990 when some rich folks tried to turn that native cemetery into a golf course. That . . .' I hesitated, deliberately to build effect, 'that . . . quite a few white academics warned me off about you when I was in Canada. Said you were "too radical" – "puts people off his own cause" sort of backbiting banter – but then, they were too much fair-weather liberals for my comfort. Seemed to me they'd never been much exercised with anything that challenged their values.'

'They warned *you* off about *me*!' he explodes. 'Am I meant to be *dangerous* or something? Look!' he says curtly. 'Tell me what your business is. Straight up. What are you wanting?'

I explain that in a couple of months' time, autumn 1994, the British government's public inquiry into the Harris superquarry will open. I play up the fact that Ian Wilson has attributed the coming about of this substantially to the interventions of me and Ian Callaghan. I do my best to explain that I'm working with a theological analysis. 'You see, in our culture we don't have a concept of mountains being "sacred" like you do,' I say. 'But I tell you, if you felt this place, if you talked with some of the native people who live around it, if you experienced the sense of human presence that goes back to when the icecap first melted, then you'd know that this mountain is special. You'd be convinced. You'd feel that this island is too good to let the bastards rip it up.'

'Look,' he says again, 'I admire your cause, but I've got a dozen other land-rights issues happening in First Nation territories here. I can't just drop everything and come to a territory that I don't even know. My priority's with my own people.'

And I know that I'm losing him. The connection's breaking up and it's not because he's on a mobile phone. He's the right figure for the job, but I'm failing to get through because somewhere in myself I'm blocked. I'm being limply ineffectual. Sure, I'm putting my case rationally, and that's the conventional Western way, but it just isn't good enough.

I reckon I've one last volley to go before he hangs up. If we're going to get anywhere, maybe we need some passion; some poetics. There's nothing to lose, I suppose. Should I be outrageous and go for it?

'Look . . .' he comes back with a weary impatience.

'Look! You look, Mr Stone Eagle!' I shout down the telephone. 'This one's big time. This one's different. Do you know where the people behind your superquarry came from – names like MacAskill and Kelly? They came from places like the Hebrides and Ireland in the Celtic world. Over here. They got pulled like weeds from their own land and transplanted onto yours. Don't you see? We're both from superquarry-threatened communities. We're both from communities that were fucked over, yes, *fucked over*. They cleared the native people and now they're wanting even the rocks.'

Silence. Long silence.

OK, so it was over the top, intemperate. But, damn it, this was the only chance. Too rough to go slow. And if that meant leaping over potholes the size of mountains, over an ocean, then what's to be lost?

'And I'll tell you another thing,' I come back at him, passion growing. 'I know you only by reputation. But your totemic names are *stone* and *eagle*, right? Well, this mountain is about *stone*. And *eagles* nest just 400 metres from the planned quarry boundary. The eagle is my totem too. And I tell you too –' and I swallow at the brazenness of the outrageous conviction that's whelming up. 'I tell you, Mr Stone Eagle. *The eagles request you to come and help us.*'

It's a very long silence. Quite expensive too, on a transatlantic phone call in those days.

'OK,' he answers slowly, with ceremonial deliberation. 'When do you want me to fly in? What do you want me to do?'

Credited with having said that 'Adam was a crofter and only the Fall gave us landlords', the silvery-greying and smartly besuited Reverend Professor Donald Macleod defied any stereotype one might have of Scotland's most radical, controversial, hated and loved Calvinist theologian.

The Free Church of Scotland to which the professor belongs is one of several faces of Highland Presbyterianism. It's the one for which old Murdo had sung as precentor in some of its post-Disruption general assemblies. Radical in its origins, especially on the need for land reform, it now maintains an austere front; and yet you need only experience the warmth of many of its adherents to see that the basic message of 'love your neighbour' is deeply alive. Many of their beliefs can be portrayed as antique, but even their pronounced views on, say, keeping the Sabbath as a day set aside to punctuate a busy world with rest and reflection, can find fresh relevance when contextualised by Professor Macleod. He calls the Sabbath an 'employment protection measure' and argues, convincingly, that it protects the vulnerable from what has, beyond the Outer Hebrides, become a twenty-four-hour, seven-days-a-week industrial whirl with no space for collective composure.

I'll never forget the time I went into Edinburgh's Free Church College, where the professor is now principal, and joked with one of his students that it felt like stepping back into the seventeenth century. Fixing my gaze, the young clergyman said with a twinkle, 'We would prefer to think that it is more like the first century.'

I'd been driven here by my telephone encounter with Stone Eagle. Here I was, facing Professor Macleod on the other side of a book-heaped desk – its authority imposing between us like a flat pulpit. A newspaper profile had said of this man: 'A liberal in the Free Church of Scotland is someone who believes that women can be admitted to church not wearing a hat . . . . Prof. Macleod's fundamental beliefs . . . would mark him out as a dangerous fundamentalist in almost every other branch of the Christian church.'[1]

Oh well. Ho hum.

'So, Alastair, I hear that you are quite a wild character yourself,' he said as I sat down, his wry smile suggesting that wildness was a characteristic with which he was not entirely out of sympathy.

Ho hum. For some reason I had this expression running though my mind. It made an amusing counterpoint to the formality of the circumstances. Of course, it would have been a very relevant expression too, I am sure, for the circumstances of Professor Macleod. Opponents of his radical preaching had attacked him so fiercely that he must have been forced to entertain a few doubts about his fondness for a theology of 'realised eschatology' – the Luke 17:21 view that Heaven is, in some sense, present in the here and now. Precisely such a paradox between the idyllic and brute daily reality was captured by a popular T-shirt back in my Papua New Guinea days. Printed on the front was a palm-fringed beach and on the back: 'Ho hum – another shitty day in Paradise.'

But back to the professor.

'Wild? Yes. So I've heard,' I replied, 'But I have to confess that my own version is more of a pagan-leaning Quaker variety than a Calvinist one.'

Quakers, as it happens, have a long history of what is called 'working under concern'. A 'concern' arises when a Friend, as Quakers call themselves, derived from John 15:15, feels led by the inner Spirit, hopefully that of God within, to take on some act of testimony, witness or work. The trepidation of being so moved can literally make the body shake – hence the originally derogatory nickname 'Quaker'. In theory, such prompting of the 'Holy Spirit', that 'spirit of kindliness' as John Smith of Lewis called it, is recognised by all branches of Christianity. But in practice, Spirit-led theologies nearly always cause discomfort to church hierarchies. The Religious Society of Friends has therefore been unusual throughout its three-hundred-year history. In Britain the 'peculiar people' who comprise it have moved from an era of strict austerity to modern participation on such frontiers as interfaith work, the creative arts, justice and peace campaigns, and even, in some meetings, the celebration of relationships other than heterosexual marriages.

Quakerism, like the professor's Calvinism, embraced what might be termed a radical orthodoxy.

'So – a Quaker with a Calvinist background,' the professor mused, knowing that I had originally grown up within the established Church of Scotland on Lewis. 'Oh well, I don't think we'll be holding that too much against you.'

I smiled to hear the Hebridean 'we' instead of 'I'; the professor was someone whose sense of self was grounded in community and not just individuality.

'But, you know,' he continued, 'judging by some of your writings, I think you'd rather enjoy John Calvin. Very rational, you see.'

'Yes, I fear as much,' I said.

'So tell me,' he said, 'how did you come to bring theology into the superquarry inquiry?'

'By reading your own columns in the *West Highland Free Press*!' I quipped.

We both laughed. The flattery was contrived to a sufficiently blatant degree as to loosen things up, but it was not without truth.

'Seriously,' I added. 'It's partly to do with the way in which you've been arguing for a resurgence in Highland liberation theology. And specifically on the quarry question, I'd picked up on comments you made when sharing a platform with Prince Charles at the 1993 Scottish Crofters' Union conference. If I read between the lines rightly, you made veiled criticism of the scheme. You saw it as exploiting people's alienation from their land, from the Creation.'

'And how did you come to bring that into a government planning inquiry?'

'The inquiry's remit includes cultural factors,' I said. 'It seems to me that in the context of Hebridean culture you can't avoid looking at the theology behind such a development. Of course, it would be nice if the churches were doing that as part of their business. That way, people like me could avoid the discomfort of folks saying, "Who the hell does he think he is?" But as you'll know, the churches are limiting their concern only to whether or not the quarry would work on a Sunday. I've been round all the Harris ministers. They're hamstrung about the quarry, whether they want to be or not. Their own memberships are divided on it. They can't push the issue any further than saying, in effect, "It's all right to destroy God's Creation, provided you only do so between Monday and Saturday." And at least one minister believes that the quarry would be a good thing anyway. It's the jobs.'

'So what did Miss Pain think of your proposed case?' he asked.

Miss Gillian Pain was the senior Scottish Office inquiry reporter. Single-handedly, she would have to gather all the evidence in an antiquated British administrative procedure that relied on one person's work and judgement to give government ministers crucial advice.

'Well, she was good enough to listen. I presented it in the light of the World Council of Churches' concern for the "integrity of the Creation".'

'And she accepted your argument? She agreed to its inclusion?'

'Yes,' I chuckled. 'If she hadn't, I was ready to challenge how come the very doors of the Scottish Office have an inscription of Jesus's emblazoned across them: the one about being "fishers of men".[2] And then there's the constitutional point like you yourself have made – that the very basis of British sovereign power is represented as deriving from "divine grace" via a supposed "Defender of the Faith". You know: the letters DG and FD on all British coins – that kind of pomp and circumstance. And then there's Lord Stair saying that the bottom line of Scots law is "divine law", with Blackstone throwing in something similar for the English.[3] So she couldn't very well disagree that God has a bearing on British law! It's in the nation's constitution. But I must admit, I chuckled inwardly because the Church and the political establishment have prevented these things from being much recognised and used in the past. Yes, I chuckled right enough! The pre-inquiry meeting was such a deadly serious business in its setting-out of the terms of engagement. We all of us, all the interested parties, sat round a huge oval table in the Scottish Office, and there was me begging permission to bring theological testimony as deadpan as a kirk elder. The learned lawyers for Redland looked like their poker faces would crease up – it was so medieval, so ridiculous-sounding!'

'And Redland let you away with it? They didn't object?'

'Not at all! In fact, I'm given to understand that they think I've shot myself in the foot. I mean, there was me, previously making hardcore economic, cultural and ecological arguments against the quarry – the sort of thing that public inquiries are meant to be about. And all that was probably a bit of a threat to them but nothing that they couldn't outwit by paying the odd professor here and there to testify against. Then what do I do but go and disqualify myself from consideration as a serious runner. I rule myself out from being taken seriously alongside such stalwarts as Kevin Dunion of Friends of the Earth and the Scottish Wildlife and Countryside Link team. I go orbiting off into bizarre spiritual arguments that, given how Redland see the world, nobody in their right minds would give credence to. And what with Stone Eagle's participation, the company executives looked like they reckoned it would be good for nothing more than their own entertainment.'

'Indeed,' the professor said knowingly, as if he was almost inclined to see their point. 'And what would you like my role to be?'

I explained that I had in mind to make a submission that would operate at both psychological and spiritual levels. It was aimed in several directions – towards the voluntary organisations, the planning authorities, the councillors, and the Government; but above all, towards the community of ordinary people in the Hebrides and their church leaders.

I said that I fully recognised that not all my aims were ones to which the professor would necessarily subscribe. The Quaker understanding of consensus is not to seek uniformity, but to find points of unity around which people can unite. It was my hope that, on at least some objectives, he, Stone Eagle and I could find mutual accommodation. The aims that I had in mind were:[4]

- To stop the ripping apart of the Earth, both on Harris and elsewhere, wherever that extraction is thoughtlessly undertaken for greed rather than vital need. The basis of using natural resources should be *reverence*: profound respect for the Creation.
- To explore the use of liberation theology in Scotland, particularly in heightening awareness of the bond that exists between people and the land. This bond is central to advancing social and ecological *responsibility*.
- To do these things in a way that builds understanding of what 'sustainable development' really means. Sustainability, in biblical terms, means to 'keep' the Earth for 'as long as the Earth endures'.[5] Geologically, our four-billion-year-old planet is only in middle age. It can be expected to remain capable of supporting life for maybe as much as another four billion years, until the sun goes into supernova. That should be our requisite human-planning horizon for living sustainably on this planet.
- To encourage Calvinist Scots, whose theology has tended to focus upon a transcendent otherworldly God, to reflect also upon the *immanence* of God: the presence of God in this world as expressed through ongoing creative process.
- To understand the history behind oppression, disempowerment and poverty that knocks on from one generation to the next: the roots of intergenerational poverty. That is to say, to explore a spiritually informed cultural psychotherapy. This could be revealed, I hoped, by comparison between disempowered Scottish communities and North American native reservations.

'So that's why I'm moved to ask your help,' I told the professor, 'and why your voice is important in this inquiry. Stone Eagle's presence will be attractive to the media. His message will speak about the alienation of indigenous peoples from the land on both sides of the Atlantic. But he and I on our own can't cut the heavy theological ice. To do that we need a heavyweight. We need at least a loose association with you.'

'You know I'm not popular in some of those heavyweight theological circles, don't you?' he said, cautiously.

'Of course, in the same way as Jesus warned that those who carry the cross will always be unpopular,' I replied. 'It's what you yourself once wrote – something to the effect that not every non-Christian will be "crucified" in our modern society. But every Christian most certainly will be. You see, I'm not worried about your unpopularity. You know better than I do where the church is a mere dead hand. I'm interested in stimulating the places where life can come alive. I'm interested in taking from our culture's past those elements that offer future strength. And that's what Redland is giving us the opportunity to do. It's like the company are saying to the Hebrides, "Well, if you're that much of a graveyard, we'll just walk in and carry the place away." No wonder some of the old folk on Harris are saying that the quarry would be a "judgement from God". They see the nature of the beast that they're up against. And that's why I'm asking you to stand with us. I do believe this quarry demarcates the frontline of corporate idolatry.'

I paused. The preacher was being preached at.

Then I leaned over the desk and faced the Presbyterian professor square-on. 'So, would you be willing to make a platform of the three of us at the inquiry? I know it will be difficult for you. I know you'll get shot at. I know that you'll be uncomfortable with some of the theology of Stone Eagle and myself. But I also know that you'll see the points of unity and,' I thought, echoing the Syrophoenician woman's challenge to Jesus on the need not to keep exclusive company, 'remember that even "dogs under the table eat of the children's crumbs".[6] So will you, then, help us to present a spectrum of theological testimony?'

The preacher smiled gently, warmly and with a profound dignity. I suspect that he was bemused by my protestations more than impressed, but he had sympathy, and wanted to stop the people of his native region from getting walked over.

'Very well,' he answered. 'When will it be?'[7]

19. The Womanhood of God

Donald Macleod had already seen the draft of my own testimony. I had published it as a detailed letter in the *Stornoway Gazette* to draw out any local objection or protest at theological error.[1] None had been registered. Indeed, privately, businesses and local people who felt they could not speak openly gave me encouragement and even some £500 to help with costs. 'You have my blessing,' I was resolutely told by one native of the village of Lingerabay, which the quarry threatened with partial annihilation. That was important, especially in a community where blessing, as distinct from more formal permission, has real meaning.

The cornerstone of my side of the argument was to be *reverence*: profound respect for the Creation. 'Reverence,' I would conclude at the public inquiry

> is concerned with the integrity of a thing or person; to value it for itself; to work with it symbiotically, in celebration of its being, with that grace which is consistent with the 'saying' of grace, and not with a graceless spirit of mere utility. The superquarrying of Roineabhal at Lingerabay would be theologically justified only if it can be undertaken reverentially; if it can be felt as part of the movement of love. It would mean enquiring whether government have considered reappraising national transportation policy to minimise the need for further motorway construction . . . recycling used rock otherwise dumped in landfill sites . . . [and] assessing whether [new quarries] are best located in National Scenic Areas, or at sites already despoiled by industrial activity. I would hold that these considerations have not been addressed by proponents of the Lingerabay quarry. Proceeding would therefore inexcusably violate the integrity of Creation.[2]

If the superquarry was the presenting symptom of a more general malaise in the world, the wider focus as far as I was concerned was Christian culture. Much post-Reformation theology on these islands, indeed, much church teaching in many parts of the world, has been necrophilic: obsessed with death and what would happen thereafter. And this, it seemed to me, was not a healthy understanding of death. It was not about seeing the darkness as soft soil from which new life can grow. Rather, it was the outcome of a fear-driven, victim-blaming, dominator-wins history. It was a politically constructed churchianity rather than the spiritual dynamics of cosmic love that Jesus actually taught.

Yes, people in the past had often suffered heavily. Culloden and the Clearances had cut deep. But what made it all doubly wicked was that, like the worst forms of Hindu karmic retribution, people had often been persuaded that their suffering was their own fault.[3] They had internalised victim-blaming. Scotland's 1712 Patronage Act, which gave landlords the power to appoint clergy, was only one symptom of a long political process that colonised the soul and so made colonisation of the land easy. Here, and more widely in the world, the Powers that Be had long since learned that to wield the sword effortlessly with one hand, you pick up the cross, or the crescent, or the Star of David, or whatever, with the other. The one cuts externally; the other, abused to the point where it can be beaten soft into secularism, crushes internally.

Seen in this light, liberation theology is the liberation of nothing less than theology itself. It was precisely for such liberation that figures like Jesus, the Hebrew prophets and Mohammed (peace be upon him) stood – if we can find the sympathy within ourselves to understand them in their cultural and historical contexts. When it is said that Jesus came to bring liberation from 'sin', we maybe need to understand that internalised bonds of oppression, including the oppression that living in unjust relationship brings upon ourselves, were precisely the bonds that his message of forgiveness sought to break. As the Hindu–Catholic scholar Raimon Panikkar says, 'Only forgiveness breaks the law of karma'.[4]

It was precisely to turn hypocritical religion on its head that Jesus repeatedly attacked the temple authorities, with their airs and graces and their fancy titles. They were 'whitened sepulchres . . . a nest of vipers'. The Roman Empire generally allowed indigenous freedom of religion, but it colluded in suppressing Jesus because he didn't quite fit their version of the 1712 Patronage Act. He caused people to think too deep and to feel too strongly. Similarly, we today must be careful about dismissing true religion – the work of growing collectively into love. We must be careful about rejecting spirituality just because religion, as its social expression, speaks so powerfully to the human condition that it inevitably attracts those who seek to hijack and co-opt it. As a Sudanese student told me, 'In our country we have a saying: The brighter the light, the darker the shadows that gather around.'

The eighteen evicted families of Glen Calvie are a powerful example of spiritually internalised oppression. Huddled into a village graveyard while waiting for an emigrant ship to come in 1845, they etched on the windowpane of Croick Church, there to be seen to this day: '*The people of Glen Calvie, the sinful generation.*' It was Professor Macleod's grasp of such psychohistory and his determination to promote change that contributed to his being such a significant and controversial reforming theologian. It was these factors, too, that enabled him to appreciate the full spiritual depth of the superquarry debate. 'I represent the Church,' he was to say in a 1995 sermon commemorating the Glen Calvie Clearances.

> I confess that it instilled a spirit of resignation which went far beyond Christian humility. I confess its guilty silence. Like the German Christians under the Nazis, the clergy of the Highlands failed to open their mouths for the dumb. That is a guilt which I feel [together with] the lawyers and their clerks, the police and the bailiffs, the politicians and the journalists. All were willing coadjutors in our Holocaust . . . . Never again, if we can help it, will our land see such injustice . . . . Above all, let us resolve to undo the damage, to stem the haemorrhage of people from our Highlands, to reinstate our lost culture and to bring back under our own stewardship and protection those straths which violent hands stole from us.[5]

The same world-denying pie-in-the-sky-when-you-die theology of deferred gratification that allowed those mouths to stay closed was still commonplace in the Highlands of the twentieth century. As one Harris minister of religion told me in a discussion about the superquarry: 'Our concern is with salvation and not with the matters of this world.' It was a belief in a God up there, transcendent, rational, domineering and dispassionate (except when angry), like a fearsome feudal king – or perhaps like a projected absent father figure.

As I deepened my teaching and understanding of human ecology in the rich environment that Edinburgh University provided, I felt a profound sense that to relegate the spiritual to the realm of otherworldliness was no longer adequate. True enough, humankind may be stuck with the hardware that evolution has given it. Our brains may, in many respects, be hard-wired. But that doesn't stop us from constantly upgrading the software. Indeed, that's what culture is for: culture is the social software. And if the spiritual work of an activist is, as I was being drawn to conclude, shamanic, it will involve stepping outside of existing social programming to glimpse a wider panorama and new options. It will involve seeing or being shown where consensual reality has become dysfunctional. And it will then mean stepping back into the 'world' again, to sound the alarm, to nourish growth and to point towards cultural healing. As such, the deepest social activism must draw the spiritual constantly back down to Earth. Equally, such activism must draw the spiritual up, so to speak, from a ground-sense with the Earth. The 'above' and 'below', the transcendent and the immanent, need to be connected along a common axis – along what mythology calls the *axis mundi* or 'axis of the world'. This is where fresh creativity reaches consciousness. We have already seen this demonstrated by the Highland bard whose poems ran down from the eaves of her blackhouse, and by the Persian Sufi poet whose pillar, of course, symbolically connected 'Heaven' and 'Earth'.

In coming to know the cultural ground that we dig, a key observation is that the Western mindset comprises two interwoven strands. It is essential to understand these if we are to know ourselves. One is the Hellenic strand, represented by the Greek philosophers and Greek influence on the New Testament. The other is the Hebraic strand, coming from the biblical tradition of the Old Testament. (Of course, to our Jewish friends there is nothing 'old' about it; but allow me to go on, speaking from a Christian cultural context.)

The Hellenic way of looking at reality, in the footsteps of Plato and Aristotle, is broadly rational and empirical. It works by logic and leads to the refinement of scientific truth and explicit order. It sees objective principles, such as atomic theory, as the bedrock of reality, and it understands time as marching on in a linear progression. The Hebraic way, by contrast and as a generalisation, is mythic and poetic. It works by elaborating story and parable to portray poetic truth, implicit order. It accepts mystery or 'unknowing' as the bedrock of reality, and it understands time as dream-like and cyclical. This does not make the Hebraic 'irrational,' but it could be said to be 'arational' – something other than rational alone.

The difference between the two might be demonstrated like this. Consider the question: 'What is love?' Go to the academy and ask a modern representative of Hellenic thought – Richard Dawkins at Oxford University, say – and you might get a response like: 'Love is a biologically evolved neurochemical stimulus by which the selfish gene mediates its own replication.' Now, this would be a response from the *logos* – the principle of reason, the principle of strict causality that gives order to the universe. On the other hand, ask the same question of a Hebraic sage, and you might be told: 'Holy, Holy, Holy!' It's like when Moses asked God who 'He' was, and God replied (with block capital letters in most translations): 'I AM THAT I AM.'[6] That's *mythos*. Pure poetry – acausal and non-linear to the point of self-referential circularity. Very Zen. And some thinkers would say there's a third way of knowing that is poorly developed in either the Hellenic or the Hebraic mainstream. This is the way of *eros*. The *eros* reply to the question might be: 'Love, and you will know.' It's all in the experience. As such, it falls outwith the range of either discourse or narrative.

The issue is not that any one of these mindsets is necessarily wrong and another invariably right. The point to grasp is that each represents a different facet in the totality of knowing. The Hellenic is more inclined towards the exteriority of reality as approached through reductionist analysis using the head. And the Hebraic inclines towards the interiority of things as perceived by the heart. Ultimately, however, such *logos* and *mythos* polarities are a false dichotomy. They ought not be split apart. It is as if *mythos* is the landscape on a dark night, knowable only in dreams and visions; and *logos* is a penetrating torchlight by which the traveller might illuminate the next few steps, but not the totality of the journey. Their separation, according to Raimon Panikkar, is at the root of many of our troubles today. In defending the place of myth in a world of reason, he says:

> A myth is something we believe in because we take it for granted . . . . [It] makes the understanding understandable, the reason reasonable . . . . A myth defies a further foundation. It is beyond any possible definition, because the myth is the horizon which makes the definition possible. The *mythos* cannot be separated from the *logos* . . . . [Such is] the irreducibility of Reality to an intellectual principle . . . . [This] is the explanation why to impose our *concept* of peace does not bring Peace [because] the nature of peace is grace. It is a gift.[7]

The rational mind, if bereft of the soul's touchstone of beauty that poetry offers, may come to know the world with great precision, but at the cost of fragmentation. The butterfly of *mythos* is crushed by the holding. It will not tolerate the disrespect of too much prodding and dissection. By contrast, however, if the poetic mind is stripped of *logos*, it will lose its co-ordinates. It will lose its sense of proportion, of the ratio, of order – and so readily fall prey to fanaticism, demagoguery, neurotic nostalgia and chaos. That is why we need both *mythos* and *logos* together. Indeed, we need the driving passion of *eros* too. It is what gives us the motivation to get things done. In total then, holistic human involvement in life requires the heart, head and hand. Set out like this it seems pretty obvious. So why is it, then, that we do not see more of a self-evidently good thing in the world around us?

The answer, I think, rests substantially with Plato and the philosophical hero about whom he wrote, Socrates. Socrates seemingly lived in an era when the balance between *logos* and *mythos* was swung in the other direction, and *eros* was considered suspect. He saw rhetorical skill being abused by politicians and lawyers (his hated Sophists), and believed that reasoned argument was the path to justice. However, Plato was living two-and-a-half millennia ago. He was living in a military city-state based on aristocracy, patriarchy and slavery. His sense of what justice meant was very different from ours. To him it meant a regimented 'right ordering' of society whereby everybody kept their place in a militarised feudal system. The problems that he identified and his solutions are therefore not necessarily fitting to our era. They have, however, left a considerable legacy. They have been engaged by Renaissance thinkers onwards to gentrify and legitimise Europe's ruling robber-barons, the monarchies, with neo-classical formulations of learning, honour and glory. The Renaissance was precisely that: a renaissance of Greek and Roman ideals that were, underneath it all, imperial ideals; and this was what fuelled the early-modern mindset of King James.

Greek philosophy before Plato's influence had been very like much Eastern mystical thought. Heraclitus, for instance, taught that 'All things come out of the one, and the one out of all things'.[8] Most thinkers believed that reality was interconnected. Plato, however, split up this rather Taoist unitary view of things. He said that we should begin by distinguishing between this world, the Earth, 'which is always becoming and never is', and the philosopher's world of ideas, the eternal, 'which always is and has no becoming'.[9] We should turn our backs on this world, he urged, and spurn the body, because 'true philosophers make dying their profession'. Their goal is 'a freeing and separation of soul from body'.[10]

As such, Plato became the father of dualistic thought: the idea of a sharp split between body and mind, or Heaven and Earth. This is important for environmentalists to understand, because although Plato was acutely aware of environment degradation in his times,[11] parts of his philosophy reinforced the idea that we can legitimately cut ourselves off from this world.

What is damaging about Plato is not that he demonstrated the power of reason, but that in certain key texts he placed *logos* above, rather than alongside, *mythos* and *eros*. It is reason, as he saw it, that leads the soul to God. Accordingly, he urged that those arts that stir up passion, especially poetry and music, should be censored.[12] The ideal state or republic should only permit arts 'which will fittingly imitate the tones and accents of a man who is brave in battle . . . who, if he fails, or sees before him wounds or death, or falls into any other misfortune, always grapples with his fate, disciplined and resolute'.[13]

Here we see a template of stiff-upper-lip leadership. By requiring censorship to shut out other ways of knowing, it was totalitarian. It entailed exerting control over the psyche. And so the backbone of Plato's politics developed: that 'no man, and no woman, be ever suffered to live without an officer set over them'.[14] The upright citizen would be led into the ways of God by aristocratic philosopher-kings who were to be kept genetically robust by eugenics, fed only on roast meat ('Homer never mentioned sauces,' Plato quips), schooled in philosophy and sport from childhood at elite schools so as to become 'warrior athletes', expressing their homosexuality Platonically, and worshipping, in effect, at the church of reason.[15]

In the course of all this, Plato deftly makes sure that God as the 'maker and father of this universe' takes the show over from God-as-Goddess.[16] Some of the ancient Greeks had, after all, been rather fond of cults expressing what Bertrand Russell's *History of Western Philosophy* called 'a curious element of feminism' that 'husbands found . . . annoying, but did not dare to oppose'. Some Bacchic cults even involved large companies of women dancing in mystical ecstasy on the hills all night, rejecting prudence, intensifying feeling, and generating enthusiasm – a word that means, we might remember, 'being filled with God'. In the end, however, the Greeks (according to Russell) 'were saved from a religion of the Oriental type' as well as from the rustic spirituality of their Eleusinian mysteries. It was 'the existence of the scientific schools,' Russell concludes, 'that saved Greece'.[17] In other words, the triumph of *logos*.

In these ways the ground was perfectly laid for opening the ideological doors of Europe's Renaissance nearly two millennia later. During that time Rome had come and gone. It had fallen, we might note, substantially due to 'barbarian' or, one might say, anti-imperialist and substantially Germano-Celtic tribes. In the 'Dark Ages' that followed, learning was kept alive in Celtic Ireland and Scotland, on that western edge where the Romans had scarcely penetrated, and the later Normans would never leave behind much more than the odd castle. It was from the Celtic fringe, from the sixth century onwards, that learned monks communicated knowledge back into the courts of Europe. From its foundation in the mid-twelfth century until the Reformation in the sixteenth, the Sorbonne, the great university of Paris, had as many as eighteen Scottish rectors. Similarly so with Scots colleges that were set up in various other European cities. Some of these scholars returned home and, in turn, established the Scottish university system with its distinctive emphasis, as was traditionally the case, on holistic, generalist, internationalist and communitarian thought. This was the famous Scots principle of the 'democratic intellect' – the notion that while knowledge inevitably creates specialists, the value of that specialism will be fully disclosed only when its inevitable blind spots are put to the test in real-life service and accountability to the community.[18]

So what went wrong? What caused mainstream Western thought to turn its back on the holistic approach and to abstract the rational from its rightful mythic and erotic context? A significant part of the answer probably lies in what Karl Popper called the 'spell of Plato' – in Plato's ability to present authoritarian aristocracy as being necessary for the rational ordering of society.[19]

The values underlying a 'good classical education' must, as aforementioned, have been only too comforting for Europe's medieval robber-barons, caught between secular expediency and the Church, as they fought to consolidate their monarchies. As such, the Renaissance can be seen partly as a gentrification of feudalism, one that led to early modernity's Enlightenment or 'Age of Reason'. Reason, and its gift of scientific method, facilitated many positive developments. But it also rapidly advanced military strategy, weaponry and naval technology – all prerequisites for conquest. Furthermore, a Trojan horse accompanied Greek thought. Classical mores carried with them archetypal principles. These were the gods of Homer and associated warrior ideals – ideals that provided the emerging ruling classes with a legitimising frame of reference a world apart from Christian nonviolence. For the Homeric gods and heroes, like the European elites themselves, were a conquering aristocracy. As Gilbert Murray says in *Five Stages of Greek Religion*:

> The gods of most nations claim to have created the world. The Olympians make no such claim. The most they ever did was to conquer it . . . . And when they have conquered their kingdoms, what do they do? Do they attend to the government? Do they promote agriculture? Do they practice trades and industries? Not a bit of it. Why should they do any honest work? They . . . conquering chieftains, royal buccaneers . . . find it easier to live on the revenues and blast with thunderbolts the people who do not pay.[20]

Continuity between classical warrior cults and later European empire is evident in much imperial propaganda. One example, drummed into generations of British schoolchildren, is 'The British Grenadiers' – a song adulating the macho qualities of throwing grenades:

> Some talk of Alexander, and some of Hercules,
> Of Hector and Lysander, and such great names as these,
> But of all the world's great heroes,
> There's none that can compare,
> With a tow, row row row, row row row,
> To the British Grenadiers.

All this took place under (and remains under) the banner of a British state; a state that rests its constitution on a monarch purporting to be 'Defender of the [Christian] Faith'. But interestingly, the Hebraic God was never very happy with the idea of the early Israelites having a this-worldly monarchy. Was God alone not sufficient as their king? A human king, God warned them, would inevitably become a feudal tyrant. He would, according to Samuel, 'take your sons and appoint them to his chariots' and 'take your daughters to be perfumers and cooks and bakers'.[21] How prescient! But the Israelites didn't listen. They wanted to have the trappings of every other tribe and those trappings trapped them.

Renaissance classical thought may have helped us, today, to have become 'modern', but it did so by underpinning a Christendom that could justify wielding the sword in one hand and the cross in the other, with a cruel eye on the compass to navigate the way. As the rest of the world awaited crusade and inquisition, the gift of peace on Earth remained elusive. Suffering humankind could but wait, and watch all points of the come-to-pass.[22]

When you realise that you're powerless to navigate overwhelming seas, just keep watching all points of the come-to-pass. Try neither to sell out nor burn out. Don't yield to addictions or distractions; remain fully present, painfully conscious, but alive to what is happening. That way you can watch for the cracks that will inevitably appear in the Domination System, and you will be ready to intercede. That way you might even get some laughs.

Consider the monolithic Plato. 'The safest general characterization of the European philosophical tradition,' Alfred North Whitehead famously said, 'is that it consists of a series of footnotes to Plato.'[23] Inasmuch as this is true, it is so because Plato is actually so contradictory that it is often more revealing to observe what is *selected* of his teachings than what he actually said. Yes, there is the totalitarian Plato who we have just reviewed, and who frequently has been used to justify authoritarian social structures. But there is also another side; one that is overgrown and overlooked by the mainstream groves of Western thought. A side that is, however, powerfully relevant to ecology. We find it most strikingly in Plato's *Phaedrus*.

In this text, Socrates is persuaded by Phaedrus to take a day out in the countryside. The barefoot philosopher is reluctant to go. 'You must forgive me, dear friend,' he says. 'I'm a lover of learning, and trees and open country won't teach me anything, whereas men in the town do.'

However, on arrival in a secluded glade, Socrates, his senses now opened, is deeply impressed. 'Upon my word,' he enthuses, 'a delightful resting place, with this tall spreading plane, and a lovely shade from the high branches of the *agnos*. Now that it's in full flower, it will make the place ever so fragrant. And what a lovely stream under the plane tree, and how cool to the feet!'

The two thinkers have, as it happens, come to a sacred grove. 'Judging by the statuettes and images I should say it's consecrated to Achelous and some of the nymphs,' says Socrates. 'In fact, my dear Phaedrus, you have been the stranger's perfect guide.'[24]

An enthused Socrates then moves on to describe himself as 'a seer'. He tells his friend: 'The greatest blessings come by way of madness, indeed of madness that is heaven-sent.' And this includes, he admits, 'rapt passionate expression' in lyric poetry.[25] Tellingly, he associates such an alternative way of knowing with women – with the ministry of prophetesses and priestesses. Elsewhere, in expounding 'Platonic love', Socrates names one of these as Diotima of Mantinea. He says: 'It was she who taught me the philosophy of Love.'[26]

As the two men prepare to return to the city, Socrates, who once likened the philosopher's art of birthing ideas to his mother's profession of midwifery, or *maieutics*, prays aloud:

Dear Pan, and all ye other gods that dwell in this place, grant that I may become fair within, and that such outward things as I have may not war against the spirit within me. May I count him rich who is wise, and as for gold, may I possess so much of it as only a temperate man might bear to carry with him.[27]

What we find expressed in Socrates if we look hard enough, then, is a holistic approach to knowledge; one in which 'sense of wonder is the mark of the philosopher'.[28] But it was mainly by getting out of the human-made city with its socially constructed realities, and into the natural environment, that Socrates could learn to see and smell the world so richly. And look at how he resisted, at first, going into the wildness with Phaedrus, into the realm of nymph and faerie! That's the trouble with the rational mind, and why it can be so censorious of passion as it wrestles to maintain its precious control. It 'panics' that if Pan gets a look in, 'pandemonium' will break out. It clutches on to order, to the seeming stability of gold. It gets bewildered by Pan's challenge to these things in drawing attention to God's providence in nature. That is the significance of the Prayer of Socrates. It reminds us that we cannot worship both God and Mammon. It warns that placing confidence in outward riches will only undermine the faith needed to build inner wealth and experience the fruits of providence.

By overemphasising rational Hellenistic roots, the Western mind has unwittingly damaged its capacity to appreciate Hebraic thought and other more mythopoetic approaches – approaches like the Celtic mind and, indeed, the erotic side of Socrates. The malestream Western mind has tried to apply reason to stories, such as to the Genesis creation myth, or to the parable that is the life of Christ, and in so doing did not realise that its tools were the wrong ones. It was like trying to explain a space rocket through scientific principles contained in the Psalms. *Mythos* thereby became incredible rather than being the reference frame for laying out the parameters of what is actually credible. Bereft of poetic knowing and the emotional engagement of feeling, the rich and warm metaphorical meanings that can be discerned in the Holy Scriptures and other sources of wise story have withered. Singled out on its own, *logos* itself has dried up from lack of a nourishing context, becoming a desiccating parody of what passionately fired-up reason could actually be. This was why the early Quakers called the Devil 'the Reasoner': it was precisely because of 'his' propensity so very cleverly to miss the point! The erotic nature of authentic relationship with God got lost as the light of reason was forced into its mystery. Biblical writings that testify to the spiritual erotic, like the Song of Solomon and Chapter 7 of Luke's Gospel, consequently fell into that treasure-filled backwater of passages about which few sermons are ever preached. The very *passion* of Christ's empathy in solidarity with the world got overlooked. Devoid of meaning, and disabled in the capacity to feel, the modern human being ended up too often characterised, as we have seen, by anomie.

And so cue Nietzsche: 'God is dead. God remains dead. And we have killed him.'[29] In God's place 'the Superman lies close to my heart . . . . He is my paramount and sole concern – and *not* man: not the nearest, nor the poorest, not the most suffering, not the best.' So it was that Nietzsche prophetically testified to (or did he believe it all?) the culminating idolatry of the modern project. He identified the question at the heart of a world that had become blind to love incarnate in the scent of a flower, in the song of a bird, in the touch of a moist kiss. It was the question that Nazism, like other supremacist ideologies predicated on violence, would answer in its own utterly vacuous way, namely: 'How shall man be *overcome*?'[30]

This, then, is the central spiritual issue of our times. How can we invite and accept the spirit of life back into our world? In the words of the Lewis bard John Smith, where can we find that Holy Spirit – that 'arrow of the Lord' – with which to pierce 'the skin of surly selfishness'?

For me, then, and I cannot speak for Professor Macleod or Stone Eagle on this, the underlying aim of testimony in the superquarry public inquiry was to appeal for a theology of immanence. It was to add passionate fuel to a growing shift in Western thought. The superquarry was only a presenting symptom of the Powers that lay behind it. The bigger hole in the ground, or rather, the hole in reality, was the Western mind's tendency to behave as if 'man and his environment' were separate, thereby allowing destruction to be carried out without realising that it was, ultimately, self-destruction.

For these reasons I felt impelled through my public-inquiry testimony to remind people of the Celtic triple union of community with one another, with nature and with God. The Earth, says Matthew 5:35, is the 'footstool' or 'resting place' of Christ, and so must not be abused. In particular, I wanted to focus on Jesus's words in Luke 17:21, where he affirmed a this-worldly realm of God that is 'within' or 'among' us. I wanted to draw out the sensuality of what the Orthodox tradition means when it says, 'the Church is the world transformed into the body of Christ and vivified by the Spirit'.[31] And I wanted to remind people, at least in my Hebridean home community, of the rich nature spirituality of Genesis 1, Job 37–9, Psalms 104 and John 1; a spirituality that knows God to be panentheistic – as being present in this world – as well as being transcendent.[32]

And as for any suggestion that these were dilettante concerns, in Matthew's gospel alone there are eight occasions when Jesus goes off up the mountains to teach, pray and find composure of soul in solitude.[33] Native peoples often pick up these points much more readily than do Westerners. I was struck by some words of Guboo Ted Thomas, an Australian Aboriginal:

The special places are usually in the mountains . . . . Jesus himself went up into the mountains to pray, saying to his disciples, 'You wait here.' . . . You can knock down a church and build it up again and it remains a sacred place. But an Aboriginal sacred place is made by the Master . . . . Aboriginals do not even set up stones to make any spot sacred. Certain significant, beautiful rocks are enough – as Nature put them there – to call a place a cathedral. Such a place is made by God, not by human hands like a big church in Sydney.[34]

But as the date of our appearance at the public inquiry drew near, I found myself wrestling inwardly over the wisdom of speaking on a religious platform. The tactical strength of such testimony was evident. The media would love it. But the deeper theology to which I was trying to give expression was hard and sometimes embarrassing to articulate. Christianity had done so much damage in the past, including damage to nature.[35] Would we be better off junking the whole thing? Better off Buddhist? But if we did discard Christianity, would we not need to reinvent much of the same story? And could we knowingly follow a Buddhism of integrity without engagement with that most exemplary of Bodhisattvas, Jesus Christ? Certainly, the Siamese Buddhist scholar and activist Sulak Sivaraksa would say not. 'If our Christian friends would extrapolate Christ's teachings on love and morality,' he writes (indicating that he has no problem with the concept of 'God' where it is a mystical understanding), 'we would have a lot in common.'[36] Jesus was persecuted because he challenged traditional values: he disowned his own mother and, yes, brothers; accepted the sensual love of a 'loose' woman; was considered to be a crazy healer in league with the Devil; engaged in direct action against the powers of money and religion; and was suspected of being mad or a drunkard. You don't hear much about these incidents, but they're all in the Bible.[37] Is this the kind of man that we, who might purport to be social activists, should abandon simply because the same sort of people who might set out to frame us have also, over the past two thousand years, done a pretty good job of framing him? Should we deny one of the likes of us just because adversaries have managed to put the cringe factor on him?[38]

Gradually, I found myself coming to accept that what I was working with was more than just a tactical campaigning device. Ecodefence was, in a manner that people like Guboo Ted Thomas could perhaps understand, an act of worship. It demanded a deepening of my own spirituality. Often that felt like taking a step and not knowing if the ground upon which it would fall would be solid, then taking the next step out of nothing more than confidence that the last one had not broken the ice. Sifting spiritual gold from the superquarry's gravel became a new imperative. It required watching all points of the come-to-pass and learning to see a new panorama – a Pan-orama; a new worldview. It required, in Quaker parlance, being prepared to follow peculiar 'leadings' to avoid casting God in an image that was too small, too conservative. Chief among these was integrating the femininity of God.

> The reason why the hairs stand on end, the eyes water, the throat is constricted, the skin crawls and a shiver runs down the spine when one writes or reads a true poem is that a true poem is necessarily an invocation of the White Goddess, or Muse, the Mother of All Living . . . . Houseman offered a secondary test of true poetry: whether it matches a phrase of Keats's, 'everything that reminds me of her goes through me like a spear'.[39]

So said Robert Graves; and in writing about the superquarry, in writing many of the passages in this book, I came to know that feeling. I knew that watering of the eyes; that spear; aye, that 'arrow of the Lord'.

There is a body of philosophical insight known as 'ecofeminism'. It equates what Carolyn Merchant calls the 'death of nature' with the rise of patriarchy – the domination of 'male' power structures over both women and nature.[40] By insisting on representing God as 'He', most organised religion bolsters patriarchy; indeed, it is a primary source of patriarchy's power. It plays Plato's game of downplaying the femininity of God. It venerates death and neglects life.

The glee with which Ian Wilson had described turning Roineabhal into one of the biggest holes ever to be made felt to me like an incomparable assault on the Earth. The equivalent of six atom bombs in one place is quite some violence, and the more I pondered this, the more I found myself drawn to exploring ecofeminist dimensions of the Bible.

There are, of course, the standard textual references in the Bible to the spiritual feminine: the fact that Genesis describes the 'image' of God as being both female *and* male;[41] the two references in Job 38 to God having birthed nature from out of the 'womb'; and St Paul's remark that in Christ there is 'neither male nor female'.[42] But perhaps the most powerful material comes to us in the person of an Old Testament figure known as *Hokmâ* in Hebrew, or *Sophia* in Greek. Indeed, as every PhD student or 'doctor of philosophy' doubtless realises, it is from her Greek name that we derive the very word philosopher – *philo-sophia* – meaning, of course, 'lover of the Goddess of Wisdom'.

'Woman Wisdom', as she is sometimes called, first appears in a body of Old Testament material called Wisdom Literature, particularly in Proverbs, Ecclesiastes, Job and, implicitly, in the magnificently erotic Song of Solomon. Theologically, she is identified with the Holy Spirit, our 'spirit of kindliness'.[43] Both the Hebrew word for Spirit, *Ruah*, and the Hellenic *Sophia* are feminine gendered. Here is a very beautiful passage from Proverbs 8, 2600 years old, in which she describes herself:

The Lord created me at the beginning of his work,
the first of his acts of long ago.
Ages ago I was set up,
at the first, before the beginning of the earth.
When there were no depths I was brought forth,
when there were no springs abounding with water.
Before the mountains had been shaped,
before the hills, I was brought forth –
when he had not yet made earth and fields,
or the world's first bits of soil.
When he established the heavens,
I was there,
when he drew a circle on the face of the deep,
when he made firm the skies above,
when he established the fountains of the deep,
when he assigned to the sea its limit,
so that the waters might not transgress his command,
when he marked out the foundations of the earth,
then I was beside him, like a master worker;
and I was daily his delight,
rejoicing in his inhabited world
and delighting in the human race.
And now, *my children*, listen to me:
happy are those who keep my ways.
Hear instruction and be wise, and do not neglect it.
Happy is the one who listens to me,
watching daily at my gates, waiting beside my doors.
For whoever finds me finds life
and obtains favour from the Lord;
but those who miss me injure themselves;
all who hate me love death.[44]

No wonder few sermons are preached about this passage. To the patriarchy it
is terrifying. What could speak more clearly to the Domination System than,
'all who miss me injure themselves; all who hate me love death'? So what is
the full spiritual significance of Woman Wisdom?

One way to answer that question is to look at what has emerged from theologies that overlook her: from those mindsets of the cold and religious that
focus on death and on the graven image of a transcendent male deity, divorced
from the idea of God's immanence in nature and community. That mindset,
as we have seen, has distinct classical roots which propelled it into
Christendom from the Middle Ages onwards, but it also came from a Hebraic

mythopoetic direction in some of the Old Testament stories, where we find God portrayed as a figure to be simultaneously loved and feared; a God who, astonishingly, may even broker deals with his old buddy the Devil, or so it seems.[45] This God required sacrificial propriation of his easily roused anger. The cornerstone of piety was not so much to be God loving, as 'God fearing' – a feature that developed particular potency in the Highland Church. I have asked Hebrew scholars if the verb translated in the Bible as 'to fear' really does mean that, and, sadly, I am assured that it does.

To understand the appeal of the God-fearing approach, it may be helpful to observe a core human response to a dominating power: namely, that it is common for the oppressed to come to love the oppressor. The evolutionary psychology of this is readily understandable. Quite simply, if you side with the oppressor, if you become a part of his or her retinue, then your immediate chances of survival will probably be higher. It's a case of bowing to the principle that 'might is right'. The integration of love and fear that this invokes was the principle by which the medieval feudal family extended itself and, indeed, by which empires could be controlled by small elites using terror as their ultimate sanction. But respect born of fear can also be seen in many commonplace contexts where justified authority may slide over the mark and into authoritarianism – in families, schools, workplaces and systems of land ownership. Indeed, we may find it wherever one person exerts disproportionate, illegitimate, unaccountable or unasked-for power over another. Sometimes it is called 'the Patty Hearst syndrome', after the heiress who came to venerate her kidnappers while being held for ransom. In her case, born into a superrich newspaper-owning family, there may have been some justification for coming to think that her captors had a valid point. But we also find many examples where that could hardly have been the case. For example, in Highland history the great bard Màiri Mhòr nan Oran, 'Big Mary of the Songs', herself having endured unjust imprisonment ('Prison is a fine college,' she wrote[46]), nevertheless found it hard to believe that the laird himself could have sanctioned her people's suffering. She reserved her invective, instead, for his servitors – for functionaries like Sheriff William Ivory, whom she likened to Satan. Interestingly, the child psychologist Alice Miller emphasises that one of the biggest obstacles to recovering from being raised in a dysfunctional family is facing up to never really having had the love that every family likes to think it gives – getting beyond the myth that 'our parents always loved us. Any ill-treatment was deserved and for our own good'.[47]

The Russian writer Mikhail Bulgakov, in his vicious allegory of the Soviet regime, traces compliance with evil to ordinary and eminently understandable human cowardice. 'Among human vices be considered cowardice one of the first,' he writes, '. . . because all the rest come from it.'[48] The end point of cooption by corrupt power, he suggests, is satanic. Indeed, the Black Mass (which Bulgakov uses to symbolise the core of Stalinism) represents love con-summated with evil personified. While Bulgakov's imagery might seem a little incredible to the Western reader perhaps not versed in the Russian fairy-tale tradition, his point that totalitarian terror demands loyalty to the point of love is important. As such, evil constantly puts real love to the test. Ironically, love grows in being proven in this way. Says the Scots poet Edwin Muir: 'But famished field and blackened tree/Bear flowers in Eden never known./Blossoms of grief and charity/Bloom in these darkened fields alone.' [49] To insist upon having love as one's god in the face of terror that would pull the psyche into the service of some lesser god requires the greatest courage. And there lies one of the central challenges of life. As the oil in the lamp of youth burns low in mid-life, new supplies must be found to ward off that dying of the light that is the onset of spiritual death. Either it comes tem-porarily from the route of cowardice, by tapping into energy from 'below' by means of retail therapy, addictions, and other false satisfiers; or it comes last-ingly from 'above', which demands exacting courage. It means that as we go through life we need to evolve from finding our satisfaction mainly in outer things and look, instead, to the inner life. This is why people who are not coming alive spiritually are dying, and become very boring.

It was precisely this exacting courage, to hold steadfast to God, that Jesus embodied. That is why we cannot ignore him. However, understanding him is not easy. Consider the meaning of the Crucifixion. Traditional Christian theology saw its function as having been to appease, once and for all, God's wrath at human wickedness. This remarkable 'doctrine of the atonement' makes out that God was so angry with humankind because of Adam's sin, yet loved His Creation so much, that He sent His son to be the blood sacrifice to appease His own wrath! Christ, as St Augustine puts it, 'was made a sacrifice for sin, offering himself as a whole burnt offering on the cross of his pas-sion'.[50] Well, if that's really how God operates, most folks might be forgiven for thinking that God should get professional help. These ideas derive mainly from Paul, the Church Fathers and later reformers, rather than Jesus's own words in the gospels. They derive from attempts by a patriarchal mindset to interpret tragic events within the constraining framework of their own world-view dominated by Roman imperialism. Unfortunately, the doctrine of atonement remains the diet of reactionary fundamentalist preachers. If the metaphorical Devil is watching all this, he must derive very great satisfaction from seeing religion so perverted.

One can, however, look at the Crucifixion in a very different way. It is that Jesus's plight drew a line under the sacrificial religious practices of his culture and time. Jesus, after all, was trying to transform the psyche of humankind, not that of God. The effect of his crucifixion was to say, in effect, 'Let's stop these barbaric sacrificial practices once and for all: take me, who will exact no revenge, then be done with it.' After all, he not only drove the money-changers out of the temple: he also fashioned a whip and drove out the sacrificial animals, thereby saving them.[51] By challenging the Law of Moses with its 'eye for an eye' retributive justice that would, as Gandhi said, 'turn the whole world blind', Jesus arguably sought to break the chain reaction of blood spilling more blood. By turning his own cheek on the cross and praying that his tormentors be forgiven, he demonstrated the power of love over the love of power. He showed that nonviolence can cut sharper than the sword. Confronted and refuted by such courage, totalitarian terror could no longer exert its terrible control. Death lost its sting. Life, if we are willing to let it, could be resurrected.

This is why, I think, an understanding of the cross is essential to the work of liberation. Similar understandings of divine suffering are found in other faiths, even if reactionary Christians would rather fit their God to the Bible than the Bible to God. These are truths common to the human condition because they are foundations of human psychology. It is not that the activist necessarily wants to be a Christian or a Buddhist or a Wiccan or a Ba'hai or however it is that God reaches out to their particular cultural and historical context.[52] Rather, it is that if your courage is really tested, if you are really exercised (which is not the same as the vanity of 'looking for martyrdom'), then you will unavoidably find spirituality speaking to you. Authentic spirituality offers the activist a very deep and practical strength. The point is that this strength, this courage, comes not from the ego, but from that of God (or the Goddess) within. It comes from innermost being. It comes from that depth of community where our individuality is transcended but not revoked, as St Paul so beautifully put it, in membership of one another.[53]

These reflections, incidentally, point to why it is that anti-Semitism is so profoundly anti-Christian. There may be much happening in present-day Palestine with which we can and should take issue, but to blame Jews for being the 'Christ killers' is to fall into the very pattern of recrimination that Jesus himself was trying to halt. To be anti-Semitic, or to be racist or unfairly discriminatory in any form is, in fact, to be one of the latter-day Christ killers: one of those who prevent Christ from getting down from the cross. The tough reality for the reactionary fundamentalist Christian is that Jesus stood for precisely those values for which the political right of the late twentieth century invented an expression of special ridicule: 'political correctness'. And so to the evidence of Christ's feminism.

It was women who anticipated the most radical political dimensions of what Jesus stood for;[54] women who financially supported his ministry;[55] women (some of them bleeding) who he touched and whose kisses, caresses, tears and anointing oil he accepted even though it caused him to be scorned and would have made him ritually unclean;[56] women he taught even when others thought they 'ought' to have been busy in the kitchen;[57] women who he defended from the death penalty for expressing their sexuality;[58] women who stretched his own thinking towards becoming ethnically inclusive;[59] women who witnessed his being denied;[60] women who stayed with him to the end after the male disciples had all let him down;[61] and women to whom he first revealed that death had no ultimate grip upon him.[62]

Indeed, Jesus's association with women goes very deep indeed. In Matthew 11:19 and Luke 7:35 he identifies himself, personally, with *Sophia* – 'Woman Wisdom'. Speaking of himself, and, furthermore, under circumstances where his persecutors are recorded as having thought him to be either drunk or mad, he concludes a statement by saying, 'Yet wisdom is vindicated by her deeds.' The authoritative HarperCollins Bible commentary remarks, 'Jesus seems to be identified with *wisdom*, though the latter was mythologized as female . . . thus *her deeds* are actually his.'[63] And then, at the end of Matthew 11, Jesus lays down his great invitation: 'Come to me, all you that are weary and are carrying heavy burdens . . .'. In so doing scholars consider him to be quoting Woman Wisdom from the apocryphal book of Sirach or Ecclesiasticus.[64] Indeed, the New Revised International Version of the Bible, probably the most scholarly translation, heads this section of the New Testament: 'Jesus as Wisdom's Spokesperson'. In other words, we might make sense of Paul's statement that in Christ 'there is neither male nor female' by suggesting that while Jesus was a man, the spirit that is Christ incorporates both genders. We might therefore be as comfortable calling Christ 'She' as 'He'; indeed, not to do so would technically speaking be blasphemous.[65]

Now, what is the relevance of all this to the Harris superquarry debate, to the imperative of land reform in places like Eigg, and to the wider global ecocide of our age? Why was it that I found radical ecofeminist theology to be so life-giving and so paradoxically affirmative in mounting a Christian defence of the integrity of Creation? I find it hard to put into words, but it has something to do with the manner in which understanding of the deity is localised around the world and that, as we have seen, the Hebrides of ancient times were considered to have been under the special care of Bhrighde. We saw, if you remember, that when Christianity first came to the Isles, Bhrighde's nuns were among those who grafted a New Testament on to that of the Old. We explored how veneration, or reverence – the opposite of sadistic domination, utility and control – has remained a cornerstone of Celtic spirituality. And we have seen, too, that Bridgit of the Isles became the foster-mother of Christ – a feature that is especially strong in the Scottish tradition.

What may not be immediately apparent is that the implications of fostership in a Celtic cultural context are huge. Fostership counts for much more than blood lineage, thus the Gaelic proverb: *Fuil gu fichead, comhdhaltas gu ceud* – 'Blood to the twentieth, fostership to the hundredth degree'. Also, 'The bonds of milk [nurture] are stronger than the bonds of blood [nature]'.[66] The principle at work here is profoundly biblical, and has huge implications, if we care to uncover them, for identity and belonging in the world today, where so many people find themselves without roots. That principle is that Jesus himself was the foster son of Joseph. It was to this alone that he owed his lineage in the House of David.[67] Without it, his claim to be who he was would not have accorded with Old Testament prophecy and the whole show would have collapsed.

Applying the cultural importance of fostership to Bhrighde, Alexander Carmichael writes:

> Thus Bride is called *ban-chuideachaidh Moire* (the aid-woman of Mary). In this connection, and in consequence thereof, she is called *Muime Chriosda* (foster-mother of Christ); *Bana-ghoistidh Mhic De* (the god-mother of the Son of God); *Bana-ghoistidh Iosda Criosda nam bann agus nam bean-nachd* (godmother of Jesus Christ of the bindings and blessings). Christ again is called *Dalta Bride* (the foster-son of Bride); *Dalta Bride bith nam beannachd* (the foster-son of Bride of the blessings); *Daltan Bride* (little fosterling of Bride), a term of endearment.[68]

The significance of Bhrighde's sometime designation, the 'Mary of the Isles', is therefore immense. As a foster mother, she could be seen in the Celtic mind as standing in parallel with the natural mother, the Blessed Virgin Mary – 'Mother of God'. Indeed, in the Hebridean tradition Bhrighde herself has been represented as being virgin-born, fostered by a father who, unjustly, was accused of raping her mother, who subsequently died in childbirth.[69] In recreating the Goddess Bhrighde as the Christian St Bride, the Gaelic Celts thereby did so in a cultural context that implicitly left her Goddess status intact. Bhrighde's place as an archetype of the spiritual feminine thereby becomes, in my view, a localised expression of the Old Testament's *Sophia* – the feminine face of God Herself. The little girl remembered in Hebridean folk tales for her kindness, wisdom and gaiety becomes, one might say, a localised incarnation of the Great Cosmic Mother.

And that, to me, is the deepest symbolism of *Innis Bhrighde* – the Holy Hebrides. These islands stand in the North Atlantic as a revelation of the fullness of God, the womanhood of God, in complementary counterpoint to the masculinity of God. They stand as a symbolic place on Earth, one that if we forget or neglect, we will come undone. They stand, as Hugh MacDiarmid said in 'On A Raised Beach', as stones that 'go through Man, straight to God', bare stones that 'bring me straight back to reality . . . The beginning and the end of the world/My own self, and as before I never saw/The empty hand of my brother man . . .'.[70]

We saw how, in 'Strathallan's Lament', Robert Burns depicted that empty hand as 'a world without a friend'. Strathallan's ability to enjoy the 'crystal streamlets' and the 'busy haunts of base mankind' had been ripped apart by war – the consequence of a colonial mindset within which, as *Sophia* diagnosed, 'those who miss me injure themselves; all who hate me love death'. Strathallan's dysfunction might in turn be diagnosed as an erotic dysfunction; a blockage in the flow of the cultural life force. It is a disruption of empathetic feeling caused by violence, by war, by exploitative trade and empire. 'You were in Eden, the garden of God,' said Ezekiel (clearly using Eden as a metaphor). 'You were on the holy mountain of God and walked among the precious stones . . . . But in the abundance of your trade you were filled with violence, and you sinned.' Similarly, in Revelation, the degradation and despoilation of the Earth is traced to the city in which 'Your businessmen were the most powerful in all the world, and with your false magic you deceived all the peoples of the world!'.[71]

What is it, asked the bard, that might pierce this 'skin of surly selfishness' of these our troubled times?[72] Only, he answered, 'the arrow of the Lord'. Only the 'spirit of kindliness' – the Holy Spirit; the Spirit that, as was said of St Bride, 'turns back the streams of war'. This is the spiritual feminine that men and women alike must integrate to find life.

Whatever might be the fate of Mount Roineabhal and its precious rocks; whatever the hideous consequences if men bulldoze up heathery limbs from tranquil sea and blast down into the crucible of the Earth, these are the thoughts that this island mountain invites in my mind. For a mountain, too, has its testimony. Like the Well of the Holy Women, it too will show us ourselves.

20. Return of the Salmon

Vivid images eddied and ebbed in bleary semi-consciousness as I began to awake that November morning in 1994. Stone Eagle was flying into Glasgow in a few hours' time to participate in the superquarry public inquiry.

But for now I was dreaming, and in the dream I'm back in the village, back in the Leurbost of my childhood. Across the road from our house is the river. That was where Alex George Morrison, Derek Maciver, Duncan Norman Macleod, Donald and Calum Ian Ferguson, John Neil Montgomery, Murdo MacLeod and myself, all of us from the New Holdings and Cameron Terrace end of the village, had gone fishing as boys.

I remember once, and this was no dream, the whole river turned to lemonade! Amazing, but true. An open-topped lorry carrying crates of mineral water had skidded on ice and crashed into the stream. For weeks afterwards, we boys were fishing out the spoils from deep pools. Oh to have been a fish when that happened! (Aye, and oh to have been a fish when small boys were safely displacing their energies from hooking trout to grappling bottles of limeade, red cola and American cream soda!) For several weeks one last bottle – ginger pop, I fantasised it as being – lay at the bottom of a very, very deep pool in all of 4 feet of water. We were only little, so little, but we tried everything we could think of to fish it out. Alex George and I even made strenuous efforts to train his uncle's little dog, Timmy, to dive down for us. After all, Timmy could fetch the newspaper from the shop, so why not? Eventually, and mercifully before it occurred to us to throw either Timmy or ourselves in, a big flood came. The bottle was washed away and never seen again. I expect that it now lies somewhere under Loch Leurbost, down by the mudflats at Crothairgearaidh where we'd go to gather mussels in any month that had an 'r' in the name. And who knows, maybe in a billion years' time some humanoid palaeontologist will crack open a bottle-shaped boulder and ginger pop will spurt foaming out, tasting every bit as good as it surely would have done that day of the Great Crash.

Beneath the house of Alex's uncle and aunt was an especially wide pool. When we were little, around 1960, it had been dammed to power a hydraulic ram pump. That same year, three salmon got stuck, unable to leap the wall of the dam to reach their spawning grounds. Somebody promptly speared them with a pitchfork. Never again was the noble fish to come that way.

And now in the dream this November morning I'm standing in our house. It's the big white house that served as both my father's surgery and our home. Beside me is Ulrich Loening, my boss at the CHE in Edinburgh University. With him is George Allan, Alex's uncle. George was a crofter and weaver of Harris Tweed. He and his wife, Kateag, had always treated me like one of their own children. But in real life George had long since passed away.

And as I'm waking up, I'm dreaming this dream and part of me is simultaneously trying to figure it out. I'm seeing that George stands for the indigenous way of life. Ulrich, on the other hand, represents the wider world and its global concerns. And I'm just watching from the window there, standing watching with these two fine men, when suddenly my son, Adam, comes running inside. He carries a willow basketwork creel, one just like they used to have in the old days for bringing in the peats. It's full of salmon, overflowing. 'Dad! Dad!' his little voice excitedly quivers. 'They've come back! The salmon are returning!'

We three men raise the binoculars that, conveniently, the dream had us wearing round our necks. And the lad's right. Amazingly, the stream is leaping, alive with the big silver fish returning from its epic Atlantic migration.

In Celtic mythology the salmon is a symbol of spiritual knowledge. It acquired its spots by eating the hazelnuts of wisdom. As I waken fully, I know that later today Stone Eagle and his partner and co-worker, Ishbel Munro, will be arriving in Glasgow, Scotland, having departed from New Glasgow, Nova Scotia. The link between Canada and Scotland could hardly be more graphic. Native wisdom was migrating back from across the Atlantic. Maybe this could help us to recover an ecological wisdom lost in Strathallan's despair. It might be too late for George's generation, for Ulrich's generation, and even for mine, but maybe not for Adam's.[1]

Iona was to be our first port of call. I wanted Stone Eagle to connect with the land, with the people. I knew that in the Iona Community he and Ishbel might see something at odds with what he had encountered at Canadian reservation mission schools, with all their physical, sexual and cultural abuse of native peoples. He might see a spirituality that would surprise him.

On the road to the Oban ferry, we stopped for lunch and to show solidarity at the Faslane Peace Camp on the Gare Loch. For many years this has stood in witness against Britain's four Trident nuclear submarines being docked there. The peace campers welcomed Sulian with his 2-foot-long pigtails, turquoise jewellery and stetson; they welcomed him with a large plate of stew – vegetarian stew.

'Don't you get *moose* here?' the Chief whispered to me. 'Indians eat *moose steaks* and *chickens* – not . . .' and he disdainfully poked his chick peas, his slow verbal gait grinding to a speechless halt. 'Look,' he said pleading as politely as a guest could, 'do you think you can get that message to them up north?'

We left to a farewell serenade of bagpipes. Sulian reciprocated with a tobacco offering – a type of blessing over the campers' fire. It was all very nice. But as we drove out on to the main road and headed west, a tension was fast building. We were going to go past the main entrance to the submarine base. As we reached the razorwire that ran along the side of the road, the tension broke.

'You have to be ready to fight and kill if the chips are down,' he said. 'A lot of our people are dying because of what's been done to them by the Government and the companies. Those chips are already down. That's why I attended the action at the Oka stand-off. That's why my peers made me War Chief.'

'Yeah,' I said, 'But how do you square that with being a Sacred 'Peace' Pipe carrier, Sulian? How can you justify the AK47 in one hand and that little suitcase with your Sacred Pipe in the other?'

'Damned if I know,' he admitted frankly. 'I couldn't figure it out. I asked an elder the same question.'

'And what did he say?'

'That everything is medicine and it is only when you misuse the medicine that it becomes harmful. And to the best of my knowledge, during the time I had to carry a weapon, I never once misused it. When we were surrounded by the Canadian Army, lives were saved by many of us who took part in the stand-off. That included our own lives. In the end, the elder told me, I'm the one who has to try and work out what having both these roles means!'

I laughed. Then he good-naturedly tried to provoke me.

'*Schnachans!*' he exclaimed. 'You should know that word – *Sccchhhnachans!* At least, that's what your Gaelic people on my territory called them when they'd hire us Indians to castrate their rams.[2] I'll tell you something about this Scotland: you've got no moose to eat, no land of your own – no wonder you've got superquarry problems, because you've got *Sccchhhnachans* only the size of chick peas!'

'You've got superquarry problems too,' I remarked wryly. 'What d'you think is going to serve that cause best? Running around Mount Kluscap with AK47s? And the Mounties looking on, just itching for an excuse to wrap a bayonet around your *Schnachans* – or making front-page stories in the newspapers because we've invited your Sacred Pipe over here? This is a theological witness, Sulian, not a war dance.'

'OK, OK,' he said. 'I've not come over here to cause you any offence. I'm just making an observation. I'm just saying that it's very difficult to soar with eagles when you're running with turkeys.'

I couldn't help but laugh. Yes, I could feel the magnetism of his way and he, just possibly, of mine. We were getting to know one another, getting each other's measure. The banter about *Schnachans* was a kind of sparring, a test-ing of one another's strength and character. He could see that I was worried about what the media would do with the warrior chief stuff, and there was entertainment value for him in my squirming! And I could see that his mind was much quicker than mine. He'd throw out jokes like frisbees and I'd not get them until half a mile further down the road. 'What's wrong with you?' he'd demand. 'I keep lobbing them over and you keep dropping them. Must be the lack of *Schnachans*!'

I was about to tell him my children's favourite dig. Question: 'How do you get Dad to laugh on Saturday morning?' Answer: 'Tell him a joke on Friday night.' But by now we had reached the high-security zone. The mil-itary base to the left of the main road was fortified with heavy coils of razorwire and observation posts commanded by armed guards. Part of me, I have to admit, was feeling a bit irritated with the teasing that had been building up already over the short time we had known one another. Sure, Sulian was trying me out. But I had other things on my mind: ferry schedules, accommodation, media coverage. Then, suddenly, as we drew parallel with the main entrance, I had a wicked idea. I'd done the likes of this before on demonstrations where we'd speed along in power boats, trying to penetrate military defences. It was a cat-and-mouse game and the military actually enjoyed it; it kept them on their toes. Sometimes, hardcore protestors, of whom I could not claim to be one, had actually boarded submarines. Sometimes they managed to undertake considerable 'disarming' work. Indeed, three years later a famous court ruling at Greenock would admonish three of my friends who undertook £80,000 worth of damage to a submarine-testing laboratory. Sheriff Margaret Gimblett was persuaded that they were upholding the international law on genocide.[3] But Stone Eagle didn't know about any such context. He didn't know that we were unlikely to be arrested merely for being bloody nuisances.

So it was that without saying anything to him, I deliberately missed our turning at the roundabout by the main entrance and drove straight up to the open gates of the base and right on through them. Inside was a security check-point.

I stopped the car and wound down the window. 'Good afternoon, officer,' I said, 'This is Warrior Chief Sulian Stone Eagle Herney of the Mi'Kmaq Nation, here on a diplomatic mission at the request of the indigenous peoples of Scotland. His rank is equivalent to Field Marshall in NAiTO. Yes, that's right. NAiTO.'

Sulian stared at me, aghast. Had he come to Scotland at the behest of a nutter? No *Schnachans*, maybe. Nuts were another matter.

'Yes, sir!' I said, to the young marine, evidently caught at the junction of bewilderment and bemusement. 'NAiTO. You know, the North Atlantic Indigenous Territories Organisation – that nonviolent direct-action military alliance of native peoples to effect counter insurgency measures against rapacious lairds, superquarry magnates, Trident nuclear submarines and other violations of native territory on both sides of the Atlantic. Now, would you be so good as to lift that machine gun out of our way – I do hope it's not loaded – and call your Commanding Officer, and tell him that the warrior chief he might have read about in this morning's *Scotsman* is here to INSPECT THE GUARD. I mean to say, officer, this installation is paid for with our tax money. Your C.O. couldn't possibly mind us bringing in a bit of overseas military-advisory capacity for the INSPECTION!'

By this time, a senior officer was on the scene to take over from his dumbfounded colleague. This, of course, was just another of those regular minor irritations that the military had come to expect from the Peace Camp. And after all, there is nothing in British law to stop one from turning up at a military base and asking to inspect the guard. If you're as polite as I was, you can, at worst, be refused.

'Come along now, sir,' the officer said. 'Back up now. Off you go.'

'Well, officer, I'd dearly love to – especially since we don't have any flowers to place in the muzzle of that gun of your friend's. But you see, there's now quite a convoy of vehicles queuing up behind us. Do you think that you and your men could very kindly go out on to the main road and stop the traffic, so that what's behind us can back up, then we too can back up? Don't worry – your missiles will be quite safe while you're conducting the traffic, because Sulian Stone Eagle Herney here is a war chief . . .'

'Just drive through and go round in a circle, then come straight back out,' yapped the officer, now visibly impatient.

So we drove into the base, turned a wide, wobbly circle, snapped a few photographs, gave the junior guards a bit of relief from boredom, and as we passed back out, I yelled, 'Peace to you all! Peace to you all!'

'So, Sulian,' I said, on what proved to be the *only* occasion that I ever managed to get the better of him. 'If landing you inside a nuke base isn't *Schnachans*, tell me what is?' And we zoomed off, rolling with the prankster spirit, having stopped, shall we say, at a Station of the Cross on our holy pilgrimage to Iona.

We reached Fionnophort on the Isle of Mull that night only to find the ferry stormbound. I was deeply disappointed. The Abbey had promised to arrange a Celtic creation liturgy on the theme of stone. Sulian and Ishbel, however, were relieved at the prospect of an early night in a bed and breakfast. And anyway, as Ishbel tactfully explained, when missionaries have made your childhood a misery, the idea of sleeping in an abbey is not exactly the stuff of sweet dreams. In Canada there are an estimated 105,000 survivors of child sexual and physical abuse from native reservation schools, many of which operated under supposedly 'Christian' auspices. Sulian was one such 'survivor', and the healing of a wounded child in a grown man's frame can be a long and faltering process. Some become drug addicts or alcoholics, as Sulian himself hinted he had once been. Others find death more meaningful than life, and, convinced that they can never be accepted and healed into the fullness of their potential humanity, they take suicide as a way out. Too many become, in turn, child abusers themselves. It is as if they get stuck in a pattern of relating sexually to others at the same age as when they themselves first got drawn into the cycle of abuse. The evidence suggests that a disturbing proportion of this latter group are people holding positions of power and leadership in society. They operate under an outward veneer of respectability that leaves behind an icy comet's tail of trust betrayed. Whole communities get emotionally cut up when the truth comes out, not least because, as many churches have found out to their crippling cost, such individuals were often known for living admirable lives in other ways. There are, however, a few remarkable souls who do rise above it all – but usually, as with many members of Alcoholics Anonymous, only after being faced with the full awfulness of what they have become and discovering, by some amazing grace, what it can mean for a human being to heal.

So, the storm that prevented us from reaching Iona Abbey that night was real, yes, but it was also metaphoric. It was also an inner storm, and given the buttons being pressed in Sulian, the weather was a blessing in disguise. There were many occasions such as this when Ishbel mediated culturally between me and the Chief. I started off thinking she had just come along for the trip, and that us guys could work out the business. But within a few days it was clear that the trip would never have happened without her. With Scots-Canadian family roots and Sulian as a partner, she understood both cultures from the inside out. Coming to Scotland had meant leaving her little daughter behind; that had been a sacrifice for them both. I hoped that the little girl would understand that this is what it can mean to have a mother who is, in a very real sense, an elder.

By the next morning, the storm had subsided. As we stepped on to Iona, Sulian was immediately rapt by the atmosphere and the kindness with which the staff of the Iona Community welcomed him. He was amazed at the respect apparent in the conservation of the stones. We walked up through the ancient graveyard, where both Scottish and Norwegian kings are laid to rest, and entered into St Oran's Chapel.

'I never knew you people had places like this!' he exclaimed, examining what looked to him like the Mi'Kmaq Star on a richly foliated grave slab.

'If you're into all this, then how come your people destroyed our sacred sites?'

'Well,' I said, 'I can only presume it's something to do with the way we lost our *Schnachans*.'

The next day we journeyed on to the Isle of Eigg. At the ferry terminal we were joined by a camera crew that had flown over for *Fifth Estate*, the Canadian Broadcasting Corporation's leading current-affairs programme. Meanwhile, the *Toronto Globe and Mail* had heralded the Eigg visit with a front-page headline proclaiming, 'Scottish islanders revolt against landowner: Villagers seek Micmac chief's advice to fight wealthy car salesman'. A welter of similar headlines about Eigg and the superquarry in the British press meant that wherever Sulian went, people now recognised him. He found the warmth of the welcome bewildering.

'How come these are the same Gaelic people who came over and did terrible things to us?' he asked me. 'How come you're the same people that took our land?' he inquired of his hosts, only half-jokingly.

'I've figured it out,' he told Eigg's luxury-taxi driver, Davey Robertson. We were revving and rattling away from the pier to enjoy the hospitality of an English incomer couple, Karen and Simon Helliwell. Theirs was pretty much an alcohol-free house. It was therefore a suitable place for Sulian to leave his Sacred Pipe and bundle.

'Figured what?' asked Davey. Here was a young man who'd acquired a few acres of croft land and learned Gaelic; said he'd rather raise kids in rural wildness and frugality than in the urban wilderness of Glasgow, where he'd come from.

'You Gaelics,' Sulian continued. 'I figure you sent all the bad ones over to us, but kept the good ones for yourselves!'

The ceilidh that night was held in the farmhouse of Colin and Marie Carr. They passed round the factor's letter starkly ordering them 'to remove' by Hogmanay. The atmosphere was drum-tight, but thrilling. Sulian was astounded to see Scottish people experiencing what his people had also undergone. Earlier on he had mischievously held up a souvenir from the burnt-out Rolls. He told the unamused Canadian camera crew: 'Hey – they got wagon-burners here!' I just shuffled around, looking embarrassed, muttering something about 'an Act of God, or so it is said to be . . .'

It was vital, he told everybody, to build solidarity in carrying out acts of defiance. Equally vital was a sense of *place*, and to unhook from drugs like alcohol, and for men to listen to and respect their womenfolk. That's what having real *Schnachans* was all about. That was how the First Nation peoples in North America were going about recovering their power and dignity.

Later, Camille Dressler's history of Eigg was to describe the occasion as

... an unexpected morale-booster for the islanders. It was felt to be particularly significant that a Mi'Kmaq Indian from Nova Scotia, the descendant of the people who had welcomed and helped the people of Eigg fleeing eviction two hundred years earlier, had now come to Eigg as a gesture of solidarity with the island's own indigenous population.

Schellenberg was, she went on to write, 'astonished that the story was even attracting international attention [and] argued that he had never been serious in his intentions to carry out the threatened evictions, people had over-reacted'.[4] The eviction orders duly got quashed before they could be executed. It would be hard to underestimate the significance of this triumph. Probably for the first time in modern history, a prominent laird's plans had been thwarted in a very public manner. A community had overcome its fear of victimisation. A culture of silence had been broken down and something new, exciting and life-giving had broken through.

Before Sulian left Eigg, some of the islanders brought him gifts of tobacco. Offerings and blessings were exchanged.

'It's the kids that most impress me,' he said, watching the children play with some feathers that he had given to Brendan, Camille's little boy.

Ishbel agreed. 'It's not just a wonderful environment,' she enthused. 'It's a wonderful attitude people here seem to have to their kids. They're just so free and cared for, but without being pampered with all that consumer trash. You can see how alive they are. It shines from their eyes.'

As the ferry pulled out from the pier, a tumultuous farewell came up from half the island who had turned out to see him off. Sulian shouted back, 'Your cause is our cause!'

And so the Atlantic was bridged. But Michelle Metivier, the Canadian television producer who had shadowed everything with her camera crew, seemed uptight and increasingly tight-lipped. What was wrong? Did it not make great television that a Canadian fellow-citizen had proved such a hit? Was native peoples' solidarity not a cause for celebration? And wouldn't the folks back home on the ranch be pleased to learn that the plight of the land of their own ancestors was at last being tackled?

For some reason, her smile had gone and she seemed to be avoiding conversation with me. I felt like I was not relating, any longer, to a real flesh-and-blood human being.

21. Mother Earth Will Cleanse Herself

Another day and another day passed. We headed further north, out west. After Eigg, Tom had come and picked us up in the *Wu Wei*, ferrying us from a crossing point on Little Loch Broom over to Scoraig for a night. Then we took the Ullapool ferry to Stornoway, drove down the peaty spine of Lewis and into the rocky majesty of Harris. We visited the mountain and met with some of the people living around it. Now, at last, high noon had arrived.

And Miss Pain wanted to make her displeasure quite clear. Her public inquiry was turning into a media circus. There had been a packed press conference beforehand. Stone Eagle, newly dubbed 'the streetwise Indian who communicates with e-mail rather than smoke signals', was wearing a dramatic feather headdress given to him by Caroline Marshall, the widow of Donald Marshall Sr, late Grand Chief of the Mi'Kmaq First Nation. 'Wear this when you speak there,' she had instructed him.[1]

The inquiry proceedings had moved down to Harris for three days. Usually they were held 50 miles away in Stornoway and, as a result, rarely were many more than a dozen observers present. But today the chamber, a room in the local school, was filled to capacity. Over a hundred people pressed together, and there would have been many more attempting to come in but for a funeral in the village. Donald Macleod was busy doing an interview for Gaelic TV. Senior pupils from the school had been given time off in order to give their own testimony; the majority were opposed to the quarry. Even my mother was sitting there, trying not to look embarrassed as she doubtless pondered, 'What has he got himself into now?' Indeed; this was, in the full 1960s sense of the expression, 'a happening'.

Outside, Michelle Metivier's increasingly intrusive camera crew were breaking the rules by filming through the window with a telescopic lens. Their presenter, to my annoyance, sat in the front row and was wired so that he could bug the proceedings. By now, unless their research had dug up something they were not telling me about, I had reason to believe I had got their measure. 'They've been sent over to do a hatchet job,' a senior BBC source had warned me. 'The Canadian authorities don't like what they see as "uppity Indians" hitting the international circuit on land rights. They're out to stitch him up.' One can never be certain about such assertions, but the source, unhappily, seemed to be vindicated by the resulting programme, which dubbed the people of Eigg mere 'hobby farmers' and implied that Stone Eagle was an impostor by whom I'd been taken in. Our subsequent complaint to the Canadian broadcasting ombudsman fell on deaf ears. But in the big picture of things, this was just one bit of negative publicity in an ocean of otherwise positive material. Coverage included BBC Radio 1's news bulletin, the BBC World Service, interviews on various television stations, several Canadian radio programmes and some forty items in the newspapers.

My testimony was to be given first. In a British public inquiry, one is meant to get up and simply read a written submission. As that seems such a lifeless way to proceed, most people extemporise. I too had presumed to do this, but Miss Pain took the opportunity decidedly to rebuke me. I was ordered to read only what was written in front of me. Well, fair enough, I suppose: she wanted to make it clear who was boss, and she had, after all, been decent enough to hear our submissions.

I ploughed my way through the 1500-word text. I couldn't help feeling it was falling flat; the stolid lines of the academic written word boxed in huge surges of emotion. Well, too bad. That was how it had to be.

Donald was next. Miss Pain had already made her disciplinary point. Here, now, was a man of real gravity and high standing in the community. He was allowed the freedom he wanted both to follow his text and to extemporise. His testimony was gripping. It was the sort of thing that makes you think, 'Wow! If that's what Christianity's about, then I'm all for it.' He said:

> To an extent that has no parallel elsewhere in the world, the ideology and culture of Harris are underpinned by Presbyterian theology. So far as ecological theology is concerned, however, there is nothing distinctive in Presbyterianism and my perspective merely reflects the broad Judaeo-Christian tradition.
>
> The most important influence on that tradition has, obviously, been the Jewish Scriptures, particularly the early chapters of the Book of Genesis. But I believe that the basic emphases of that tradition have a force beyond that of a mere external canon. They commend themselves to the deepest instincts of men and women, as, interacting with their environment, they experience both awareness of the existence of God and a sense of responsibility to the world in which He has placed them.
>
> The points I would wish to emphasise may be summarised as follows:
>
> 1. God as Creator has absolute sovereignty over the environment. We must use it only in accordance with His will; and we shall answer, collectively as well as individually, for all our decisions in this area.

2. Theologically, the primary function of the Creation is to serve as a revelation of God. To spoil the Creation is to disable it from performing this function.

3. In the Judaeo-Christian tradition there is an intimate link between man and the soil. He is taken from the ground; his food is derived from it; he is commanded to till and to keep it; and he returns to it. This implies a psychological as well as theological bond. Although such facts should not be used to endorse naked territorialism, they do raise the consideration that rape of the environment is rape of the community itself.

4. The precise responsibility of man to his environment is defined very precisely in the Judaeo-Christian tradition.

4.1 Man has to 'keep' it [Genesis 2:15]. This is not simply an insistence on conservation. It designates man as guardian and protector of the ground.

4.2 Man is the *servant* of the ground [Genesis 2:15]. This is the usual meaning of the Hebrew word popularly rendered to us as *to till*. Christian theology has largely failed to recognise this emphasis. Any insistence on the more widely perceived notion of man's *dominion* [Genesis 1:28] must be balanced by the less familiar but equally important concept of man as servant.

5. There is no place in the Judaeo-Christian tradition for divided guardianship of the land. In particular, there is no place for the idea that agrarian rights may belong to the people, while mineral rights belong to someone else. This dichotomy is central to the current debate. From a theological point of view, the present arrangements, while perfectly legal, are indefensible.

6. Man's relationship with his environment has been disrupted by the Fall. One primary symptom of this is that he is always tempted to allow economic considerations to override ecological ones. In the present instance the divinely appointed guardians and servants of Lingerabay are the people of Harris. Unfortunately, these very people are now suffering a degree of economic hardship that threatens the very survival of their community. Torn between their love for the land and their need for jobs, they face a cruel dilemma. Capitalism offers to help them in characteristic fashion: it will relieve unemployment provided the people surrender guardianship of the land (thus violating their own deepest instincts).

The people of Harris live conscious of the glory of God. What I'm asking is to reflect on whether this project is to the glory of God. Do we have God's mandate to inflict on Creation a scar of this magnitude that might detract from Creation's ability to reflect the glory of God? I know that Roineabhal is not in itself an area of what you might deem to be 'beautiful'. It is nevertheless an area of magnificence and grandeur and, by being such, bears eloquent testimony in my judgement to the majesty and grandeur of God's Earth. In my view no hole in the ground could bear that testimony as Roineabhal presently does.

The professor seated himself. I could palpably sense his discomfort. I understood why: his attempts to reform the Free Church had made some powerful enemies. According to a subsequent newspaper report, in the eyes of the conservatives his testimony at the public inquiry exemplified 'the problem' with him. Although his testimony had been 'impeccably Calvinist', he had stooped to share a public platform with Stone Eagle, 'a Red Indian ... a pagan', and myself, who many would regard as 'a heretic'.[2] Evidently, the Church of the Latter-Day Pharisees remained as much in business as when it attacked Jesus, similarly, for keeping dubious company. Such uptight religious rectitude reminded me of the young rabbi who said to an elder, 'How come that in days gone by people saw God, but they don't anymore?' And the elder replied, 'Because these days, nobody's prepared to stoop that low.'

Finally, Stone Eagle rose to speak.

Greetings, Brother and Sisters, from the Mi'Kmaq territory to your territory.

As an indigenous person of North America whose grandfathers met your grandfathers on their arrival to my territory several hundred years ago, we, the Mi'Kmaq First Nations, have endured many trials and tribulations that were caused by the two nations coming together.

In the history of the Mi'Kmaq First Nation we have never been defeated in war. We never ceded our aboriginal rights that were handed down to us by the Creator.

Prior to the arrival of the visitors to our shores, we, the Mi'Kmaq First Nation, had our own traditional form of government, laws and education that was totally different from the laws that were imposed upon us by the visitors to our territory.

Our philosophy and spirituality has always been one where man was not dominant over the creation or other life forms, which we shared this territory with. It was always our belief, and still is our belief, that the Creator had placed the Mi'Kmaq people as caretakers of Mother Earth. Somewhere in the past hundreds of years the majority of the indigenous people, perhaps because of the influence of the non-natives to our territory, became parasites of Mother Earth, thus destroying her natural bounty.

It is the resurrection of our traditional values and codes of conduct that our elders reintroduced to this generation that reawakened the true Mi'Kmaq Spirit and spiritual connection to Mother Earth and the Creator. We, in Mi'Kmaq territory, continue on a daily basis to create solidarity with other nations in North America. We continue to create unity among all First Nations people with the common belief that the true philosophy of our grandfathers is the answer to save or to slow down the environmental destruction that is plaguing all of mankind.

It is my firm belief that we, of this generation, have no hope in solving the environmental deterioration that is ongoing as we speak. However, I also have firm convictions that we, of this generation, may be able to slow down the destruction of our Mother Earth enough so that the next generation that will be replacing our leaders will find the solutions and the cure for Mother Earth.

If we fail to do so Mother Earth will cleanse herself of the offending organism that is killing her. This is our teaching.

The destruction of any mountain, river or forest is horrifying to all of us, whether it be the Hebrides in Scotland, the Shetland Islands or an oil spill in Alaska or the destruction of the Sacred Mountain, Kluscap, in Nova Scotia. It is no longer tolerable to pretend [about] or ignore these assaults. Your mountain, your shorelines, your rivers and your air are just as much mine and my grandchildren's as ours is yours. To say that I am concerned about the proposed destruction in your territory is to say that I am concerned about the destruction in North America.

It is my duty and my responsibility to the Creator and all life that I must get involved, with or without your blessings. Coming from a tradition such as I come from, it is customary among our people to speak from the heart. It is customary that we place faith in the Creator to give us words of wisdom . . . . I have never been able to shed a tear on cue. However, I have shed tears because of honesty. If I fail your criteria in being unable to present a written text more than what is here, I do apologise. But I also guarantee you my belief instils me to deliver and my testimony will not let you down. For it is my firm conviction that there is a divine hand that guides me.

I am grateful and honoured to assist in your battle to protect Mother Earth. For if I can assist you in your battle for the protection of land which should be shown reverence because the work of the Creator is sacred, then I am assisting my grandchildren who must take over my position once I have entered the Spirit World.

And that was it. It was all over.

But late that night I went to the home of one of the most respected elders in the community of Harris. I was not sure where he stood on the superquarry debate. The living-room light was still on. For some reason I felt moved to knock on his door.

We talked for half an hour. It would have been tactless to ask directly what he thought of the day's proceedings, but I felt a sense of silent blessing. To be truthful, that was why I had come.

As he showed me out, I was handed a package. It was the size of a small bag of sugar.

'Give this to Stone Eagle, will you?'

'What is it?' I asked.

'Tell him that this is the summit rock of Mount Roineabhal. I broke it off for him.'

I was aghast.

'I don't think he'll be able to accept it,' I said. 'You know what his people are like about such things.'

'I know,' the elder said. 'But tell him this: tell him it's better than having a superquarry.'

The next morning we take the ferry back to the mainland, allowing time to go round by the Calanais standing stones. Wherever we had stopped during our journey together and had received a welcome, Sulian had reciprocated by singing the Mi'Kmaq 'honour song'. The drum that he carried for this purpose was inscribed with a date: 1752. This, he told me, commemorated the peace treaty between the Mi'Kmaq and the British colonists, which stated that the Mi'Kmaq were to give sanctuary to immigrants suffering under the snowbound winters. It is said that many North American families of Scots descent owe their survival to the faithfulness with which the First Nation peoples honoured their treaties in this way. The émigrés of Eigg, as we have seen, were perhaps but one of many cases in point.

'I've got something to give you at the Stones,' I say as we pull away from the Scarista House Hotel, where, right beside the ancient churchyard of Bhrighde, Jane and Ian Callaghan had generously provided us with accommodation.

'You've got something for me?' Sulian laughs. 'Oh, good. Very good. I do like presents!'

We drive north, passing stunning beaches. Taransay island, later to become famous in the BBC series *Castaway*, is immediately out to our west. Near it is *Bogha na Cille* – the Rock of the Church; the Lady's rock.

'Yeah, but there's a problem with this particular present,' I say. 'I fear you may not be able to accept it. It's something powerful. Awesomely powerful.'

I think how, to me, the power is in the metaphor. It's what the summit rock symbolises that matters; not that it *is* the summit rock, which, after all, looks indistinguishable from any other rock on the mountain. And I think that to Sulian's mind it'll probably be the other way round. For him, the symbolic power will be only the secondary quality. For him, the rock will have symbolic power precisely because it *is* the summit rock.

'Ah! You give me something that's too powerful?' he says. 'Come on – you couldn't give me anything I couldn't accept!'

'It's not from me,' I reply tightly, pre-emptively covering myself. 'It's from the elder.'

'Then there'll be no problem me accepting it.'

'We'll see.'

Our car draws up to the megalithic site. Here's Calanais, once again. Here's these amazing rocks shaped by aeons of weather. Here's the outline of a Celtic cross on the ground, built three thousand years before Christianity. Here I am, again, but this time it's different. This time, I'm here for a reason.

Once again, Sulian is astounded to see such veneration for stone.

There's a burial chamber in the centre. Before excavation it would have been covered over: a 'faerie hill', as tradition tends to think of such mounds – a liminal place where the worlds of the living and of the dead meet. 'I believe that there is a power in this place,' John MacGregor of nearby Gearrannan once told me. 'It is a power that can be used for either good or evil, and I have had personal experience of that power.'

We wander over to the centre. Ishbel, Sulian and I stand side by side; two men and a woman. We stand inside what would have been the Hill; what is the Hill.

I pass him the elder's package. He opens it as if there's a bomb inside. Which, of course, there is.

He takes out the triangular piece of rock. Freshly fractured crystal facets glint and glitter in the first morning light of two billion years.

I find myself remembering the piece of rock that I had once broken from that mountain, some twenty years ago: three-sided – a natural triquetra.

'What's this?' he asks quietly.

I feel as though he already knows, but I have to tell him anyway. It's like when the police knock on the door, and it opens, and they say nothing but just look at the parents, and their hats are in their hands – and what follows is just a formality. A terrible but banal formality.

'That . . . is the summit rock of Mount Roineabhal. It has been broken off in your honour.'

The blood drains from the Warrior Chief's face. Here and there the skin pulses and twitches, but soon even that stops. Only a desiccated, expressionless vacancy remains. This, after all, is no ordinary death. In his eyes, this is more like murder.

'They what?' He struggles for words. 'They broke it off . . . Do you know what . . .'

The big man's voice falls away. He's hit. Stunned. Floored. I feel like some perverse, reluctant referee: four . . . five . . . six . . . seven . . . will he make it up again?

He does. Again, slowly, he returns to the immensity of what he's now faced with.

'Do you know what it means?' he finally utters, teeth set on edge, each word ground and pressed out to the very last nuance; voice measured now, honed, accusative. 'Do you know what it means in our tradition to do a thing like that?'

'I do.' I say, with marriage-vow solemnity. Actually, I don't, but I can guess. And I know that maybe I dropped what he'd thrown at me previously, but this time, I have to catch it all. I have to carry the full force. This time the banter between us was no laughing matter.

Sulian just stands there, leaning on his stick, the twin eagle feathers fastened to it fluttering in the wind. He searches for words. His turquoise-ringed hands reach inwards to the molten centre, to the source of his fire. This is the real thing: for those who've always been fobbed off with second-rate petitions of mere corny piety, this is prayer.

The silence endures. Then, as a growing trickle, the words start to come. They come, but it is not anger that erupts; it is understanding. And he starts to speak, hesitatingly, but cavernously, and with an intense compassion.

'What have your people come to that they should *decapitate* their own mountain?'

'I know, and I told the elder,' I reply. 'But he said that I was to tell you this. He said, "Tell him *it's better than having a superquarry*".'

Sulian freezes again. An axe blow – an insistent intention to cut through something – is hard medicine for even a warrior chief to bear.

An empty wind blows over from nearby Loch Roag. My archaeologist friend Jim Crawford took me in his boat to the skerries far out where the inlet meets the great Atlantic, to see the ancient monastic beehive cells. One of them, he thinks, was an oratory of the Celtic Church. You see the same further south, off the coast of Ireland. Hermits may have lived in these places, alone with God and nature: anchorites interceding in the 'busy haunts of base mankind', wielding axes no heavier than the breath of their song. Such is the warriorship necessary where steel is too blunt to cut the darkness, and where steel is much too unforgiving.

Back in Harris I had challenged Sulian on this – on the different levels of engaging with conflict: physical, psychological and spiritual; a spectrum running from violent to non-violent. Michelle Metivier's team had been bugging me. They wanted to know how, as a Quaker pacifist, I could justify sharing a platform with a warrior chief, with a 'man of violence'. 'Well,' I'd replied to them, 'If I only did business with other pacifists, I probably wouldn't be talking to you!' But later I took up this point privately with Sulian. 'Look at you, for example,' I'd said to him. 'I can see two types of warrior in you. That of a military operator, yes, but also an emerging spiritual warriorship.'

'Don't you even joke about that!' he exploded. It was an uncalled-for, unexpected burst of real anger. It etched his words on my mind. I knew that I had touched on some rift, and he was not ready or willing to enter into it – at least, not with me. So I'd backed off.

We stand looking at the gaunt stones for a long time. I think of when I was little and we used to come to the Stones with visitors. I think of the bleak times. The days I'd feel small and vulnerable in the cold, very small. And I think of how the red-hot passion of spiritual work always alternates with icy dark nights of the soul. I think, too, of this world, and how the taproot of good so often gets besmirched with the grime through which it pushes. Edwin Muir said it all so well in 'One Foot in Eden':

> Yet strange these fields that we have planted
> So long with crops of love and hate.
> Evil and good stand thick around

> In fields of charity and sin
> Where we shall lead our harvest in.
> Yet still from Eden springs the root
> As clean as on the starting day.

Some of Sulian's words from the day we left Eigg come echoing back to me. 'Don't you be too apologetic about old Angus,' he'd said, in admonishment. 'If you were carrying what he carries – if you bore his weight of tradition, his burden of leadership, and everything he's been through, you'd probably be drinking too!'

And that's the difficulty with spiritual activism. It means running with the handicap of whatever your own limp might be, plus, typically, that of whoever's running with you. What's more, it usually means running on empty. Sometimes, as Siddhartha told his beloved, all that you can do is wait, and fast, and pray. That's what makes for spiritual work. It's why the deepest activism is always spiritual activism. It's the faith to hold the faith even when you can't see the object of your faith on the road ahead.

And the Chief holds steadfast in the heart of the burial chamber. We're surrounded by larger-than-life stones that look for all the world like an ancient human congregation huddled together. And the Chief is just staring in awe at the 6-inch-high pyramid of rock. Yes, it's only a tiny fragment of what Redland wanted. Tiny. But it is *the* fragment.

'I cannot accept this gift,' he says at last.

I had expected as much, and my heart sinks. What do you do with the pinnacle of a mountain rejected? You can't glue it back on again because something has changed. The mountain has changed, at least symbolically – at least in our minds. A process has started. A process to be persevered with and worked through by those of us into whose hands it has fallen. A process demanding faith in the process because, like it or not, we have now elected, in some crazy way, to carry the mountain. It feels like more than I can stomach.

'It is not within my authority to accept this gift,' Sulian repeats firmly.

White clouds sail across the sky from the distant island of Great Bernera. It would be there, some months later, with Jim Crawford, that I would find a 5000-year-old hazelnut shell, washed out from prehistoric forest debris in the peat. But for now, I just feel drained and empty, ever so empty, and kind of sick. All the energy has been sucked from my stomach as if with some great cosmic vacuum pump.

It had been an exciting ten days with Sulian and Ishbel. Exciting, but hard. We had challenged each other to the hilt. But now I have nothing left, not enough strength to carry a mountaintop.

And the Warrior Chief's gaze is fixed on some distant point. He's never stopped taking everything in, watching all points of the come-to-pass. He's here, and he's far out elsewhere too. Eventually, he speaks.

'But I'll tell you what I can do,' he says.

Sulian too is exhausted; deeply spent. Coming to Scotland, to the land of the ancestors of his oppressors, had placed him under huge psychological and spiritual pressure. The many jokes that had flashed between us had been only a form of lubrication. And now he was confronted with this 'gift' – nay, almost assaulted by it. My role was easy in comparison. I was only the messenger.

'I'll tell you what I can do,' he reiterates. And there is a sea change now. His voice swells with an impending flow, and power surges, in ruby hues, back into his red-skinned face. As I watch, I see this grown man growing before my eyes, growing with the conviction of the military commander that he is. But what I am seeing now is more than just military power, much more. What I see now is no worldly sense of authority. That's not what is shining, radiant, in this man's countenance.

What I'm seeing now is the spiritual warrior.

'Alastair,' he would write the next day, inside his decorated buckskin shirt that he would give to me before leaving Scotland. 'My friend, may you never have to prove you have Balls. I believe that your path of peace is better. I pray you never walk my path. Your friend always, Sulian Stone Eagle.' Indeed, it would come as little surprise to me a year later when he wrote saying that he had retired from the Warrior Society, but not from carrying his Sacred Pipe and bundle.

And so Sulian gazes at me. He gazes at me and through me, into the ancient landscape, beyond even the distant horizon where the Sleeping Beauty Mountain reclines replete with story, and with stories all around.

No longer is it Sulian Stone Eagle Herney who's standing here. No longer is it he who's speaking. It is the ancestors; the old people. What I hear is the silver river, the chorus of a whole nation.

Sulian raises his head to the sky. He opens his lips. We know, all three of us know, that we are caught up here, participants in a spontaneous sacred ceremony, transfigured in a sacrament of this present moment.

A deep joy wells up. Seeds of fire burst open and with a tongue of living flame the Eagle speaks before the Stones:

'In my authority as Warrior Chief and Sacred Pipe Carrier of the Mi'Kmaq Nation I shall take the summit of this mountain into sanctuary on behalf of all my people. We, the Mi'Kmaq Nation, will look on this action as coming formally under the terms of our 1752 Treaty with the British. Our ancestors always honoured their side of this treaty. We shall do likewise again today. My ancestors promised to look after your people when they had been cleared from their own lands. Now it is your rocks that are under threat of being cleared. So yes, we will help you once more. We will take the summit of your mountain . . . into sanctuary.'

22. Healing of the Nations

An unmarked white car tailed us for many miles as we headed south back down to Glasgow. It speeded up when we accelerated and crawled when we went dead slow. We didn't know why it was there, but it followed us so closely that it seemed to want us to know that we were being watched. Well, if you try to inspect the troops at Faslane, perhaps you can expect a guard of honour.

By the time Sulian flew out of Glasgow the next day, media coverage of the inquiry had made him so well known that some half-dozen strangers spontaneously came up and said things like, 'Thanks for what you're doing for Scotland.' But on the eve of his departure he made one last stop. In many ways it was the most remarkable. A group of largely unemployed youths from deprived areas of Glasgow had come together to try and reclaim a sense of meaning in their lives. Some had been involved with popular education, environmental or cultural campaigns. Others had simply struggled with hopelessness, squalor, violence and substance abuse. Hardship was etched so deep into many of their faces as to almost take away the capacity to smile. Indeed, most were the offspring of intergenerational urban poverty; the descendants of those pushed off the land a century or more earlier. Poverty had been both their birthright and their birth rite. That they held in common. But another thing they held in common was that they had decided to resist, and to do so using creativity, community and ecology as their means of achieving empowerment and securing transformation.

Central to this vision was the question of how to build a meaningful sense of belonging and identity when so much of their environment was degraded and their self-esteem often fragmentary.

'We want to create something that shows everybody what we can really do,' explained Colin MacLeod, a native of Govan. 'We're starting a carving school, making things out of wood and stone, and we're teaching ourselves about the history of this place as one of the early centres of the Celtic Church. George MacLeod of the Iona Community was based here when he started to rebuild Iona Abbey. Like he said, it's about bringing together work and worship. It's about getting back our dignity.'

Colin explained the difficulty of reclaiming indigenous identity in a multi-cultural context. 'We've got to make it so that nobody's rejected,' he said. 'That's why we've called ourselves the GalGael, and we're setting up a "GalGael Trust". The Gael were the heartland people, and the Gall were the strangers. The people of the Hebrides became known as the Gall-Gael – the strange, or foreign Gaels – because they assimilated Norse culture which came down from Scandinavia. That was in the ninth century, yet the Hebrides remained the heartland of the Gaelic world. And that's what happens when you include people in. It creates a sense of belonging. It makes a life worth living. You see, in today's world, there's a bit of the native and a bit of the stranger in us all. We're all Gall-Gael now.'

Colin explained that Govan had lost much of its confidence as the Clyde shipbuilding industry had died. 'That's why we want to move from doing carvings to building small boats,' he said, 'and from there we'll build the big one: an authentic Hebridean longship – a birlinn.'

Leading traditional shipwrights like Iain Oughtred and John MacAulay (who had represented the Isle of Harris in the superquarry inquiry), had offered to help them. And sure enough, on New Year's morning on 1 January 2000, they launched a replica Govan yawl, the first boat to enter the Clyde in the new millennium. The GalGael's vision of cultural renewal had captured every-body's imagination. Even the Army had helped them to mill the necessary timber, gathered after being blown down in a storm. Andrew Marr, now the BBC's political editor, visited the GalGael in the course of writing a book about British identity, and he had this to say:

> The[se] people were eloquent, self-confident and dignified, making a real difference to a battered place . . . . creating more human happiness than a hundred toothpaste factories or credit-card call centres. They had a sane perspective on identity . . .[1]

In Sulian's eyes, of course, these were life's fighters. Their attitude expressed an everyday stoicism; the heroism of little things that, with perseverance and integrity, was able to grow and go somewhere. Many had simply become fed up of being kicked around. They'd decided not to take any more and to get organised. They spent an afternoon showing Sulian around Glasgow's housing schemes, talking with those at the bottom of the social pile. He was introduced to people who had taken costly stances in fighting the iniquitous 'poll tax', to protesters who were trying to prevent a motorway from being built through nearby Pollok Park, and to individuals who struggled to tackle their alcohol and drug addiction by addressing the root cause – loss of meaning.

Not for the first time on this tour, Sulian was simultaneously shocked and inspired by what he saw.

'Your situation is the same as ours,' he told a gathering of 150 residents who had left their high-rise flats to assemble round a campfire in a piece of woodland that night.

> In fact, it's worse than our situation. Canada's victim has at last found someone worse off than him. We at least can hunt and fish on our own land. We have our Treaty. But you're living here in cold, damp housing conditions that we wouldn't keep our dogs in. The suits and ties will talk all day about poverty, and drive home each night on their comfortable salaries. They'll do everything for you except give up something of their privilege to help you. That's why taking control of situations for yourselves is so important. Whether [you succeed in your campaigns] or not, *the point is you've made a stand*. You've grown in strength and unity. *You've proven yourselves to be warriors*. And that's how you're different from the suits and ties who put you in these urban reservations in the first place, and keep you there to have the leafy suburbs and open country for themselves.

Before leaving, he did something that had never before happened in Mi'Kmaq history. In a move that was later formally endorsed by the Mi'Kmaq Warrior Society, he appointed Colin MacLeod a district war chief in recognition of his nonviolent 'defence of Mother Earth'.

Colin, however, had a reciprocal honour up his sleeve. He and his co-workers had been inspired and uplifted by media reports of Sulian's Scottish tour. So touched were they that he should bother to come and see them that they had carved him a huge 'gift from the Scottish people' out of a quarter-ton block of sandstone.

So it was that Stone Eagle flew back to Nova Scotia with a stone eagle.

Some months after getting home, Sulian wrote about his own anti-superquarry campaign on Mount Kluscap, or Kelly's Mountain, Cape Breton Island.

> After giving evidence . . . at Harris and sharing our solidarity and unity with other grassroots people in Scotland, our struggle here gained weight with the authorities who are now seriously considering setting our Sacred Mountain aside as a protected area . . . making life here in Canada a bit easier for the First Nations.[2]

He felt that the eagle was too big a gift to accept personally. Accordingly, the Mi'Kmaq chiefs agreed to receive it on behalf of their whole nation. They also ratified Sulian's treaty decision to take the summit of Mount Roineabhal into sanctuary. He said:

> The stone eagle is growing real fast. It is now so big that Colin and I are lost in its greatness. And I believe this is the way it should be. I see great good coming from it by way of helping our peoples heal from their first meeting.

Because the eagle and the mountaintop were of such symbolic significance, the Mi'Kmaq formally approached the white folks in Pictou town and asked if it could be exhibited in the region's Hector Heritage Quay museum. The *Hector* was the emigrant ship that had brought Ishbel's forebears from Scotland during the Highland Clearances. So it was that a special ceremony was agreed upon. The *Nova Scotia Evening News* summed it up with the headline 'Scots, Micmacs seal 200-year-old truce'.[3] Ishbel described the day thus:

The event began with a piper playing traditional Scottish music. Then Sulian offered tobacco to elder Albert Denny who is Chief of the Pictou Landing First Nations. As First Nations protocol requires, he asked permission to enter Albert's territory and asked for his protection. Then the Mi'Kmaq honour song was sung. The words of the song state that we must all honour our indigenousness, be proud of who we are and where we come from.

Sulian gave the history of how this day came to be, how we came to be at the Hector Heritage Quay, the site of the building of the replica of the ship *Hector* which carried the first Scottish emigrants from the Highlands to Pictou, Nova Scotia. The Mayor of Pictou was there, the President of the Heritage Quay, Wayne Fraser representing the government of Nova Scotia, Chief Albert Denny, Eileen Brooks who is leader of the women of the Warriors' Society, a three year old Mi'Kmaq in traditional dress, Sulian's 85 year old mother, young warriors, a 5 year old who is half Mi'Kmaq and half Scottish. A man on holidays from Glasgow happened to walk by and come in. A women who grew up on the Isle of Lewis and whose Mother was from the Isle of Harris attended. There were also direct descendants of the emigrants who left Scotland on the *Hector* in 1772.

Sulian then presented Eileen Brooks with a pouch of tobacco and spoke of how we need all aspects of society, and here today we have the warriors, the peacemakers, leaders, the children, and the elders. He talked of his first hand knowledge of the warrior life and of the Oka crisis, and he knew well the reality of hate. He spoke also of the need for us all to put away our racism and that if this ceremony caused two or three people to leave from here and change their thinking, it would be well worth it. Sulian described how he had been a very, very racist person, and he had paid a huge price. Last year he had lost a little girl due to racism. His baby was half white and he feels the baby left because his racism was so strong. At that point, Sulian could no longer speak. Many people had tears in their eyes . . .

The Ceremony was closed with another Pipe tune. People were so 'up'. It had taken two hours, with most people standing, but people did not want to leave. They talked and laughed and shared food. Mi'Kmaq people, who would never think of going to the Hector Centre, toured the displays of Loch Broom, the Battle of Culloden, the Clearances, the poverty and their first glimpse of Nova Scotia from the ship. They also went into the ship and were shocked with how tiny the passenger space was. Elderly locals thanked Sulian, elders of both people talked together and shared tea. Local people discussed racism and were surprised to learn that First Nations still consider Pictou a very racist place . . . . So it was amazing to be in this same town, with local officials and townspeople acknowledging and thanking the Mi'Kmaq Nation, making them welcome in the town.

One of the many things that can be learnt from this day is the true power we, the people, hold. A simple gift given from the heart, from one person to another, grew and became the means for the Gaelic community to make amends to the Mi'Kmaq Nation, to connect with our past, to bring it out in the light and look at where we are now and who we are. We truly honoured both our ancestors who struggled so hard for us to be here today, and we honoured all our children by walking in dignity.

In Honour of our Ancestors,
Ishbel Munro

One local newspaper ran on its front page most of the address that I had faxed across for Ishbel to read out at the event. This is part of it:

The *Hector* belongs culturally to the Nova Scotia peoples of Scottish descent. The stone eagle now belongs to the Mi'Kmaq; it is our heartfelt gift to represent all that the eagle symbolises in aspiring to new heights of friendship. And the summit of Roineabhal, that belongs to us. It is on loan to you, taken by Sulian into symbolic sanctuary at our request under the terms of the spirit of the 1752 Treaty. May the warriorship by which he and others safeguard this for us be a spiritual warriorship. May the rock be returned if and when our mountain is saved, just as we hope that Mount Kluscap will also be saved from the superquarry proposed on your side of the Atlantic. And should our mountain not be saved, may the summit remain always in Mi'Kmaq hands as a reminder that our plight is so deep that we lost not only our people in the Clearances, but also, now, our place.[4]

Towards the end of the book of Ezekiel, the prophet is shown a vision of the land that had once been broken and turned to wilderness. But the bones of the dead have come back to life.[5] The Earth, a new Eden, is restored by a stream that rises from the ground beneath a sacred place.

'Wherever the river goes,' Ezekiel is told, 'every living creature that swarms will live, and there will be very many fish.' All kinds of trees will grow. Because 'the water flows from the sanctuary, their fruit will be for food, and their leaves for healing'. Restored natural ecology is to be complemented with restored social justice. Even those of the lowest status, 'the aliens who reside among you and have begotten children' – that is to say, incomers and refugees who have chosen to stay and who seriously wish to belong to a place – these 'shall be to you as citizens of Israel; with you they shall be allotted an inheritance [of the land]'.[6]

This image of a restored human and natural ecology – a return to Eden – recurs at various points in the Bible.[7] But most importantly, it concludes the New Testament. We find it right at the end, in the last chapter of the enigmatic Book of Revelation. We find it there among muddled and heavy metaphor, but it is there nonetheless, as it is likewise in many of the world's religious traditions.

It leaves us with a vision in which loss, destruction and death have been passed through. A new world opens out, beyond all the crucifixions and the suffering. It is as if we pass back through the fire from which we were born, now stripped of ego, of craving and officious striving for control. We pass back through the flaming sword at the gateway to Eden with which the angel guards the Tree of Life.[8] We reach for fruit and leaves placed there for the 'healing of the nations'.[9] We become, as Peter put it, 'participants of the divine nature'.[10]

These things are not obscure theological rantings belonging only to the past; they are part of the cultural fabric of our present times. They replay constantly as archetypal motifs in popular culture. Take, for instance, the Christian motifs in the cult movie *The Matrix*. Or Joni Mitchell's classic 1970 song 'Woodstock', which touched the hearts of a generation. Here you have the 'child of God' walking the road, going back to the land to set his soul free. He's leaving the smog, aware that with the half-million others on their way to the Woodstock rock celebration, he's part of a great turning in the human spirit. His mind trips out and he dreams of bomber planes turning into butterflies above his Vietnam war-engrossed nation. He sees the great truth of interconnection – that each soul is stardust and golden – but that we've missed our vocations; we've been trapped in the 'devil's bargain'. Our struggle, the challenge of becoming fully human and the full meaning of our troubled times, is to make it 'back to the garden' – to return to Eden.[11]

Just after the first publication of this book, I received news that left me cut through to the core. Sulian Herney had pleaded guilty in court to having, over three years, sexually abused a girl from his reservation.

I felt hit by a missile from Hell. It tarnishes the story I have told, and yet, ironically, it underscores its importance. Humankind, especially after the September 11th attacks on America, can no longer ignore the roots of violence.

Distraught, and wrestling to rebuild a separate life, my dear friend Ishbel wrote to me. She quoted a native healer who worked with residential-school survivors: 'The dark power does not want the nations to heal, so it is attacking the children. We are in a spiritual battle. Adults must choose to heal.'

The good that Sulian did in Scotland speaks for itself. I pray with him, with my troubled friend Stone Eagle, to find the courage that he seeks to turn from death.

'Get yourselves a new heart and a new spirit!' said God through Ezekiel. 'I have no pleasure in the death of anyone . . . . Turn, then, and live.'[12]

23. Arrow of the Lord

By 1994, Ulrich and I had, between us, got the Centre for Human Ecology into a position where it was really going somewhere. It was, at last, having the impact intended by its founder, the eminent geneticist Professor C. H. Waddington, who set it up in 1972. I worked only part-time, to allow space for campaigning, and Ul was technically retired. But we managed a dozen MSc and up to eight PhD students between us. They helped to run things, bringing music, food and scholarship into the place. That was how we managed to achieve so much with very little.

Both the principal of the University, Professor Sir David Smith, and his deputy, Professor Barrie Wilson, strongly supported our work. The latter wrote: 'The Centre for Human Ecology today finds itself at the hub, its "alternative" views no longer peripheral, but at the core of common concern for the environment and the University's integrated approach, which leads the way for others in higher education.' However, by 1995, Sir David Smith had retired and Professor Wilson had tragically passed away in his professional prime. Then things changed.

Review committees were convened. Privately, and on a one-to-one basis, senior university managers admitted that 'the problem', as some of them saw it, was my work on Eigg and with the superquarry. The Centre also had a controversial track record from long before my time: housing the Medical Campaign Against Nuclear Weapons; questioning excessive meat production and so risking consternation from the meat industry; promoting organic agriculture when, as one professor irately claimed (with a technical precision that completely missed the point), 'Our agriculture is already organic!'

'The problem' with the CHE, then, was a question of radicalism, of maverick epistemology. It got up certain people's noses. But you must understand, the managers said: it was other authorities and not they who were upset. They actually supported and rather admired the work of the CHE. And it was right, said one senior professor, for the CHE 'to have an ethic'.

So you see, it was not them, but these other Powers that Be that had to be deferred to. There was no alternative. 'You know what it's like, Alastair,' they said. 'They sit on research funding committees down in London and they say, "Edinburgh University? Where's Edinburgh? Isn't that where they run around superquarries with Red Indians and cause trouble for our friends who own little Scottish islands? No. We won't fund Edinburgh, this time."'

Then there was the niggling question of my research and teaching, and in particular my 'alternative' viewpoints: ecofeminism, deep ecology, spirituality – ideas similar to those of Professor Carolyn Merchant and Vandana Shiva.

'What's wrong with those?' I asked. Weren't our courses actually making a profit for the University? Hadn't the British Council given us a massive contract to train senior governmental officials in sustainability? Were our external examiner reports not exemplary? Indeed, did they not testify that 'much important work has been conducted within the Human Ecology MSc by both teachers and students [developing] an intellectually innovative, creative and exacting approach to issues of mounting public significance'? And did they not conclude that 'the CHE has brought distinction to Edinburgh University'?[1]

Maybe, said one of the administrators. Maybe, said this man, this otherwise decent man, who in easier times, like so many of them, had actually done much to assist our work. But, he said, the essence of the problem as he saw it now was . . . *ecofeminism*.

'How so?' I asked.

The administrator's eyes sunk into their sockets, flashing. Then he startled me by snapping back, angrily, that ecofeminism was rubbish. It was a black hole, one that draws you into a morass; a closed way of thinking into which, if you enter, there is no way out.

'Maybe we don't fully understand each other,' I suggested. 'Maybe some of the students and I could offer you a short seminar . . .'

He sort of smiled, as if to suggest that I really ought to know better, and said that it would be a waste of time.

An attempt by a professor from another university to stick the knife in was wonderfully blunt. '*You really will have to gag people like Alastair McIntosh,*' he wrote, speaking of research in which I had applied an ecofeminist critique to Britain's science policy. 'His hard-hitting recent article in the Glasgow *Herald* debunking the Government's Science and Technology White Paper will alienate most, if not all, wealth creators.'[2] Two other letters that I also managed to obtain copies of – both from individuals with business connections to the proposed Harris superquarry – were of a similar tone. The University was without question under pressure to disassociate itself from me. But it was not, I was repeatedly assured, a question of academic freedom.

Now, I was asked, would I not go quietly? Would I promise no more fuss in the media; no more letters from outraged students and public about the proposed 'suspension' of our MSc course, about the impending effective closure of the CHE?

Literally hundreds of protests had poured in, some from leading thinkers around the world. At the grassroots level people were also shouting in support. A letter from the Isle of Eigg Residents' Association said:

> The people of Eigg would not be where they are now without the expertise of teachers and students from the Centre who have tirelessly helped us strengthen our resolve and morale when our small isolated community was under threat.

Well, precisely, I was told, there's the problem: academics don't campaign, do they? Yes, they may do paid work for industry. And yes, their reports may be used by industry for lobbying. But that's professional consultancy, which carries a dignity not shared by campaigning. Now, if only you would go quietly, Alastair, compromise, conform, we will make it easy for you.

A senior university official summoned me to his office. He said he would come straight to the point: he offered to do a 'deal' with me. They wanted an end to the protests coming out in the press. I could take the CHE class library and re-establish it elsewhere. (That would be worth several tens of thousands of pounds.) What's more, he would propose giving us associated institution status – if only I'd go quietly. That would allow us to continue to teach an Edinburgh University-accredited MSc programme. He said they didn't much mind what we taught, within reason, so long as it was continued semi-detached, outside of their walls. 'And why not within their walls?' I wondered. It was, he said, a question of control. He thought I would know what he meant, that there was no need to spell it out further.

I protested that there had never been an adequate explanation as to why they wanted to close a successful centre. I had eighteen pages documenting the whole ridiculous saga – meetings, phone calls, the lot. But he was not to be swayed. Indeed, I found him intimidating.

I left his office, having rejected the deal. I experienced the final months of laying down my work in Edinburgh University as an incredibly isolated and isolating period. The previous year we had earned a reprieve after intense campaigning led by our students. This time, when the managers came back at us again, it was like the doctors all knew the patient was going to die and there was nothing more anybody could do. We went through the motions of another campaign, but it was stillborn. I made the decision not to remain silent about what was happening, and, typically, this earned admiration in some quarters and vilification in others. Some felt that the high profile of my campaigns had left the University with no option. 'You force them into a corner because you won't tolerate their hypocrisies, their compromises,' I was told by a sympathetic but critical colleague. 'Your arguments are too strong. You leave them no way out, then you're surprised when they turn on you and it drags the whole show down.'

'Look,' I replied angrily, 'I worked with subtlety, almost invisible, until what I was doing started to be effective. Then I could no longer hide it. Are you saying that all our work should be mere displacement activity? Is the Socratic gadfly to have no bite? Is scholarship to have a built-in cut-out device to fail the poor and let down the broken in nature?'

And so I found myself, metaphorically, walking alone out into the garden. Very alone. And it was like they took a chainsaw to my stomach, and a hacksaw to my sinews, and cut the tree to pieces. That was what it actually felt like – a chainsaw and a hacksaw running through living tissue. 'It does cause you to ponder,' said my friend Professor Macleod, with a seriousness that could only come out of the Free Church College, 'it does cause you to ponder whether the Devil is anti-ecological.'

In the week that the fate of the Centre for Human Ecology was finally confirmed, the *New Scientist* magazine ran a leader headed 'A narrow kirk in Edinburgh'.

> Over the past few weeks, Edinburgh University has supported its controversial psychologist Christopher Brand, on the grounds that 'academic freedom' allows his studies of intelligence, race and genetics. So far, so good – intellectual freedoms are essential.
>
> How strange, then, that during these same weeks, Edinburgh University has decided to be rid of its outspoken Centre for Human Ecology, where staff and students are more likely to be debating the relationship between the profit motive and the decline of reverence for the land than whether the mean IQ of black people is less than that of whites.
>
> The centre has an international reputation, its former students and visiting researchers have published numerous books and papers, and its MSc course is in demand from students around the world. An attempt to shut it down last year was averted only at the very last moment. Now the contracts of its staff are to be ended, its MSc course closed and its library dissolved.
>
> The centre has always, of course, been far too radical for many in the university. Its members have campaigned against the development of 'superquarries' and questioned the pattern of land ownership, with 80 per cent of Scotland in the hands of 900 families. Even 'environmentally friendly growth' has been challenged by asking whether some people might be more fulfilled with less resources.
>
> Overall, there will be a considerable loss to the university's intellectual tradition. Among those to go will be Alastair McIntosh, teaching director of the institute, whose views on the relationship between science and ethics can be read in this week's *Forum*. The MSc students will finish their courses and depart, and a tradition of fearless enquiry will be broken. Edinburgh University should have been big hearted enough for both Brand and McIntosh to flourish within its walls.[3]

It is sometimes the case that the Powers of the Domination System, being brazen, materialise in a physical form. Shortly after the Division of Biological Sciences in the Faculty of Science and Engineering axed the CHE, they opened their new biotechnology centre, the Michael Swann Building. Outside it stand two bronze human figures, *Parthenope* and *Egeria*, sculpted by Sir Eduardo Paolozzi. Costing £50,000, these were the first works of art to have been commissioned by the Faculty for a very long time. Paolozzi's brief had been to reflect 'the aspirations' of those working within the building.

The figures have parts of their bodies horribly cut off. Chunks of flesh and bone are replaced by machines, metal plates and cogwheels. Poor *Egeria* is upside down. *Parthenope*'s eyes are being violently forced open. Rarely in the history of false gods could a more telling pair of graven images have been conceived. The pieces brilliantly betray a demi-humanity in which nature's proportionality has been brutally ousted by technology's angularity. *Parthenope* and *Egeria* are representations of man-become-God gone wrong. They are devoid of all femininity, a vindication for Mary Shelley, the creator of *Frankenstein*.

If anybody now asks me why Edinburgh University closed us down, I tell them that underneath the presenting symptoms like Eigg and the superquarry, it was epistemological. A conservative university holds in place the establishment mindset. It may be a largely unconscious process, but that is how it has probably been since the days of the 'first university', Plato's Academy. Our CHE was too much of a thorn in the side of the malestream mainstream; too much like that dissenting colleague in Milgram's experiment. And I demonstrate my point by taking them to see Paolozzi's sculptures. 'There,' I say, 'is what shut us down. There are the Powers; the fallen, mutant and tragic Powers.'

Happily, the CHE was re-established in 1997 by its former students and teaching staff. It was the students, supported by charitable trusts and some prominent academics – including a few brave figures from Edinburgh University – who saved the place. In January 2000 academic accreditation was restored by the Open University's validation unit. More students than ever before enrolled on the MSc degree course in human ecology.[4] But I did have cause, one day, to look into the old CHE office. It had lain unused for some time and was being stripped for renovation by workers.

Stepping inside felt like entering a tomb that still held relics of a once-wonderful and powerful spirit. Amazingly, a rose from the garden outside had forced a shoot in through the library window. It blossomed silently, a passionate red. And on our old blackboard someone unknown to me had written:

> This was once such a
> lively and exciting place to be.
> Now look at it!
> I hope the bastards who
> did it down are happy.
> Sadly, I am sure they are.
>
> – Ksirtin

So much for the University of Edinburgh. So much for that late, great, grove of academe. The Powers are fallen.

But we are undone in our humanity if we lose sight of the fact that the Powers can also be redeemed. In my last days at the University I was very touched by many things. One was a personal letter from a senior administrator, who wrote:

> You have served the University well . . . . [It] has benefited greatly from your contributions as a manager, teacher and inspirational guide. But that same University has been parsimonious where it should have been magnanimous, ill-tempered where it should have been conciliatory, loquacious where it should have been listening – faults typical of many grand old ladies!

For giving me so much over seven years, including these insightful experiences and the unique sabbatical in which to write this book, I thank the University of Edinburgh.

The backlash from the superquarry was felt at many levels. There were various casualties along the way. One seemed to be Scottish Natural Heritage (SNH), the Government's own environmental advisory agency, which finally forced the public inquiry through. In 1995 the Conservative government subjected SNH to a 10 per cent budget cut. The press suggested that in daring actually to carry out its mandate the agency

> . . . has had its wings clipped for being too good at its job . . . [having] aroused the ire of both ministers and the development lobby . . . [through such involvements as] intervention in one of the biggest environmental issues in Scotland in the 1990s, the . . . superquarry on Harris.[5]

In a 1993 referendum before the inquiry had taken place, 62 per cent of the people of Harris on a 61 per cent turnout had voted *in favour* of the quarry. The council then voted almost unanimously to grant outline planning permission. By May 1995, however, as the public inquiry closed, a repeat referendum by secret ballot recorded a massive swing to 68 per cent *against* the development, with a remarkably high 83 per cent turnout.[6] The Western Isles Council then voted 21–8 to reverse their earlier support for the quarry. The cartoon in the *West Highland Free Press* showed a mountain signposted 'To Lingerabay' in one direction, and 'To Damascus' in the other.[7] The stubborn facts that the public inquiry had uncovered had led to a sea change in opinion. Editorial leaders in the *Stornoway Gazette* concluded:

> Redland had far more resources to put into this fight than all their opponents put together will have in their entire lives. But they have lost. They have lost support from the ordinary people of Harris and they have lost the support of the Council .... It can be said clearly and without equivocation that the people of Harris have heard the evidence brought before the public inquiry and decided that they do not want a superquarry. The quarry promoters have lost the battle .... This is ... democracy at work and the very reason why we prefer it to any form of dictatorship.[8]

In what the press hailed as a 'final vindication of the quarry objectors' case', the Council adopted as its new-found policy position the case originally lodged by leading anti-quarry councillors – Norman MacDonald of Harris (who led the motion), Colin Campbell of Benbecula, Donald MacLean of Lochmaddy and Alasdair Nicholson and Roddy Murray, both of Lewis.[9] However, it was not until March 1998 that Miss Pain finally produced the first draft of her report. This comprised her summary of the evidence and 'findings of fact', but was as yet minus the conclusions. She had been required to conduct the biggest-ever public inquiry in Scotland, single-handedly, without even so much as clerical support. The political system had never been designed to accommodate such major challenges from multinationals or, for that matter, such international responses from objectors.

By the end of the millennium, the politicians in Edinburgh had still not arrived at a final decision on whether to let the scheme go ahead or not. Partly the delay was down to Miss Pain having fallen ill while writing up her report, but in addition ministers seemed to be in no hurry to decide on a political no-win situation. Either environmentalists or industry were destined to be angered by the outcome, and both lobbies were powerful.

As time had rolled on, huge political changes had been taking place. Scotland was on its way to recovering its own Parliament. This would bring about greater local control. Yet globalisation was pulling political levers in the opposite direction. Polarisation between the centre and the periphery was escalating. All this had been reflected in the quarry debate. Indeed, it was brilliantly captured in the summing-up stage of the public inquiry. Here, Dr Robert Reed QC, a member of the pro-quarry legal team, deeply offended local people by saying: 'One of the most worrying aspects of the inquiry has been the gloomy and despairing attitude of many of the Harris natives who have given evidence, and their suspicion of outsiders, commerce and enterprise.'[10]

There you have it. If you care for place and culture, if you fail to worship Mammon, you're 'gloomy and despairing'. Imagine what people might have thought if those of us opposed to the development had gone about responding in kind. Imagine if we had accused Redland of being 'a heap of trouble', stuck in a 'hole', and soon to be 'gone off the rails' to the detriment even of its 'long-suffering shareholders'. And imagine if, to bolster this incredible case against such a monolithic Leviathan, we predicted that the company's share price would nosedive from 634p to just 258p in the three years following the public inquiry, causing it to be described authoritatively as going from 'glamour stock to basket case'. Imagine, too, if we had told Miss Pain that 'loss of independence seems a foregone conclusion' for Redland, and that it was likely to fall to a predatory takeover by one of the new breed of 'pan-European monster' companies, the 'political fall-out' from which can only store up social 'tensions for the future' as these massive transnational corporations 'eliminate thousands of jobs, but can be extremely profitable'.

Imagine if we had said all that! Well, these quotations all come from the *Financial Times* of 14 October 1997.[11] They were written as Redland succumbed to a hostile takeover by the French multinational Lafarge. The astonishing reality was that, as time rolled on, a crippled Redland was brought down by its own kind. From the time the public inquiry ended, their corporate roller-coaster ride had become increasingly bumpy. The company had progressively lost face in the Hebridean press, and, it would seem, this was reflected in a wider deflation of Redland's sails.

There were many reasons why the local side of things had gone flat as people became better informed. One factor was a mounting concern that not one, but several superquarries could be visited upon the islands. Indeed, as far back as 1992 Redland had pushed its luck by proposing to establish a second huge quarry, this time in Carnish, in the beautiful Lewis district of Uig. The crofters there woke up one morning to letters saying that the company had just bought the gravel from under their fields, and they might have to move.[12] 'No way!' the crofters replied. Thereafter Redland had gone very quiet. Two years later, however, a company called Scottish Aggregates, a subsidiary of Ready-Mix Concrete (The RMC Group plc), announced that they had acquired the mineral rights on Loch Seaforth from a Swiss heiress, Mrs Panchaud. Mrs Panchaud had just sold most of the North Harris mountains to the conservation-minded Bulmer cider family. Unknown to the Bulmers, however, she had kept back one little corner for a potentially more profitable scheme on the lower slopes of the Clisham range – the northern part of the island. Ready-Mix planned to wait and see if Redland succeeded in establishing the precedent of violating a National Scenic Area.[13] If they did, Ready-Mix would push through their own quarry in this majestic fjord, also a Marine Conservation Area. As Norman MacLeod was to write in expounding his 'gravel-pit of Europe' scenario, 'the Lingerabay quarry is only the first of many [that] will prove a humiliating exploitation: Harris being ripped apart and her people ripped off'.[14] 'Imagine,' he said to me, 'if a Harris woman had gone to Switzerland and proposed superquarrying the Eiger!'

Then, to further sour the corporate cream, a raft of financial controversies began to emerge. Angus Graham, a vigorously pro-quarry councillor, was questioned about 'hospitality' received from Redland. He said there had been none, except that 'sandwich lunches were provided to council members' and that there had been a number of occasions during the public inquiry when Redland staff had offered council staff their 'spare sandwiches'.[15] That was perhaps innocent enough. However, one of the famous sandwich-eaters was Graham Barry Edwards, the Council's assistant director of administration. As journalist Mike Merritt revealed, Edwards had championed the cause of duty to the extent of refusing elected councillors access to an environmental consultancy report critical of the quarry while simultaneously copying it to Redland! A cartoon in the *West Highland Free Press* showed dissatisfied councillors at Edwards' desk, saying, 'He won't tell us what was in the sandwiches either . . .'. But the fan really hit the, shall we say, cream, when it was revealed that upon Edwards' retirement from his post with the council, he accepted a new job – as public-relations advisor on island matters to Redland! 'The ethics did not worry me in the slightest,' he said demurely. The council, however, were sufficiently incensed that they moved to sever all contact with Redland, thereby doubtless giving Edwards a more relaxing retirement.[16]

Meanwhile, the bardic tradition had wound itself up to full declamatory volume. The *Stornoway Gazette* published Gaelic poems about the beauty of Roineabhal and letters from islanders as well as visitors lamenting the proposed desecration. Many of these revealed profound concerns about global capitalism coming to town. One writer, Norina MacLean from Stornoway, with a sharp eye for particularising the global from the local, put it like this: 'Redland has little respect for culture and roots even at an hour of remnant . . . . The battle is for Lingerabay; the war is for the spirit of a people and of a nation.' And my old schoolfriend Ian Stephen, the Benside poet, wrote of how Roineabhal had long been used as a line of sight when fishing far out at sea. He concluded laconically, 'Maybe we'll lose/only our bearings'.[17]

It was during the run-up to the 1997 general election that the heat really piled on to the company or, arguably, was piled on by it. The candidate for the SNP, Dr Anne Lorne Gillies, claimed that Redland intermediaries had made three approaches to get her party to drop its opposition to the superquarry. Her election agent, Angus Nicolson, told the press, 'I was the subject of one approach and the figure of £30,000 was mentioned [to bankroll the election campaign]. I am not a liar.' Dr Gillies also said she had been telephoned by a person introducing himself as 'a consultant for Redland' who offered her information that could have been useful in the election. She claimed that he told her 'they could influence the vote in Harris and if I supported the superquarry they could get the people of Harris to vote for me'.[18] Dr Gillies, outraged at this ostensible attempt to pervert the course of democracy, filed a complaint with the Stornoway police. This prompted the islands' green-leaning Labour MP, Calum MacDonald, publicly to ask the company: 'What is the size of the slush fund set aside by Redland Aggregates to try and influence opinion in the Western Isles?' Redland executives retorted that the allegations were 'totally unacceptable'. But rather than offering to help the police to get to the bottom of the matter and deal with any renegade consultant who might have acted beyond his remit, they threatened the SNP with libel action. The police complaint was promptly dropped, but only after, in the words of the *West Highland Free Press*, the SNP started 'shifting the blame to the mineral giants' PR company, Barkers'.[19]

Whatever the truth or otherwise in local talk about political corruption, about Freemason networks and about inflated 'consultancy fees', it was certainly the case that Barkers, a major London-based PR and advertising company, had been deeply involved behind the scenes. During 1996 a group of pro-quarry Harris residents had formed a body called the Coastal Quarry Local Supporters' Network (CQLSN) to advance their interests. 'We will be asking questions and raising any issues that come up because we are totally independent,' asserted Catherine MacDonald, a former councillor who had recently failed to be re-elected on her pro-quarry platform. However, as Callum Ian Macmillan of the council's Labour group retorted:

> The supporters' network claims to be independent of Redland yet newspaper articles costing thousands of pounds . . . have been paid for. The network's helpline, which purports to be based in Harris, is in fact run by Redland's PR firm, Barkers, in Glasgow. So much for the claims that the network is independent.[20]

Early in 1997 the CQLSN announced that it had negotiated an £18 million compensation deal with the company for the community. Calum MacDonald MP responded that this was 'like buying a round of drinks' on the eve of a general election. In addition, the lobby group had circulated a glossy mailshot to Harris residents. This proffered 'findings of fact' about the quarry's many benefits. But the 'facts' were to backfire. Shortly after their circulation, Catherine MacDonald, in a remarkable expression of principle, abruptly resigned her role in the lobby group. She put out a statement saying:

CQLSN's 'findings of fact' document sent out recently had Barkers' name at the top of it. They used my name and attributed comments to me without even asking my permission to do so. I also feel that other letters which they say have come from the CQLSN have in fact been written by Redland's consultants.[21]

In addition, Ms MacDonald alleged that even the CQLSN's constitutional principles had been 'drawn up by Redland's lawyers'. She said that while she still supported the idea of a quarry, she felt that Redland were now 'imposing their will' on the local community.

However, the CQLSN's vice-chair staunchly denied these claims. It was an authentic community organisation, he insisted; certainly not a corporate front. He said, 'Redland are not involved in drafting the constitution. It has absolutely nothing to do with Redland. We are doing this off our own back.' Well, it was a nice try, but the same *Stornoway Gazette* report went on (oh how stubborn facts can be) to disclose that the paper had obtained a copy of a fax from Burness, Redland's solicitors. It was addressed to John Lievers, the Redland director responsible for driving the scheme through. The fax showed conclusively that not only had Burness conceived the CQLSN constitution, they had even baptised the baby: the CQLSN had been given its cumbersome name by Redland's own lawyers.[22]

When pressed by Calum MacDonald MP on the CQLSN's funding, John Lievers was forced to issue an admission. He conceded: '[It] is completely correct ... that Redland Aggregates Limited has met the costs of the CQLSN's mailshots to the people of Harris. The company will continue to meet other reasonable expenses where appropriate and when requested to do so.'[23] In response to a request I made for further information in August 2000, Mr Lievers acknowledged that Redland had also given 'modest' sponsorship to the Harris football team, a student bursary and the Leverburgh agricultural show. He refused to disclose the level of the CQLSN's funding, saying, 'The total amount reimbursed over the years is the concern only of this company and the CQLSN . . .'.[24] It was Mr Lievers, incidentally, who in 1993 had argued: 'A public inquiry would be a complete waste of money. What will happen is you will get an awful lot of people going over an awful lot of issues that we have already gone over.'[25]

As the 1990s progressed, then, Redland had indeed, and in more ways than one, gone from being 'a glamour stock to basket case'. The takeover by Lafarge now meant that any go-ahead for the quarry would be in the French national interest rather than the British one that had been so fervently argued over during the public inquiry. Henceforth we were to be dealing with Lafarge Redland Aggregates Ltd – a tiny subsidiary of the biggest cement producer in the world; a company run by a chief executive, Bertrand Collomb, whose office desk, according to the business pages of the *Scotsman*, is built of the company's own product: concrete![26]

As for Harris, what had been a poorly informed public in the early 1990s was now no longer so. By the beginning of the new millennium, Harris Development Ltd, a group set up by local people to stimulate alternative employment,[27] had created more jobs in tourism, electronics and fish processing than the quarry would have done had it been up and running. A new consciousness had arisen on Harris. People had faced the fundamental set of strategic questions: Where are we? Where do we want to go? And how are we going to get there? They had undertaken this not for personal enrichment, but for community benefit. And 'daily bread' for many of the employable unemployed had come to them.

Nowhere was the island's new-found confidence in its own identity more obvious than in the public-inquiry summing-up speech delivered by its chosen representative, John MacAulay of Manish. In contrast to Robert Reed's corporate sense of gloom and doom, MacAulay described a resurgent empowerment resulting from 'the education' that Harris had undergone. Much of this, he said, had necessarily been self-education. It had entailed weighing up the cases of the pro and anti lobbies, as well as substantial unpaid research to enable the community to represent itself at the inquiry without the enormous expense of a legal advocate or QC. In a style remarkably resonant with Noel O'Donoghue's writing about 'the mountain behind the mountain', he concluded:

At this inquiry we have heard Harris described as 'poor'. We have tried in our own evidence to point out the importance to the people of Harris of the non-material benefits of living here and how these transcend material considerations . . .

[Mount Roineabhal] provides peat for fuel from the lower slopes; clean fresh water from the upper streams for public water supplies; grazing for sheep; salmon and trout from the surrounding lochs; the very best of shellfish from around its coastline. It is of excellent educational and recreational value, both from the geological and historical significance of the area. It quietly dominates the townships of Strond, Borosdale, Rodel, Lingerabay and Finsbay, as well as the main southerly village of Leverburgh. *It is not a 'holy mountain' but it is certainly worthy of reverence for its place in Creation* . . .

The overwhelming effect and, in the long term, total dependency on one major industry would bring about irreversible changes to the culture and way of life, unacceptable risks to existing local industry, and the sterilisation of future compatible development. Few, if any, fears have been totally eliminated. It is increasingly harder to see how the island and its people could be adequately compensated if such a project was to proceed – a project described by one of the oldest residents in Lingerabay as a *breitheanas* – a judgement.[28]

Indeed, these words came from the same John MacAulay – shipwright, scholar and crofter – who had written about the Hebrides being Bhrighde's Isles and who would assist the GalGael with their desire to learn the art of Hebridean boatbuilding. What's more, the first work later completed by the GalGael Trust in Glasgow was an immaculate scale model of the birlinn, or Hebridean longship, featured in stone on the wall of St Clement's Church in the heart of this ancient parish, once called Kilbride. Cultural reconnection was happening!

I have seen it written in the plethora of material on Celtic saints that one Gaelic meaning of the name Bhrighde is 'Fiery Arrow'. I have so far been unable to confirm this, but it certainly seemed to me that in John's remarkable speech, a bardic 'arrow of the Lord' had found its mark.

Lafarge Redland Aggregates, however, were unimpressed at being nailed. In fact, they were incandescent. Having invested over £6 million so far, John Lievers was determined not to let his shareholders down. As for Ian Wilson, the mineral-rights owner, he had gone very quiet. After all, he had always said he would never let a superquarry go ahead if local people didn't want it. It now seemed they didn't want it, but he was dug too deep into the hoped-for 'glory hole', as he called it, to wriggle back out.[29]

In her final report, eventually completed in 1999, Miss Pain concluded that the quarry would create about a hundred jobs – not the several hundred originally speculated upon. And this figure included the indirect jobs that would be generated by knock-on effects in the wider economy. Harris itself, she said, would only gain thirty-three direct jobs. A further ten induced jobs would bring the probable total to forty-three, thereby boosting the island's employment by 10 per cent. It was, she added, 'not possible to predict the impact of the quarry on the tourist industry'. As no reliable studies had been undertaken, it was not possible to know if the quarry's gains would be offset by losses in other employment sectors.

Her conclusions had little to say about human culture, focusing mostly on the single issue of Sabbath observance – which was really a non-issue because the company had already agreed not to work unnecessarily on Sundays. The eagles, she said, could go and hunt elsewhere; there was 'no conclusive evidence' that they would abandon their nesting sites as half their mountain got blasted away. The otters would be displaced from their holt, but 'any disturbance would not be unreasonable', and her discussion erroneously spoke of *Lutra vulgaris*, the common otter, instead of *Lutra lutra*, the species which lives on the site and which happens to be protected by European law.[30] As for the National Scenic Area (NSA) designation, this was a bit of a problem. She said:

I find that the proposed quarry will completely change the landscape characteristics of Lingerbay by changing the scale and character of its coastline and its hinterland . . . . I find that the impact cannot be described as minimal – on the contrary, it would be locally severe . . . . The quarry would create an area of massive disturbance, involving man-made industrial features, heavy plant, and disruptive noise, etc . . . . The present remote, peaceful, and traditional ensemble of a semi-natural and croft-ing agriculture environment would be disrupted by the intrusion of a man-made excavation and associated quarry and harbour installations on an enormous scale . . . . Altogether, I find that this would have a very disruptive effect on the character of the immediate area affecting local residents . . . . Unless there are overriding reasons relat-ing to national benefit, which is a matter for my conclusions, the acceptance of such an intrusive feature within such an important landscape would set a precedent that would undermine the continued successful operation of policy for NSAs.[31]

That justification, however, was duly provided. Miss Pain broadly accepted gazumping estimates from government and the industry that British primary aggregate production would increase from 304 million tons in 1989 to 426 mil-lion by 2011. However, as Ian Callaghan of Scarista House and Kevin Dunion of Friends of the Earth Scotland repeatedly pointed out, actual demand was matching only 50 per cent of these forecasts.[32] Not only that, but in England the industry already had huge stocks of unworked quarrying material – mas-sive reserves that it called 'landbanks'. Miss Pain nevertheless considered that there was a justified need 'for minerals operators such as Redland to look for alternative sources of aggregates in order to maintain their landbanks to serve the English market for the future'. Accordingly, she summed up her report by saying: 'The potential for coastal superquarries does not derive from any need for the material in Scotland but is primarily related to the market in South-East England, with the possibility also of export outside the UK.' In this respect, aggregates from superquarries would represent 'an important nat-ural resource [which would] make an essential contribution to the nation's prosperity [and] can assist the balance of payments, either through exports of minerals or import substitution'.[33]

All this, in the view of Miss Pain, justified 'the conclusion that overall, the proposed development would be in the national interest'. The harm to the National Scenic Area would be offset by the economic benefit. In any case, after 'restoration' the crater

. . . would undoubtedly be a dramatic feature and would eventually create a diversity of landscape which would not be out of place in an area of scenic beauty. The new road around [the hole] would also provide interesting views out to the Minch and the cliff itself would be attractive to geologists, mountaineers, botanists and even wildlife.[34]

In short, Miss Pain presented the Scottish government with her recommen-dation. She said, 'On balance, the proposals would be beneficial . . . . Accordingly, I recommend that the application . . . be approved.'[35]

24. Storming the Bastille

It happened very quickly in the end. During March 1995 Maxwell MacLeod had broken the story in *Scotland on Sunday* that a German artist, Professor Maruma, claimed to have secretly bought Eigg for £1.6 million ($3 million). Sir Maxwell, who was well connected to the landed establishment and close to some of Schellenberg's family, could not reveal his sources. However, the story flew in the face of all other evidence. Not least, Schellenberg was issuing adamant denials. He claimed:

> The island has *not* been sold. I can't answer why this chap [Professor Maruma] is saying he has bought it. The island is not for sale and has not been put on the market. The more this type of thing appears, then the less likely any changes will occur at all.[1]

The media revelled in such headlines as 'Two "owners" scramble for possession of Eigg' and 'Tussle of Teutonic eccentricity'. But sold the island proved to be. The threat that there would be no changes if people continued to express their legitimate interest proved to be Schellenberg's final blast of bluster. When it came to the crunch, the Last Emperor lay exposed, naked, for all to see – a man unable to admit reality and no longer able to control its representation. He had reportedly signed the island away to Maruma over dinner 'on a table napkin, prompted by the approval of his friend, the captain of Clanranald' – whose ancestor had first sold Eigg into private ownership in the first place.[2]

The ex-laird made his swansong appearance on Eigg when he went to collect remaining belongings on 4 April 1995. 'Just look at that!' said Davey Robertson to an incredulous *New York Times* journalist, pointing to mangled water pipes in the Lodge's kitchen. 'You read about people taking even the kitchen sink with them. He's actually done it!'

As two helicopters full of reporters swooped down and swooned at such a delectable yarn, Schellenberg, with fixed grin, stepped off the Eigg pier and on to a landing craft heaped up with the kitchen sink and even the light fittings.

He glowered at the assembled islanders who'd turned out *en masse* to witness this historic event. 'It's great to see everyone here without any work to do!' he snapped.

'Don't you know? It's Eigg's official holiday,' quipped Wes Fyffe, the fisherman husband of Maggie, she now being the towering power behind the Isle of Eigg Trust.

As the landing craft chugged away from the pier, Schellenberg's mood suddenly inverted in that manner so characteristic of people who are divided within themselves. His head lifted, a smile broke through the thundercloud, and, bizarrely, he called out for 'three cheers'. Ecstatic islanders responded unreservedly. Three raucous 'hoorays' went off like carnival fireworks. Never before had the laird and vassals of Eigg been so united. Never had there been such cause for celebration.

'You never understood me,' he shouted back plaintively, across the ocean's widening gulf. 'I always wanted to be one of you.'[3]

A quiver of excitement ran through Scotland after the massive media coverage of the day's events. A newspaper poll revealed that two in three Scots now wanted regulation of the land market.[4] Eigg had not yet come into community ownership, but something had shifted. A transformation had taken place both on this tiny island and in the national psyche. For the first time in Scottish history a community had cleared their own laird. A new space in the mind had opened up. It was now seriously legitimate to think of challenging landed power.

A French tourist visiting Eigg summed the situation up. 'It feels,' she told me, 'like being present at the storming of the Bastille.'

The pasty-faced Professor Maruma, all of forty-one years in age, was rarely without a cigarette in hand, wearing blue jeans taut over a bulging backside, a revolutionary-looking red shirt, and his trademark black beret slouched sideways over thinning, lank, black hair. His persona was less laid-back than smeared-back. He must, given his new status as the Grand Old Laird of Eigg, have been a very rich man indeed to expect to carry it off.

Media reports claimed that he was a fire-worshipping New Age 'holistic artist' – the reputed nephew of Nazi field marshal Karl von Runstedt.[5] He claimed to have made his fortune selling pictures at up to half a million pounds each on the international art market.[6] He wanted to turn Eigg into a paradise for ecologically sound 'soft tourism'. The spirited fight that the residents had put up in seeing off Emperor Schellenberg had specifically attracted him. Maruma presented himself as the first of a new breed of right-on laird.

'Look, it's all about energy,' he told a bemused Lesley Riddoch (who once told me that the secret of her popularity as a campaigning journalist was 'teaching people how to say *bog off*'):

It's all about energy. Schellenberg had craziness and he put it outside himself on everyone who lives here. I admire you for standing up to him. That shows a healthy energy. That's what I need to make my plans work .... We will build a new pier and get a boat. Islanders will use it for free. Tourists will pay .... We will make a revolution here together – all we need is positive energy and courage.[7]

He had been given the name Maruma when a guru saw it while staring into a muddy puddle in Abu Dhabi. His art involved setting fire to painted canvases to create a mystic fusion of the artist and the elemental. Volcanic Eigg was, of course, a mecca for a fire artist. And he was especially attracted to the Massacre Cave, where, in a tribal war back in 1577, the island's 400-strong population had reputedly been kippered to death while trying to hide from the invading MacLeods of Harris.

'We will live here soon,' Maruma said, nodding to his demure German girlfriend as he warmed to his *Scotsman* interview with Lesley. The girlfriend spoke hardly any English and was scarcely old enough to be out of school, but she doted admiringly on this man of passion – the professor who, having spent just a few hours on Eigg, could say:

I love this island. When I went to the cave, I knew this was the right place to be. The cave is the island's soul because this is where it has been hurt. That's what the Maoris believe – the cave is special. It is like the birth canal of a woman . . . the uterus. All the pain is there and yet all the energy is there too. Do you understand?

However, apart from sending a studiously polite letter at the beginning, Maruma carefully avoided all contact with me. This made me uneasy. My suspicions were not alleviated when, in June 1995, on one of only three occasions that he visited the island, he called a residents-only public meeting and declared, 'You don't need the Isle of Eigg Trust now. You've got Maruma.'[8]

Meanwhile, investigative journalists from around the world were swarming in and trying to check out his background. None of them could get a grip on his past. Finally, Germany's *Stern* magazine disclosed that he was unheard of in the art world and dubbed him 'the German fairy-tale prince'. His claim to be a professor at 'Athens University, New York' was found to be without foundation. His real identity was plain Herr Marlin Eckhardt and the only distinctive letters attached to his name were for a string of unpaid debts. The German courts attempted to settle these by auctioning off the paintings in his 'Maruma Centre' gallery in Stuttgart. They were worthless.

A promise had been made to invest £15 million in 'the Maruma Concept for sustainable development'. Thankfully, it never materialised. Amid much media speculation about laundered drugs money from the Russian mafia, it turned out that the real game had probably been to make Eigg a tourist resort for rich Germans. Maruma had cobbled together the buying price from a funding consortium. It was reportedly backed by half a dozen German businessmen including the financier Dr Heinz-Dieter Kals, a retired scientist called Willy Hermann and a Stuttgart hotelier by the name of Zimmerman.[9] There was speculation that these were all friends of Schellenberg's and that he had cooked the whole thing up as a way out and a Teutonic joke, with Maruma as the fall guy. Whatever the truth of the matter, the Maruma Concept got no further than the 'professor' asking John Cormack, Eigg's postman, to move his little house away from the sea 'to make way for the Maruma beach concept'. John had the redoubtable pleasure of telling him that this coastal strip fell under crofting tenure and therefore its tenants were protected under the 1886 Crofting Act. Strangely enough, one got the impression, doubtless mistaken, that neither Keith Schellenberg nor his selling agents had bothered to tell the hapless Maruma that any development plans for this beautiful spot would be built on sand.

So it was that come early 1996, the final act in Schellenberg's 'greatest soap opera of all time' was making front-page headlines up to three times a week. Maruma had failed to pay wages. He had failed to sign over the plot he promised for a community hall. He had failed to sign agreement for the community's initiative on native forest regeneration, leading to the loss of a large job-creating grant for replanting. And he was even in the process of having to sell the island's remaining cattle to pay the bills of his Edinburgh-based lawyer, this being the same lawyer, incidentally, who had originally told me that he had seen good and bad landlords over the years, but the professor was one in whom we could almost certainly place confidence!

Enough was enough, and on 29 January 1996 the Eigg Residents' Association went public and issued a statement of no confidence. Maruma was to shape up or shake out. In that week alone, the *Scotsman* devoted four front-page stories to Eigg and mentioned it in two leaders. Other newspapers similarly clamoured for the action. It was like *Whisky Galore* – an absurd tale that could only come from the 'furthest Hebrides', but a tale that was striking chords in the furthest corners of the world.

With the general election just over a year away, the Conservative government recognised that it had a political problem on its hands. Ministers could no longer abdicate concern for matters that they might have preferred to remain outwith their 'locus to intervene'. A *Scotsman* editorial called on Margaret Thatcher's notorious poll-tax architect, Michael Forsyth, the Secretary of State for Scotland, to *do something*. It concluded:

Last week, in the wake of renewed worries over the intentions of the laird of the island of Eigg, we lamented anew the idiosyncratic and anachronistic system of land ownership in Scotland and underlined the need for reform at the roots. Michael

Forsyth . . . [must now find] courage to address the fundamental iniquities of land ownership.[10]

As press cuttings faxed through the ether like intercontinental ballistic missiles from Alaska, Bonn and Buenos Aires, and television teams parachuted in from Japan, France, New Zealand and the United States, Maruma was forced by Heinz-Dieter Kals to put Eigg back on the market. Kals wanted over £2 million for it. Poor Maruma was in a tailspin, shot down from a £15 million high by the paparazzi. He'd just wanted a good trip. Now he just wanted, one suspected, to clamber back up the birth canal and hide in the famous uterus. He seemed to be going mad. He had started to mirror the unreality of Schellenberg; it was as if Schellenberg's infection was catching. Everybody knew that Eigg was unofficially back on the market, but Maruma flatly denied any prospect of a sale. 'I love Eigg,' he insisted, 'and in the next couple of weeks I will visit the island to clear things up. I am the owner and want to stay the owner . . . . I have taken out a new loan to develop the island.'[11]

The scene could have been straight out of Tolkien's *Lord of the Rings*. Whoever held and used the ring of power was progressively destroyed by it. The ring had to be released. The ancient Celtic volcano was pumping energy again. These were heady times. In a dream, I saw the legendary dragon of Eigg provide the gold that would be needed to buy the island. It was just a dream, but it gave me a peculiar surge of confidence. It seemed to symbolise the resurgence of people power and, specifically, the power of the Big Women. And it wasn't just me being touched by archetypal forces. At around the same time, Colin Carr, the almost-evicted tenant farmer, and Scruff, the fisherman, went out one Sunday afternoon with a digger. They went to where a massive basalt column had lain for generations in grass by the roadside, dug a hole, and erected the pillar over a bottle of whisky. It was the same spot where I'd had that strange experience in the back of Mairi Kirk's Land Rover several years previously. 'We'd always talked about making it a standing stone and now felt like the right time to do it,' Colin told me.

The island had become too hot to handle. The privacy of any individual who presumed to wrest control of it would be undermined by intense media scrutiny. Private ownership had to be dropped, symbolically, between the cracks of the basalt columns of the island's Sgurr. It had to be dropped, just as in Tolkien's tale Frodo Baggins (by Gollum's agency) finally drops the ring of power: it falls down through the gaping jaws of the Crack of Doom, deep inside the territory of Sauron, the Dark Lord.

Title over the island of Eigg had to be set free. It had to be returned to the soil; to the people of the soil; to the wildlife of the soil – aye, to the very God of the soil. As the folk singer Dougie MacLean puts it, 'You can't own the land; the land owns you.'

No lie can stand the test of time. So it was that shortly after Maruma's Schellenbergesque denial of any intention to sell, a selling agency was appointed. This was the remarkable and amusingly named Vladi Private Islands, run by one Farhad Vladi, who describes himself as an 'international island broker'. It was he who reportedly struck the original deal between Schellenberg and Maruma.

Vladi had first accompanied Maruma to Eigg as a translator. He told the press: 'Scottish islands are the Van Goghs on the international island market, masterpieces of mother nature.' His agency had 120 other islands worldwide on their books, each having been graced by a personal visit from Vladi. 'There is a sense of romance in buying islands,' he enthused. 'It is the ultimate purchase you can make, a complete miniature world of which you can be king . . . owning your own domain, surrounded by water and with the privacy to enjoy it alone with just family and friends.'[12] To the Eigg islanders this Canadian from Nova Scotia of Iranian and German descent, who boasted members of the Shah of Iran's family among his five hundred satisfied customers, was but 'some kind of enigmatic Buddha who gave us all the creeps'.

In September 1996 the British general election was just eight months away. The Conservative Party knew that they were electorally vulnerable, having, among other sins of commission and omission, abdicated governance over the question of landed power. They had failed to protect the Community of the Realm. The Union of Scotland and England itself was under threat, with mounting demands for, if not a full divorce, then certainly an amicable separation and semi-detached relationship. Accordingly, Michael Forsyth helicoptered into Eigg for breakfast one day, just to show that his party really did care. The residents told him that without security of tenure, they could not even apply for development assistance under his own Rural Partnership Fund for sponsoring community self-help projects. Forsyth came away saying:

> Frankly, I was rather appalled by the description they presented of an island whose infrastructure is crumbling and which is suffering from very serious neglect. The present situation is pretty shocking and is not sustainable. The islanders have a right to a degree of security.[13]

The following May, however, would see the 'melt-down' scenario whereby every Scottish Conservative seat, including Forsyth's, was wiped out. The election of a new Labour government would see a referendum giving 75 per cent backing to the restoration of a Scottish Parliament. The new millennium would usher in a completely new era in Scottish politics. It would, many hoped, start to reverse policies that James I had initiated some four hundred years earlier following the 1603 Union of the Crowns, policies that led to the loss of Scottish autonomy in 1707. The consciousness and conscience-raising process of conscientisation, spurred by outrage over the land question and other triggers for popular education like the superquarry debate, had certainly played their respective parts in this.

By early 1997, the Isle of Eigg Trust was in full and serious fundraising swing, running a series of fabulous events including a 'Not the Landowner's Ball' at which major Scottish artists performed. Dr Heinz-Dieter Kals, as principal creditor, now called the shots. Maruma, like some wicked prince (or was it court jester?) had been banished by the good faerie. He was never, ever, heard from again in the Eigg soap opera. Somewhere on Eigg there will be a flat rock, perched on a pinnacle like a black beret. In years to come, hundreds of years ahead in the future, old storytellers with a twinkle in the eye and a dram to warm the belly will tell tourists: 'Ah yes, the legend of Maruma's Cap . . . they say he is still down there, and if we don't look after this island right, then one day . . .'

But we weren't at that stage yet. For a week or two, our hearts sank when it was announced that the island might be bought by a richly endowed operation – the Pavarotti Foundation. Its smarmy and ever-smiling besuited consultants were to meet with the local authority, Highland Council, to discuss using the island to establish a college for three thousand opera students under the Italian tenor, Luciano Pavarotti. However, the mirage evaporated when Pavarotti disclaimed sponsorship; and the Foundation's manager proved to be, yes, one Heinz-Dieter Kals![14] It was all just a ruse to up the ante in the bidding stakes.

My own role in the Eigg Trust was by now, in early 1997, extremely minimal. Although I was still a trustee, the islanders had run it all themselves since 1994. They had achieved this with efficiency, vision and courage. Those who had predicted that everybody would 'fight like cats in a bag' were confounded: men and women alike had pulled together like a pack of workhorses. A new trust, The Isle of Eigg Heritage Trust, was now being set up to subsume the original one. This incorporated the residents of Eigg, who would have four trustee places, Highland Council, representing the wider democratic constituency, with two places, and the Scottish Wildlife Trust, representing the birds and the bees, also with two places. Its chair, Simon Fraser from Lewis, a Gaelic-speaking crofting lawyer, held the casting vote.

The idea of the Heritage Trust was not to make the residents into owners in the private sense of that word. Rather, most would remain tenants, but effectively become landlords unto their own democratic accountability. This would be a 'third way' approach to land holding: 'communitarian' rather than capitalist or communist. Under crofting law, tenancies can be inherited and remain secure if the crofter continues to be resident and does not abuse the land. This can allow for individual entrepreneurial freedom within a framework of mutual accountability and democratically controlled planning safeguards. Such a system offers a pattern and example for land reform that could perhaps spread much wider than Eigg or Assynt. Indeed, were it to be coupled with land value taxation – particularly where such taxation is loaded against owners who do not have the support of their communities – then a buy-out fund could be generated and the capital value of land would decline. By such means landlordism in rural and urban areas alike could be brought into check, turning market forces against themselves, and the lairds could, thereby, progressively finance their own clearance.

Land, after all, is the one commodity that God doesn't make anymore. It is therefore wrong for its ownership to be highly concentrated. Indeed, land comprises the natural nature in which human nature comes to know itself. Access to it is therefore important – even if exercised only in the wild and magical regions of the mind. Community land trusts are therefore an answer to providing people with the opportunity to live in a more authentic relationship *with* the land, even if not necessarily *from* the land. This matters, because it builds a sense of 'bioregion' that is human-scaled. Such a sense of place in turn contributes towards a sense of belonging. And that builds a sense of identity which in turn can carry the collective values that can sustainably generate the responsibility necessary for upholding both the social and the natural environments.

As such, the human sense of who we are and what we are about can be re-rooted. It can be built up from the ground upon which we stand. Global problems can then be tackled not just from the top down, which is important, but also from the local level up, which is even more important, because this is the level at which most people find themselves. The possibility then emerges of building a harmony of soil and soul: of releasing emergent properties that are positive, being based on right relationship between humankind and the natural world. Such are the potential fruits of building community on the bedrock of reverence.

So, Eigg was openly back on the market and Dr Kals had no scruples over who it should be sold to. We expected to have to pay about £1.5 million – half of what had been anticipated by Schellenberg when the Isle of Eigg Trust was first established in 1991. The Scottish Wildlife Trust and its English sister organisations mailed out an appeal using their huge membership lists. However, the Government's lottery-funded National Heritage Memorial Fund still refused to help. This was a disappointment, but again, it helped to up the ante. As Peter Peacock, the convenor of Highland Council, put it: 'You get the impression the lottery are under huge pressure behind the scenes from certain establishment figures not to give money as it might set a dangerous precedent in land ownership patterns in Scotland.'[15] Meanwhile, Nick Reiter, the council's head of policy, was helping to keep the market-spoiling temperature hot. He was busily telling the press, 'I don't think anyone would be foolish enough to buy the island having seen what is happening here. This is not just a piece of land for someone to pick up, there is an entire movement here.'[16]

While all this was going on, the people of Eigg were coming under pressure from the 'suits and ties'. They were actually being very helpful. But as always, they were worried about the movement's PR image. It was being suggested that island ceilidhs might best be kept out of sight of visiting journalists. But this was roundly rejected. It would have conflicted with that deepest instinct embraced by Eigg natives and incomers alike: Highland hospitality. So it was that one day along came a young journalist working for the *Guardian*. It happened at the time of the annual outing to the neighbouring island of Muck. During this sea voyage, people have a wee dram on the way there (to keep the cold at bay), another while on Muck (just to be friendly), and a third on the boat home (to assuage seasickness). Sometimes, however, the sea is very rough, there is a lot of sickness, and those worst affected engage in much assuaging.

Such was the fate on this occasion of poor Maggie Fyffe, and the *Guardian* accordingly ran a most lurid article. It would have been a betrayal of hospitality were it not for the fact that it was all true. It concluded: 'A fiddler played on the back of a truck and Fyffe lay in the middle of the road, asleep with a can of Export beside her head.'[17]

Poor Maggie. It looked like the worst possible PR. She felt like she'd betrayed the cause and let everyone down. However, an English millionaire, a woman who happened to be a *Guardian* reader, was rather touched by the article. Smart millionaires, after all, get wise to chancers who put on false faces to please them. This one rather liked the way the Eigg islanders were putting on airs and graces for nobody. All through the campaign they had simply been themselves – crofters, fishers, bed-and-breakfast providers, unemployable alcoholics, doctors, teachers, shepherds, builders, caterers, writers, artists, historians, retired military, ecologists, the lot. They had used the media to seek security of tenure for themselves and the island's wildlife, and they had, in so doing, advanced the wider cause of land reform. But they had never put on one face for the media and another for private life. They had never tried to master the stiff upper lip. And that was what had impressed so many journalists so very much. It impressed even those sent up from London with commissions to do hatchet-job stories; even these had been disarmed, dazzled by what they found on the Road to Damascus.

The funniest case was a private detective commissioned by a pop star to find out if the people's revolution was for real. The pop star wanted to know whether he and his proposed VIPs' hotel development scheme would be acceptable. Well, the detective turned up, plied all the usual informants with the usual lubricants, and concluded that not only was the revolution for real, but that he wanted to join it himself! His subsequent attempt to get a job on

Eigg failed, but he ended up moving from his city home to just a few stones' throws away from Tom Forsyth's place at Scoraig.

The solicitor of the *Guardian*-reading millionaire wrote to Tom Forsyth, who passed the letter to me, who gave it to Maggie. Maggie had to agree that she would be the only trustee to know the identity of the 'mystery woman', who offered the campaign half a million pounds. Meanwhile, thousands of small donations rolled in from the public. Many enclosed touching covering letters. Typical was that from an unemployed London man enclosing £2 and simply saying, 'It gives me hope.' Everybody joined in the task of opening envelopes, sending thank-yous and adding up the daily total. 'It started out at £1000 per post,' recalls Scruff (who, I can now safely reveal with appreciation, was the fisherman who had secretly given us his £100 right at the beginning). 'And it went up to thirty grand! It was just brilliant, pure magic!'[18]

We raised £600,000 from 10,000 small donations. This was still not going to be enough, so the mystery woman doubled her contribution. The Isle of Eigg Heritage Trust then put in its offer of £1.6 million. It narrowly exceeded the bid of an Oxfordshire farmer who had hoped to capitalise on our market spoiling! There were no other offers.

On 12 June 1997 the island of Eigg, representing fully 1 per cent of the privately owned land in the Scottish Highlands, formally came back into community ownership.

In the telling of this story I have drawn deeply upon spirituality. I have drawn upon the magic inherent in all miracles with which theology concerns itself. Much of the foregoing has been very personal, indeed risqué. In this my Australian rainforest friend, John Seed, has fortified me: 'When they tell you to tone it down, Alastair, just you turn it up.' I make no apology, proffer no excuses. This has been a theology of insistence. It has pushed me beyond myself. I want only to emphasise that this story is told as seen through my own eyes. As with the account of the superquarry, others would have described the landscape very differently. Adrienne Rich puts it like this: 'I stand convicted by all my convictions – you, too.'

My concern has been to honour the source of that spring-fed Well of the Holy Women – that cool pool of silver-running metaphor into which we have been gazing; that revelation of the creativity of God in nature; that passion in all the meanings of the word that is, in the community from which I come, understood as 'Christ'. And yes, these things will be mocked in some quarters. The Christians will say it is all too pagan and the pagans will say it is too Christian. I say to such hair-splitting: 'Too bad.' *Poesis* will always be discounted by the prosaic – by those stalwarts of the banal who miss, in the words of Adrienne Rich, 'the true nature of poetry. The drive to connect. The dream of a common language.'[19]

These things, I believe, need to be understood in our troubled times. They're needed by those called to the ancient and honourable work of unblocking wells. This sentiment, this hard-headed analysis, is not my own invention. It has a perennial life, an intelligence of its own. Only today as I wrote these concluding paragraphs, I came across a newly translated Gaelic poem by the Rev. Dr Kenneth Macleod. Listen, then, to part of 'An Fhuar-Bheinn' – 'The Cold Hill', the hill that is a source of cool refreshment, like that which feeds the Well of the Holy Women. Listen, in Ronald Black's rendition, to nature personified in the words of a poet who was born on Eigg in 1871 and is still warmly remembered by indigenous islanders to this day.

> My desire and my dreams in the cold hill, the cold hill,
>> With her pure spring water roaring down through a mist,
>> The sun and the starlight kissing her tresses
> While I want her and crave her as long as I live.[20]

I do accept that to many observers, spiritual meaning in the Eigg campaign would have been quite invisible, indeed nonsensical. These people would probably think that the only theology involved was when three clergy from the Presbyterian, Roman Catholic and Episcopalian traditions (a mini 'healing of the nations' in itself) gathered down by the pier on 12 June 1997 and jointly blessed Eigg's second newly erected standing stone, *Clach na Daoine* – the Stone of the People.

Others – at least, those who had missed seeing the school of 150 dolphins leaping around the boat bringing honoured guests that morning – these others might say that the most inspired piece of 'ministry' was when Brian Wilson MP, soon to become minister for trade and industry in Tony Blair's Cabinet, stood up in a packed marquee erected over the erstwhile Schellenberg's tennis court and declared, 'Game, set and match to the people of Eigg!'

And still others would have quipped that the most valuable spirit came out of the barrel of Talisker malt whisky, donated by a distillery founded on the neighbouring Isle of Skye by the MacAskill brothers of Eigg in 1825.

Well, of course, there is spirit and there is Spirit. I believe that both were at work during the island's land-reform campaign, and I would certainly be recommending a little of the Talisker too.

But it was Fiona Cherry's remark that gave me most pleasure during the three days of round-the-clock dancing that marked the end of seven generations of landlordism.

'What does it feel like, Fiona?' I asked, as we blethered and made music in Marie Carr's spacious kitchen.

'Well,' she replied. 'Yesterday I had a house. Today I have a home.'

25. Revolutionary Love

Within a year of the community buy-out, members of three indigenous house-holds were able to secure tenancies and come back to Eigg. One family did leave Eigg for the mainland, but an island is not a prison; there will always be a flux. The shoddy little tea-room on the pier gave way to a fabulous new visitor centre with a licensed restaurant, craft shop, post office and shop. A magnificently equipped hostel was privately built for backpackers and student groups, and the first use made of the Lodge (riddled with rot and in need of major investment as it is) was for a European conference on sustainable development.

Music was flooding back into the island. Alexander Carmichael had recorded that during the nineteenth century a famous fiddle player on Eigg had been persuaded by a preacher to discard his violin, made by a pupil of Stradivarius. Carmichael claimed that in lamenting 'the parting with it! the parting with it!' the old man had faltered, wept, and 'was never again seen to smile'.[1] Before he passed away, I asked Eigg's tradition bearer, Angus MacKinnon, if he thought this story was true. 'It certainly is true,' Angus replied. 'That man was of my own family. A visiting preacher made him do it, not one of our own clergy. And that fiddle had such a clear tone that if he played it at one end of Cleadale, you'd pick out every note at the other.'

Well, music had come back, and smiles accompanied it. The local economy was booming, and by the end of the millennium a local construction company had been established. Everybody was working on everybody else's projects and housing renovations. A five-year woodland regeneration programme employed six people, replanting native trees and fencing overgrazed areas to allow for natural regrowth. In May 2001 the corncrake, a rare bird absent for twenty years, returned. Visitors pumped three thousand bed-nights over the summer months alone into the tiny economy. Much of this work was seasonal and piecemeal, but taken together it made for the vibrant patchwork of livelihood that crofting at its best can be. But for Wes Fyffe, Maggie's husband, it was not without its downside.

'Well, Mr Fyffe,' the sympathetic woman in the unemployment benefit office said when he had to sign off, 'it must be very nice for you to have found a job after so long on the dole.'

Wes was for once lost for words. What could he say? After all, he'd been doing the rounds telling everyone, 'Ah, the spectre of full employment has at last returned to Eigg.'

And so it had. People were standing on their own feet more and more. They were getting it together and becoming self-reliant to a degree never before possible – because they had access to the local resource base with which to do it.

Yes, there are stresses in post-revolutionary Eigg, and yes, people will fall out and have to wrestle with the tensions of small-mindedness, fear and jealousy; but these things are all a normal part of being a real community. Conflict is a normal part of the human condition. If people can take responsibility and deal with it themselves instead of having to refer to the laird as a higher authority, then they can grow and increase their human understanding; even their love. Learning forgiveness and reconciliation is part of what community is for. We need more space for this in the world today if we want peace in the world of tomorrow.

In a wider Scotland, land reform has since shifted from being one of the driving forces to create the new Scottish Parliament to becoming a flagship policy within it. Brian Wilson MP told an unimpressed London Committee of the Scottish Landowners' Federation (the lairds' trade union) that an 'irreversible shift' has taken place 'in public policy towards the issue of land ownership in Scotland'. Land reform, he said, has now become 'a litmus test by which the Parliament and Executive would be judged'.[2] Alasdair Morrison MSP, the Minister for the Highlands and Islands in the Scottish government, said, 'Landlords have for generations been obsessed with control, but today are gripped with fear at the prospect of losing the illegitimate power they've exerted over Highland communities . . . . Notice has now been served on rapacious landowners who have abused wealth and privilege. An unstoppable reforming process has begun.'[3]

In January 1999 the Government published its Green Paper on land reform. This promised to address matters 'not as a once-for-all issue but as an ongoing process'. It continued:

The objective for land reform is to remove the land-based barriers to the sustainable development of rural communities . . . . To achieve this there needs to be increased diversity in the way land is owned and used . . . and increased community involvement . . . so that local people are not excluded from decisions which affect their lives and the lives of their communities.[4]

Meanwhile, the lairds held panic meetings and their magazine *The Field* spoke of 'Cuba visited upon the Highlands' and the threat of 'archaic socialist principles of the sixties'. Reform, it said, was something that the market 'would treat as very burdensome'.[5] A leader in *The Times* described the Scottish Parliament's thinking as 'rashly inflammatory', while the *Daily Telegraph* cranked like a creaking tank about 'Stalinism'.[6]

In May 2000 the Scottish Parliament unanimously passed a bill that, after nine hundred years, abolished feudal tenure. An £11 million fund was created to assist community buy-outs. And in February 2001 a draft land-reform bill was published, aiming to redress the inequitable ownership pattern left behind by feudalism. It offers crofting communities an automatic right to buy out their land at any time based on a government valuation. A more limited provision for other rural communities is proposed, which will give rights of pre-emptive purchase if and when land is put on the market.[7] While these measures are limited, they should help to constrain both the lottery of ownership and the lairds' behaviour. Inasmuch as they might be considered to represent a market impediment, they should contribute to market spoiling. To be a laird will no longer carry the automatic kudos that it once did.

In short, a gradual 'ongoing process' of land reform has begun. The litmus paper will remain under scrutiny. Scotland does not expect overnight miracles, but Scotland certainly expects positive change.

Scotland, however, did not know what to expect with the proposed and opposed Harris superquarry. Neither, it seems, did Lafarge Redland Aggregates Ltd.

In July 2000 Sarah Boyack MSP, the Scottish government's environment minister, announced that she was considering designating the mountain a Special Area of Conservation. Lafarge reacted by taking out a defensive lawsuit to try and force the Government's hand. Remarkably, they claimed that the long delay in concluding the inquiry process had violated their 'human rights' under Article 6 of the European Convention on Human Rights! Nobody questioned the justification of their claim that things had dragged on too long – we all felt that – but to make it an issue of corporate 'human' rights was quite something. In law, as we have seen, a corporation is considered to be a 'fictitious person'. It represents a collective of persons: the shareholders. Worryingly, Lord Hardie seemed to agree with the company that this meant that the corporation, in effect, had 'human' rights in the interest of representing the property rights of its owners. Lafarge won their case.

Needless to say, this gave me ample opportunity to expound the doctrine of corporate personhood to a rather incredulous public in the media. The notion had its origins, I was able to point out, in America in the case of Southern Pacific Railroad v. Santa Clara County, 1886. A corrupt Supreme Court judiciary decided that corporations had the same rights under the American constitution as people had.[8] The implication more than a century later across the Atlantic, I pointed out, was that the corporate Mammon was not only after our rocks: by hijacking human rights he was also redefining what it means in law to be a human being. It was, I suggested, a blasphemous and idolatrous use of law. Blasphemous, because it misrepresents the nature of God by implying that a man-made entity can be deemed 'human'; and idolatrous, because it does this in the worship not of God, but of profit.

Lord Hardie's decision gave the Scottish government two weeks to make up their mind on the quarry. Their hand had at last been forced, which was no bad thing, and the decision fell on the plate of Sam Galbraith MSP, now the environment minister following a cabinet reshuffle. On 3 November 2000 I was making my way to London to meet with Aurum Press to discuss their interest in publishing this book. On the way, I heard a radio report that the decision was imminent. When I arrived at Aurum's offices, I called the BBC's newsdesk – and I would imagine it is not often that a publisher's first encounter with an author is characterised by his filling the office with a great whoop of joy!

Sam Galbraith's letter to Messrs Burness, Lafarge's lawyers, detailed various points of disagreement with Miss Pain's conclusions and points of law where she had 'misdirected' herself. Perhaps out of sympathy for the crushing weight of the task that had been landed on her to deal with single-handedly, it mostly made light of these. But it came down heavily on two points. First, in stressing that she had interpreted the 'national interest' as 'primarily related to the market in South East England' and to export revenues, 'she has made inappropriate connections between Scottish policy . . . and English policy'. Accordingly, she had come to the wrong conclusion about what constituted an overriding 'national' interest. And second, ministers took the view that 'the Reporter has, in her overall conclusions, seriously understated the impact of the proposed development on the National Scenic Area'.

'Accordingly,' the letter concluded, 'the Scottish Ministers hereby refuse to grant planning permission in respect of the extraction, processing and transport by sea of anorthosite from land near Rodel, Isle of Harris.'[9]

We had won.

Except for Lafarge's appeal.

We had to wait the full six weeks that they were permitted before, at the very last moment, the company announced that they intended to appeal.

What's more, they were determined to fight it on two legal fronts. One would try to overturn the rejection of their planning application. The second would attempt to re-invoke an earlier planning permission granted back in 1965. Most people thought this 'grandfather' concession was no longer valid, but the company's lawyers believed they could prove otherwise.

On the first matter we suffered an immediate defeat. The Scottish government were forced to agree that their political decision rejecting the superquarry had not been sufficiently robust in law. Accordingly, they withdrew their letter of rejection and announced they would have to consider the matter afresh. The long waiting process would begin all over again.

The other prong in Lafarge's strategy could, equally, take years to work its way through the courts. For the island of Harris, it was the worst possible outcome. When the economy of an area depends heavily on tourism, people need to know where they stand. There would be no point planning for the future and investing in it if that future was perhaps going to be compromised by forced transition to an industrial economy.

So it was that we were all thrown back again onto watching all points of the come-to-pass. It was then, in the summer of 2002, that I received an intriguing e-mail. It came from a Monsieur Thierry Groussin, Chargé de la Formation des Dirigeants in the Confédération Nationale du Crédit Mutuel – the big French bank that, unlike capitalist banks, is owned and controlled by regionally based committees of its clients.

Thierry, as I came to know him, explained that he had bought a copy of *Soil and Soul* while on holiday in Scotland. He was particularly struck by the early section discussing the village economy in which I grew up: he realised I was describing the same ideals that had originally been the motivating force that drove the ethos of Crédit Mutuel. Staff needed to be reminded of these values to understand what was special about the organisation for which they worked. Would I, he therefore wondered, consider coming to Paris to address a conference of senior management? He didn't want anything fancy. None of my high-falutin' theories from MBA days about discounted cash-flow investment appraisal techniques discounting the children's future, or anything like that. Simply stories about mutuality in practice – the building of each others' houses, the sharing of fish, and so on. As an Irish priest had once advised me, 'Tell them it in stories, and they'll never forget.'

Well, Thierry's event ended up as not one conference, but four in total, also involving Camille Dressler from Eigg and my French wife, Vérène Nicolas, who specialises in community-empowerment work – which, actually, is what locally based mutual banking is a part of.

During these visits I was introduced to the 'Co-evolution Project' – a small Paris-based ecological think tank that Thierry ran jointly with Mme Dominique Viel, an economist with the French Ministry of Finance, and a few other thinkers. They were interested in the role of corporate ethical responsibility in addressing the present problems of the world. It troubled them considerably to learn that it was a French company, Lafarge, that was now behind our superquarry threat.

In the summer of 2003 Thierry and his son, Adrian, visited the Isle of Harris. He was delighted by the way local cars on the single-track roads would go out of their way to stop and let you past, sometimes causing mini-hold-ups as both parties flashed their lights, inviting the other to come on. 'Look,' I was able to say to him, laughing: 'this is the island where people compete to co-operate!'

We drove along a mixture of modern roads, where large volumes of stone had been blasted and bulldozed into place, and the old Golden Road, where much more modest quantities had been laid with care to provide beautiful ter-raced support. The contrast between profligate and respectful use of resources leapt out to the educated eye. Mind you, it has to be admitted that the Golden Road was named not after the island's haunting sunsets, as tourists like to think, but the construction cost! But maybe that is, in part, the way to go. Maybe, if we want to use resources more sustainably, we have to learn anew how to restore the human by mixing our creativity more fully with what nature provides. And maybe that's the beauty of it all.

The highlight of Thierry's visit was, of course, the ascent of Mount Roineabhal. As we sat on the summit, admiring the incredible view that remained so much under threat, he pulled out his mobile phone and started calling up various business colleagues! They, he told me, knew senior people in Lafarge.

'You know,' he said, 'Bertrand Collomb, who's now the chair of Lafarge, has developed an admired reputation in France for raising standards of eco-logical responsibility. It would shock French people if they knew what his company were threatening to do in Scotland. Indeed, I wonder how aware they are in Paris of what their newly acquired English subsidiary is doing?'

The outcome was that in October 2003, Thierry, Dominique and I were invited to visit Lafarge's headquarters in Paris. There we met with Michel Picard, Vice President for Environmental Issues, and Gaëlle Monteiller, Senior Vice President Public Affairs and Environment.

I must admit that I was not very optimistic about this meeting. Lafarge had, indeed, always appeared to us like the 'pan-European monster' about which the *Financial Times* had warned. However, my prejudices were rather challenged when I got there. The company's vice presidents seemed like thoughtful and concerned human beings, determined to use their positions to act as ethically as they could. They told me frankly that Harris 'has become a problem for us' and asked if I could set up a fact-finding visit so that they could come and listen to the positions of both sides of the community.

I returned to Scotland, my costs having been generously covered by a charitable foundation, the Network for Social Change. Working closely with Morag Munro, the elected councillor for South Harris, and John MacAulay, the community-appointed chair of the Quarry Benefit Group, I set up a series of meetings for 15 January 2004. The same two executives I'd met with in Paris, together with Philippe Hardouin, the company's Senior Vice President Group Communications, duly flew in to the island. They came, they saw and they listened carefully – particularly to concerns from those on both sides of the debate about ongoing planning blight afflicting the island's future.

They went away again, but on 2 April they came back on a chartered private jet. This time they brought with them two of their most senior English executives. In a simple meeting in the Harris Hotel, an event that felt almost ceremonial, they announced that they would be withdrawing from the project. They had seen that further years of legal argument would not be good either for the company or for the local community. In making this announcement, Philippe Hardouin told the press:

> We have to create value for shareholders, but we want to do it by respecting some values. The combination of both dictates our decisions. We recognise that if we are acting in the best possible way from an environmental standpoint, we will get a competitive advantage.

Responding to Michel Picard, Morag Munro wrote on behalf of the island's council:

> I wish to express my gratitude and the gratitude of this community to you for bringing the uncertainty of the past thirteen years to an end. We are very appreciative of the fact that you came to Harris to see for yourselves and then came back to give your decision directly to the community before anyone else. Your courtesy was greatly appreciated by both supporters and opponents of the project.

The Lafarge decision had come about partly because of 'push' from pressure groups like Friends of the Earth Scotland and the Royal Society for the Protection of Birds Scotland, and partly through 'pull' from other groups working with them to raise corporate standards. It later transpired that the Swiss-based WWF International (the World Wildlife Fund) had been particularly instrumental working jointly with its Scottish branch in this respect, threatening to pull out from its corporate partnership for sustainability with Lafarge if the superquarry went ahead.

But pressure like this can be effective only if it finds a point of attachment among those at whom it is aimed. After announcing their dignified exit strategy from Harris, I was subsequently invited by Michel Picard to spend three days with eighty-seven Lafarge managers, including the new chief executive, Bernard Kasriel, at a conference on quarrying and environmental responsibility in Bergamo, Italy, co-sponsored by WWF International. It was impressive to witness the workings of a large company, some of whose staff were being dragged kicking and screaming into a greener future and others who were very much doing the dragging, arising out of a genuine personal concern for the world.

I came away all the more convinced that it is the people that matter and can make a difference: as Jung said, individuals are the 'make-weight' that can tilt the balance. A large company is, indeed, a mindless monster, unless people all the way through the system devote themselves to making it otherwise. Then, and only then, can it start to become more like a community with values, and maybe even something of a soul. But this means, as with Groupe Crédit Mutuel, having an ethic that serves profit but transcends mere money-making. It is only human goodness that can bring this about and so humanise the otherwise inhumane world created by emergent properties of greed.

I am not saying here that Lafarge is always exemplary, or that somebody like myself may never find themselves standing against them in the future. I just wish to place on the record that, at the end of the day, the company did right by us. We have made friends and have, at their request, opened a public debate about future aggregate supply. The first airing of this appears in the summer 2004 issue of *ECOS*, the journal of the British Association of Nature Conservationists. It includes contributions from Nigel Jackson, Executive Director of Lafarge Aggregates UK, Dan Barlow of Friends of the Earth Scotland, and myself writing jointly with Jean-Paul Jeanrenaud and Luc Giraud-Guigues – the WWF International staff members who lobbied Lafarge so effectively as 'critical friends' from Switzerland.

It has to be said of this happy outcome that things probably would have turned out much the same even if Lafarge had exhausted their legal avenues. But by acting the way they did, they probably did themselves as well as us a favour. The involvement of the Paris executives most certainly accelerated the process. As one of them put it, 'The visit to Harris was the key in the lock that unblocked the process and moved it along.' For that, we genuinely thank them, and as Morag Munro's letter indicates, we do so most warmly.

On the eve of Lafarge making their historic announcement, a small group of people assembled in the Elder's house on Harris. We re-read Stone Eagle's public-inquiry testimony together and gave thanks for the wonderfulness of what he, with the crucial support of his former partner, Ishbel, had helped to achieve.

We recalled his request to us, before he went to jail, simply to be prayed 'with and not for'. 'During the darkest moments in your life,' he wrote in an e-mail, 'you'll find that even your shadow is gone.'

In July 2004, after being released from prison, Sulian wrote to us again. 'While I was in Waseskun healing lodge,' he said, 'the Elder there worked with me and showed me so many things that I must deal with and so many good things I must dust off and bring to the front. He saved my life! The long house society has made me a mask keeper but it is not time yet to think in what way I have to use this healing mask. They did not break me in jail; they healed me at the Mohawk treatment lodge.'

Only time will reveal the progress and completeness of that healing. It will inevitably be a slow and even faltering process. Cognitive skills not acquired in childhood are easily caught up with later on in life. But putting right emotional apparatus that never fell properly into place at the right time is very much harder. Healing this requires far more than cognitive therapies. It takes nothing less than spiritual power. No 'medicine' can go deeper. None is more needed in today's wounded world.

'And the next thing,' said the Elder on Harris softly, as we sat beside a roaring fire in his stone-built home by the sea beneath the sacred mountain, 'the next thing . . . will be to bring the mountaintop home.'

Of course, unlike the Irish, modern Scotland doesn't really 'do' sacred mountains. Theologically they're dodgy, and in secular terms they're bonkers! Yet that is what I have heard some folks calling Roineabhal. As one native islander said, 'If it wasn't before, it is now.'

And the Elder leaned back in his chair. He lifted his eyes in the direction of the mountain out of which so many good things had come for so many of us.

'It may be some years before the summit rock is brought back,' he concluded, 'but the mountain can wait. And that too . . . yes, that homecoming too . . . will be for the healing of us all.'

Paulo Freire says, 'I am more and more convinced that true revolutionaries must perceive the revolution, because of its creative and liberating nature, as an act of love.' He goes on to quote the enigmatic Che Guevara, who wrote in *Venceremos:* 'Let me say, with the risk of appearing ridiculous, that the true revolutionary is guided by strong feelings of love. It is impossible to think of an authentic revolutionary without this quality.' Freire then states a truth that is of the utmost importance and, for the campaigning activist, the greatest challenge. He says:

> This, then, is the great humanistic and historical task of the oppressed: to liberate themselves and their oppressors as well. The oppressors, who oppress, exploit, and rape by virtue of their power, cannot find in this power the strength to liberate either the oppressed or themselves. Only power that springs from the weakness of the oppressed will be sufficiently strong to free both.[10]

The Keith Schellenbergs, the Ian Wilsons and the John Lieverses of this world will all know how far short I fall from this ideal. 'All life entails violence,' says Gandhi. We cannot walk across a field of grass without causing hurt to the creatures that live there. However, he concludes, our duty is to minimise the violence we personally exert. And to forgive and ask forgiveness: for as William Blake says, 'The cut worm forgives the plough.'[11] Mutual continual forgiveness liberates the ongoing expression of life. It's a question of forgiveness, Jesus said, 'not seven times, but I tell you, seventy times seven times'.[12]

Hearing truth spoken inevitably troubles the chrome-plated peace of the oppressor. Stirring things up like this, however, is a duty, even an act of love. If done right, which is so hard to achieve as to be rare, it will speak to the oppressor's own deep self as well as on behalf of those who they oppress. A social activist cannot expect to be loved by the ego of a Keith Schellenberg. But if they fail to speak to and remember the soul, then that activist will fail in the greater work that liberation is about.

'You never understood me: I always wanted to be one of you,' were Schellenberg's parting words at Eigg's pier.

Well, we did understand, Keith. Dear Keith Schellenberg, who was born of a mother, who has nursed his children and whose little dog, Horace, was run over and killed in the same week that Eigg changed hands.

Yes, Keith, we invited you to stand, as an equal, as one of us. You have the letters. We even asked for your blessing on Eigg's new growth, and, perverse though it might seem, some of us would yet value that blessing.

You see, you helped us. Like Lafarge/Redland on Harris, your challenge injected a shot of energy into the cultural immune system. You pushed us, as a Scottish people, to rethink our priorities, to better understand oppression, to explore liberation and to get our act together. You helped us to see that true power is service.

And I'll tell you something, you old rogue. I cannot write this conclusion without a bemused sense of, damn it, affection.

Afterword

Inside the water butt by our old croft house at *Druim Dhubh* was an inky darkness. But as my eyes became more accustomed to the light, the dance emerged. Tiny creatures darted to and fro. Life-giving jewels of oxygen traced meteoric paths. There was maybe little point to it all, except as an expression of life's magic. And when I think back, when I remember standing there just four years old in my Wellington boots and yellow oilskin coat, that was precisely the beauty of what I watched; its rapturous beauty.

And maybe that's the way it is in the wider world today. As people concerned about the Earth and all that it contains, we are required to look courageously into the darkness. It is a daunting task; one where it is all too easy to burn out, or sell out, or to sink to the bottom, paralysed, when faced with the enormity of our own limitations and hypocrisies. And yet, if we let ourselves be overwhelmed – if we do nothing because we think we cannot do enough – we misread, profoundly, the game of life. We miss each season's fleeting blossom.

The darkness, after all, is a place of gestation. From here, life and consciousness grow. Consider the water beetle. The dance takes place precisely because these creatures have the capacity to carry, into deep and dark places, just sufficient oxygen for their needs. And it is the same with us. We too potentially have the capacity to live life to the full, to find the remnant of like-minded people, to hear the music quicken and to make community.

In this book we have explored some emergent properties of human ecology – the study of human communities. I have focused on islands, because it is easier to tell a story around places with a fixed boundary. But it will have been clear, I hope, that this story is connected in with the whole world. It speaks to many peoples and places, rural and urban.

We have seen how change that violates interconnectedness causes degradation, loss and extinction. But equally, we have seen how virtuous cycles can be set in motion. These, too, have emergent properties. Look at Eigg. The purchase of Eigg eventually came about because a millionaire was inspired by the struggle; but some 10,000 lesser contributors paved the way for that inspiration, and many dozens of people beavered away behind the scenes putting their hearts into the campaign. Each individual was a link in the chain; a step of faith.

That is why, if humankind is to have any hope of changing the world, we must constantly work to strengthen community. We need, first, to make community with the soil, to learn how to revere the Earth. In practical terms, that means ecological restoration, walking lightly in the demands we make of life – sufficiency rather than surplus, quality rather than quantity, and buying (if and when we can) products like organic food and sustainable timber that are produced by working with rather than against nature's providence.

Second, we need to make community of human society. We need to learn empathy and respect for one another simply so that people get the love they need. In practical terms, that means developing an inclusive sense of belonging, identity and values. It means understanding and overcoming the psychology of racism and exclusion; sharing wealth and skills; putting the children and the elderly first; understanding how our family dynamics shaped our worldviews; insisting on psychological honesty; finding the courage to face necessary confrontation with equanimity; shifting from competition to co-operation in politics and economics; and buying 'Fair Trade' products that avoid exploitation. For there's no such thing as 'cheap' when it comes to right relationship.

And third, but not least, we need community of the soul. Whatever our religion or lack of one, we need spaces where we can take rest, compose and compost our inner stuff, and become more deeply present to the aliveness of life. We need to keep one eye to the ground and the other to the stars. We need to remember that when we let loose our wildness in creativity, it is God-the-Goddess – or call it Christ, or Allah or Krishna or the Tao – that pours forth. It does so from within, as a never-ending river.

This tripartite understanding of community is the root, trunk and branch of right relationship. It is how love becomes incarnate.

Where, then, might we start? 'If in doubt what to do,' says Ram Dass, 'feed the hungry.' Test any course of action with the touchstone of service. Ask: does it help the poor? Does it restore the broken in nature? Does it bring music to the soul?

In short, is it concerned with the blossom?

Enjoy!

Alastair McIntosh
Scotland, 2001

Endnotes

Where an endnote specifies 'see endnote extensions', further details will be found on the *Soil and Soul* website at www.AlastairMcIntosh.com.

Introduction

1 *Lycidas*, lines 149–51, in Palgrave 1986, 55–60.
2 *Reflections in a Slum*, in Bold (ed.) 1984, 85–6.
3 Rich 1978, 67. The lines from 'Natural Resources' are taken from *The Dream of a Common Language: Poems 1974–1977* by Adrienne Rich. Copyright © 1978 by W. W. Norton & Co. Inc. Used by permission of the author and W. W. Norton & Co. Inc.
4 Peavey 1986; Sheilds 1991.
5 Winona La Duke (Ralph Nader's Native American 2000 US election running mate), pers. com., Ireland, 1994.
6 See Rabindranath Tagore's play *The Cycle of Spring*.

PART ONE

1. Digging Where We Stand

1 Areas from Wightman 1996, 120. There are about 2.5 acres to the hectare.

2. Earmarks of Belonging

1 Grant 1811, 51.
2 *North Star and Farmers' Chronicle*, 4 July 1896.
3 Mainzer 1844. See endnote extensions.
4 Lynch 1992, 186.
5 McGrath 1997, 437–49.
6 'A Famous Precentor: the Late Mr Murdo MacLennan', obituary (communicated), *North Star and Farmers' Chronicle*, 8 June 1899.
7 John MacInnes, pers. com., c. 1996. For history of *na Daoine*, see Hunter 1976, 100–3 and MacilleDhuibh 1994. For the Disruption, see Ansdell 1998.
8 Hunter 1976, 101.
9 An Lanntair 1995.
10 O'Cathain 1995 is an excellent scholarly modern source. Carmichael 1994 provides much Hebridean material, especially 580–6. Condren 1989 discusses vestal virgin

and feminist considerations. Fiona Macleod (a.k.a. William Sharp) retells several of the Hebridean stories – see McNeill (ed.) 1990. John Duncan represents her transportation in his splendid painting *St Bride* (1913), which rests in the National Gallery of Scotland.

11 MacAulay 1996, 6–7. Note that MacAulay is speaking here partly from oral tradition.

12 Meek 2000, 232.

13 Meek 2000, 242. See also Celtosceptic critiques by Macleod 1997, Márkus 1997a (a Dominican) and in Sutcliffe and Bowman (eds) 2000.

14 MacilleDhuibh 2000b (in his critique of Professor Meek's book).

15 Meek 1995, 34. What we seem to be looking at in Celtic thought, then, is a polarity: austere institutional religion on the one side and nature spirituality on the other; Apollo and Dionysus; original sin and an appreciation of original blessing. Arguably we miss the point if we deny the truths of either of these poles. Such is the nature of mystical paradox.

16 Meyer 1911 is a classic statement of this position, as is de Kerckhove 1992. On Matthew Arnold, see endnote extensions to Arnold 1910, 18–23.

17 The folklorist F. Marian McNeill calls this 'The Vision of Ethne' – McNeill 1990, 19. The parallel with Luke's *Magnificat of Mary* is evident. Also, see Tacitus 1970 on the matriarchy of some Celtic and Germanic peoples, pp. 140–1.

18 Gathorne-Hardy 1993, discussing the English nanny.

19 *The Republic*, III:413.

20 Márkus 1997b, 9, 14.

21 Kinsella (trans.) 1970, 28–37.

22 Condren 1989, 77. See endnote extensions.

23 A parallel may be observed today in Papua New Guinea where the fear of sorcery (see McIntosh 1980 and 1983) – often itself exacerbated by social breakdown – can drive the spread of Christianity. See endnote extensions.

24 Pers. com. with Tom Henigan of Killaster, 1996.

25 Hardy 1993, 130–43 (chapters XVII–XX); Norberg-Hodge 1991, 106; Posey (ed.) 1999. As I wrote this, Darrell passed away. He will be of most blessed memory to many indigenous peoples.

26 On blackhouse architecture and human ecology at Arnol, see Fenton 1989. For research into the old ways of conserving nutrient cycles and building soil fertility see Dodgshon and Olsson 1988 and Dodgshon 1993. Also Fenton 1999 and Hunter 1976.

27 Liam Horan, Balintubber, Co. Mayo, 1999.

28 Shaw 1986, 7. During the Eigg campaign I had the privilege of being given a blessing by Margaret. She translated it from the Gaelic as: 'May I be with you both when I am thinking about you and when I am not thinking about you.'

3. Globalisation and the Village

1 MacAlister (ed.) 1938.

2 For documentation of this see McIntosh 2000a.

3 *Stornoway Gazette*, 14 June 1940; reprinted *ibid*. 15 June 2000.

4 Illich 1981.

5 Schumacher 1974. Many of these ideas are taken forward by Satish Kumar in *Resurgence* magazine and at the excellent courses he teaches at Schumacher College in England.

6 See Sachs 1992.

7 See MacilleDhuibh 1996.

8 Cordova 1997, 33–4.

9 Sachs 1992.

4. Celtic Ecology

1 Goldsmith 1996, 3.

2 Wilson 1992, 247, 255.

3 Elliot, C., '"Common" birds at risk', *Guardian Weekly*, 8 February 1998.

4 Myers and Simon 1994, 74.

5 In Miller 1995, 82.

6 Rackham 1986, 26 and 28.

7 Myers and Simon 1994, 77.

8 *Ibid.*, 76.

9 May and Lawton 1995, 6.

10 World Conservation Monitoring Centre, 1992, 197.

11 Martin 1994, 106–7.

12 MacKenzie 1919, 144–5; my emphasis.

13 Ransford cited in Black 1999, 711 (from the *Scotsman*, 5 December 1992); Ronald Black a.k.a. Raghnall MacilleDhuibh, cited by John MacInnes in his preface to the 1994 single-volume edition of Carmichael. Note the review of the *Carmina* and of Carmichael's life and the question of whether he elaborated material in Black 1999, 709–12. Black quotes Professor Mackinnon's view that Carmichael 'got to know, as few have ever known it, the inner life of the people'. Black also gives a revealing gender analysis of sources. He points out that whereas another contemporary collector, J. F. Campbell of Islay, drew on 102 males and only twenty-one females for his sources, with Carmichael 'it is startling to find that the number of males is almost identical at 103, but that the number of females has shot up to 112'. This might beg the question as to whether there is a gender dimension to Highland green consciousness and its related Celtosceptic debate.

14 In addition to the complete Penguin Classics edition, selections from Adomnán, along with much splendid 'Twilightist' material, are anthologised in McNeill 1990. See Meek 2000 for a catalogue of this genre of anthology.

15 In Hyde 1894, 25–6. Hyde warns that, 'No faith can be placed in the alleged date or genuineness of Amergin's verses. They are, however, of interest, because Irish tradition has always represented them as being the first verses made in Ireland.' Compare with, say, chapter 9 of the *Bhagavad Gita* – a Hindu passage that in many respects summarises Christian mysticism.

16 Bain 1951. Note Bain's correspondence with Coomaraswamy on comparisons with Indian art, p.20.

17 Meyer 1911, xii–xiii. Note that the Historiographer Royal for Scotland, Christopher Smout, appears to overlook much of the material here in suggesting that there was very little indigenous Highland green consciousness (Smout 1991).

18 Jackson 1971, 28–9.

19 Stewart 1970. See endnote extensions.

20 MacInnes 1997, 5.

21 Grant 1898, 143.

22 Hunter 1995b.

23 See, for example, the appendices to Stewart 1990 edition of Kirk's *Secret Commonwealth*.

24 Kipling 1993, 10–14. Puck remarks that he is the last fairy in England. See endnote extensions.

25 Evans 1981, xiii.

26 MacInnes 1997, 2.

27 Eliade 1989; Halifax 1980.

28 Heaney 1984, 19.

29 From Heaney 1984, 20, 43, and Jackson (trans.) 1971, 255.

30 Campbell 1994, 51–62. Indeed, it is possible that the exchange was two-way; see endnote extensions.

31 Knight 1990, 13.

32 Bloomfield and Dunn 1989; Eliade 1989; Halifax 1980.

33 Commission on the Future of Multi-Ethnic Britain 2000, 103, 3, 14.

5. By the Cold and Religious

1 Quoted in Fraser 1994, 3; my emphasis.

2 See Middleton-Moz and Dwinell, 1986. On traumatic stress, see also Cairns 1999 and Gillegan 1997.

3 MacLean 1993, 101.

4 For example, Theodore Beza – see McGrath (ed.) 1995, 235–6. For a sympathetic modern biography of Calvin, see McGrath 1990.

5 Visser and McIntosh 1998. Christ taught against usury in Luke 6:34–5. In these notes I indicate biblical versions only where the choice of translation matters. Most of my usages are NRSV (New Revised Standard Version – preferable for scholarship) or the KJV (the King James or 'Authorised Version' – preferable for poetry).

6 Polanyi 1945.

7 McIntosh 2000c.

8 Korten 1999, 183–6.

9 Mander 1992, 126.

10 *Institutes of the Christian Religion*, III:xxi:1, 5, in McGrath 1995, 233.

11 Weber 1976; note Anthony Giddens's critique of Weber in his introduction to this edition.

12 See sources in McIntosh 1996a, and on Bacon's contribution to military intelligence, Whaley 1982, 191.

13 Merchant 1980. I am grateful to Monica Sjoo (pers. com., 2001) for the expression 'malestream'.

14 Bacon 1974, 241; see my critique of 1992 White Paper on science policy, McIntosh 1996a.

15 Hill 1992, 157.

16 MacInnes 1978, 452; Macinnes 1988, 70, and 1993, 31 and 49; Dodgshon 1989, 181.

17 Lipson 1959; Hill 1992.
18 Campbell 1994, 29.
19 MacInnes 1982a; MacInnes 1999. See also Hunter 1975 on Irish influence.
20 In Withers 1988, 74.
21 Macdonald 1990, 27–32.
22 Mackenzie 1903, 241; Macinnes 1993, 34; MacilleDhuibh 1998b.
23 Martin 1994, 288. Also Johnson and Boswell 1993, 141–2.
24 *Internal Colonialism: The Celtic Fringe in British National Development, 1536–1966*, cited in McCrone 1992, 60–1.
25 Campbell 1994; O'Baoill 1994; MacInnes 1981.
26 Macinnes 1993, 40, 47, 52; Withers 1988, 113.
27 In Meek 1996, 20–1. Similar ideas emerged near-contemporaneously from colonial Ireland. For example, Edmund Spenser; see endnote extensions.
28 See discussion in Daly and Cobb 1990, 160.
29 Smith 1986, 107.
30 *Ibid.*, 489.
31 Newton 2000.
32 MacilleDhuibh 2000a.
33 Griffin 1992, cover quotation.
34 MacLean 1937, 9–13; now in print again from Hodder and Stoughton, 1999.
35 Magnetic imprint dating locates the emplacement of the South Harris Igneous Complex, of which Roineabhal is a part, to about 1870 million years ago – Piper 1992. Some of the world's oldest rocks, dating back to 2–3 billion years ago, are found on the Hebrides, which form part of the Baltic and Canadian Shields. The Precambrian 'Lewisian' geological period is named after Lewis.
36 Graves 1961, 24–5, 69–73. Professor Ronald Hutton in his eminently reasonable, decent and sympathetic way debunks Graves's 'White Goddess' and 'Triple Goddess' – the source of some contemporary Wiccan thought (Hutton 1991, 335–41). However, as Graves reminds us in quoting Ovid, 'Her power is to open what is shut; to shut what is open' (p.69). Graves sees with a poetic eye and so, arguably, glimpses that which the cutting edge of scholarship otherwise cuts up. I suspect that Ronald Hutton might, when off duty, concur.

6. The Admiral's Birthday Surprise

 1 Pers. com. with Jim Crawford, Garynahine, 1998.
 2 MacLean 1993, 68–70.
 3 Campbell 1994, 29.
 4 Cited in Campbell 1994, 25.
 5 MacilleDhuibh 1998c.
 6 Macinnes 1993, 40.
 7 MacInnes 1999.
 8 Hyde 1894, 28.
 9 MacilleDhuibh 1998b.
10 Campbell 1994, 44–50, 60.
11 Ó Baoil 1994.
12 Ó Baoil 1994, 6.

13 Spenser c. 1589, 526.
14 Bloomfield and Dunn 1989, 31.
15 MacInnes 1978, 451.
16 Bloomfield and Dunn 1989, 39.
17 McIntosh 1983 and 1980. See endnote extensions.
18 MacInnes 1978.
19 MacilleDhuibh 1996.
20 Donald John MacDonald in Black (ed.) 1999, 754.
21 Johnson and Boswell 1993, 113–14.
22 Corkery 1967, 73–5, presents both of these. The Irish one is from the 1722 *Memoirs of the Marquis of Clanricarde*. MacInnes 1999 also discusses each case in depth.
23 Grof 1985; Tart 1969.
24 O'Cathain 1995, 157–63.
25 Martin 1994, 176–7.
26 MacInnes 1999, 325–6.
27 Ellis 1995, 174–5, citing Professor Hennessy in the Kilkenny Archaeological Journal, 1885.
28 MacInnes 1989b, 16–17; MacInnes 1981, 160.
29 To my knowledge by far the best source on this is Newton 2000.
30 See discussion in Donald J. MacLeod's (undated) introduction to Martin, 1994, 23–4.
31 MacInnes 1997, 18–19, my emphasis.
32 MacInnes 1968, 40.
33 MacInnes 1989b, 10; MacInnes 1968, 41; Cohn 1999.
34 Black (ed.) 1999, 751.
35 Laviolette and McIntosh, 1997.
36 *Our Gaelic Background*, cited in a MacDiarmid exhibition, An Lanntair, Stornoway.
37 St Bride's Day lecture, Edinburgh University Celtic Society, 1996, unpublished; see also MacInnes 1997, 10.
38 cf. Tart 1988.
39 MacInnes 1968, 41.
40 Khan 1988, 24.
41 Sofer 1998.
42 Bloomfield and Dunn 1989, 31, 24.
43 Bloomfield and Dunn 1989, 11.

7. Such Happy Times

1 Durkheim 1951.
2 From *The Ramparts We Guard*, 84.
3 Secretaries of State for Environment etc. (1990), 59.
4 McIntosh 1991.
5 Smout 1993, 41.
6 Wightman 1996. More precisely, about 1300 owners control 67 per cent of the land (Wightman, pers. com.). Some of these owners are, of course, corporations and tax-avoiding trusts.

7   See Newton 2000, 183–8, for examples and corroboration of Donald's perspective.
8   de Leeuw 1996, 386.
9   Etherington-Smith, M., 'Look Who's Stalking', *Harpers & Queen*, August 1992.
10 Anon., 'Land of the rising gun', *Tatler*, 291:9.
11 Ross Benson, cited in 'Clippings from the phrase shed', *West Highland Free Press*, 29 December 2000.

8. Gunboats and the Old Man of Eisken

1   Hunter 1976.
2   *Ibid.*, 172.
3   *Seaforth Papers* in *ibid.*, 41–7. See also Macdonald 1990, 33–8.
4   www.jardine-matheson.com.
5   In MacLean and Carrell (eds) 1986, 11.
6   Family information pers. com. by kind courtesy of Captain Audley Archdale, 1998.
7   Matthew 8:20.
8   Hunter 1976, 171–3, 270.
9   *The Deer Drive*, in Meek (trans.) 1995, 279–80. Translations used with Professor Meek's kind permission.
10 *The Old Man of Eishken*, in Meek (trans.) 1995, 275–8.
11 The figure cited is Hunter's, drawing from five sources. The official report in the *Northern Chronicle*, 30 November 1887, suggests that the slaughter did not exceed a dozen. Captain Audley Archdale considers this more reliable (pers. com.).
12 In MacLean 1993, 152.
13 *Such a Parcel of Rogues in a Nation*, in MacKay (ed.) 1993, 460–1.
14 In MacLean 1993, 157.
15 Lynch 1992, 319.
16 Cited in Brown, McCrone and Paterson 1996, 39, from Colley, L. (1992), *Britons: Forging the Nation, 1707–1837*, Yale University Press, 5.
17 Lynch 1992, 338–9.
18 Campbell 1994, 94–106; Dressler 1998, 28–40.
19 Cited in Jarvie 1991, 45.
20 Allan Torrance, pers. com., 1996.
21 See Jarvie 1991; McCrone 1992; MacArthur 1993; Smout 1991 and 1994; Nairn 1991.

9. Voice of Complicity

1   Blamires 1996 and pers. com. It is rare to find such estimates; see endnote extensions.
2   See reproductions in the excellent photo-essay of MacLean and Carrell (eds) 1986.
3   Carmichael 1994, 632.
4   In Hunter 1976, 83.
5   Corkery 1967, 35–6.
6   Harting 1973.
7   In Shaw 1988, 22. See also Newton 2000, and Smout 1991 and 1993.

8 Newton 2000.
9 Duncan MacLaren, *Clydebank*, pers. com. and by kind permission, 1989.
10 *Books of the Fues*, in Craig of Riccarton 1934, 1175; also, Kingston 1992.
11 Cited in the *Ecologist* (ed.) 1993, 24, from Collins, J., *Land Reform*, Green & Co., London, 1908, 144–5.
12 *Ecologist* (ed.) 1993, 25.
13 Hill 1992, 154, citing Dr Kerridge's recent work.
14 Unnamed poet cited in MacDonald 1891, xxii–xxiv.
15 Hill 1991, 132–3. Also note the appendix to Hill 1994: 'A Note on Liberation Theology'.
16 Prebble 1969.
17 Cited by Wilson 1997 (cutting from the *Herald*).
18 See Craig 1996 for eyewitness accounts of the Clearances, critiquing Bumsted, J. M., *The People's Clearance*, Edinburgh, 1982.
19 In MacLean and Carrell (eds) 1986, 17.
20 In Hunter 1976, 27.
21 In Lester 1936, 7.
22 *The Social Anthropology of Economic Underdevelopment*, no. 70, 302, cited in *Ecologist* (ed.) 1993, 22.
23 In Neihardt 1979, 9–10.
24 Citation and figures from Boff and Elizondo 1990, vii.
25 In Minh-ha 1989, 132.
26 Fanon 1967. James Hunter (1995b) in his masterpiece of psychohistory quotes Fanon and suggests: 'Substitute "Highlander" or "Gael" for "Arab" . . .' (p.36).
27 Said 1993.
28 Corkery 1967.
29 Freire 1971, 121–2.
30 Meek 1995, 14.
31 *Dusgadh*, North Lochs Historical Society, no. 11, June 1998.
32 C. and R. Macdonald in Morton 1991, 66, with their kind permission.

10. Echoes Down the Glen of Landed Power

1 *Taking on Trident*, Scottish CND briefing paper, Glasgow, 1997.
2 MacLean and Carrell (eds) 1986: a bilingual community arts production to accompany an exhibition of the same name, produced by Malcolm MacLean from Lewis and Christopher Carrell from England.
3 For detailed background on the Napier Commission and the Crofters' Holdings (Scotland) Act, 1886, see Cameron 1996 and Hunter 1976.
4 'No One Can Watch the Wasichu', Walker 1985, 59–60, by kind permission of the author, The Women's Press and David Higham Associates.
5 In Mackay (ed.) 1993, 287.
6 'A Song Between Dugald and Donald', trans. (unpublished) by Professor Donald Meek, from A. and D. Stewart's collection, 1804.
7 Joel 1:2–3, 12.
8 *Highlander*, 31 July 1875.
9 Daniel 3:19–30.

10 Conrad 1995, 55–95; my emphasis.
11 de Mello 1992, 182.
12 Fromm 1978.
13 Matthew 22:20, NRSV.
14 HarperCollins NRSV commentary, Meeks *et al.* (eds) 1993, 1898.

11. World Without a Friend

 1 Matthew 6:24; Luke 16, KJV. Mammon is an Aramaic name Jesus used for the evil personification of money.
 2 Black 1999, xxvii–xxviii (my emphasis), and MacilleDhuibh 1999. The narrative above is my own extemporisation based on Ronald Black's translations and commentary.
 3 Tart 1988.
 4 *The Undiscovered Self* in Storr (ed.) 1983, 360. My thanks to psycho-entomologist Professor Stuart Hill for the 'energy vampires' concept.
 5 Shor 1969, 241, 253; my emphasis.
 6 Bloomfield and Dunn 1989, 4.
 7 Araoz 1984; my emphasis.
 8 See, for example, the tale of *The Fairy Queen in the Form of a Frog* in MacDougall 1978, 21–25, where the glamour is removed from the eyes with a magic soap. The eminent folklorist Dr Alan Bruford in his introduction to the reprint of this collection (pp.v–xi) warns of the faeries, 'They can be helpful, but in an unpredictable way: the safest advice is to have as little as possible to do with them'. See endnote extensions on the implications of 'glamour' for the psychology of perception.
 9 Mercedes-Benz (France) mailshot promotional brochure, September 2000; Alpha Romeo advert in the *Observer Sport Monthly*, February 2001.
10 Pierre Martineau, 1956, in Packard 1960, 46; my emphasis. For more recent applications of depth psychology to marketing see works on 'consumer behaviour' such as Sheth, Mittal and Newman 1999, and my work on Eros and Thanatos in tobacco advertising, McIntosh 1996c.
11 *Uses of the Erotic: The Erotic as Power*, Lorde 1984, 53–9.
12 At a conference on *The Impact of Identity on Local Development and Democracy*, South-North Network Cultures and Development, Belgium, 2000. The North African scholar Hassan Zaoual also played an important affirmative role in these conversations. See, too, my interviews with Hearo Mukari of Akapiru, the Papua New Guinean cannibalistic sorcerer, in McIntosh 1983. Also, McIntosh 1980 for intercultural comparisons in one particular aspect of PNG sorcery belief.
13 To be fair, King James later put an end to burning as the means of witch execution; indeed, after departing to England, where he found the English to be much less paranoid about witches than the Scots had been, his interest substantially diminished, though not before several witches were burnt in Lancaster to curry his favour.
14 Skidelsky 1992, 454, quoting St Paul in 1 Timothy 6:10, KJV.
15 As cited in Wink 1992, 50, from Steinbeck, Viking Press, 1939, 42–5, reproduced by permission of Penguin Books Ltd.
16 Marcuse 1964; Wink 1992.

17 Arendt 1963.

18 Haney, Banks and Zimbardo 1973.

19 Milgram 1974, xii–10. For critical discussion of such experiments see, for instance, Miller 1986 and Rosenbaum (ed.) 1983.

20 *Corporations as Machines*, in Mander 1992.

21 The song is on the *Plastic Ono Band* album; permissions information from Sony ATV, pers. com., 22 March 2001.

22 Anon., 'Long in the Truth', *Scotsman*, 10 February 1996, 13; Wightman 1996, 136.

23 Johnson 1997; Gillegan 1997. James is the spouse of the eminent feminist psychologist Carol Gillegan. For Bob's recent work on personality disorder with the James Naylor Foundation, see www.jnf.org.uk.

24 *Guardian*, 27 and 31 January 1996.

25 See especially Miller 1987, 8–63.

26 Fromm 1977; Reich 1972. See also Theweleit 1987 and 1989.

27 Gillegan 1997, 47.

28 Freud 1984, 380–1.

29 The Frankfurt School also included Adorno, Horkheimer and Marcuse. For application of their studies to ecology in the wake of Nazism, see Merchant (ed.) 1994.

30 Fromm 1977, this citation from 1994, 51, 52.

31 For instance, Leviticus 18:21 and 20:2–5; 2 Kings 23:10 and Jeremiah 7:31, 19:5 and 32:35.

32 By her kind permission, first published by Pomegranate Women's Writing Group 1992, 64–5.

12. Seeds of Fire

1 Deuteronomy 30:15,19, NRSV; my emphasis.

2 'The Undiscovered Self' in Storr (ed.) 1983, 380.

3 Genesis 18:16–33.

4 Jeremiah 5:1. See Jung's 'Answer to Job' on ethical challenges between humankind and God (Jung 1972).

5 The Centre for Human Ecology website is at www.che.ac.uk.

6 Luke 12:49, NRSV.

7 John 15; Romans 12:5; Colossians 1:18.

8 Seed, Macy, Fleming and Naess 1988, 16.

9 Luke 17:21, KJV.

10 Romans 13:1, KJV.

11 Wink 1992, 10.

12 Wink 1992, 297–8. Wink's trilogy is now available in synopsis as *The Powers that Be* (1998), Galilee, London.

13 I am particularly grateful to Jill Beavitt, Djini van Slyke and Tess Darwin for insights on these matters; see Darwin 1995 for an excellent discussion of creativity in relation to ecological education.

14 Starhawk 1982, 13.

15 Numbers 11:29. See also Acts 2:17–21 citing Joel 2:28–32.

16 1 Kings 19. See also, for example, Isaiah 11:21–2.

17 Jeremiah 1:6.

18 Jeremiah 20, NRSV.
19 Isaiah 6:5, 20:3, NRSV.
20 Exodus 4:10.
21 Ezekiel 1 and 2:6; cf. Revelation 4, especially verses 6–8 – the lion, ox, human and
    eagle from Ezekiel's vision are taken in Christian tradition as totems of the four
    apostles – John being the eagle.
22 1 Kings 17:4.
23 1 Kings 2. A Jungian take on this might see the she-bears as failure to integrate the
    anima – his feminine side.
24 Jonah 1–2.
25 Freire 1972.
26 'The Song of the Wandering Aengus' (adapted) in Jeffares (ed.) 1962, 27.
27 Genesis 3:24.
28 Corkery 1967, 70.
29 'Walking the Coast', in White 1990a, 42, with the author's kind permission.
30 Derick Thomson, 'Strathnaver' in Dunn (ed.) 1992, 214–15, by kind permission
    (Strathnaver is in Sutherland, north-east of Skye).
31 In MacLean and Carrell (eds) 1986, 37; cf. translation in Meek (ed.) 1995, 57–8,
    192–3.
32 God to Moses before the burning bush in Exodus 3:5, KJV.

PART TWO

13. Well of the Holy Women

 1 'Leaves of Grass', Whitman 1986, 26.
 2 de Tocqueville 1966, 146.
 3 A. Wightman, 'Estate Duties', *Sunday Times (Ecosse)*, 10 January 1999.
 4 Grulin material all sourced from Dressler 1998, 83–4.
 5 Cited in Dressler 1998, 83.
 6 Dressler 1998, 99.
 7 Dressler 1998, 122.
 8 Sir Steven Runciman's obituary, *Guardian*, 3 November 2000.
 9 Dressler 1998, 154.
10 Porter 1991, unpaginated.
11 *Daily Mail*, 29 January 1995, cited in Dressler 1998, 159.
12 Cited in Dressler 1998, 156.
13 Some twenty volumes of High Court proceedings from his failed libel case against
    the *Guardian* in 1999 amply testify to these perspectives.
14 See endnote extensions for examples.
15 Porter 1991, unpaginated.
16 Hennessey 1992.
17 S. Lindsay, 'Eigg's new laird runs into trouble', *Herald*, 3 June 1976.
18 See Wright 1997 for exposition of this. Interestingly, Canon Kenyon Wright (who
    chaired the executive of the Constitutional Convention that brought Scotland
    back its Parliament in 1999) tells me that he learned his liberation theology while
    working in India.

19 Menuhin's foreword to Hunter 1988, vii.
20 Meek (trans.) 1995, 213–20, except the third stanza where I have used Derick Thomson's translation in Hunter 1976, 91.
21 See endnote extensions on the meaning of Tara.
22 Dressler 1998, 8; Martin 1994, 304.
23 Heaney (trans.) 1984, 50.
24 Acts 17:16–33; see endnote extensions.
25 Spenser 1589, 550.
26 I owe this insight to Colin MacLeod of the Gal-Gael Trust, Govan. The Parekh Report has picked up on some of these ideas from our national-values discernment work, *People and Parliament*, in Scotland – see Commission for the Future of Multi-Ethnic Britain, 2000, 6–7; 261–2, 346. Likewise, the BBC's political editor in Marr 1999, 73–5.

14. The Mountain Behind the Mountain

1 Kirk 1993.
2 Research (Companies House, pers. com.) shows that Wilson or his wife, Maureen, have had directorships, major shareholdings or prominent interests in many now dissolved or bankrupt companies; see endnote extensions.
3 This conversation is paraphrased from notes. The 'silt from the Elbe' story has been independently documented by Lewis-based journalist Mike Merritt.
4 C. D. Gribble and C. I. Wilson, *Potential for a large coastal quarry in Scotland*, Scottish Development Department, 1980, as cited in Kirk 1993, 23.
5 Wilson 1991, 6; my emphasis.
6 Luhmann 1995. Note also Savory 1988, 26.
7 Gelderloos 1992.
8 O'Donoghue 1993, 30–1.
9 O'Cathain, 1995, and other sources.
10 This version from Ann Campbell of the Isle of Eigg, 1997.
11 Cited in Dressler 1998, 192.
12 MacNeill and Richardson 1996, 15. See MacDougall 1978, 35–8, for an account of how MacCrimmon was given a silver chanter by the Banshee (faerie woman) of the Cave of Gold, and how she taught him to play the faerie music by emulating the deftness of her fingers on his chanter.
13 Maoilious Caimbeul (Myles Campbell), 'And So Somersault' in Black 1999, 616–17, by kind permission.
14 Carmichael 1994, 575.
15 Okri 1998, 63.
16 'Elegy Written in a Country Church-Yard' in Palgrave (ed.) 1986, 145–8.
17 Job 1:1; 22:5.
18 Mark 7:24–30. For Murdo's obituary, see next endnote.
19 'Golden Wedding at Jamestown', 4 July 1896, and obituary, 'A Famous Precentor: The Late Mr Murdo MacLennan', 8 June 1899, both in *North Star and Farmers' Chronicle*, citing Dr Beith's account of Dr Candlish's tour of the Highlands in 1845.
20 Cited in Dressler 1998, 192.

21 From publicly tape-recorded proceedings.
22 Pain 1999, vol. 1, 39, 64. Figures actually in metric tonnes, but these are close to imperial tons.
23 See Monbiot 2000, 281–3.

15. Under Enemy Occupation

1 Porter 1991.
2 Constructed by Jim Crawford.
3 Hunter 1976, 171–4.
4 Allardyce 1991. The article actually refers to a 'vintage Bentley', an error I have corrected.
5 Alexander, Shucksmith and Lindsay 1988, 5.
6 Rousseau 1973, 76 (opening to Part II).
7 For sociological analysis of this see McCrone 1992, and the fascinating use made of Pierre Bourdieu's schema (1984) as applied to Scottish lairds in Samuel 2000.
8 Berger and Luckmann, 1971.
9 Trying to fit into the institutional structures of the Roman Catholic Church, it must be said, places a narrow focus on to some of Gutiérrez's work; see endnote extensions.
10 I dedicate this expression to Tara O'Leary, who so encouraged me to have fun with it.
11 Gutiérrez 1988, xxxvii–xxxviii; 24.
12 Cited in Macleod 1998, 198.
13 I recommend the Penguin Classics versions of these and of the Buddhist *Dhammapada*, as Juan Mascaró's introductions to his translations wonderfully weave oriental and occidental spirituality into a seamless whole. For pointers towards a feminist liberation theology within Islam, see, for example, Watt 1991 (or see my website for the *Coracle* interview with Professor Montgomery Watt, conducted by Dr Bashir Maan and myself).
14 Or possibly, as Jung suggests in 'Answer to Job', an evolution of God 'himself', confronted by occasionally superior human morality (Jung 1972)!
15 Gutiérrez 1983, 20.
16 Esquivel and Graf-Huber 1991. I believe this expression comes from the English theologian Sheila Cassiday.

16. Too Rough to Go Slow

1 Pers. com. to me, 18 July 1991.
2 *Daily Telegraph*, 24 July 1991.
3 For example, two ships that left the Highlands for Nova Scotia in 1801 had 700 'passengers', whereas they would have been permitted only 489 if they had been putting out with slaves from the Gambia – MacLean and Carrell (eds) 1986, 13.
4 Cited in Dressler, 1998, 176–7.
5 *Daily Telegraph*, 23 May 1994, cited in Dressler 1998, 178.
6 'A man with Eigg on his face', *Scotland on Sunday*, 25 May 1999.
7 Pers. com., 1 October 1992.
8 Freire 1972, 21.

9 H. Porter, 'Scrambled Eigg', *Harpers & Queen*, October 1991.
10 Bourdieu 1984.
11 Hesse 1973, 52.
12 White 1992, 173–4.
13 White 1990c, 85, by kind permission.
14 White 1991, 3.
15 Dressler 1998, 171–2.
16 John 14:15–31; 16:4–15.
17 Meek 2000, 12–13; see endnote extensions.

17. The Emperor's New Island

1 Ezekiel 37:1–16.
2 McIntosh 1992.
3 'Gigha's break is all that the islanders ask', *Scotland on Sunday*, 22 March 1992.
4 *Hansard*, 4 June 1992, 'Island Communities (Argyll)', 1019–28; my emphasis.
5 Pers. com. to me from Ken McCorquodale, 26 June 1992.
6 Pers. com., 3 February 1992.
7 *West Highland Free Press*, 3 July 1992.
8 *An e Farmad a ni Treabhadh*, Grampian Television, broadcast 13 December 1993.
9 Pers. com., 12 June 1997.
10 Pers. com., Edinburgh 1992.
11 *The Crofter*, December 1993.
12 1 July 1992, published in *Reforesting Scotland*, autumn 1992.
13 Sourced from Dressler 1998, 175–6.
14 'Deep-rooted doubts as the laird returns', *Scotsman*, 10 July 1992.
15 Their ref: TMSAC 3715005, 15 October 1992. The organisation has since started up again with an interesting website that insists they are not racist.
16 B. Dow, 'Mohamed of the Glen?', *Daily Record*, 18 January 1999.
17 'A message from the people of Eigg', *West Highland Free Press*, 21 January 1994 (initiated by D. J. Kirk).
18 Pers. com., 21 May 1998.
19 Henderson 1982, 256 and 260–1. See also Ellis 1995 on Celtic women, Condren 1989 on Irish mythology, and Ehrenberg 1989, 142–70, on the Iron Age archaeological and literary evidence. A contrary position is presented by Gilbert Márkus 1992, who urges a cautious approach to ancient and early sources.
20 Fiona Cherry, Duncan Ferguson, Margaret Kirk, Katie MacKinnon, Christopher Tiarks, Barry Williams.
21 *Good Morning Scotland*, Radio Scotland, 17 July 1994.
22 *Dirty News*, BBC Radio 5, 19 July 1994. The French Revolution was actually in 1789.
23 *Dirty News*, BBC Radio 5, 19 July 1994.

18. Stone Eagle to Fly In

1 Wright 1995.
2 Matthew 4:19, KJV.
3 Stair 1981, 1.1.1; Blackstone 1829, 1.2.38–41; see also papers on my website.

4 For a full presentation of the superquarry inquiry testimonies and discussion of background issues, see our *Journal of Law and Religion* paper together with Professor Maltz's commentary on it: McIntosh, Macleod and Stone Eagle Herney 1995; Maltz 1995.

5 Genesis 8:22.

6 Mark 7:28, KJV.

7 I have recreated the spirit of our conversation here rather than the exact words.

19. The Womanhood of God

1 'Theology Goes Against Superquarry', *Stornoway Gazette*, 31 March 1994.

2 McIntosh, Macleod and Stone Eagle Herney 1995, 781–2.

3 Bruce 1983; Hunter 1974; Ansdell 1991; Meek 1996.

4 Panikkar 1991.

5 This sermon (published as Macleod 1995) drew heavily on points made in his superquarry theological testimony. The professor humbly plays down here the fact that his own church, the Free Church of Scotland, emerged out of the Disruption partly in response to these injustices. However, its voice was often disappointingly quiet – perhaps out of the conservativism that commonly sets in when a breakaway movement harbours unresolved doubts about its legitimacy, causing it to hold with asphyxiating rigidity to charter texts and cornerstone positions.

6 Exodus 3:14, KJV. The NRSV offers: 'I AM WHO I AM', 'I AM WHAT I AM', OR 'I WILL BE WHAT I WILL BE'.

7 Panikkar 1991.

8 In Russell 1961, 59.

9 *Timaeus* (Jowett), 27 (I am using standard referencing rather than pagination for Plato). In other words, Plato splits the Tao and says it has to be either Yin or Yang. It is to this passage that, I think, the fundamental difference between Eastern and Western thought can be traced. Pre-Socratic philosophers such as Heraclitus and Empedocles did not make this distinction; to them, all was one.

10 *Phaedo*, 67–8. In mitigation, we might remember that the Platonic Socrates (through whom these words were spoken) was, like Jesus, under sentence of death. They may have been very appropriate words in his predicament, but are questionable as a more generalised philosophy of life. The *Timaeus* nevertheless portrays this world as beautiful; indeed, it is 'a god'. As such, Plato blows hot and cold as to the status of this world, thereby enhancing the flexibility of his subsequent footnotes.

11 *Critias* 110–12, where he describes prehistoric soil erosion, saying, 'You are left (as with little islands) with something rather like a skeleton of a body wasted by disease', and tells how this leads to the loss of springs and rivers, compounded by deforestation, and resulting in desertification.

12 *The Republic*, Book III.

13 *The Republic*, 399.

14 *The Laws*, 942.

15 *The Republic*, chapter 3. 'Church of Reason' from Pirsig 1976.

16 *Timaeus*, 24–8. In just a couple of paragraphs the *Timaeus* thereby effects a remarkable theocratic gender shift. The Platonic Socrates patronisingly presides over the

replacement of Critias's Goddess-predicated worldview with a superior male-God schema proposed by Timaeus.

17 Russell 1961, 25–43. Russell mentions the *Bacchae* of Euripides as one of his main sources. For a popular feminist take on prehistory and what followed it, see Sjoo and Mor 1993.

18 Andrew Lockhart Walker 1994, pers. com. (on the Sorbonne). Also Davie 1986; MacDonald 1993; Broadie 2000.

19 Popper 1962.

20 Cited in Russell 1961, 32.

21 1 Samuel 8; see also Deuteronomy 17:14–20. The 'upside-down kingdom' of Jesus is, accordingly, a restoration of the original settlement, though St Paul seems to have missed the point.

22 Expression courtesy of 'Kenny Leather' Stephen, Shawbost.

23 Whitehead 1929, 53.

24 *Phaedrus*, 230.

25 *Phaedrus*, 242–5.

26 *Symposium*, 201–12.

27 *Phaedrus*, 278. On Socrates' maieutic vocation, see the *Theaetetus*, 149–51. Tom Forsyth often cited this in claiming that the Isle of Eigg Trust played a maieutic role.

28 *Theaetetus*, 155d.

29 *The Gay Science*, 125, cited in Nietzsche 1961, 14.

30 Nietzsche 1961, 297.

31 Nellas 1987, 154–7. See endnote extensions on exegesis.

32 St Paul described how, because of human wickedness, 'the whole Creation has been groaning in labour pains . . . . For the Creation awaits with eager longing for the revealing of the children of God' (Romans 8:18–25). John Calvin also saw the importance of knowing the Creation as the expression of God's Providence. He called it 'this most beautiful theatre', and added, 'Let us not decline to take a pious delight in the clear and manifest works of God' (*Institutes of the Christian Religion*, 1:XIV:20; see also 3:X:2).

33 Why is it, then, that we miss the significance of such connection with nature? A good part of the reason is that Jesus frequently lays condemnation upon what is translated as 'the world'. However, the Greek word being translated is actually *kosmos*, which might be more fully translated as, 'the human sociological realm that exists in estrangement from God' (Wink 1992, 51). In other words, Jesus's attacks on 'the world' were aimed not at God's Creation – nature – as has sometimes been assumed, but at the 'worldly' Domination System.

34 Thomas 1987, 92–3.

35 White 1967.

36 Sivaraksa 1999, 81.

37 Matthew 12:48 and 10:34–9; Luke 7:36–50; Matthew 9:34; John 2:13–22; Matthew 11:19.

38 John 13:38; 18.

39 Graves 1961, 24.

40 Merchant 1980.

41 Genesis 1:27.

42 Galatians 3:28.

43 Camp 1996; Long 1992.

44 Proverbs 8:22–9:6 NRSV; my emphasis. See also the HarperCollins Study Bible commentary, Meeks *et al.* (eds) 1993, 954.

45 See Job 1 – remarkably, God puts the Devil up to torturing the 'God-fearing' Job into proving his faith.

46 'Song on Ben Lee', in Meek (ed.) 1995, 266; see also discussion of her poetry in MacInnes 1999.

47 Miller 1987.

48 Bulgakov 1997, 329, and as expanded in one of his letters in the translator's end-note, p.410.

49 'One Foot in Eden', in Dunn (ed.) 1992, 29–30.

50 Cited in McGrath 1997, 391. McGrath, a leading reformed theologian, acknowledges that theories of the atonement have of late become unfashionable.

51 John 2:13–25.

52 The reactionary fundamentalist Christian who objects to this syncretism must demonstrate in what ways we are not entitled to see, for example, Christ as Buddha nature and Buddha nature as Christ. That is to say, before condemning syncretism he or she must show that it is not possible for the Holy Spirit to have been operative in other cultures at other times in history, and for there to be many 'masks of God'.

53 Romans 12:5. Note that this implies that spiritual activism, while often a lonely task such as Gethsemane and the Cross demonstrated, is ultimately grounded in community. This is the true meaning of that much-misunderstood word 'church'.

54 'Magnificat of Mary', Luke 1:46–55, especially verses 52–3. For a powerful and important counterpoint to the case I make here, but one that, possibly, under-estimates the cultural difficulties that Jesus was labouring under, see Hampson 1990.

55 Luke 8:1–3.

56 The 'prostitute' and/or the woman with the oil: Luke 7:36–50; Matthew 26:6–13, etc. Note that the story of Jairus's daughter and the woman with the haemorrhage are ostensibly unconnected, but nevertheless interwoven. The daughter is twelve years old (the age of puberty) and the older woman has been bleeding for twelve years. This might hint that her problems were the problems of being a woman in that society. Jesus resurrects and heals the little girl by saying to her '*Talitha cum*', which means 'Little girl, get up!' It was her father, Jairus, who pleaded for her to be brought back to life. Jesus immediately told him and his wife to give her nour-ishment (Matthew 9:18–26, Mark 5:21–43, Luke 8:40–56). Perhaps men and women who nourish are what women need to heal from patriarchal structures that drain the blood and suck life.

57 Mary and Martha: Luke 10:38–42.

58 The woman caught in adultery: John 7:53–8:11.

59 The Syrophoenician woman: Mark 7:24–30.

60 The servant girl who witnesses Peter's denial: Mark 14:66–72.

61 The male disciples fell asleep on him and variously betrayed or denied him: Matthew 26. The women at the foot of the cross: Matthew 27:55–61 etc.

302 Endnotes

62 Jesus's appearance to Mary Magdalene and other women: Matthew 28:1–10, etc.

63 HarperCollins NRSV commentary, Meeks *et al.* (eds) 1993, 1878. Note also how the prologue to John's gospel (John 1), in expressing the pre-existence of Christ (see Macleod 1998, chapter 2), seems to incorporate *Sophia*'s qualities from the Wisdom Literature into the Christ-principle of the *logos*. The *logos*, however, is very much a male rational principle. Early church fathers like Justin Martyr spoke of God scattering 'the seeds of his Logos' (Martyr's *First Apology*). The *logos* was, in effect, the sperm of God – the *logos spermatikos* as they called it. Through it, 'The world of Greek philosophy is thus set firmly in the context of Christianity: it is a prelude to the coming of Christ' (McGrath 1997, 331–2). Accordingly, we might ponder whether John, wittingly or unwittingly, has subsumed the feminine principle into the male in that rather Greek manner as we discussed earlier with Plato's *Timaeus*, where a Goddess-predicated world was superseded by a male God (John, of course, was writing in Greek and using the *Septuagint* or Greek translation of the Hebrew scriptures). However, what Jesus says in Matthew 11 and Luke 7, and what Paul says about gender being transcended in Christ in Galatians 3:28, is a little different. In these more Jewish passages the feminine principle is acknowledged rather than merely subsumed. Rather than being lost sight of, Woman Wisdom is given her place in the integrated transcendent fullness of God. Christ thereby overtly owns his own anima integration – his femininity – and he does this fully mindful that the 'world' will think him mad or drunk.

64 Sirach 24:19; 51:23.

65 Ruether 1984.

66 The first is from Carmichael 1994, 581; the second is cited in Nicholson's *Gaelic Proverbs*.

67 Luke 2:4. This is not to deny that in Celtic cultures fostership was also important for all the usual reasons of strengthening military allegiances, etc.

68 Carmichael 1994, 581. See O'Cathain 1995 for an immense body of new pan-European scholarship on Bhrighde.

69 'The Sin-Eater and Other Legendary Moralities' in McNeill 1990 (ed.), 63–4. I take this from the writings of that arch Twilightist, Fiona Macleod (a.k.a. William Sharp (1855–1905)), who many would dismiss as a 'romanticiser', but whose work has a beautiful spirit and was based on Hebridean legends current in the nineteenth century.

70 'On a Raised Beach' in Dunn (ed.) 1992, 56–68. This work of mystical geology, which I consider to be Scotland's greatest twentieth-century poem, formed part of my public-inquiry testimony.

71 Ezekiel 28, NRSV, adapted; Revelation 18: 11–24 TEV. Ezekiel's is a remarkable chapter, both in its critique of capitalism in the King of Tyre's city of trade, and in its manifest use of Eden not as a real location, but as metaphor – a point about which, doubtless, few sermons are preached.

72 Smith in Meek (trans.) 1995, 213–20.

20. Return of the Salmon

1 For Adam's treehouse brand of ecopacifism and the full text of Barnie McCormack's poem 'Listen to the Wind' quoted at the start of this book, see www.AdamMcIntosh.com.

2 This word does not seem to exist in contemporary Scottish Gaelic.
3 'Saboteurs cleared as "Trident is Illegal"', *The Times*, 22 October 1999. A higher court later overturned this ruling, though the fact that the senior judge announced the decision without wearing his wig suggested dissentience.
4 Dressler 1998, 180.

21. Mother Earth will Cleanse Herself

1 This was Plains style as is now used by many Nations. Donald Marshall had appointed Sulian in 1989. His successor, Grand Chief Ben Sylliboy, endorsed this mandate in a letter copied to me confirming that Sulian was on a mission from which 'he has not ever been discharged . . . to do whatever he can to preserve our sacred mountain . . . to keep [Mount Kluscap] safe for our future and the future of our children'. Sulian was acutely aware that solidarity in helping to save the mountain on Harris would also help the case of his own.
2 Wright 1995.

22. Healing of the Nations

1 Marr 2000, 72–5.
2 Pers. com. to me, 1 June 1995.
3 *Evening News*, Nova Scotia, 2 August 1996.
4 *The Casket*, Antigonish Nova Scotia, 7 August 1996.
5 Ezekiel 37.
6 Ezekiel 47:12, 21–3, NRSV.
7 Ezekiel 36:35; Isaiah 51:3; Jeremiah 31:28.
8 Genesis 3:24. I am grateful for Tom Forsyth's insight on this point.
9 Revelation 22:2.
10 2 Peter 1:4.
11 'Woodstock' first appeared on Mitchell's *Ladies of the Canyon* album; Crosby, Stills and Nash also released an excellent cover version. See endnote extension on *The Matrix*.
12 Ezekiel 18:31–2.

23. Arrow of the Lord

1 Final external examiner's report, 16 October 1996, from Professor Robin Grove-White of the Centre for the Study of Environmental Change, Lancaster University.
2 This was sent by a Glasgow-based professor of engineering to my former boss on 21 October 1996 in the month after our closure, but it demonstrates the kind of atmosphere that could be felt in the run-up to closure. See McIntosh 1996a for my full critique of the Government's militarised and industrialised science policy.
3 *New Scientist* editorial comment, 4 May 1996, by kind permission. 'Forum' appeared in the same issue. Christopher Brand was subsequently dismissed by the University for running a website on which it was suggested that paedophilia was not damaging to children, provided they are of above-average intelligence.
4 'New era for "eco" college as relaunch approved', *Scotsman*, 7 February 2000.
5 'Government sacks top conservationist', *Herald*, 8 March 1996; J. Watson, 'Red light puts brake on green quango', *Scotland on Sunday*, 24 December 1995.

6 'Massive swing of opinion against superquarry', *West Highland Free Press*, 26 May 1995.

7 'Council's road to Damascus crowded', *West Highland Free Press*, 9 June 1995 (cartoon by 'Chris').

8 *Stornoway Gazette* leaders (Fred Silver), 25 May 1995 and 8 June 1995.

9 'Triumph for superquarry objectors', *Stornoway Gazette*, 25 January 1996.

10 'Harris natives "gloomy and despairing" says council QC', *West Highland Free Press*, 9 June 1995.

11 Pages 1, 21 and 26 in four related articles.

12 'Outrage over plan for massive quarry in Lewis township', *West Highland Free Press*, 17 April 1992.

13 'Plan No. 2 for coastal quarry in Harris', *Stornoway Gazette*, 10 March 1994.

14 MacLeod 1994.

15 'Row leads to bid to ban council contact with superquarry firm', *West Highland Free Press*, 8 December 1995.

16 *Ibid.* (includes the 'Chris' cartoon). Planning advisor John Marshall was another sandwich-eater with major influence on the council.

17 Poems, both entitled 'Roineabhal', in the *Stornoway Gazette*, 25 May 1995 (Iain Aonghas Macleòid) and 1 June 1995 (Raonaid Chaimbeul); Norina MacLean's letter, *Stornoway Gazette*, 10 July 1997; Ian Stephen's poem, 'Under Roineabhal', in Stephen 1993, 90, with his kind permission. See endnote extension on the developers' misuse of poetry during the inquiry.

18 'Superquarry mystery over £30,000 offer to SNP', *Stornoway Gazette*, 27 March 1997; 'Bribery claim by SNP', *Herald*, 24 March 1997.

19 'Isles SNP climb down on "bribe" claim against superquarry firm', *West Highland Free Press*, 28 March 1997; 'Quarry firm may take SNP to court', *Herald*, 25 March 1997. Captain Bill Macdonald, managing director of Stanton Marine in Birkenhead, a Redland consultant on shipping, denied that he had offered the bribes during his admitted contacts with the SNP.

20 'Quarry group's "independence" challenged', *West Highland Free Press*, 12 April 1996.

21 'Quarry supporter quits over "interference"', *West Highland Free Press*, 21 March 1997.

22 'Quarry group in company plan', *Stornoway Gazette*, 17 April 1997.

23 'Redland admits payments', *Stornoway Gazette*, 10 April 1997.

24 Pers. com. 23 August 2000. He adds that no payments were made to individuals. In a further handwritten note from his home address (28 December 2000), Mr Lievers said to me, 'We are I think both in our different ways supporters of the Island communities and in that regard any help anyone can give, however small, is almost certainly welcome.'

25 'Decision on quarry is expected today', *Scotsman*, 24 June 1993.

26 D. Morrison, 'Master builder cements his reputation with takeover deal', *Business Scotsman*, 15 January 2001.

27 This was, in significant part, a conscious response by environmental and community activists including myself and Ian Callaghan to show that we also had positive economic ideas for the future of Harris – see 'Harris group to look at quarry alternatives',

West Highland Free Press, 29 May 1995, and letters from some of us to the *Stornoway Gazette* around the same time.

28 'Let the people of Harris decide on their own future', *West Highland Free Press*, 9 June 1995; my emphasis.

29 See my letter, 'Come Clean on Coastal Quarries, Mr Wilson', *West Highland Free Press*, 29 October 1999.

30 Pain 1999 (released 2000), vol. 1, 13.276–13.296; vol. 2, 19.107–19.119; vol. 3. 27.19, 27.36; Scottish Executive Development Department 2000.

31 Pain 1999, vol. 2, 14.322–14.327.

32 See, for example, Dunion's letter in the *Herald*, 15 July 2000, and analysis in Friends of the Earth 1996. One factor behind this was road protesting, knocking the political wind out of motorway-building. See endnote extensions.

33 Pain 1999, vol. 1, 13.183; vol 3, 27.59–63.

34 Pain 1999, vol. 3, 27.75. Where I have interpolated 'the hole', Miss Pain had 'the loch'. This is because a last-minute change was mysteriously slipped through in the legally binding 'Section 50' restoration plans by council staff. Whereas the original stipulation was that the crater would be flooded to create a new sea loch, the final condition merely read that it 'may' be flooded. And whereas the original stipulated 'there shall be no depositing of material in the restoration of the quarry', the final version specified 'dredged material'. Accordingly the door is left wide open to the possibility of dumping toxic waste, such as the 26 million tonnes of chemical waste that, in 1986, Redland attempted to deposit in old workings at Flamborough, just across the Atlantic in Ontario! The site in Harris is also one of a number shortlisted by NIREX for possible nuclear waste dumping. Accordingly, the worry remained, as originally probed with Ian Wilson, that a hidden agenda existed to put something of value back into the island.

35 Pain 1999, vol. 3, 27.83.

24. Storming the Bastille

1 *Daily Express*, 25 March 1995.

2 Dressler 1998, 186.

3 Dressler 1998, 183.

4 *Scotland on Sunday*, 29 October 1995, cited in Dressler 1998, 184.

5 E. Clouston, 'Hebridean island becomes domain of fire-worshipper from Germany', *Guardian*, 30 March 1995.

6 M. Vaughan, 'Lord of the troubled isle', *Herald*, 30 March 1995.

7 L. Riddoch, 'He is the Eigg Man', *Scotsman*, 12 April 1995.

8 30 June 1995.

9 A. Dalton and J. Ross, 'Pavarotti denies links with Eigg Music venture', *Scotsman*, 1 February 1997.

10 *Scotsman*, 1 February 1997.

11 G. Burke, 'Left in limbo by their elusive laird', *Daily Mail*, 1 February 1996.

12 M. Hannan and R. Edwards, 'Islanders launch bid to buy Eigg', *Scotsman*, 26 July 1996; Dressler 1998, 189; www.vladi-private-islands.de.

13 A. Dalton and J. Ross, 'Forsyth says plight of Eigg is appalling', *Scotsman*, 26 September 1996.

14 A. Dalton, 'Eigg's financial web revealed', *Scotsman*, 31 January 1997.

15 J. Ross, 'Anger as Eigg fails to win lottery cash', *Scotsman*, 23 January 1997.

16 J. Ross, 'Islanders launch appeal for Eigg', *Scotsman*, 28 August 1996.

17 R. Nicoll, 'Scrambled Eigg', *Guardian*, 31 July 1996.

18 Dressler 1998, 187.

19 Rich 1978, 7 and (above) *ibid.*, 13. The lines from 'Origins and History of Consciousness' and 'Hunger' are taken from *The Dream of a Common Language: Poems 1974–1977* by Adrienne Rich. Copyright © 1978 by W. W. Norton & Co. Inc. Used by permission of the author and W. W. Norton & Co. Inc.

20 Translation in Black (ed.) 1999, 45, by kind permission. Note Sorley MacLean's 'Road to the Isles' Celtosceptic satire on this sort of Twilightism, *ibid.*, 319, and Black's discussion of Macleod ('He was a gentle, unworldly man, diffident but a good preacher'), *ibid.*, 720–2. Black quotes Macleod as having said '. . . you could not always be certain whether this thought or that verse was really your own, or something out of the past. Not that it greatly matters . . .'. In many ways Kenneth Macleod and Sorley MacLean represent a polarity in twentieth-century Gaelic literature: the age-old Dionysian and Apollonian counterpoint; Phaedrus and Socrates.

25. Revolutionary Love

1 Carmichael 1994, 29.

2 15 June 2000, text of address courtesy Wilson's office.

3 *Scotsman*, 15 June 2000.

4 Land Reform Policy Group 1999, 1, 4.

5 M. Wigan, 'Scottish Land Reform – or Who Should Control Private Property', *The Field*, March 1999. In *The Field* of June 2001 Sir Michael Wigan goes on to say: 'The bill contains threats for anyone owning rural assets . . . . The new law encourages a green-eyed rural culture of perpetual revolution . . . . The proposals would be astounding outside Scotland.'

6 Leader, *Daily Telegraph*, 6 January 1999, on launch of the Green Paper.

7 Scottish Executive Development Department 2001.

8 McIntosh 2000c; Korten 1999.

9 Scottish Executive Development Department 2000.

10 Freire 1972, 62, 21. Just to confirm Keith Schellenberg's fears about 'Islamic fundamentalists' on Eigg, I notice that radical Islam has its own equivalents to Paulo Freire's 'conscientisation', for example, Ali Shariati of Iran, with his concern that 'real intellectuals . . . had a social responsibility and mission to communicate the objective abject conditions of the masses to the masses, until they attained a level of consciousness that would lead them to revolt' – in Rahnema (ed.) 1994, 219.

11 'Proverbs of Hell', Blake 1991, 54; Blake, of course, reverses constructs of 'Heaven' and 'Hell' in pointing to their 'marriage'.

12 Matthew 18:22, NRSV alternative. In other words, forgiveness effectively without limit.

Bibliography

Newspaper features of a substantive nature are included below, but items of merely ephemeral interest are referenced only in the appropriate endnote. This bibliography comprises mainly direct citations. An extension, reflecting wider influences, may be found on the *Soil and Soul* website at www.AlastairMcIntosh.com; my papers and articles and a readers' forum may also be accessed at the site.

Agnew, J. (1996). 'Liminal Travellers: Hebrideans at Home and Away', *Scotlands*, 3:1, 32–41.

Alexander, D., Shucksmith, M. and Lindsay, N. (1988). *Scotland's Rural Housing*, Shelter and Rural Forum, Edinburgh.

Allardyce, Jason (1991). 'Will Schellenberg be the last emperor of Eigg?', *West Highland Free Press*, 22 November 1991.

An Lanntair (1995). *Calanais*, An Lanntair, Stornoway.

Ansdell, Douglas (1991). 'The 1843 Disruption of the Church of Scotland in the Isle of Lewis', *Records of the Scottish Church History Society*, 24, 181–97.

— (1998). *The People of the Great Faith: The Highland Church 1690–1900*, Acair, Stornoway.

Araoz, D. L. (1984). 'Hypnosis in Management Training and Development' in Webster and Smith (eds) 1984, 558–73.

Arendt, Hannah (1963). *Eichmann in Jerusalem: A report on the banality of evil*, Viking, New York.

Arnold, Matthew (1910). *On the Study of Celtic Literature and Other Essays*, Everyman, London.

Bacon, Francis (1974). *The Advancement of Learning and New Atlantis*, Clarendon Press, London; first published 1605.

Bain, George (1951). *Celtic Art*, Constable, London.

Black, Ronald (1999). *An Tuil: Anthology of 20th Century Scottish Gaelic Verse*, Polygon, Edinburgh; see also MacilleDhuibh, Raghnall, a.k.a.

Blackstone, Sir William (1829). *Commentaries on the Laws of England*, 18th edn, S. Sweet & A. Maxwell, London.

Blake, William (1991). *Selected Poems*, Everyman, London.

Blamires, Steve (1996). *The Highland Clearances: An Introduction*, The Highland Clearances Memorial Fund, Juneau, Alaska.

Bloomfield, Morton W. and Dunn, Charles W. (1989). *The Role of the Poet in Early Societies*, D. S. Brewer, Cambridge.

Boff, Leonardo and Elizondo, V. (eds) (1990). *1492–1992: The Voice of the Victims*, Concilium Special, SCM, London.

Bold, A. (ed.) (1984). *The Thistle Rises: An Anthology of Poetry and Prose by Hugh MacDiarmid*, Hamish Hamilton, London.

Bourdieu, Pierre (1984). *Distinction – A Social Critique of the Judgement of Taste*, Routledge, London.

Bradley, Ian (1990). *God is Green*, DLT, London.

Broadie, Alexander (2000). *Why Scottish Philosophy Matters*, The Saltire Society, Edinburgh.

Brown, Alice, McCrone, David and Paterson, Lindsay (1996). *Politics and Society in Scotland*, Macmillan Press, Basingstoke.

Bruce, George (ed.) with Rennie, Frank (1991). *The Land Out There: A Scottish Land Anthology*, Aberdeen University Press, Aberdeen.

Bruce, Steve (1983). 'Social change and collective behaviour: the revival in eighteenth-century Ross-shire', *British Journal of Sociology*, 34, 554–72.

Bulgakov, Mikhail (1997). *The Master and Margarita*, Penguin, London.

Cairns, Kate (1999). *Surviving Paedophilia: traumatic stress after organised and network child sexual abuse*, Trentham Books, Stoke on Trent.

Calvin, John (1986). *Institutes of the Christian Religion*, Collins, Glasgow; first published 1536.

Cameron, Ewen A. (1996). *Land for the People? The British Government and the Scottish Highlands, c. 1880–1925*, Tuckwell Press, East Lothian.

Camp, Claudia V. (1996). 'Sophia/Wisdom' in Russell, L. and Clarkson, J. S. (eds) 1996, *A Dictionary of Feminist Theologies*, Mowbray, London.

Campbell, John Lorne (1994). *Canna: the Story of a Hebridean Island*, Canongate, Edinburgh.

Carmichael, Alexander (1994). *Carmina Gadelica*, Floris Books, Edinburgh; originally published from 1900 onwards in Gaelic/English in 6 vols.

Cohn, Shari A. (1999). 'A Historical Review of Second Sight: the Collectors, their Accounts and Ideas', *Scottish Studies*, 33, 146–85.

Commission for the Future of Multi-Ethnic Britain (2000). *The Future of Multi-Ethnic Britain: The Parekh Report*, Profile Books, London.

Condren, Mary (1989). *The Serpent and the Goddess: Women, Religion and Power in Celtic Ireland*, HarperCollins, New York.

Conrad, Joseph (1995). *Heart of Darkness*, Penguin, Harmondsworth; first published 1902.

Cordova, V. F. (1997). 'Ecoindian: A Response to J. Baird Callicott', *Ayaangwaamizin: International Journal of Indigenous Philosophy*, 1:1, 31–44.

Corkery, Daniel (1967). *The Hidden Ireland*, Gill & MacMillan, Dublin; first published 1924.

Craig of Riccarton (1934). *Jus Feudale* [incorporating the twelfth-century *Books of the Feus*], William Hodge & Co., Edinburgh; first published 1606.

Daly, Herman. E. and Cobb, John B. (1990). *For the Common Good*, Greenprint, London.

Darwin, Tess (1995). 'Creativity, Ecology and Becoming a Person', *The Trumpeter*, fall 1995, 145–7.

— (1996). *The Scots Herbal: The Plant Lore of Scotland*, Mercat, Edinburgh.

Davidson, Hilda E. (ed.) (1989). *The Seer in Celtic and Other Traditions*, John Donald, Edinburgh.

Davie, George E. (1986). *The Crisis of the Democratic Intellect: The Problem of Generalism and Specialisation in Twentieth-Century Scotland*, Polygon, Edinburgh.

de Kerckhove, D. (1992). 'Asterix Against the Romans' in O'Driscoll (ed.) 1982, 585–8.

de Leeuw, A. D. (1996). 'Contemplating the Interests of Fish', *Environmental Ethics*, 18:4, 373–90.

de Mello, Anthony (1992). *Awareness: the perils and opportunities of reality*, Image Doubleday, New York.

de Tocqueville, Alexis (1966). *The Ancien Régime and the French Revolution*, Fontana, Glasgow.

Devine, Tom M. (1989). 'Social Responses to Agrarian "Improvement": The Highland and Lowland Clearances in Scotland' in Houston and Whyte (eds) 1989, 148–68.

Diamond, Irene and Orenstein, Gloria F. (1990). *Reweaving the Web: The Emergence of Ecofeminism*, Sierra Club, USA.

Dodgshon, R. A. (1989). '"Pretense of Blude" and "Place of Thair Duelling": the Nature of Scottish Clans 1500–1745' in Houston and Whyte (eds.) 1989, 169–98.

— (1993). 'Strategies of farming in the western highlands and islands of Scotland prior to crofting and the clearances', *Economic History Review*, XLIV:4, 679–701.

— and Olsson, E. G. (1988). 'Productivity and Nutrient Use in Eighteenth-Century Scottish Highland Townships', *Geografisika Annaler*, 70B, 39–51.

Dressler, Camille (1998). *Eigg: The Story of an Island*, Polygon, Edinburgh.

Dunn, Douglas (ed.) (1992). *The Faber Book of Twentieth-Century Scottish Poetry*, Faber & Faber, London.

Durkheim, Emile (1951). *Suicide*, Free Press, Glencoe, Illinois.

Ecologist (ed.) (1993). *Whose Common Future? Reclaiming the Commons*, Earthscan, London.

Ehrenberg, Margaret (1989). *Women in Prehistory*, British Museum Press, London.

Eisely, L. (1962). *Francis Bacon and the Modern Dilemma*, Montgomery Lectureship on Contemporary Civilisation, University of Nebraska.

Eliade, Mircea (1989). *Shamanism: Archaic Techniques of Ecstasy*, Arkana, London.

Ellis, Peter Berresford (1985). *The Celtic Revolution: A Study in Anti-Imperialism*, Y Lolfa, Wales.

— (1995). *Celtic Women: Women in Celtic Society and Literature*, Constable, London.

Esquivel, Adolfo Pérez and Graf-Huber, Maria (1991). *The Way of the Cross from Latin America*, Cafod, SCIAF and Trócaire, London, Glasgow and Dublin.

Evans, Estyn E. (1981). *The Personality of Ireland*, Blackstaff Press, Belfast.

Evans-Wentz, W. Y. (1977). *The Fairy-Faith in Celtic Countries*, Colin Smythe Humanities Press, Atlantic Highlands; first published 1911.

Fanon, Frantz (1967). *The Wretched of the Earth*, Penguin, Harmondsworth.

Fenton, Alexander (1989). *The Island Blackhouse*, Historic Scotland, HMSO, Edinburgh, 2nd edn.

— (1999). *Scottish Country Life*, Tuckwell Press, Phantassie.

Festinger, Leon, Riecken, H. N. and Schacher, S. (1956). *When Prophecy Fails: a social and psychological study of a modern group that predicted the destruction of the world*, University of Minnesota Press, Minneapolis.

Fox, Matthew (1983). *Original Blessing*, Bear & Co., Santa Fe.

Fraser, D. (1994). 'Making Waves', *Scotsman Weekend*, 1 October 1994.

Freire, Paulo (1972). *Pedagogy of the Oppressed*, Penguin, Harmondsworth.

Freud, Sigmund (1984). *On Metapsychology: The Theory of Psychoanalysis*, Penguin Freud Library, vol. 11, Penguin, London.

Friends of the Earth (1996). *The Case Against the Harris Superquarry*, FoE Scotland, Edinburgh.

Fromm, Erich (1977). *The Anatomy of Human Destructiveness*, Penguin, London.

— (1978). *To Have or to Be?*, Abacus, London

— (1994). *The Erich Fromm Reader*, ed. R. Funk, Humanities Press, New Jersey.

Gathorne-Hardy, Jonathan (1993). *The Rise and Fall of the British Nanny*, Weidenfeld, London.

Gelderloos, Orin (1992). *Eco-Theology: The Judeo-Christian Tradition and the Politics of Ecological Decision Making*, Wild Goose, Glasgow.

Gibb, Peter (2000). 'Civil Society, Governance and Land Reform [in Scotland]', *Geophilos*, Land Research Trust, London, 00 (1), 70–91.

Gillegan, James (1997). *Violence: Reflections on a National Epidemic*, Vintage, New York.

Gimbutas, Marija A. (1991). *The Civilization of the Goddess: The World of Old Europe*, HarperCollins, San Francisco.

Glacken, Clarence (1973). *Traces on the Rhodean Shore: nature and culture in Western thought from ancient times to the end of the eighteenth century*, University of California Press, Berkeley.

Goldsmith, Edward (1996). *The Way: An Ecological World View*, Themis, Totnes.

Grant, Anne of Laggan (1811). *Essays on the Superstitions of the Highlanders of Scotland*, Longman, Hurst *et al.*, London.

Grant, Elizabeth of Rothiemurchus (1898). *Memoirs of a Highland Lady 1797–1827*, John Murray, London.

Graves, Robert (1961). *The White Goddess: A Historical Grammar of Poetic Myth*, Faber & Faber, London.

Griffin, Susan (1992). *A Chorus of Stones: The Private Life of War*, The Women's Press, London.

Grof, Stanley (1985). *Beyond the Brain: Birth, Death and Transcendence in Psychotherapy*, SUNY, Albany.

— and Grof, Christine (eds) (1989). *Spiritual Emergency: When Personal Transformation Becomes a Crisis*, Tarcher, New York.

Gutiérrez, Gustavo (1983). *The Power of the Poor in History*, SCM, London.

— (1988). *A Theology of Liberation: History, Politics, Salvation*, rev. edn, SCM, London.

— (1990). 'Towards the Fifth Centenary [of the colonisation of the Americas]', in Boff and Elizondo (eds) 1990, 1–9.

Halifax, Joan (1980). *Shamanic Voices: The Shaman as Seer, Poet and Healer*, Pelican, Harmondsworth.

Hampson, Daphne (1990). *Theology and Feminism*, Blackwell, Oxford.

Haney, C., Banks, C. and Zimbardo, P. (1973). 'Interpersonal Dynamics in a Simulated Prison', *International Journal of Criminology and Penology*, 1, 69–97.

Hardy, Thomas (1993). *Tess of the D'Urbervilles*, Wordsworth, Ware; first published 1891.

Harting, J. E. (1972). *British Animals Extinct Within Historic Times with Some Account of British Wild White Cattle*, Paul Minet, Chicheley.

Heaney, Seamus (1984). *Sweeney Astray*, Faber & Faber, London.

Henderson, Hamish (1982). 'The Women of the Glen: Some Thoughts on Highland History' in O'Driscoll (ed.) 1982, 255–64.

Hesse, Hermann (1973). *Siddhartha*, Picador, London; first published 1922.

Hill, Christopher (1991). *The World Turned Upside Down: Radical Ideas during the English Revolution*, Penguin, Harmondsworth.

— (1992). *Reformation to Industrial Revolution*, Penguin, Harmondsworth.

— (1994). *The English Bible and the Seventeenth-Century Revolution*, Penguin, Harmondsworth.

Hope, A., Timmel, S. and Hodzi, C. (1995). *Training for Transformation: A Handbook for Community Workers*, 4 vols, Mambo Press, Zimbabwe.

Houston, R. A. and Whyte, I. D. (eds) (1989). *Scottish Society 1500–1800*, Cambridge University Press, Cambridge.

Hunter, James (1974). 'The Emergence of the Crofting Community: The Religious Contribution 1798–1843', *Journal of Scottish Studies*, 18, 95–116.

— (1975). 'The Gaelic connection: The Highlands, Ireland and nationalism 1873–1922', *Scottish Historical Review*, 54, 178–204.

— (1976). *The Making of the Crofting Community*, John Donald, Edinburgh.

— (1995a). *Towards a Land Reform Agenda for a Scots Parliament*, John McEwen Memorial Lecture, Dingwall.

— (1995b). *On the Other Side of Sorrow: Nature and People in the Scottish Highlands*, Mainstream, Edinburgh.

Hunter, James (1988). *The Fiddle Music of Scotland*, eds A. and W. Hardie, Hardie Press, Edinburgh.

Hutton, Ronald (1991). *The Pagan Religions of the Ancient British Isles*, Blackwell, Oxford.

Hyde, Douglas (1894). *The Story of Early Gaelic Literature*, T. Fisher Unwin, London.

Illich, Ivan (1981). *Shadow Work: Vernacular Values Examined*, Open Forum, UK.

Isle of Eigg Trust (1990). *Eigg* [original Trustees' manifesto], Edinburgh [also on www.AlastairMcIntosh.com].

Jackson, Kenneth H. (1971). *A Celtic Miscellany*, Penguin Classics, Harmondsworth.

Jarvie, Grant (1991). *Highland Games: The Making of the Myth*, Edinburgh University Press, Edinburgh.

Jeffares, A. N. (ed.) (1962). *W. B. Yeats: Selected Poetry*, Macmillan, London, 1962.

Johnson, Bob (1997). *Selected Articles*, James Naylor Foundation, York and Isle of Wight.

Johnson, Samuel and Boswell, James (1993). *A Journey to the Western Islands of Scotland* and *The Journal of a Tour to the Hebrides*, Penguin, Harmondsworth; first published c. 1773.

Jung, Carl Gustav (1972). *Collected Works*, Routledge & Kegan Paul, London.

Khan, Inayat (1988). *Music*, Hunter House, Claremont.

Kingston, William (1992). 'Property Rights and the Making of Christendom', *Journal of Law and Religion*, IX:2, 373–97.

Kinsella, T. (trans.) (1970). *The Táin (Táin Bó Cuailnge)*, Oxford University Press, Oxford.

Kipling, Rudyard (1993). *Puck of Pook's Hill* and *Rewards and Fairies*, Oxford University Press, Oxford.

Kirk, Martin (1993). 'Coastal Quarry or Superquarry? A review of strategy for hard-rock coastal quarries', *Quarry Management*, August, 19–23.

Kirkwood, Gerri and Colin (1989). *Living Adult Education: Freire in Scotland*, Open University Press, UK.

Knight, Gareth (1990). *The Magical World of the Inklings: J. R. R. Tolkien, C. S. Lewis, Charles Williams, Owen Barfield*, Element, Longmead.

Korten, David C. (1999). *The Post-Corporate World*, Kumarian Press, USA.

Land Reform Policy Group (1999). *Recommendations for Action* [Green Paper on land reform], The Scottish Office, Edinburgh.

Lawson, Roderick (ed.) (1991). *The Shorter Catechism*, Knox Press, Edinburgh; first published 1647.

Laviolette, Patrick and McIntosh, Alastair (1997). 'Fairy Hills: merging heritage and conservation', *ECOS: Journal of the British Association for Nature Conservation*, 18:3/4, 2–8.

Lester, W. R (1992). *Unemployment and the Land*, Centre for Incentive Taxation, London; first published 1936.

Lipson, E. (1959). *The Growth of English Society: A Short Economic History*, 4th edn, A. & C. Black, London.

Loades, Anne (ed.) (1990). *Feminist Theology: A Reader*, SPCK, London.

Long, Asphode Pauline (1992). *In a Chariot Drawn by Lions: The Search for the Female in Deity*, The Women's Press, London.

Lorde, Audre (1984). *Sister Outsider: Essays and Speeches*, Crossing Press, USA.

Luhmann, N. (1995). *Social Systems*, Stanford University Press, California.

Lynch, Michael (1992). *Scotland: A New History*, Pimlico, London.

MacAlister, R.A.S. (ed.) (1938). *Lebor Gabála Érenn: The Book of the Taking of Ireland*, Parts I and 2, Irish Texts Society, Dublin.

MacArthur, Mairi (1993). '"Blasted heaths and hills of mist": the Highlands and Islands through travellers' eyes', *Scottish Affairs*, 3, 23–31.

MacAulay, John (1996). *Birlinn: Longships of the Hebrides*, White Horse Press, Isle of Harris.

MacDonald, D. C. (1891). *Preface to Birthright in Land by William Ogilvie*, pamphlet reprint, Kegan Paul, Trench, Trubner, London.

Macdonald, Donald (1990). *Lewis: A History of the Island*, Gordon Wright, Edinburgh.

MacDonald, Murdo (1993). 'The democratic intellect in context', *Edinburgh Review*, 90, 59–60.

MacDougal, Rev. James (1978). *Highland Fairy Legends*, D. S. Brewer, Cambridge; originally published 1910 as *Folk Tales and Fairy Lore in Gaelic and English*.

Macey, Joanna (1993). *Despair and Personal Power in the Nuclear Age*, New Society, USA.

MacilleDhuibh, Raghnall (1994). 'The Seeing Detective' [*na Daoine*], *West Highland Free Press* [*WHFP*], 30 September 1994; see also Black, Ronald, a.k.a.

— (1996). 'The Highland Welfare State', *WHFP*, 21 June 1996.

— (1998a). 'The Identity Business is Booming', *WHFP*, 3 July 1998.

— (1998b). 'Thigging and Sorning', *WHFP*, 4 December 1998.

— (1998c). 'On the Sneck of the Door', *WHFP*, 16 and 23 October 1998.

— (1999). 'MacCallum's Heart and Lamont's Conscience', *WHFP*, 11 November 1999.

— (2000a). 'There's a New Fad in MacLean Lands', *WHFP*, 25 August 2000.

— (2000b). 'Communion Forever Unbroken?', *WHFP*, 8 September 2000.

Macinnes, A. I. (1988). 'Scottish Gaeldom: The First Phase of Clearance' in Devine, Tom M. and Mitchison, R. (eds) (1988), *People and Society in Scotland: Vol. 1, 1766–1830*, John Donald, Edinburgh, 70–90.

— (1993). 'Crown, Clans and Fine: The "Civilizing" of Scottish Gaeldom 1587–1638', *Northern Scotland*, 13, 31–55.

MacInnes, John (1968). 'The Oral Tradition in Scottish Gaelic Poetry', *Scottish Studies* 12, 29–43.

— (1978). 'The Panegyric Code in Gaelic Poetry and its Historical Background', *Transactions of the Gaelic Society of Inverness*, 435–98.

— (1981). 'Gaelic Poetry and Historical Tradition' in MacLean (ed.) (1981), *The Middle Ages in the Highlands*, Inverness Field Club, Inverness, 142–63.

— (1982a). 'The Gaelic Continuum in Scotland' in O'Driscoll (ed.) 1982, 269–81.

— (1982b). 'Religion in Gaelic Society', *Transactions of the Gaelic Society of Inverness* LII (1980–82), 222–42.

— (1989a). 'The Gaelic Perception of the Lowlands' in Gillies, W. (ed.) (1989), *Gaelic and Scotland: Alba Agus A' Ghàidhlig*, Edinburgh University Press, Edinburgh.

— (1989b). 'The Seer in Gaelic Tradition' in Davidson (ed.) 1989, 10–24.

— (1997). 'Looking at Legends of the Supernatural', *Transactions of the Gaelic Society of Inverness* LIX (1994–96), 1–20.

— (1999). 'The Bard Through History' in Neat 1999, 321–52.

Mackay, James A. (ed.) (1993). *Robert Burns: The Complete Poetical Works*, Alloway Publishing, Darvel.

Mackenzie, A. Fiona D. (1998). '"The Cheviot, the Stag and the White, White Rock?" Community, identity, and environmental threat on the Isle of Harris', *Environment and Planning D: Society and Space*, 16, 509–32.

Mackenzie, W. C. (1903). *History of the Outer Hebrides*, Simpkin, Marshall & Co., London.

— (1919). *Book of the Lews*, Alexander Gardner, Paisley.

MacLean, Alistair (1937). *Hebridean Altars: Some Studies of the Spirit of an Island Race*, Moray Press, Edinburgh.

MacLean, Fitzroy (1993). *Scotland: A Concise History*, Thames & Hudson, London.

MacLean, Malcolm and Carrell, Christopher (eds) (1986). *As An Fhearann: From the Land*, Mainstream, Edinburgh.

MacLean, Samuel (Sorley) (1939). 'The Poetry of the Clearances', *Transactions of the Gaelic Society of Inverness*, 38, 293–324.

Macleod, Donald (1995). 'Our Highland Guilt', *Scotsman*, 25 May 1995.

— (1997). 'Focus' [on "Celtic spirituality" as "New Age"], *West Highland Free Press*, 7 March 1997.

— (1998). *The Person of Christ*, Inter-Varsity Press, Leicester.

MacLeod, Norman (1994). 'What profit for Harris from Lingerabay Superquarry?', *West Highland Free Press*, 24 June 1994.

Macpherson, James (1996). *The Poems of Ossian and Related Works*, ed. H. Gaskill, Edinburgh University Press, Edinburgh.

McCrone, David (1992). *Understanding Scotland: The Sociology of a Stateless Nation*, Routledge, London.

McGrath, Alister E. (1990). *A Life of John Calvin: A Study in the Shaping of Western Culture*, Basil Blackwell, Oxford.

— (1995). *The Christian Theology Reader*, Blackwell, Oxford.

— (1997). *Christian Theology: An Introduction*, 2nd edn, Blackwell, Oxford.

McIntosh, Alastair (1980). 'Beliefs about out-of-the-body experiences among the Elema, Gulf Kamea and Rigo peoples of Papua New Guinea', *Journal of the Society for Psychical Research*, 50:785, 460–78.

— (1983). 'Sorcery and its Social Effects Amongst the Elema of Papua New Guinea', *Oceania* [Journal of the Department of Anthropology, University of Sydney], LIII:3, 224–32.

— (1991). 'Wokabout Somils in Sustainable Forestry: New Hebrides to Old', *Tree Planters' Guide to the Galaxy, Reforesting Scotland*, no. 4, 5–7.

— (1992). '"A collector's item" or community ownership – The Isle of Eigg debate', *Edinburgh Review*, 88, 158–62.

—, Wightman, Andy and Morgan, Daniel (1994). 'The Scottish Highlands in Colonial and Psychodynamic Perspective', *Interculture: International Journal of Intercultural and Transdisciplinary Research*, XXVII:3, 1–36, Montreal.

— (1994). 'Journey to the Hebrides', *Scottish Affairs*, 6, 52–67.

—, Macleod, Donald and Stone Eagle Herney, Sulian (1995). 'Public Inquiry on the Proposed Harris Superquarry: Witness on the Theological Considerations Concerning Superquarrying and the Integrity of Creation' [including appendix on 'The Fallacy of the Presumption of Symmetrical Depreciation in the Substitutionality of Natural and Human-Made Capital'], *Journal of Law and Religion*, Hamline University Law School, USA, XI:2, 755–91.

— (1996a). 'The Emperor has no Clothes . . . Let us Paint our Loincloths Rainbow: A Classical and Feminist Critique of Contemporary Science Policy', *Environmental Values*, V:1, 3–30.

— (1996b). 'Community, spirit, place: A reviving Celtic shamanism', *The Trumpeter: Journal of Ecosophy*, 13:3, 111–20.

— (1996c). 'From Eros to Thanatos: Cigarette Advertising's Imagery of Violation as an Icon into British Cultural Psychopathology', Occasional Paper, Centre for Human Ecology, University of Edinburgh.

— (1997), 'The Gal-Gael Peoples of Scotland', *Cencrastus: Scottish and International Literature, Arts and Affairs*, 56, 8–15; also in Pearson, Roberts and Samuel (eds) 1998, 180–202.

— (2000a). 'Saint Andrew: Nonviolence and National Identity', *Theology in Scotland*, VII:1, 55–70.

— (2000b). 'A Sabbath of the Land', *Stornoway Gazette*, 20 July 2000.

— (2000c). 'When Mammon Comes Marching In . . . Challenging the Claim of Corporate "Human" Rights', *Stornoway Gazette*, 28 September 2000.

McLeod, Donald (1892). *Highland Clearances: Donald McLeod's Gloomy Memories*, Archibald Sinclair, Glasgow (Nevisprint facsimile reprint, undated).

McNeill, F. Marion (1989). *The Silver Bough*, Canongate Classics, Edinburgh.

— (1990). *An Iona Anthology*, New Iona Press, Iona.

Mainzer, Joseph (1844). *The Gaelic Psalm Tunes of Ross-shire and the Neighbouring Counties*, John Johnstone *et al.*, Edinburgh.

Maltz, Alesia (1995). 'Commentary on the Harris Superquarry Inquiry', *Journal of Law and Religion*, XI:2, 792–833.

Mander, Jerry (1992). *In the Absence of the Sacred: The Failure of Technology and the Survival of the Indian Nations*, Sierra Club, San Francisco.

Marcuse, Herbert (1964). *One Dimensional Man: Studies in the Ideology of Advanced Industrial Society*, Routledge, London.

Márkus, Gilbert (1992). 'Early Irish "Feminism"', *New Blackfriars*, July–August, 375–88.

— (1997a). 'The End of Celtic Christianity', *Epworth Review*, 24:3, 45–55.

— (1997b). *Adomnán's 'Law of the Innocents'*, Blackfriars Books, Glasgow.

Marr, Andrew (1999). *The Day Britain Died*, Profile Books, London.

Martin, Martin (1994). *A Description of the Western Islands of Scotland Circa 1695*, Birlinn (facsimile reprint), Edinburgh; first published 1698.

Mather, Alexander S. (1992). 'Land use, physical sustainability and conservation in Highland Scotland', *Land Use Policy*, April 1992, 99–110.

Matthews, John (1991). *The Celtic Shaman: A Handbook*, Element, Longmead.

May, R. M., Lawton, J. H. and Stork, N. E. (1995). 'Assessing Extinction Rates' in May and Lawton (eds) (1991), *Extinction Rates*, Oxford University Press, Oxford.

Meek, Donald E. (1987). '"The Land Question Answered from the Bible"; The Land Issue and the Development of a Highland Theology of Liberation', *Scottish Geographical Magazine*, 103:2, 84–9.

— (1993). '"As Some of Your Own Poets Have Said . . ."', *Scottish Studies*, 31, 9–13.

— (ed.) (1995). *Tuath is Tighearna: Tenants and Landlords – An Anthology of Gaelic Poetry of Social and Political Protest from the Clearances to the Land Agitation (1800–1890)*, Gaelic Texts Society, Scottish Academic Press, Edinburgh.

— (1996). *The Scottish Highlands: The Churches and Gaelic Culture*, World Council of Churches, Geneva.

— (2000). *The Quest for Celtic Christianity*, Handsel Press, Edinburgh.

Meeks, Wayne A. *et al.* (eds.) (1993). *The HarperCollins Study Bible: New Revised Standard Version*, HarperCollins, London.

Merchant, Carolyn (1980). *The Death of Nature: Women, Ecology and the Scientific Revolution*, Wildwood House, London.

— (ed.) (1994). *Ecology: Key Concepts in Critical Theory*, Humanities Press, New Jersey.

Meyer, Kuno (ed.) (1911). *Selections from Ancient Irish Poetry*, Constable, London.

Middleton-Moz, Jane and Dwinell, L. (1986). *After the Tears: Reclaiming the Personal Losses of Childhood*, Health Communications Inc., Deerfield Beach.

Milgram, Stanley (1974). *Obedience to Authority*, Tavistock, London.

Miller, Alice (1987). *For Your Own Good: The Roots of Violence in Child-Rearing*, Virago, London.

Miller, A. G. (1986). *The Obedience Experiments: A Case Study of Controversy in Social Science*, Praeger Scientific, New York.

Miller, G. T. (1995). *Environmental Science: Working with the Earth*, Wadsworth, California.

Minh-ha, Trinh T. (1989). *Woman, Native, Other*, Indiana University Press, Bloomington.

Molloy, Dara (1996). 'Refounding the Celtic Church', *The Aisling*, 18, 5–13.

Monbiot, George (2000). *Captive State: The Corporate Takeover of Britain*, Macmillan, London.

Morton, Tom (1991). *Going Home: The Runrig Story*, Mainstream, Edinburgh.

Myers, Norman and Simon, Julian L. (1994). *Scarcity or Abundance? A Debate on the Environment*, W. W. Norton, London.

Nairn, Tom (1991). 'Scottish Identity: A Cause Unwon', *Chapman*, 67, 2–13.

Neat, Timothy (with MacInnes, John) (1999). *The Voice of the Bard*, Canongate, Edinburgh.

Nellas, Panayiotis (1987). *Deification in Christ: Orthodox Perspectives on the Nature of the Human Person*, St Vladimir's Seminary Press, New York.

Newton, Michael (2000). *A Handbook of the Scottish Gaelic World*, Four Courts Press, Dublin.

Norberg-Hodge, Helena (1991). *Ancient Futures: Learning from Ladakh*, Routledge, London.

Northcott, Michael (1996). *The Environment and Christian Ethics*, Cambridge University Press, Cambridge.

O'Baoill, Colm (1994). *Gair nan Clarsach: The Harps' Cry – An Anthology of 17th Century Gaelic Poetry*, Birlinn, Edinburgh.

O'Cathain, Seamus (1995). *The Festival of Brigit: Celtic Goddess and Holy Woman*, DBA Publishing, Co. Dublin.

O'Donoghue, Noel D. (1993). *The Mountain Behind the Mountain: aspects of the Celtic tradition*, T. & T. Clark, Edinburgh.

O'Driscoll, Robert (ed.) (1982). *The Celtic Consciousness*, Dolmen/Canongate, Portlaoise/Edinburgh.

Okri, Ben (1998). *A Way of Being Free*, Phoenix, London.

O'Madagain, B. (1993). 'Song for Emotional Release in the Gaelic Tradition' in Gillen, G. and White, H. (eds) (1993), *Irish Musical Studies, 2: Music and the Church*, Irish Academic Press, Ireland, 254–75.

Packard, Vance (1960). *The Hidden Persuaders*, Penguin, Harmondsworth.

Pain, Gillian (1999). *Report of Public Local Inquiry into Extraction of Anorthosite at Lingerbay, Isle of Harris*, Scottish Executive Inquiry Reporters Unit, 4 vols, Edinburgh.

Palgrave, F. T. (1986). *The Golden Treasury of the best songs and lyrical poems in the English language*, Oxford University Press, Oxford.

Panikkar, Raimon (1991). 'Nine Sutras on Peace', *Interculture*, XXIV:1, 49–56.

Pearson, Joanne, Roberts, Richard and Samuel, Geoffrey (eds) (1998). *Nature Religion Today*, Edinburgh University Press, Edinburgh.

Peavey, Fran (1986). *Heart Politics*, New Society, Philadelphia.

Piper, J. D. A. (1992). 'Post-Laxfordian magnetic imprint in the Lewisian metamorphic complex and strike-slip motion in the Minches, NW Scotland', *Journal of the Geological Society*, 149, 127–37.

Pirsig, Robert (1976). *Zen and the Art of Motor-Cycle Maintenance*, Corgi, London.

Plant, Judith (ed.) (1989). *Healing the Wounds: The Promise of Ecofeminism*, Greenprint, London.

Plato (1961). *Plato: The Collected Dialogues including the Letters*, eds E. Hamilton and H. Cairns, Princeton University Press, USA.

Plumwood, Val (1993). *Feminism and the Mastery of Nature*, Routledge, London.

Polanyi, Karl (1945). *Origins of Our Time: The Great Transformation*, Victor Gollancz, London.

Pomegranate Women's Writing Group (1992). *Pomegranate*, Stramullion Publishing, Edinburgh.

Popper, Karl R. (1962). *The Open Society and its Enemies: Vol. 1, The Spell of Plato*, Routledge, London.

Porter, H. (1991). 'Scrambled Eigg', *Harpers & Queen*, September.

Posey, Darrell Addison (ed.) (1999), *Cultural and Spiritual Values of Biodiversity*, United Nations Environment Programme, Intermediate Technology Publications, London and Nairobi.

Prebble, John (1969). *The Highland Clearances*, Penguin, Harmondsworth.

Rackham, Oliver (1986). *The History of the Countryside*, Dent, London.

Rahnema, Ali (ed.) (1994). *Pioneers of Islamic Revival*, Zed Press, London.

Reich, Wilhelm (1972). *The Mass Psychology of Fascism*, Souvenir Press, London.

Reid, David (1995). *Sustainable Development: An Introductory Guide*, Earthscan, London.

Rich, Adrienne (1978). *The Dream of a Common Language: Poems 1974–1977*, W. W. Norton, New York.

Ritchie, J. (1920). *The Influence of Man on Animal Life in Scotland: A Study in Faunal Evolution*, University Press, Cambridge.

Roberts, Richard. *Religion, Theology and the Human Sciences*, Cambridge University Press, Cambridge, in preparation [I have not yet seen the finished text, but having worked closely with Professor Roberts, a leading expert on globalisation, I would expect it to offer a highly academic complement to many of the themes in this book].

Rosenbaum, M. (ed.) (1983). *Compliant Behaviour: Beyond Obedience to Authority*, Human Sciences Press, New York.

Roszak, Theodore, Gomes, Mary and Kanner, Allen (1995). *Ecopsychology: Restoring the Earth; Healing the Mind*, Sierra Club, San Francisco.

Rousseau, Jean-Jacques (1973). *The Social Contract and Discourses*, Dent, London; *Discourse on the Origin of Inequality* first published 1755.

Ruether, Rosemary Radford (1984). *Sexism and God-Talk: Toward a Feminist Theology*, SCM, London.

Russell, Bertrand (1961). *History of Western Philosophy*, Unwin, London.

Sachs, Wolfgang (1992). 'Progress and development' and 'Poor not different' in Ekins, Paul and Max-Neef, Manfred (eds) (1992), *Real-Life Economics: Understanding Wealth Creation*, Routledge, London, 156–61 and 161–65.

Said, Edward W. (1993). *Culture and Imperialism*, Chatto & Windus, London.

Samuel, Andy M. M. (2000). 'Cultural Symbols and Landowners' Power: The Practice of Managing Scotland's Natural Resource', *Sociology*, 34:4, 691–706.

Savory, Allan (1988). *Holistic Resource Management*, Island Press, Washington DC.

Schumacher, E. F. (1974). *Small is Beautiful*, Abacus, London.

Scottish Executive (2001). *Land Reform: The Draft Bill*, Scottish Executive, Edinburgh.

Scottish Executive Development Department (Planning Division) (2000). *Lingerbay Decision*, letter to Martin Sales of Messrs Burness, Lafarge Redlands' solicitors, giving the public inquiry decision, 3 November [see superquarry pages at www.AlastairMcIntosh.com].

Scottish Office (1998). *Land Reform Policy Group: Identifying the Problems*, The Scottish Office, Edinburgh.

Secretaries of State for Environment etc. (1990). *This Common Inheritance: Britain's Environmental Strategy*, HMSO, London.

Seed, John, Macy, Joanna, Fleming, Pat and Naess, Arne (1988). *Thinking Like a Mountain: Towards a Council of all Beings*, New Society, USA.

Sellner, Edward C. (1994). 'A Common Dwelling: Soul Friendship in Early Celtic Monasticism', *Cistercian Studies Quarterly*, 1, 1–21.

Shaw, C. B. (ed.) (1988). *Pigeon Holes of Memory: The life and times of Dr John Mackenzie, edited from his manuscript memoirs*, Constable, London.

Shaw, Margaret Fay (1986). *Folksongs and Folklore of South Uist*, 3rd edn, Aberdeen University Press, Aberdeen.

Sheth, Jagdish N., Mittal, Banwari and Newman, Bruce I. (1999). *Customer Behaviour: Consumer Behaviour and Beyond*, Dryden Press, Fort Worth.

Shields, Katrina (1991). *In the Tiger's Mouth: An Empowerment Guide for Social Action*, Millennium, Australia.

Shor, R. E. (1969). 'Hypnosis and the Concept of the Generalised Reality-Orientation' in Tart (ed.) 1969, 239–56, from *American Journal of Psychotherapy*, 13, 1959, 582–602.

Sivaraksa, Sulak (1999). *Global Healing: Essays and Interviews on Structural Violence, Social Development and Spiritual Transformation*, Thai Inter-Religious Commission for Development, Bangkok.

Sjoo, Monica and Mor, Barbara (1993). *The Great Cosmic Mother*, HarperCollins, London.

Skidelsky, R. (1992). *John Maynard Keynes: The Economist as Savior, 1920–1937, Vol. II*, Macmillan, London.

Smith, Adam (1986). *The Wealth of Nations*, Penguin Classics, Harmondsworth; first published 1776.

Smout, T. C. (1991). 'The Highlands and the Roots of Green Consciousness, 1750–1990', *Proceedings of the British Academy*, 76, 237–63.

— (ed.) (1993). *Scotland Since Prehistory: Natural Change & Human Impact*, Scottish Cultural Press, Aberdeen.

— (1994). Perspectives on the Scottish Identity, *Scottish Affairs*, 6, 101–13.

Sofer, Leo (1998). 'Once Upon a Time . . .', *Kindred Spirit*, 42, 27–30.

Spenser, Edmund (undated, author's original introduction dated 1589). 'View of the State of Ireland', *The Works of Edmund Spenser*, Routledge, London, 503–56.

Spretnak, Charlene (1991). *States of Grace: The Recovery of Meaning in the Postmodern Age*, HarperCollins, San Fransisco.

Stair, James Dalrymple (Viscount of) (1981), *Institutions of the Laws of Scotland*, Edinburgh & Glasgow Universities' Press, Edinburgh; first published 1681.

Starhawk (1982). *Dreaming the Dark: Magic, Sex and Politics*, Beacon Press, Boston.

Steiner, George (1989). *Real Presences*, Faber & Faber, London.

Stephen, Ian (1993). *Providence II*, The Windfall Press, Isle of Lewis.

Stewart, R. J. (1990). *Robert Kirk: Walker Between Worlds – A New Edition of The Secret Commonwealth of Elves, Fauns and Fairies*, Element, Longmead.

Stewart, W. Grant (1970). *Popular Superstitions of the Highlanders of Scotland*, Ward Lock Reprints, London; first published 1823 as *The Popular Superstitions and Festive Amusements of the Highlanders of Scotland*.

Storr, Anthony (ed.) (1983). *Jung: Selected Writings*, Fontana, London.

Sutcliffe, Steven and Bowman, Marion (eds) (2000). *Beyond New Age: Exploring Alternative Spirituality*, Edinburgh University Press, Edinburgh.

Tacitus (1970). *The Agricola and the Germania*, Penguin, London.

Tart, Charles T. (ed.) (1969). *Altered States of Consciousness*, Doubleday Anchor, New York.

— (1988). *Waking Up: Overcoming the Obstacles to Human Potential*, Element, England.

Taylor, Bron R. (1997). 'Earthen Spirituality or Cultural Genocide?: Radical Environmentalism's Appropriation of Native American Spirituality', *Religion*, 27, Academic Press, 183–215.

Theweleit, Klaus (1987 & 1989). *Male Fantasies*, vols 1 and 2, Polity Press, Cambridge.

Thomas, Guboo Ted (1987). 'The Land is Sacred: Renewing the Dreaming in Modern Australia' in Trompf (ed.) 1987, 90–94.

Thompson, Frank (1984). *Crofting Years*, Luath Press, Barr.

Trompf, Gary W. (ed.) (1987). *The Gospel is not Western: Black Theologies from the Southwest Pacific*, Orbis, Maryknoll.

Verhelst, Thierry (1991). *No Life Without Roots*, Zed Books, London.

Visser, Wayne and McIntosh, Alastair (1998). 'An evaluation of the historical condemnation of usury', *Journal of Accounting, Business & Financial History*, 8:2, 175–89.

Volgyesi, F. A. (1966). *Hypnosis of Man and Animals*, Bailliere, Tindall & Cassell, London.

Walker, Alice (1985). *Horses Make a Landscape Look More Beautiful*, The Women's Press, London.

Walker, Andrew Lockhart (1994). *The Revival of the Democratic Intellect: Scotland's University Traditions and the Crisis in Modern Thought*, Polygon, Edinburgh.

Watt, William Montgomery (1991). 'Women in Earliest Islam', *Studia Missionalia*, 40, 161–73.

Weber, Max (1976). *The Protestant Ethic and the Spirit of Capitalism*, Allen & Unwin, London.

Webster, W. C. and Smith, A. H. (eds) (1984). *Clinical Hypnosis: A Multidisciplinary Approach*, J. B. Lippincott, Philadelphia.

Weinberger, J. (1985). *Science, Faith and Politics: Francis Bacon and the Utopian Roots of the Modern Age*, Cornell University Press, USA.

Whaley, Barton (1982). 'Towards a General Theory of Deception', *The Journal of Strategic Studies*, 5:1, 178–92.

White, Kenneth (1990a). *The Bird Path*, Penguin/Mainstream, London/Edinburgh.

— (1990b). '"Tam O' Shanter": An Interpretation', *Scottish Literary Journal*, 17:2, 5–14.

— (1990c). *Handbook for the Diamond Country: Collected Shorter Poems*, Mainstream, Edinburgh.

— (1991). 'A Shaman dancing on the Glacier', *Artwork: Burns, Beuys and Beyond* (supplement), 50, June–July, 2–3.

— (1992). 'Elements of Geopoetics', *Edinburgh Review*, 88, 163–81.

— (1998). *On Scottish Ground: Selected Essays*, Polygon, Edinburgh.

White, Lyn (1967). 'The Historical Roots of Our Ecologic Crisis', *Science*, 155, 1202–7.

Whitehead, Alfred North (1929). *Process and Reality*, Free Press, Glencoe, Illinois.

Whitman, Walt (1986). *Leaves of Grass*, Penguin Classics, Harmondsworth; first published 1855.

Whyte, Christopher (ed.) (1991). *An Aghaidh na Sìorraidheachd: In the Face of Eternity – Eight Gaelic Poets*, Polygon, Edinburgh.

Wightman, Andy (1996). *Who Owns Scotland*, Canongate, Edinburgh.

Wilson, Charles Ian (1991). *Scotland's Hidden Wealth: Large Coastal Quarries and their Potential Role in Developing a Scottish Integrated Mineral Strategy*, Royal Institute of Chartered Surveyors in Scotland, Edinburgh.

Wilson, E. O. (1992). *The Diversity of Life*, Belknap, Harvard.

Wink, Walter (1992). *Engaging the Powers: Discernment and Resistance in a World of Domination*, Fortress Press, Philadelphia [also from the same publisher are *Naming the Powers* (1984) and *Unmasking the Powers* (1986)].

Withers, Charles W. J. (1988). *Gaelic Scotland: The Transformation of a Culture Region*, Routledge, London.

World Conservation Monitoring Centre (1992). *Global Biodiversity: Status of the Earth's Living Resources*, Chapman & Hall, London.

Wright, Kenyon (1997). *The People Say Yes: The Making of Scotland's Parliament*, Argyll Publishing, Glendaruel.

Wright, R. (1995). 'Fundamental Feud', *Scotsman*, 25 May 1995.

Yeats, W. B. (1990), *The Celtic Twilight: Myth, Fantasy and Folklore*, Prism Press, Bridport; first published 1893.

Index

324 Index